Sir Glyn Jones

By the same author:

Seeds of Trouble: Government Policy and Land Rights in Nyasaland, 1946–1964
Development Governor: A Biography of Sir Geoffrey Colby
State of Emergency: Crisis in Central Africa, Nyasaland 1959–1960
Retreat from Empire: Sir Robert Armitage in Africa and Cyprus
Johnston's Administration: A History of the British Central Africa Administration, 1891–1897
Education and Research in Public Administration in Africa (with A. Adedeji)
The Evolution of Local Government in Malawi
Ife Essays in Public Administration (with M. J. Balogun)

Sir Glyn Jones
A Proconsul in Africa

COLIN BAKER

BLOOMSBURY ACADEMIC
LONDON • NEW YORK • OXFORD • NEW DELHI • SYDNEY

BLOOMSBURY ACADEMIC
Bloomsbury Publishing Plc
50 Bedford Square, London, WC1B 3DP, UK
1385 Broadway, New York, NY 10018, USA
29 Earlsfort Terrace, Dublin 2, Ireland

BLOOMSBURY, BLOOMSBURY ACADEMIC and the Diana logo
are trademarks of Bloomsbury Publishing Plc

First published in Great Britain by I.B. Tauris 2000
Paperback edition published by Bloomsbury Academic 2021

Copyright © Colin Baker, 2000

Colin Baker has asserted his right under the Copyright,
Designs and Patents Act, 1988, to be identified as Author of this work.

All rights reserved. No part of this publication may be reproduced or transmitted in any form or by any means, electronic or mechanical, including photocopying, recording, or any information storage or retrieval system, without prior permission in writing from the publishers.

Bloomsbury Publishing Plc does not have any control over, or responsibility for, any third-party websites referred to or in this book. All internet addresses given in this book were correct at the time of going to press. The author and publisher regret any inconvenience caused if addresses have changed or sites have ceased to exist, but can accept no responsibility for any such changes.

A catalogue record for this book is available from the British Library.

A catalog record for this book is available from the Library of Congress.

ISBN: HB: 978-1-8606-4461-0
PB: 978-1-3501-8026-0

Typeset by Ewan Smith, London

To find out more about our authors and books visit
www.bloomsbury.com and sign up for our newsletters.

Contents

	Maps and Illustrations	vi
	Abbreviations	vii
	Glossary	viii
	Note on Terminology	ix
	Preface	xi
1	Early Life	1
2	Northern Rhodesia: the Districts	18
3	Northern Rhodesia: the Provinces and Secretariat	47
4	Nyasaland: Chief Secretary	61
5	Nyasaland: Governor	95
6	Nyasaland: Self-government	160
7	Malawi: Governor-General	201
8	Retirement	258
9	Proconsul of the Wind of Change	280
	Notes	311
	Biographical Notes	333
	Sources	338
	Index	341

Maps and Illustrations

Maps

1 Northern Rhodesia and Nyasaland in Central Africa   xiv
2 Northern Rhodesia   xv
3 Nyasaland   xiii

Illustrations

1 Agnes, Glyn, Nesta and Gwilym Jones, 1919
2 King's School boat crew, 1925
3 Oxford, 1930
4 Barotseland, 1950
5 Northern Rhodesia, Provincial Commissioners, 1958
6 Governor of Nyasaland, 1961
7 Executive Council, Nyasaland, October 1961
8 Lord Alport, Sir Evelyn Hone and Sir Glyn Jones, 1963
9 Sir Glyn Jones, relaxing outdoors
10 Sir Glyn Jones, relaxing indoors
11 London, 1963
12 Prime Minister and Governor, July 1964
13 Sir Glyn Jones and the Duke of Edinburgh, Independence Day, 1964
14 Sir Glyn and Lady Jones in Government House grounds, Zomba
15 Departure from Malawi, July 1966
16 Sir Glyn and Lady Jones, 1992

Abbreviations

ADC	Assistant District Commissioner
BHC	British High Commission
BNG	Barotse Native Government
CDP	Christian Democratic Party
CIA	Central Intelligence Agency
CID	Criminal Investigation Department
CRO	Commonwealth Relations Office
DC	District Commissioner
DO	District Officer
DPP	Director of Public Prosecutions
FCO	Foreign and Commonwealth Office
HMG	Her Majesty's Government
KAR	King's African Rifles
LMY	League of Malawi Youth
MBTA	Malawi Buying and Trade Agency
MCP	Malawi Congress Party
MLA	Member of Legislative Assembly
MP	Member of Parliament
OAU	Organization of African Unity
PC	Provincial Commissioner
P&DA	Provincial and District Administration
SNA	Secretary for Native Affairs
UFP	United Federal Party
WNLA	Witwatersrand Native Labour Association

Glossary

boma	district headquarters
chikote	hippopotamus-hide whip
Coloured	person of mixed race
dambo	open grassy plain
kuta	chief's council
Litunga	the paramount chief of the Barotse
machila	a hammock carried by porters carrying another person
Malawi police	Dr Banda's private bodyguard
Mbadwa	a political party in opposition to the MCP
'vespers'	an evening meeting of the security and intelligence committee

Note on Terminology

The names of countries and places are spelled as they were at the relevant time, and not in their present-day form where this is different. For example, Nyasaland and Northern Rhodesia, pre-independence, are so called; they are referred to as Malawi and Zambia, post-independence. Similarly, places such as Port Herald and Fort Johnston are so called instead of Nsanje and Mangochi as they subsequently became.

Preface

British rule in the Central Africa protectorates of Northern Rhodesia and Nyasaland covered little more than seven decades, and at the time of independence in 1964 there were a few officers who had served in their administrations for nearly half that period. Glyn Jones was one of them. The changes which he witnessed during his thirty-five years' service were enormous.

In Northern Rhodesia one could scarcely think of greater changes than those which occurred, for example, in the Zambezi valley, where he was first posted, from the primitive and isolated villages of the early 1930s to the huge Kariba hydro-electricity dam twenty-five years later. Lusaka, the seat of government and a large and bustling commercial centre, where he lived in the late 1950s, did not even exist when he first arrived in the country a quarter of a century earlier. In Nyasaland, a less wealthy country, the physical and economic changes over the same period were significantly less impressive. The political changes thereafter, however, were immense, and were the more startling because they were compressed into the space of less than half a decade.

When Jones was appointed chief secretary of Nyasaland early in 1960, the executive council – presided over by the Governor – and the legislative council were both heavily dominated by officials and Europeans. The country was being governed under a state of emergency declared eleven months earlier. The leaders of the Nyasaland African Congress, together with a large number of their followers, were in detention and had been since the emergency had been declared. Nyasaland, with Northern and Southern Rhodesia, was a constituent territory of the Central Africa Federation, imposed, against the manifest and strong opposition of the African people, in 1953. Successive secretaries of state declared that it was there for all time.

Then the wind – the political wind of change – veered. It did so suddenly, and it simultaneously increased in strength, promisingly for most but disconcertingly for many. Few saw it coming.

Four and a half years after Macmillan addressed the joint houses of the parliament in Cape Town – on 3 February 1960 – the executive council in Nyasaland had been replaced by a cabinet presided over by an African prime minister, with a membership comprised entirely of members or supporters of the Malawi Congress Party. The legislature had fifty African elected members, all belonging to Congress, and three non-African, special roll, elected members; there were no official members. The Federation had been abolished and was already starting to be accepted, even by many former supporters, as having been what nearly every African knew it would be: an unwise, unnecessary and unhappy imposition. Nyasaland had become independent, as Malawi, and Northern Rhodesia, as Zambia, was to follow three months later.

From initially preferring a career as a teacher, and being thought by his tutor to be unlikely to be confirmed in his appointment in the colonial service because he paid too much attention to football, Jones rose steadily and successfully, though not dramatically, in the Northern Rhodesia administrative service over the following three decades, from cadet, via district commissioner, commissioner for native development and provincial commissioner, to become minister for native affairs. Thereafter his professional progress *was* dramatic: he was appointed chief secretary of Nyasaland early in 1960, Governor in 1961 and Governor-General of Malawi in 1964.

Studying the life of one who rose from the bottom to the top of the colonial administrative service in this way, over this particular period, involves a study not only of the man and the changing nature of administration in Africa, but also of British colonial policy and the shifts in it. Jones's life covered the greater part of the twentieth century. He was born eight years after it opened and died eight years before it closed. He spent the middle third of it – 1931 to 1966 – in Africa. It was a period of quite remarkable change in that continent; the pace and impact of change were nowhere more spectacular than in Nyasaland; and no one was more dramatically involved than Jones.

This book sets out, by studying Jones's life, in the first part to examine a fairly typical successful colonial administrative service career and, in the second part, to examine an unusually successful and remarkable continuation of that career. It involves studying, during Jones's Northern Rhodesia service, his work in rural African administration in the 1930s and 1940s in different parts of the country and then in two of the provinces and in the Lusaka secretariat. From 1960, when the setting, nature and pace of his work changed significantly, it involves studying his work in Nyasaland–Malawi; the part played by nationalist politicians, especially that extraordinary man, Hastings Kamuzu Banda; the role of successive British secretaries of state – Macleod, Maudling, Sandys and, most importantly, Butler; and Jones's interaction with each of these. In particular, it seeks more fully to understand those interactions, especially the Jones–Banda relationship.

Map 1 Northern Rhodesia and Nyasaland in Central Africa

Map 2 Northern Rhodesia

Map 3 Nyasaland

CHAPTER I

Early Life

JANUARY 1908 was a bitterly cold month in Chester. Water surfaces were frozen hard and there was a good deal of skating on ponds and canals. 'Owing to the severe weather and the consequent distress among the poorer members of the community', soup kitchens were opened and gave sustenance to over thirteen hundred people. Two hundred school children were given free mid-day meals and 'many of the poorer people of Chester ... received their new year gift of coal from his Grace the Duke of Westminister'. At the other end of the city's social scale, the lists of those attending the New Year dinners and balls were resplendent with the names of the distinguished and the gentry.[1]

In a well built, three-bedroomed, red-brick terraced house in Edna Street (number 24) in a quiet area of Hoole, a district of Chester beyond the railway line which separated it from the city, Agnes Jones, aged twenty-one, a milliner, was facing the final days of her pregnancy before her first child was born. She was well insulated from the cold and poverty affecting many other families in Chester, for her modest house was warm and her husband, Gwilym Ioan, aged thirty-one, was in good employment as a grocer's assistant. They were a Welsh-speaking couple and regularly attended the Welsh Calvinist Methodist church, built in 1866, in St John's Street. In October 1902 Gwilym had been admitted as a full member of the church, having moved to Chester from Buckley in Flintshire where he had been a member of the same church. Two years later, Agnes also had become a full member, having moved from Bangor where she too had been a member of the Calvinistic church. Before 1907 their contributions to church finances were separate but after their marriage in the summer of 1907 their contributions became joint. All the services in the Chester church, which accommodated 550 worshippers, were conducted in Welsh, and it was the chief of the seven Welsh churches in the city at that time.[2]

These churches catered for the large number of Welsh people who crossed the border to find work at the turn of the century. Many of the men were employed on the railway and many of the women in the hospitals as nurses, or in the domestic employment of the richer Chester families. Some returned to their home country while others moved on to the larger English cities. Many, like Gwilym and Agnes, stayed and settled down in Chester.

Gwilym's family came from Cymau in the country near Wrexham, where he was born on 6 August 1877, the only son of John Jones, an auctioneer, and Elizabeth Eleanor, née Smallwood, a poet. Gwilym had two sisters – Madeline, known as Linnie, three years his senior, and Bertha, one year his senior. John's father was a ship's captain who visited Patagonia and was known thereafter as Patagonia Jones. John married Elizabeth Eleanor in 1872. She was one of four children of Edward Smallwood and his wife Mary, née Davies (known as Mair y Cymau) born in 1813. Edward was the son of William Smallwood and his wife Mary, née Bishall, whose other chidren were Edward William, born in 1847, and two younger daughters, Mary Ann and Sarah Jane.

Edward William never married. He was the village schoolmaster at Cymau and for sixty-one years the church warden there. He became a man of some wealth, acquiring Oak Mountain and some ten Welsh smallholdings. He died in 1930 at the age of eighty-three years and is buried in the churchyard at Cymau. His grave, and that of his father who died in 1880 and his mother who died in 1874, is the closest to the church and the school which was attached to it. He offered to pay the fees for his nephew to be educated at Wrexham, but Gwilym refused. The family, believing Gwilym needed to be disciplined, sent him to work as a grocer's errand boy. Somewhat footloose, and moving from one employer to another, he none the less stayed in the grocery trade. [3]

In January 1908, however, Agnes Jones was much less concerned with her husband's family history than with the immediate future of her own family. Her baby, a son, was born on Thursday 9 January 1908, they named him Glyn Smallwood and he was baptized the following year in the Calvinist Methodist church. After a few years, the family moved from Edna Street closer to the centre of Chester, to another well-built red-brick terrace house, 15 Priory Place. The houses in Priory Place had been built in 1898 and 1900, and it was here that their only other child, a daughter, Nesta, was born in October 1914.

Although Gwilym and Agnes spoke Welsh they did not bring up Glyn to speak it; indeed, while they continued to attend the Welsh church they sent their son to the Wesley Methodist church, on the other side of the road, opened in 1839 as the Methodist Sunday School. It was not unusual for parents attending the Welsh church to send their children to a non-Welsh-speaking church. The children of Welsh parents made friends with English children at school and it was natural for them to wish to attend church with their friends. Some parents, too, felt that if their children went to a non-Welsh-speaking church, they would develop better competence in the English language upon which their future careers would depend. Others, who may have been ambitious for their sons, sent them to English-speaking churches for status reasons and to take advantage of the educational benefits of attending the Sunday Schools there.[4] Nesta went with her parents to the Calvinist Methodist church, where she was admitted as a full member in 1927. It was common for the girls of families attending the Welsh church to accompany their parents rather than be sent to an English-speaking church. The Calvinist church was a centre for the Welsh in Chester and, like the Wesley church, catered for all levels of society. For example, the day Glyn was born, a former and much admired lord mayor of Chester, Dr John Roberts, died, and his obituaries described him as 'an intensely patriotic Welshman' and a fluent Welsh speaker who regularly worshipped at the Calvinist church.[5]

Many years later, a schoolfellow of Glyn's revisited Priory Place where Glyn was brought up: 'They are very small two up and two down red-brick terraced houses ... they look tidy enough, but I am amazed that it had been possible to accommodate even a single lodger' – as had been the case at one stage for at least a short time when Glyn was about seven years old – 'Glyn came from a rather more humble background than most boys at the school although I was never aware of it at the time.'[6] Another contemporary 'suspected' that Glyn's family were 'what used to be called "working class"'. Throughout his life Gwilym rented, rather than owned, the houses in which he and his family lived.[7]

Glyn went to the council-run junior elementary school, opened in 1909, in Love Street just round the corner from Priory Place and about two minutes' walking distance away. The boys' entrance to the school was closer than the girls', so he would have had a few seconds running advantage if he were late in leaving home. In 1919 he started at the King's School in Chester.[8] The school was attached to the cathedral and, while further from Priory Place, was still only ten minutes' walk from Glyn's home. At King's he was known as 'Ocky Jones' because he was the eighth Jones in the school and was entered on the register as 'Jones Octavius'. Though a day school, it was represented at the Head Masters' Conference. The school was no longer purely a cathedral foundation although the connection with the cathedral and the Anglican church generally was close. When he first went to the school, five of the ten masters were clergymen. On the governing body of twenty members, the bishop – who was chairman – and the dean were *ex officio* members and three other members were appointed by the dean and chapter. The school in the early 1920s aimed 'to provide a thoroughly liberal and practical education, to prepare boys for the universities and professions, or for commercial life'. Fees were £18 a year and in Glyn's case were, it seems, paid by his great-uncle Edward.

The school uniform comprised a blazer and a cap in the school colours. The blazer, worn only out of doors and normally on sports occasions, was of blue, green and white stripes. The cap was also in these colours in repeated narrow horizontal bands, save that prefects' cap colours were in segments, not bands, carried a metal badge, HR (*Henricus Rex*), and had a tassel. School colours for sports were worn on the breast pocket of the blazer. School hours were from 9 a.m. to noon and 1.45 p.m. to 4 p.m. although there were half-days on Wednesdays and Saturdays, when school finished at 12.45 p.m. The long mid-day break was to enable the boys to have lunch at home. In Glyn's case, he lived sufficiently near the school for him to be able to get home for lunch quite quickly. 'Evening Preparation' was a required part of the day's work, and consisted in the lower forms of an hour at school and half an hour at home, in the middle forms one and a half hours at home and in the senior forms two hours at home. Located in the city, the school had no playing fields on its premises. Instead the fields at the junior school and the suburban playing field owned by the Duke of Westminster were used. [9]

The school was divided into houses, primarily to promote interest in games but also to facilitate the 'efficiency competition' that was introduced in 1923. In this competition, plus or minus marks were given for school work, 'acts of public service to the school, punctuality, regularity of attendance at games of all kinds, and attendance at games practice'. The object of the somewhat complicated marking system was 'to make it possible for every boy to feel that by his successes or his failures, of whatever kind, he [was] contributing something, not so much for his own good or bad name, as for the good or bad name of the House group of which he [was] a member'. A second object was to 'give encouragement to the efficiency and good spirit of the average, rather than the exceptional, member of each House'. The boys were obliged to attend football and cricket practices at least one half-day each week. Swimming in the municipal swimming baths was compulsory in the summer term. Parents were urged to encourage their sons to take part in games, since 'these afford the best means of obtaining regular physical exercise, and help very largely to promote a healthy School feeling'.

Another important part of school life during Glyn's first few years was the Cadet Corps, which was started in the school in 1915 because it was felt that:

> the boys would gain greatly in discipline and physical development and would welcome their part in a national system of training for defence ...

A School contingent might do good work in supplying both officers and men to the local Territorial Corps. [It was] not in essence a military movement at all. Its object was essentially educational and its aim to link the varied activities and powers of the boy so as to fit him for citizenship in the fullest sense.

So highly did the school value the work of the corps that it made membership compulsory for all boys over the age of twelve. Despite its original importance, however, the corps was disbanded in 1923.

King's School was proud of its university and other successes, and the yearbook recorded achievements at Oxford, Cambridge, Liverpool, Manchester, Dartmouth, Sandhurst and a variety of army regiments as well as in the Home, Ceylon and Indian civil services and Eastern Cadetship examinations. It was already a tradition that the head boy went on to Oxford or Cambridge. Many former pupils had joined the army during the war and the school was proud of their award of five Distinguished Service Orders, fifteen Military Crosses, two Military Medals, two Croix de Guerre and several mentions in dispatches. A significant number of pupils went to work overseas when they left school. In 1919 Old Boys were writing from Ontario, Los Angeles, Nevada, Rio de Janeiro, Buenos Aires, Mysore, Rangoon, East Africa, Melbourne, Norway and China.

There had long been a large number of applicants for admission to the school, and in the immediate post-war years, including the year when Glyn entered, fewer than half the applicants could be admitted each September. The school, with 260 boys, continued to be 'full and more than full' for the next several years.

Glyn spent eight years at the King's School, from the age of eleven to the age of nineteen. During this period, 1919 to 1927, he developed into an outstanding pupil in each of the important fields of academic work, sports, extra-curricular activities and posts of responsibility.

In the academic field, the quality and characteristics of the staff were varied. French was taught by B. T. Williams, ' a strong character [who] never used the cane but had no trouble in keeping order'. Physics, on the other hand, was taught by T. W. Thomas, who 'could not keep order and on one occasion complained to the headmaster that the boys had been throwing Bunsen burners at him!'[10] Seventy years later a school friend recalled:

> There were certainly some characters on the staff. 'Jerry' Duncan was the typical old country parson; T. W. Thomas taught physics and was ragged by us mercilessly; nevertheless he was a persistent man, rarely lost his temper, and did teach us something. Charlie Holt, chemistry, was also a good teacher but *he* was the prankster. The house master of Evans house, of which Glyn became captain, was H. H. Willis, 'a first rate

teacher of history' and 'in every way a most admirable man; a quiet-spoken, gentle fellow who had the respect of everybody'.[11]

Scholastically Glyn was considered 'a late starter [but his] academic performance increased in later school days'.[12] He took the School Certificate examinations in 1924 and, with eleven others from the King's School, passed, though only he and two others did sufficiently well to matriculate. The following year he passed the Higher School Certificate examination in English literature, history and Latin at the principal level, with a subsidiary-level pass in French, although he had studied it at the principal level. He did not pass the examinations in Greek and in biblical history and literature, which he had studied at the subsidiary level. He studied the same subjects at the same level and with the same results in the following year. In 1926 he yet again took and passed the examinations in the same subjects, this time securing a distinction in Latin, but again failed to pass the subsidiary level examination in biblical history and literature. He was awarded the Captain's prize in 1926 and again in 1927, in which latter year he also won the divinity and history prizes.

It was in games and athletics that Glyn most excelled. Towards the end of his second year, the annual sports day was revived after a break when the war started. Glyn came second in the under-fifteens' 100-yard race – a small but important beginning to his athletics career. In each of the following two years, despite being small in stature, he won the under-fifteen high jump; he came second in throwing the cricket ball and was a member of his house relay team and of the school squadron race team. In 1925 his athletic successes widened: in the swimming club championships he came first in the neat dive and second in both the 50-yard free-style and the 100-yard open river races; his house, Evans, won the swimming shield for the third year running; at the sports day he won the throwing the cricket ball competition, came second in the 100-yard and third in the 440-yard races; and he was house champion. In 1926 he was first in five swimming events, came second in six athletics events, and won both the house and school championship cups. He was school swimming captain in 1924 and 1925, and was awarded his swimming colours: 'We have a most capable and enthusiastic captain in G. S. Jones.' In his last year he came first in four swimming events and second in two. Again he won both the house and school championship cups. He also represented the school in the Chester County Schools relay swimming race championships and, although they did not win, each other member of the King's team swam one length while Glyn swam two.

He also learned to box, again with considerable success. During the winter of 1923 several 'interesting boxing bouts' were staged, each house sending six students twice a week for training. Among these was Glyn, and in the finals of the competitions it was recorded that 'Jones was much too good for his class, and hardly received a blow in any of the bouts'. The following year he was awarded a 'walkover', no one apparently being prepared to take him on. He was also one of the two official judges at boxing matches.

Impressive as these athletics, swimming and boxing achievements were, they were outshone by his accomplishments at soccer and rowing.

Soccer does not seem to have been a particular strength of the school during his early years there. For example, in the twelve matches played by the first eleven in 1921-22 the school scored a total of twenty-four goals and conceded fifty-one. The standard was also somewhat haphazard. In their most successful game they won 9-0 and in their least successful games they lost 14-0 and 10-0. In the following year, 1922-23, the school magazine recorded of Glyn: 'Kicks well with both feet, shoots hard ... Very unselfish, and has turned out a more than useful outside-left.' Things began to pick up a little from 1923-24 when he was made vice-captain, and the magazine reported that 'other teams had not played ducks and drakes with [them] as they were accustomed to'. The magazine began to carry fuller notes and criticisms of the team members: 'Jones. G. S. (centre-forward and vice-captain). A most reliable player who never spares himself. Well supported, he should make an unusually successful leader.'

He was awarded his First XI colours and made captain of football in 1925. In this year the magazine reported that their standard was 'above the general average attained since the war ... G.S. Jones is the stalwart of old'. By 1926, soccer had become so important in the school that a full-page photograph of the First XI – with Glyn in the centre – was reproduced in the magazine, and detailed accounts of each major match were given. The magazine reported: 'Jones. G. S. (captain and centre-half). The life and soul of the team; an untiring worker, a conscientious captain and an inspiring leader. This year's success is mainly due to his keenness and his extraordinary ability as a player.'

He played very little during his final season at school because he sprained his ankle after the first match and was out of the game for the following eight weeks. Nevertheless the First XI lost only one of its seven matches: 'This is an excellent record but G. S. Jones would have made that little difference upon which we have always counted.' Of the match which they lost, the magazine said: 'To have to take the field against such powerful opponents without G. S. Jones ... was to court defeat.' In the season after he left school, his successor as house captain said that 'in football, as in all other departments, we miss our late captain'.

Glyn also excelled at rowing. The school rowing club had been founded in 1883 but for a period of twenty years after 1903 there was no organized rowing. Although it was surprising that a school on the banks of the river Dee had not continuously maintained a rowing club, re-starting it was not easy: funds were limited and the costs were high. The success of the club owed much to the boys themselves. Funds were raised through subscriptions and by holding concerts. In the first year of the club's revival there were only fourteen members, including Glyn, and all were enthusiastic and hard-working. A year later there were twenty-eight members – the most that could be accommodated – and a strong second crew was doing well. Glyn was made captain of boats from 1924 until he left school in 1927. He rowed at number three, and the 1925 notes on him said: 'It is not a "pretty" oar, and swings out of the boat; but he is strong and a real worker, and probably contributed as much as any member of the crew to the speed that was obtained. A thoroughly good captain, and by his example kept up the crew to the high standard of keenness required in rowing.'

The following year he rowed at stroke and the magazine reported: 'Rowing has made great progress, culminating in the winning of the Sheriff of Chester's Prize at the Chester Regatta – a real triumph upon which we congratulate the Rowing Club.' It reported, too, that Glyn was 'a champion worker', could now 'swing straight', had been a 'distinct success' at stroke, and both in that capacity and as school captain of boats had 'continued to set a fine example and [had] enhanced the confidence felt in him by the crew and the whole Club'. In his final year at school it was said of him: 'In his fourth year as captain he has well maintained the standard of efficiency and energy which he has set himself in past years. A steady and trustworthy stroke, who had the entire confidence of his crew.' The master in charge of rowing said of Glyn: 'When I first knew him he was already ... captain of the school Boats ... The rowing club was then in its infancy; by his energy and example during his four years' captaincy he has given invaluable help in making it a flourishing school institution.'[13] Some six decades later, the brochure for the centenary of the rowing club recorded that 'only one member of the School ever had the distinction of being Captain of the Rowing Club for as long as four seasons'.[14]

Glyn also played a full part in the more cultural aspects of extra-curricula activity. He studied piano playing, and in March 1921 passed the intermediate examination of the Trinity College of Music, London.[15] He also played the organ in the school chapel.[16] In the 1923–24 school year in an inter-house music competition he came second in the senior piano solo and in the senior singing solo. 'School singing, which takes place once a week, is enjoyed by all who can sing.' A fellow schoolboy recalled:

We visited each other's houses. Our fathers were both in the grocery trade in Chester ... I still have the piano which Glyn and I used to play on. He was a much better player than I was, but we were very fortunate in having several of the staff at school who encouraged us in the musical line, and we had a good musical competition. [Glyn] was certainly very able ... I cannot say for certain that they had a piano in their own house but I think it highly likely that they did. In fact I can not see how he could be such a good pianist otherwise ... Then we had a close association with the Cathedral, where the standard of organ and choral music was high.[17]

Early in 1926 Glyn performed at the school concert, singing a trio from *Iolanthe* with one of the masters and a fellow student. During the rag concert he performed again: 'a historical playlet wherein G. S. Jones stalked the stage with true Napoleonic demeanour.' At the school prize-giving, immediately following the bishop's address and the headmaster's annual report, and just before the prizes were awarded by the mayor, Glyn sang two songs: 'Danny Boy' and 'O Mistress Mine'. He joined the Literary Society, soon became vice-president – the president was a master – and read a number of papers.

As his years at the King's School progressed, Glyn filled a number of posts of increasing responsibility. In 1923–24 he was made a prefect, one of eleven in the school. Two years later he was appointed senior prefect, head boy and captain of the school; he held these posts for his last two years. We have already noted that he was captain of football, of rowing and of swimming, Evans house captain and vice-president of the literary society. The master in charge of Evans said of Glyn's five years as captain of the house:

> I have nothing but praise. In all the many activities of House life, athletic and musical, he has always displayed intense keenness, a sense of responsibility and leadership beyond his years. His outstanding success was due, I believe, more to his modesty and force of personality, than to the fact that he was Captain of School football, of swimming and of boxing. He was, moreover, an excellent organiser and a congenial co-operator in all House activities. I have seldom met with a boy who has, by his personal qualities, gained to such an extent the respect and regard of boys and Staff alike.[18]

In his report given on commemoration day three months after Glyn left the school, the headmaster publicly paid 'a warm tribute to G. S. Jones, the School Captain of the last two years'. At this time it was also said that Glyn was 'One of the best people we have ever had in the school in late years.' As head boy he 'exercised great influence on the body of prefects', 'was responsible to the Head for general school discipline and was expected to organize the prefects so that general behaviour – in corridors, playground, streets, for example – was exemplary; this included organizing the routine for general functions, such as Speech Day.' It was customary for the head boy to read the lesson at the annual commemoration day service in the cathedral and attend the annual dinner of the Old King's Scholars' Association and respond to the toast of The School. Other students recall that 'the head boy was looked on as an "idol" who exercised a firm control of all the boys in the school'. To the head boy of the junior school, Glyn, head boy of the senior school, 'was certainly the subject of hero worship'. Over four decades later he received a letter from a boy who had been in the fourth form when he was head boy, admitting to 'hero-worshipping' him. [19]

We have already seen how the French master, Williams, was admired for being able to keep order without recourse to using the cane, and Glyn's own attitude to corporal punishment is interesting. A fellow prefect recalled:

> He definitely disapproved of some of the methods used by the prefects in dealing with the younger boys ... As in many schools of that time, prefects were allowed to use corporal punishment on offending juniors. I think GSJ probably never did. Shortly after he went to Oxford, I as a prefect had beaten a boy. Some time later this news had reached him in Oxford and he wrote ... that he was sorry to hear that I had had to resort to this 'method'.

One other important event in Glyn's school career was his attendance in August 1925 at the Duke of York's Camp at New Romney, Kent. Only a very few boys from King's were chosen each year to attend. To be selected was a considerable honour. One who attended two years after Glyn recorded:

> The highest honour ... to be conferred upon anyone at a School is to be sent to the Duke of York's Camp. The camp is attended by 200 boys from industrial centres and 200 representatives of the public schools of the country. The fact that you get to know many of these other campers is the reason for my statement concerning the highest honour, for you meet the best set of fellows you're ever likely to meet after you've left school.

Another boy from Chester said those who were at camp learned lessons which they would never forget: 'They gained a new outlook upon life, learned to appreciate more each other's point of view and to regard themselves as members of a family.'

King's School had a significant overseas and especially colonial tradition. It was a member of the public schools emigration league, and the

Early Life · 11

school yearbook carried information on the league's work and on training before and after emigration as well as the selection of emigrants. The headmaster devoted a large part of his speech on prize day 1926 to 'the crying need of our Colonies for immigrants of sound physique and good education'.

During Glyn's years at the King's School there were three different headmasters. The Reverend J. T. Davies, 'Jit', who had been head since 1892 – with many of his colleagues being of the same vintage – and 'belonged to a passing age', retired in 1923. He was replaced by the Reverend H. H. Symonds, 'who swept away the old regime, a necessary but uncomfortable and unpopular operation', but stayed only two years. His successor was H. W. Ralph, 'a classicist and a fine headmaster', who was head during Glyn's last four years the King's School and of whom it was said: 'What stands out most in our recollection is his never-failing kindness and sympathy; he could be firm and even severe when occasion arose, but he always sought to rule by inspiring loyalty and affection rather than fear.' Under Ralph the school 'settled down to a new order and [began] a very happy time in the school's history'.[20] Ralph thought highly of Glyn and his all-round ability and contribution to the life of the school:

> Jones was a member of my sixth form at The King's School, Chester, from 1924 to 1927 and for two of those years was Senior Prefect, Captain of Football and Captain of Boats. In each of these capacities he gave the school the most ungrudging service, and by his own enthusiasm and the scrupulous fairness with which he controlled the activities of others commanded the respect of both boys and staff. He was in addition a sound scholar and played a leading part in the musical and dramatic activities of the school. As Senior Prefect he had very considerable responsibilities which he accepted without hesitation and exercised with discretion, combining with a natural gift of leadership a sound common-sense.[21]

Glyn was long remembered by his schoolmates. 'He was a most popular boy at school, very pleasant and set an excellent example in behaviour, never putting a foot wrong! He was such a nice polite fellow I can't imagine [that his] coming from a more humble background [than most of the boys] caused any problems for him.'[22] He left the King's School in July 1927. He never forgot the support given to him by his masters: for many years he sent bottles of sherry to three members of staff to whom he felt most grateful.[23]

Although it had become the tradition for the head boy of the King's School to go on to Oxford or Cambridge, it seems that Glyn made no application to be admitted to one or other of these universities before he left school in July 1927. He successfully applied for a 'Government grant by the Oxford University Department for the training of Teachers', and it was this which placed him in a position, at a late stage, to apply for admission to study at Oxford. At that time, and for many years after that time, young men from families of modest means and whose offspring had not previously gone to university, sought admission as non-collegiate students. His inquiries as to vacancies were not made until early September and he then asked for 'an estimate of the total annual expenses incurred by a non-collegiate student'. His letter of application was not written until late September. He explained that the lateness was due to his 'financial circumstances [which] made it impossible for [him] to make an application before now'. With the teachers' training grant, a modest one-year exhibition awarded by the trustees at the King's School and £25 obtained for him by the authorities in Oxford, he was able to go up to Oxford, to St Catherine's Society, as a non-collegiate student, to read English Language and Literature, in October 1927.[24]

He immediately entered fully into undergraduate life, a fellow student recalling: 'Glyn was a real leader among the Non-Collegiate students in nearly all our activities.' He joined the St Catherine's musical society and at the freshmen's concert on 28 October 1927, sang two songs: 'Phyllis Hath Such Charming Graces' and 'Sigh No More Ladies'. He sang this latter song on other social occasions at Oxford. He became general secretary and president of the junior common room in 1930. The Society encouraged 'all students to take part in social and sporting activities and to build up a team spirit in St Catherine's, and with Glyn leading the way', a contemporary recalled, 'it was a pleasure to do so'.[25]

During his first year at Oxford he wrote a number of fairly lengthy letters for publication in the King's School magazine which reproduced letters from the major universities. Since there were only three former King's scholars at Oxford during Glyn's time there, it fell to him to write the letters. In one of them, written when he had been at Oxford only one term, he wrote: 'An undergraduate for three years or more lives a very cloistered kind of existence, and is deprived of the opportunity of gaining many of the experiences which quite commonly come to those who are less sheltered. University life, judged under the terms of life in the outer world, is possibly a little unreal.'[26]

He played a very active part in St Catherine's debating society. In his second year he was treasurer and became president the following year. Of the non-athletic activities the debating society was the premier club. It brought together 'the sportsman, the scholar, the older man and even the occasional aesthete' within its fold.

Here it was that Glyn Jones acquired a reputation as a debater. If he was proposing a motion he would spend considerable time in preparing his brief, and the undergraduate opposing the motion was apprehensive of Glyn as an opponent at the despatch box. In the course of the debate, if an interjection appeared justified, Glyn's acute mind would more often than not demolish the opposing argument. He was very quick to pick on a salient point, enabling him to counter it efficiently and finally. He was a formidable debater.

The *St Catherine's Magazine* mentioned his presence at the debating society on a number of occasions after his presidential year of 1928-29 when he 'occupied the chair with becoming grace and impartiality': 'G. S. Jones ... we are pleased to say, occasionally turns from football to rhetoric. I don't know anything about football, but he can speak'; and in his year after graduating: 'G. S. Jones still continues to delight the House with his candour and his intimate knowledge of obscure diseases.'[27]

In the 1928-31 seasons he was awarded a soccer blue and *The Times* referred to him as 'a daring and pertinacious little outside right, who did not in the least mind exchanging charges with much bigger men'. The King's School magazine saw his selection as 'a tribute to the adaptation of a born footballer' because until he went up to Oxford he had never played on the wing but rather at centre-half.[28] He had in fact played outside-left for a while at King's, as well as centre-forward. During the Hilary term of 1928 he was made captain of St Catherine's football team.[29]

The Times and other national newspapers carried reports on the matches which Oxford University played against other leading teams, and Glyn kept copies of these articles in his private papers for the rest of his life. Initially he played at outside-right and then at inside-right but he then 'found his most effective place at centre-forward'[30] which is where he played most frequently and in nearly all the major matches. The fullest collection of cuttings is of the matches which Oxford played each year against Cambridge University, usually in very bad weather. He was one of only two Cestrians awarded Oxford blues for soccer up to this time; the other had been in 1890.[31]

In the spring of 1929 Glyn was invited to travel with the Wales junior team as 'reserve to travel' with the party to their match against the junior Ireland team at Belfast on 3 April. The card for this match, published in advance and giving times and instructions to members of the party, leaves the centre-forward position blank although all other positions had the names of the players filled in. A manuscript note in the papers which he retained, written in his own handwriting, suggests that he did play at centre-forward in this match but it seems that, for whatever reason, it was not decided that he should play until very late in the arrangements.[32]

Early the following year he was invited to play in an amateur trial game, North Wales against South Wales, at Hereford on 18 January 1930. He had been invited to play, for North Wales, only three days earlier, and two days before that he had been asked by the secretary of the Football Association of Wales to telephone him to say where he was born, his preferred position, his height, age and weight. Presumably, since the invitation to play arrived two days later, Glyn's replies satisfied the secretary on all counts, including his place of birth – which was of course England and not Wales.[33]

At St Catherine's he continued his rowing, stroking the second eight, and a fellow student recalled: 'I rowed bow; we made several bumps and were about to make another when we ran into the bank – apparently the cox had steered the wrong way. Had we made that bump we should have earned the right to keep our oars – every crew member his own oar – and it was a great disappointment to Glyn that we did not do so.'[34]

During the early part of his undergraduate final year Glyn applied for a number of appointments. Most of these were for teaching posts – the government grant would have made this a condition of the finance being granted. It seems that in some of the applications he may have set his sights so high that he was unlikely to be appointed. He applied for a position at Repton School, one of the major public schools, then headed by Geoffrey Fisher, later Archbishop of Canterbury, who thought he sounded 'interesting'. He applied, too, for a professorial chair in English at the Muslim University at Aligarth in India and, rather than accept a lesser post, was 'inclined to stipulate for the professorship or nothing'. He was accepted for neither the Repton nor the Aligarth post. He also thought of applying for a job with the Bombay Burmah Trading Corporation, but was alarmed by the revelation that 'few men serving in the forests altogether escape malaria', and again nothing came of it. More modestly – compared to the Repton and Aligarth posts – and more safely – compared to the Burmah post – he applied for a teaching post in East Suffolk. With these job applications being unsuccessful, he turned to the colonial service, a month or so before completing his final examinations.[35]

One of his general referees for these various posts was A. J. Carlyle, lecturer in English Literature, of Lincoln College and St Catherine's. He gave his reference in February 1930:

> Mr G. S. Jones has been reading for the Honours School of English during the last two years under my direction. His work is of excellent quality, and shows both intelligence and industry, and I should expect him to obtain an excellent class in the Honours Examination. He has read carefully and with sound judgment and insight; indeed he is a man of real

capacity as well as diligence. He is also a man of very pleasant and attractive bearing, modest and unassuming, but also self-reliant and independent. I have the greatest confidence in recommending him for any position which requires ability and character.[36]

Glyn graduated in the summer of 1930. Carlyle did not appear himself to enjoy the sound judgement which he attributed to his tutee, for Glyn did not obtain the excellent result which his tutor expected. Instead he was awarded a third-class degree.

Applications, such as that which Glyn made in the early months of 1930, to be appointed to the colonial service were handled or overseen by Sir Ralph Furse.[37] For over thirty years, from just after the First World War to a few years after the Second, he occupied the important post of appointments private secretary to the secretary of state for the colonies. In many ways it was he who moulded the service. He wrote of his job that the service demanded of its recruits 'initiative, hardihood, self-sacrifice, and a spirit of adventure'.

> Qualities of character and personality (not excluding physical presence and bearing, and some rather elusive facets of a man's intelligence and temperament like imaginative sympathy) were therefore factors of prime importance. ...
>
> The chief attractions of the Colonial Service to the type of man it needed were, and remain, spiritual: the challenge to adventure, the urge to prove himself in the face of hardship and risk to health, the loneliness often and not infrequently danger: the chance of dedicating himself to the service of his fellow men and of responsibility at an early age on a scale which life at home could scarcely ever offer; the pride of belonging to a great service devoted to a mighty and benificent task; the novelty of life in unfamiliar scenes and strange conditions. In such things lay the real appeal.

It was these aspects on which Furse lay great stress when interviewing candidates. He never tried to induce a man to apply but he 'merely put the challenge to him and emphasised the difficulties'. The chief attractions which Furse listed were precisely those which would appeal to a young man like Glyn: the challenge, the urge to prove oneself, responsibility and the novelty of unfamiliar scenes and strange conditions – especially in view of his comments on Oxford's cloistered life which deprived him of gaining experiences quite common to those less sheltered.

Early in October 1930, C. W. Dixon of the Colonial Office wrote to say that, subject to his passing a medical examination – for which he would have to pay the fee of one and a half guineas – he was provisionally selected for appointment to the colonial service as an administrative officer cadet in Northern Rhodesia. His salary was to be £400 a year, rising by annual increments to £920 after sixteen years. He would be required, prior to proceeding to 'East Africa', to attend a course at Oxford, starting on 13 October and lasting three terms. If he failed the course, or if the secretary of state received adverse reports on his conduct, the selection could be cancelled and he would have to refund the allowances paid to him during the course.[38]

He spent the academic year 1930–31 on the Tropical African Services course at Oxford, studying surveying, civil and criminal law, British rule in tropical Africa, forestry, African arts and industries, and Chinyanja.[39] This extra year had the distinct advantage for him that he was able to play soccer for the university for one year longer and to be paid an allowance by the Colonial Office. He continued to live a full social life. He became a close friend of James Betts, an Edinburgh graduate attending the colonial services course before joining the forestry department in Nigeria. Very shortly before he left Oxford, Glyn was asked by James to partner his sister, Barbara, at the Pembroke commemoration ball to make up a sixsome. The sister recalled many years later:

> Glyn was a gentle, sensitive, slightly built young man whom I rather liked, and the imminence of his departure lent a romantic poignancy to our short acquaintanceship ... It was a tradition of the balls that, having drunk champagne all night, one drove out to [the] Spread Eagle Inn at Thame for breakfast. This we duly did, piling into [a] little four-seater car. The fresh morning air gave us an enormous appetite and – tradition again – the men had to push the ladies in their long ballgowns on the garden swings. We drove back to Oxford in broad daylight, [one of the other girls] and I perched on the young men's knees ... Such glamorous occasions were very rare.[40]

Over sixty years later Barbara recalled that their meeting was 'indeed a brief encounter' but that she 'formed a very pleasant impression' of him and that 'he was a very nice lad'.

Early in June 1931 he received another letter from the Colonial Office saying that a satisfactory report had been received of his progress and as a consequence he had been 'finally selected for probationary appointment as an Administrative Officer (Cadet) in Northern Rhodesia'. The 'satisfactory report' in fact contained a passage written by the tutor in charge of the course – Kenneth Bell of Balliol – which read: 'Of all the students in this batch the one least likely to be confirmed is Jones. He thinks far too much of football.'[41] The appointment took effect from the date of his sailing, and a formal letter of appointment awaited his arrival in Northern Rhodesia.[42] Some time before he left Britain he asked his cousin, Hilda, if she would marry him. He would not have been allowed to take his wife with him to Africa during his first tour and she declined. By the time he returned on leave she was already married.[43]

On 9 July 1931 he sailed from England for Cape Town, South Africa, *en route* for Livingstone, Northern Rhodesia. Eleven other cadets for Northern Rhodesia were appointed that year and there had also been twelve the previous year. Thereafter, however, applicants were less fortunate as the deepening world economic recession reduced the number of appointments made to the colonial administrative service from a peak of 133 in 1928 to a trough of twenty in 1931. Northern Rhodesia received only six cadets in the year following Glyn's appointment.[44]

CHAPTER 2
....
Northern Rhodesia: the Districts

NORTHERN Rhodesia, to which Jones was now appointed, is a 290,000 square miles landlocked country lying in the southern part of Central Africa. Essentially a plateau country varying in altitude from 1000 feet to 5000 feet above sea-level, it is drained by the Zambezi river in the west and along its southern border, by the Kafue in the centre, the Chambeshi in the north and the Luangwa in the east. It lies between 8 and 18 degrees south of the equator and is 450 miles from the Indian ocean to the east and 600 miles from the Atlantic ocean to the west. Its economy in the early 1930s was based on subsistence agriculture so far as the African population was concerned and on mining and agriculture so far as the European population was concerned. When Jones arrived the population consisted of 1,372,000 Africans and 13,300 Europeans, of whom there were twice as many males as females.

The country was administered by a governor, advised by an executive council of five officials, with a legislature of nine officials and seven non-officials. It was divided into nine administrative provinces, in the charge of provincial commissioners, each with a number of administrative districts in the charge of district commissioners. It was the task of these officers to administer the African population 'as far as possible through their own chiefs or headmen', collect tax and maintain law and order. The provincial and district administration was well staffed in comparison with, for example, neighbouring Nyasaland. Although the area of Northern Rhodesia was much greater than that of Nyasaland, its African population was smaller. Each member of the provincial and district administration in Northern Rhodesia had an average of 2594 square miles and 12,362 Africans to administer, whereas in Nyasaland each had an average of 1065 square miles and 35,553 Africans to administer.[1]

Jones sailed on the *Edinburgh Castle* from London to Cape Town, South Africa, a journey of two weeks, calling at Las Palmas and Saint Helena on the way. From Cape Town he travelled by rail through South Africa – where a colleague accompanying him recalled his remark, 'My

God, I wouldn't stand for that!' when he saw a European kicking an African[2] – on through Bechuanaland and Southern Rhodesia, to arrive four days later at Livingstone, the capital of Northern Rhodesia.

Here he was posted to the Zambezi valley in the south of the country where he spent the next eight months living under canvas. His work there, in the Gwembe valley, was among the most primitive people in the protectorate. It was a low-lying and hot district, summer temperatures rising to well over 100°F and on occasions reaching 120°F. The most uncomfortable month was October, just after he arrived, when the heat and humidity built up before the rains. Because of this great heat there were no European settlers and no European missionaries lived there consistently. The heat and humidity also persuaded villagers to sleep outside their huts at night, and occasionally hyenas attacked them while they were sleeping and bit viciously at their bodies, often their faces. Jones saw fifty such cases with large areas of the faces torn away.[3]

In February 1932, he was posted from the Zambezi valley to Mwinilunga in the north-west corner of the country where he stayed for the next two and a half years, until his first home leave. Soon after he arrived, a colleague brought to him a young African, Kenema, and told him that he would work for him as a domestic servant for as long as he wanted him. Kenema remained a member of Jones's domestic staff for the next thirty-four years.[4]

Mwinilunga district consisted of sandy but well watered plains, cut by ravines and the Kabompo river gorge. At 4000 to 5000 feet above sea-level, the district's climate was temperate for much of the year, maximum temperatures reaching 98°F and minimum 35°F. During the wet season, from mid-October to late April, 55 inches of rain fell. The vegetation was, as over most of the country, sub-tropical.

> [The population of the district] was 42 Europeans and ... approximately 22,400 Africans ... The birth rate ... was approximately 41 per thousand of which twenty-four would die before the age of two years [fourteen of them having died under the age of one year]. The people were ... physically not robust and liable to die from malaria and pneumonia ... The belief in witchcraft [was] strong, and resort to the medication and remedies of the witchdoctors was common ... The sources of food were scarcely adequate: from October to December the people had to subsist principally on wild fruits, roots and rats while awaiting the advent of the new season's crops. [Crops were frequently destroyed by baboons, wild pigs and occasionally marauding elephants.] The chief foods grown were maize, cassava, finger millet, bananas and mangoes. As much of the district was in the [tsetse] 'fly belt' it was not possible to keep cattle, although some possessed sheep and goats and chickens ... In general the

people were not keen agriculturists and hardly grew enough for their own needs, let alone for sale.[5]

Most of Jones's time was spent on tour away from the district headquarters – the *boma*. He recorded in his private diaries, often in detail, his days and weeks spent in the bush on tour, but there are large gaps in the diary for the times he spent at the *boma*. He would briefly summarize what had happened, indeed belittling the small amount of office work he did: 'Grappled with the ration account at the office. I think I managed it fairly successfully. But it is a desperately small thing to be proud of in the achievement.'[6] Nevertheless, there was usually a good deal to do: 'While at the *boma* [the young officer's] duties consisted of keeping the cash accounts, issuing the weekly ration of maize, meal, nuts and salt to the African staff [and preparing] a number of periodical returns, such as monthly financial statements, and returns of judicial cases heard. As his experience increased he took some of the simpler cases of theft, assault, etc.'[7] It was also part of his job at district headquarters to order new supplies for the office. On one early occasion he ran short of string and thought he should order a substantial quantity in order to keep a good supply. He consulted the requisition catalogue, noted what he believed to be the appropriate item number and placed his order. The stores officer at Livingstone wrote to ask if he intended to hang the whole of the population of Mwinilunga district since he had in fact ordered hangman's rope, in worryingly large quantities![8]

The official purposes of the touring undertaken by administrative officers in Africa were to maintain law and order, collect taxes, maintain contact with the African people – demonstrating the presence, indeed the existence, of the government – hear judicial cases and settle disputes and complaints. With young officers it was important, too, that they should learn as much as possible about the district, its geography, resources, its people and their problems and way of life. In Jones's case during his time at Mwinilunga, his work on tour was almost exclusively checking and revising the census rolls upon which tax collection was based. He did not collect much tax, for a number of reasons. First, there were fewer than 6000 tax-payers in the whole of the district, large as it was. Second, in the economic depression of the early 1930s, the means of earning money with which to pay tax were very limited, especially in remote rural areas. Alternatively, it is possible, but unlikely, that the people regularly and promptly paid tax and there was little need for Jones to collect it himself. None of this means that he was inactive in collecting taxes, as his diaries reveal:

Interviewed four villages before breakfast and laid the law down about tax ... Interviewed about eight of Kangombi's villages. Did some very grim talking to them all ... All Mwanambi's people who were in the village fled at my approach ... bad villages I suspect ... I am attempting to fix Mwanambi ... Last night I organised a raid on Mwanambi and Chiteka villages. Two messengers and five carriers played the drum to lull all those who ran from the villages into a sense of security. At dead of night they went to the villages concerned and were successful in catching about ten people. Rather a good night's work.

This work of 'censussing' and collecting tax inevitably involved him in a great deal of travelling, the vast majority of which was undertaken on foot though sometimes he used a motorcycle – which was frequently out of action – sometimes he borrowed a messenger's bicycle for short distances and occasionally, especially in marshy areas during the wet season, he was carried in a *machila*, a hammock slung on poles carried on the shoulders of the Africans accompanying him.

He regularly covered long distances on foot and meticulously recorded the distances of the various stages. Walking seemed to be both natural and almost compulsive with him. Occasionally, but not usually, he recorded that he was tired after a long day's walk. This was not because of the distances covered but rather because of the conditions under which he walked. For example, one morning he visited eight villages before starting his day's journey and did not get under way until 10 a.m. Then his 'byke conked out' and he had to walk 22 miles, virtually without stopping, to arrive at Chibwika's village 'as tired as hell'. He then went early to bed! It is clear that he enjoyed walking and often the scenery through which he passed:

> Got to Kaunda before breakfast – a matter of nine miles across marvellous country with large airy *dambos* [open short grass 'pans']. The air was wonderfully sweet and cool ... Cold, fresh wind and beautiful country.
>
> Up at five and on the road before six. Did the eleven miles ... before breakfast. Afterwards went eleven miles to Chinyanta's village but decided not to camp [there]. Went on a further two miles to Nguvulu. [The next day I was] up at 4.30 and off before 5.30. Did fifteen miles to Kana stream by 8.30. Breakfasted and then did the thirteen extra miles to Ntambo's village. [After two more days of walking] rose at 5. Off about 5.30 ... twelve miles to Chifuwe river by 8.30. Breakfasted there. Then ten miles to Kangulu's village.
>
> There are some fairly pretty flowers to be seen these days in the *dambos*. One *dambo* I passed today looked rather like a field of dog daisies and buttercups at home. Before I came out to Africa I was led to believe that flowers in Africa had no scent and the birds don't sing. A disgusting libel.

For the past month there have been wonderful, powerful scents in the bush, and the matinal choirs of birds have been much more harmonious than anything I heard at home.

This last passage, written after he had been in the country for not much more than a year, is an early illustration of the way in which he was ready to jump to the defence of Africa, its flora and fauna, and was already becoming 'an old hand'.

Part, at least, of his satisfaction in walking these long distances was the physical exercise it gave him and the outlet it provided for his competitiveness. For example, in March 1932, when he was first travelling to Mwinilunga from Solwezi, he was aware that another European had started out on the same route five days ahead of him. The travelling conditions through swamps were often most unpleasant. The streams were unbridged, he was soaking wet, footsore, blistered and lame. His carriers, too, were footsore and tired. Starting at 5.30 a.m. and covering 20 miles a day, the journey took Jones eight days and, although he did not say so, he was determined to overtake the man ahead of him. For limited parts of the way he used a bicycle which would have increased his speed, and for other limited parts he was carried in a *machila*, but while this latter mode was less strenuous for him it was no quicker.

> The European who is ahead of me still retains his lead of one day. He left Solwezi on Sunday 13th, I on the 18th. [By 21st] I got to within one stop of him [and on 23rd] caught the old man up at about 3.30. He had made his camp some hours before. We camped at Muzunga's village. Drank several whiskies with him and he told me a lot of remarkable stories, most of which I strongly suspected to be apocryphal. He has been in the country nearly 30 years and is 64 now. He has served many native women and has drunk much whisky.

Jones's most prominent activity on tour, apart from walking, even more than 'censussing' and tax collecting, was hunting game animals and, less frequently, birds. The wild animal population of his district was undoubtedly very much greater than its tax-paying human population. He did very little fishing, making only one reference to it in his extant diaries. Hunting was an activity he could carry on while moving from one set of villages to another and in the late afternoon when his day's work was done. He bought a shot gun before he left Britain.[9] At an early stage, too, he acquired a Mannlicher rifle. He recognized that he lacked gun expertise, and soon after arriving in Mwinilunga he wrote: 'I have decided to attempt to improve my skill with a shotgun ... there being no partner for tennis or golf, there will not be much else to do. It certainly appears that competency with all sorts of firearms is necessary here.

One wants to be able to hit a leopard on the verandah from 20 paces or under.' Again he shows how fast he was becoming an old Africa hand.

To start with, he was not a successful shot, but as time went on he improved, learned more about bushcraft and was much more successful. In March 1932 he wrote: 'Went out hunting at night Missed a pigeon and a partridge ... I was pretty poor and bagged nothing.' But in April: 'I have begun to have rather more success with my shooting these days.' Even so, towards the end of May: 'Shot a duiker and everyone agreed I must have knocked it silly, but we could find no trace of it or its blood. Shot a sitting partridge. Hit it hard but it got away. Shot at a bunch of duiker after sundown – hit nothing.' Then, right at the end of May, after crawling on his hands and knees for an hour and firing eight shots he 'managed to get a reedbuck, with quite a good head, and an owl'. There were several more unsuccessful days but he had made a start and a week or so later 'shot a duiker, 60–100 yards in thickish bush. Hit it hard in hind quarters with a soft nosed bullet'. He enjoyed the chase, and wrote in his diary of a wild pig which he encountered late one afternoon while walking with his two dogs and taking a shot gun with him:

> It approached me along a small game track and when it was so near to me that I could have stretched my hand out and stroked it, I gave it a right and a left in the eyes. It fell immediately and began to kick up an awful din which increased twofold as soon as [the dogs] started to worry it ... I gave it another one for luck and that killed it. I found it was a half grown female. A damn good chase, in which the dogs performed very creditably!

He shot duiker, bush pig, mpuku ('most annoying animals [which] lead you quite a dance'), eland, reed buck, zebra, hartebeest, water buck, roan ('queer animals, very aloof') impala, hippopotamus, warthog ('a great native delicacy') and crocodiles.

Some killing of animals was necessary to provide food for himself, his twenty-three carriers, two messengers and his personal staff of two men and three boys, and to provide barter with villagers for other food and services. But his diary entries give the impression that he reached the stage where he would shoot almost any animal which came his way. He possessed the ability of many hunters – incomprehensible to others – to appreciate and enjoy the beauty of wild animals and then violently destroy them:

> Saw an impala on a small dambo and stalked it. It looked absolutely marvellous in the sun – chestnut and black. Waited a long time for a good shot. Eventually got it through the heart.
> We had the strange joy of seeing a bull waterbuck walk straight towards

us and by careful manipulation we got him within six yards of us. But he charged off just as I was about to fire and my bullet went wide. A magnificent creature. Immediately afterwards I killed a female reedbuck. Shot it through the neck and it took over half an hour to die.

Parallel with the carnage, he was able to appreciate the beauty of nature. For example, in October 1933 he shot a number of hippopotamuses and a crocodile: 'The stench of stale blood was everywhere this morning ... In contrast with the scene of blood and slaughter immediately round the camp, nature was in her serenest mood this morning. A light breeze over the river and the sun giving only a foretaste of the heat to come. Birds singing and a general feeling of peace around.'

His work in keeping the censuses up to date and collecting tax, and his hunting, enabled him to learn more about the district and its people. In the course of his tours he performed a number of incidental and in some cases strange functions. He had shown at Oxford his 'candour and intimate knowledge of obscure diseases' and he retained this interest in Africa: 'Before leaving the village I inspected Kapasu's penis. I think he has syphilis, poor man'; 'Women sometimes abort by shoving a root up their fundamental orifice. One woman shoved it up too much and died.'

In the middle of the following year Jones carried out a number of exhumations over a period of several days because he suspected – he did not say why – the deaths had been caused by witchcraft. Initially, he could not find the bodies but he then dug deeper and found them. They were all intact with nothing suspicious about them. Although witchcraft was not involved in this instance, he quickly became aware that it was a potent factor in African life:

> Mombelo's nephew had a child which died, so the nephew and his brother went straight to old Chizere in the Balovale District to try and find out who was responsible for the death. Too many deaths had occurred in Mombelo's village recently. Chizere was of the opinion that there were witches at work and ... after a period of deep meditation the belt round his belly was seen to be moving up and down propelled rhythmically by the rise and fall of his stomach muscles. The verdict was not long forthcoming. Mombelo and his aged sister, Nyampasa, were undoubtedly the witches and had brought about the death of the child by magic. Nyampasa undoubtedly had a manikin always hungry for victims whom she sent on her nefarious errands. And Mombelo had a pet snake which he sent out from time to time to cause the death of some person or other. Both the manikin and the snake ... had to be kept alive by a continual supply of victims ... Thus Nyampasa and Mombelo were accused of being witches, but [we] got to hear of this and instead of them being killed, their accusers got one year each with hard labour.

District life, especially in remote districts such as those in which Jones served during his first tour of duty, were full of many other fascinating features. For example, he received reports that a disbanded corps of Congolese soldiers had settled in Angola only 50 miles from Mwinilunga and that they were cannibals, having eaten twenty local Africans. Since this had taken place outside Northern Rhodesia there was nothing he need – or could – do about it, but no doubt he was anxious that the practice should not spread across the border. Also, in successive years he saw clouds of locusts 'in vast hoards [and] in such numbers that the atmosphere was thick and wherever they settled the ground became literally black with them'. Again, he encountered colleagues who had been badly mauled by lions and leopards. Potentially dangerous, too, was the occasion when he discovered that 50 pounds of gelatin dynamite had become unstable and he had to blow it up. But not all the encounters were violent or unpleasant and he deeply enjoyed, for example, being taken to a secret lake:

> Njeke took me to see the hidden lake. I am the fourth European to see it ... It is a wonderful sight ... A stretch of water about half a mile in diameter and one and a half miles in circumference. Beautiful, clear and with a girdle of marvellous sub-tropical trees surrounding it. Abounding in fish so Njeke says. No natives go there for they are afraid. It is not an ordinary rainy season lake but a perennial affair – 'lake of god', a natural lake.

This, for the right kind of person – the sort Furse had in mind – was a fascinating life, but it was isolated, very different from life in Britain. How did Jones react to it? There are three aspects which help us to answer this question: health, for even the most fascinating of jobs can be rendered unbearable in the absence of at least fair health; relaxation, for one needs to be able to withdraw from even the least onerous of jobs and relax through leisure pursuits if life is to be fulfilling; and the ability to cope without the company of other people when necessary and to make the most of such company when opportunity presents itself. His own philosophizing also helps us to understand how he coped with the sort of life he was living.

First, health. Northern Rhodesia lies entirely within the tropics. Landlocked, it does not benefit from any moderating influences which the ocean otherwise might bring. The Gwembe valley was about 2500 feet above sea-level – low for the Central Africa plateau and, though having less than 30 inches of rain annually, it was not a particularly healthy area. Mwinilunga, at 4500 feet above sea-level, was much wetter, the annual rainfall exceeded 55 inches and malaria was common in the hot season. At an early stage he noted '*Glossinae morsitans* at [his] camp' even in the cool season. Indeed, he helped to nurse a colleague – D. S. Cleak, an assistant surveyor – who suffered badly from it.

Jones himself enjoyed remarkably good health. There were a few minor worries. For example, in the hot season he was badly bitten by 'maddening' tsetse flies all over his body which became 'very swollen' and he as a consequence 'irritable'. Soon after arriving in Mwinilunga he decided to see one of the doctors at a mission station nearby 'about [his] internal trouble'. A little later he said he had 'looseness of bowels consequent on massive meals and lack of exercise'. Exercise was important to him and he got plenty of it on tour, but in the short break between Gwembe and Mwinilunga, while staying at Mazabuka, he went with a colleague for early morning runs before breakfast and for long walks in the late afternoon; they 'did P.T. until 6.30 a.m.' and 'physical jerks' early on other mornings; he did skipping exercises and played a good deal of tennis. For most of the time he seems to have eaten quite well. The district commissioner at Mwinilunga had a vegetable garden from which Jones was also provided. When he visited the few settlers' farms he was able to enjoy 'good food: fresh milk, cream, oranges, fish etc.' Game meat was never a problem, and chickens and goats could always be purchased from local Africans. The list of provisions which he took on tour, in kitchen boxes carried by six of his porters, was extensive, and although much of it was tinned it provided a balanced diet. Usually he did not consume all the provisions he took on tour but on one occasion he recorded that he had 'no butter or flour today – in fact on the bread line'. Since the previous day he had had what he described as a 'rather a poor breakfast of fried chicken, native mushrooms and potatoes', perhaps the breadline was a little more distant than he thought. In these ways he kept himself in good physical shape and was fortunate to enjoy good health.

Next, recreation. There were two non-physical forms of relaxation in his leisure hours which helped make his life fulfilling: music and reading. He had sung and played the piano and organ at school and university, but he was unable to pursue to any great extent either of these interests in his early days in Africa. This did not mean, however that he forsook the pleasures of music. In the days he spent at Mazabuka before going on to Mwinilunga he went several times to a local school where he practised Beethoven's *Pathétique* piano sonata. With a number of young ladies he listened, on the gramophone, to *The Pirates of Penzance* and no doubt sang it too. He took out to Africa a gramophone and a number of records which he listened to at Mwinilunga. On his way through Ndola he bought more records: Beethoven and César Franck symphonies and Elizabeth Schumann and Richard Tauber singing. He also enjoyed the singing of Africans, particularly the women. He commented on how the people of one remote area he visited sang very well; on the way in which women would often accompany him, singing, on his journey between villages and greet him when he arrived at the next village, singing and dancing. He was also interested in, but not invariably enamoured of, other forms of African music, some of which he described as 'A pretty frightful din!'

His other form of relaxation was reading and this he did both at the station and on tour. The books which he read included Edgar Wallace's *Red Aces*, Galsworthy's *Forsyte Saga* and Reitz's *Commando*, the 'most amazing journal of the Boer War, much more interesting than any book I have yet read about the Great War probably because the Boer War was the more interesting war of the two'. He got a 'tremendous thrill' every time the author mentioned the English column appearing 'in a cloud of dust' over the horizon. 'There are grand open plains in the Union. Here you can rarely see the horizon, the bush being much too thick.'

Most of the activities in which he engaged – touring, hunting, listening to the gramophone and reading – were solitary pastimes. The solitariness is suggested in the front of his diary for 1933. Here, the first two pages are headed 'Frequently Used Telephone Numbers', one printed, the other in Jones's handwriting. Both are completely blank. Only once did he record in his diary 'thinking how nice it would be to meet a white man'. He seems to have coped well and to have been quite content without the company of other people when, as was usually the case, it was necessary to do so. Equally, however, when opportunities – relatively rare as they were – to enjoy the company of others presented themselves he took full advantage of them. Such opportunities took two forms, not necessarily separate: the company of other government officers and the company of women.

When officers, all male, from bush stations visited more populous district headquarters, their social reunions tended to be somewhat raucous and bawdy: 'I got rather merry and told smutty stories'; 'Facey told me the one about the bargee and the couple in the punt and I told him the one about Peter the Yorkshire policeman'; C. H. Hazell, an administrative officer of some seniority, 'came at dusk and carried me off to sundown. Fairly hectic night'; 'Spent the day at Hazell's place. Opened bottle 11.30 am. and continued at my place 6 pm. Dinner at Hazell's. Had *akazi anai* [four women] in to sing to us. *Onse awiri tinali ni moa ambiri* [Both of us had much beer]'; 'Returned to J's house and drank up till 4 a.m. Pretty wobbly'; 'Dinner at Hazell's wilder than ever ... After others had gone to bed, Robinson, Hazell and I stayed up drinking'; 'About 12 Hazell said he must go. We then decided we ought to finish the bottle. We did. Hazell left at 4.30 a.m.'.

A forest officer who had been on the colonial services course with him at Oxford, and whom he occasionally met when they both happened to be in the same larger centre on visits, recalled:

> Most of us spent our pre-war days as lively carefree young bachelors. There were games and hearty booze parties when we came in to the line of rail from long spells of touring in the African bush, where one lived camping in primitive and often very trying conditions. Jones and I were once summoned before the provincial commissioner at Ndola and warned that we would be thrown out of the house we occupied if we didn't stop our riotous parties and stop behaving like noisy undergraduates.[10]

Nor were such goings on confined to periodic social meetings with fellow officers; they also extended to other male company. The forest officer also recalled a later visit they made to a mission station and 'a bunch of catholic fathers. Very quiet, austere lot, in retreat or something.' The journey was a long and bumpy drive and they arrived late in the afternoon, were welcomed in, shown their plain quarters and told that the evening meal would be after prayers.

> The meal was simple but with it they served mead, made from local forest honey, and very strong. There were six priests or fathers from unexpectedly varied backgrounds. Taking more mead with us they led us to a hall-like room with a harmonium in it. I thought we were going to attend an evening service. But no: conversation flowed and the mead flowed also. Jones produced a few low stories. These were capped by a couple of the younger priests with doubtfully reputable songs. More mead was circulated. One of the priests had once been a Wurlitzer player in a dance hall in Montreal. He got on to the harmonium. In no time the others were pulling up their cloaks, kicking their legs out, dancing can-can, and bellowing out good old bawdy songs – Frankie and Johnny, The Harlot of Jerusalem, Bollicky Bill the Sailor ... Drink overtook me at that point.[11]

Just as the opportunity for those from bush stations to enjoy the company of fellow officers was largely restricted to infrequent visits to the larger centres, so also with female company. In 1931 there were only 3000 European women in the country, and 6500 European men.[12] In the Mwinilunga district there were not more than twenty settlers and most of these were men. There were very few white women indeed in the remoter outstations. Officers from such stations tended, therefore, to take advantage of their visits to larger stations to enjoy the companionship of European women.

Jones seems to have appreciated the close and frequent company of a particular young lady during his transit stay at Mazabuka. He was a keen and usually, but not invariably, admiring observer of the female form both white and black. His diaries at this time contain frequent descriptions of the physical attributes of the females he came across and occasionally ended with such expressions of desire and regret as 'a rather tempting fruit', and 'she is more than enough to give you bad dreams in this place'.

The woman he mentioned most frequently in his diary at this stage, however, was a person in Britain called Babs. During his first year in Northern Rhodesia Babs wrote to him quite frequently and on occasions he received two letters from her in the same mail. For about three months when first at Mwinilunga he did not reply to her letters although he said from time to time, 'I must write to Babs and swallow this stupid pride.' His reticence in writing – in addition to the unexplained 'pride' – was probably due to his having other things to do rather than to a cooling in their relationship, whatever its nature. He did miss her ('I thought of Babs a lot and wished to God that she was with me') and commented in his diary when the mail arrived without a letter from her. Eventually he wrote and continued to do so from time to time until at least well into 1933. He felt guilty when he did not write and realized that she was 'getting a trifle weary of writing without getting an answer'. He felt too that some of the letters he did write were 'not frightfully interesting'. He was concerned when she wrote to his mother: 'Babs has written to Mother to enquire. My God!' It is unclear whether his concern was that Babs was becoming over-serious or that he was incurring the wrath of his mother for not writing to Babs. She was the only female outside his family to whom he wrote in his early days in Northern Rhodesia.

There are a few 'philosophical' entries in his diary which give an indication of how he himself thought he was reacting to his life in Africa. First, it is possible that he was not too much bothered by what fellow officers might think of him. Of his district commissioner in the Gwembe valley he recorded in his diary: 'Could obtain no inkling of what precisely he thought of me. Decided not to worry too much on that score.' Then, when he became a Fellow of the Royal Empire Society, he wrote: 'Glyn Jones, B.A., F.R.E.S.: how perfectly bloody!' More genuine, probably, are a number of other entries in his diary. For example, after he had grappled with the ration account in the office, he wrote:

> One has to get used to mastering the small things after coming down from the 'Varsity and one has to get used to adopting the spirit of humility. There are not many big things left to do in the Service, and as for the little things, one feels glad that no conspicuous credit may be gained from them. Yet it is a big thing to be able to be here. Africa, I feel convinced, is rather like one of the major experiences of life – like having a woman or going up to Oxford.

Have come to the conclusion that I am not a diarist. I lack the concentrative powers which are necessary [and] a diary can be a dull record of the exact times of feeding, or a medium of introspection, or it can be Pep[y]sian. I never get beyond the first of these possibilities, and, thank God, I am not pettifogging enough even to persist in that!

The new year for me brings along a very necessary resolve to economize and save money. Hitherto I have been unwisely generous and have spent with a certain amount of bad taste. The payment of debts and the aggregation of a decent sum of money against contingencies must now be my aim. I now wonder if there is any wisdom in despising the hoarding spirit. Can there be anything despicable in husbanding the strength of one's body and being desperately careful about the spending of one's money? The idea in itself is not despicable, but frequently the people who hold it are.

These entries in his private diary suggest that while he realized he would have to get used to the humble, mundane and possibly trivial aspects of his work, he did not see himself as pettifogging in his approach to them. He felt that he should attempt to pay off his debts and start to save, possibly, although he did not say so, because he realized that wiser spending and more thrift would be necessary if he were to marry. The remarks about unwise generosity, spending in bad taste and the merits of 'husbanding the strength of one's body' may together reflect a feeling that he had over-indulged himself socially.

The essence of Jones's reaction to his life in Northern Rhodesia in his early days there was that he enjoyed the 'major experience' of being in Africa and he enjoyed his work, particularly that on tour. They were bonuses, but important ones, that he enjoyed good health; had within himself the ability to relax through his leisure pursuits; was content with his own company when, as was generally the case, there was little or no other company, and to make the most of the opportunities of enjoying male companionship and thinking about female companionship.

How was he developing in his attitude towards and relationships with Africans, the people he had come to administer? There were signs that he was prepared to be somewhat tough with them. For example, when the wife of his Gwembe district commissioner lost her handbag when staying with him at Mazabuka, he called his house servants together and promptly 'sacked Isaac on account' of it, although he did not profess to have any evidence to show that Isaac had stolen the handbag. When he suspected that another of his servants, who was going back to his village to mourn the death of his father and mother, had stolen a blanket, he had him waylaid about four miles out, brought him back and searched his kit, only to discover nothing incriminating. When he got up late one morning because his house servant had not been sufficiently persistent in waking him and feared being reprimanded if he did so, Jones 'ticked him off because he didn't' do so. There was an occasion when he had been in the country just under a year, when he took exception to the noise of drumming while he was camped on tour. He sent messengers to tell them to stop and when they refused he personally beat two of the drummers, seven strokes each, with a hippopotamus-hide whip. Indeed, when he shot hippopotamuses he gave away most of the carcass, but he usually retained for his own use parts of the hide with which to make *chikote* whips. When on tour he reprimanded village headmen who failed to register their people, or neglected to maintain the paths leading to their village, or whose people were excessively tardy in paying their tax. On the other hand he did not despair of recalcitrant headmen:

> Spent most of the morning with Kangoni, telling him what was expected of him. He is a weak and characterless man essentially. But he possesses a certain obstinacy which is said to be characteristic of all weak willed people. There is no reason to despair of this obstinacy being converted into force of character. I wish the man well and will certainly give him all the help I can and recommend that others do so too.

It may have been a day in which he was in a particularly gentle mood, for later that afternoon he 'went for a quiet stroll with a pipe [and then] wrote to Babs'.

While he was at Mwinilunga he sat and passed the government language examination in Chinyanja. He had been taught Chinyanja on the colonial services course at Oxford and as a consequence took the examination in this language although it was not spoken in that part of the country in which he was living. He was helped to brush up on the language by a young African who worked in a local store. A close friend recalled – as did others: 'What always amused me was the appalling English accent with which Jones spoke Chinyanja – and that despite his good ear for music and his cultivated taste for it.'[13]

In August 1934 he took his first home leave and travelled by rail to Cape Town and thence by ship to Britain. He spent his leave largely with his family at Chester and his cousin, Hilda, and her family at Bangor, with visits to Oxford and elsewhere. He played a number of football matches for the Chester Old Boys.[14] His leave lasted six months and in addition he received an additional six weeks' travelling time. He returned to Northern Rhodesia in March 1935.

On his return from leave he was posted to the Luanshya district on the Copperbelt, a very different environment from Mwinilunga. Like the other Copperbelt towns, Luanshya had its adjacent mine township housing the employees of the Roan Antelope mine. Luanshya was a small district, of only 425 square miles, but it had the largest European population in the country – over 2000 – and there was a large African population, most of whom worked in the copper mines.

Social life at Luanshya was very different from what Jones had experienced at Gwembe and Mwinilunga and he was able to enjoy the facilities of the Roan Antelope club with its golf course and swimming pool. He played a good deal of football and was a member of the Northern Rhodesia national team in 1936 and 1937. There were a number of young officers in the administration, education, surveys and forestry departments, some of whom were married, who formed a fairly close social group. The country was pulling out of the recession, and the young officers, keen on their work, were optimistic about the improved prospects and, until rather later, not too troubled by developments in Europe. Jones led a pleasant and contented life on the Copperbelt. '[He] was single and [had] a modest manner, a somewhat "shaggy" look, and his trousers, which were then rather baggy in style, always appeared as if they were about to slip off his hips. Although [he] was not lacking in self-confidence ... the ladies in the group treated him in an almost protective way.'[15]

For some years past the government had been exercised by the inequities of the African tax system under which all districts, regardless of wealth, paid the same rate. In January 1935 a differential system was proposed with the higher rates being levied on the Copperbelt. The legislation to effect this, passed in May, was backdated to January. Soon after this, disturbances took place on the Copperbelt, first at Mufulira, then at Ndola and finally at Luanshya.

Jones had not long been in Luanshya when the district commissioner, A. W. Bonfield, and the officer in charge of police, Inspector Maxwell, with his assistant, Pipe, learned that the African mine-workers at Roan Antelope intended to strike. Since the Luanshya police were very few, Maxwell called on the larger unit at Nkana for reinforcements. Early the following morning, 29 May, Superintendent Fold, two other European officers and seventy-nine African policemen arrived from Nkana. These and the Luanshya men escorted those mine-workers who wished to go to work. They also protected mine plant at strategic points. Maxwell and Pipe each took out a patrol in a vanette and Jones drove Pipe's vanette. Together they dispersed several groups of strikers who, although armed with sticks, used no actual violence against them. There was, however, considerable violence in other parts of the mine. A large mob shortly stormed the compound office but was turned back by the police who made a number of baton charges which the subsequent commission of inquiry found to be unnecessary and provocative and led to bitter feelings against the police. A number of policemen were injured before the crowd withdrew. The two vanettes were heavily stoned. The district commissioner returned to the compound office and tried unsuccessfully to reason with the strikers. Maxwell drove to collect rifles and ammunition from Luanshya.

On his return journey Maxwell and his men were again stoned. The ammunition box was taken into the compound office and the rifles distributed among the members of the Luanshya detachment ... The police were lined up in front of the office facing the howling mob and subjected to further stoning and threats. One charge was repulsed but a second drove the thin line back onto the verandah. One policeman was knocked unconscious and several others hurt by a hail of stones, iron bars, pieces of piping and other missiles. Finally the line broke and the ... African police appear to have helped themselves to cartridges. Several opened fire out of the windows. As the crowd withdrew, the police followed beyond the verandah, still firing until ... Fold knocked up their rifles, ordering them to cease fire. Seven rioters were killed and 20 wounded.[16]

There was then a lull until late in the morning when soldiers of the Northern Rhodesia Rifles were flown in from Lusaka and rioting broke out again. After a further two hours, during which no more shots were fired, the rioters dispersed. One hundred and fifty troops arrived during the night and it was dawn before the police, the district commissioner and Jones, exhausted, returned to Luanshya. The government inquiry into the riots recorded that when the firing ended and before the arrival of the military, 'Superintendent Fold and Mr. Jones, with two or three police, went out and brought in some badly wounded natives ... at considerable personal risk.'[17]

At the end of his second tour of duty in Northern Rhodesia Jones went on leave to Britain. During his leave he met Margaret Florence McWilliam, the daughter of Peter McWilliam, then the manager of Tottenham football club. McWilliam was an unusually distinguished footballer, having been eight times capped for Scotland before he was injured in an international against Wales and was unable to play again. Instead he became a manager and a very successful one. It is probable that Jones met Margaret when he was visiting his sister, Nesta, who had left Chester in 1936 to live in Ilford, Essex. By the time he met Margaret, who was also living in Ilford, he was well into his leave. She was a very attractive young woman of twenty-six years. He was thirty. They fell in love and were married by special licence at the Marylebone register office on 21 May 1938. The witnesses signing the marriage register were James Bennett Pigg, a close friend who had been at St Catherine's with him, and Colin Duff, a forest officer from Northern Rhodesia. The couple then went on a 'whirlwind honeymoon on the continent and returned to Britain towards the end of his leave'. Indeed, so near the end of the leave was it that they had but a very short time left together in England. It was at this point that Margaret – whom he called Peggy – turned to him and said that if he thought she was going to 'that bloody place Africa' with him, he was mistaken. Devastated, Jones returned to Africa by himself and never saw his bride again.[18]

On his return to Northern Rhodesia Jones was posted back to the North Western Province, this time to Balovale, 'a remote, wild and lonely station with only two other Europeans on it, the doctor and his wife' in addition to the district commissioner and the district officer. Balovale, was the most northern of the administrative districts in Barotseland and had about 40,000 Africans whose villages, especially those of the Lovale, were located along the lines of the rivers. The other main tribe was the Lunda. The soils, as over much of Barotseland, are of Kalahari sands and on the west bank of the Zambezi travel was always on foot since there were no roads, and goods were carried by barge. There were three mission stations in the district, one of which was primarily a leper colony, all run by Plymouth Brethren. These were the only non-government Europeans in the district. Balovale had a very small airstrip, used mainly for carrying mail. Jones became fluent in the Lunda language during his period here.[19]

The first administrative station at Balovale was built by the British South Africa Company in 1907 under an agreement with the Litunga, the paramount chief of the Barotse, which gave the company the right to administer all the 'Lozi and its dependencies'. When the administration was assumed by the British government, the Lovale and Lunda peoples continued to pay what they felt were voluntary gifts to a powerful neighbour and what the Litunga thought was mandatory tribute paid to him as a duty by those subject to him. The long dispute came to a head after the government started to lay down rules for native courts and considered setting up native authorities. The Lunda and Lovale refused to cooperate with the Litunga, refused to pay tax to his treasury and boycotted his courts. Then, as a result of an appeal to the British government to settle the issue, a commission of inquiry was set up in September 1938. There was a single commissioner, Sir Philip MacDonnell, who was assisted by George Suckling, the doyen of missionary education in the Balovale district, for the Lunda and the Lovale, and by Gervas Clay, a district officer, for the Lozi. Jones was appointed secretary. The commission took almost two years to gather evidence, summarize it and make recommendations to the British government.[20]

In March 1939 when the commission was sitting in Mongu, Jones took the opportunity to visit the prison specifically to see a prisoner who had been convicted of rape receive twelve strokes of the cat. He believed that every magistrate should 'have a clear idea of the nature of the sentences he is liable to impose', and he recorded:

Actually, as far as I could see, the whipping today, although effective, was not as violent as it can be when performed by an expert. The native warder who administered it was by no means used to the job and lacked the touch which makes the operation so severe. The weals on the prisoner's back at the end of it were large, but actual laceration was little. The prisoner was difficult to begin with but obviously suffered considerable pain before the end. Not an elevating sight: but necessary.[21]

This entry in his private diary is interesting for the light it casts on his developing attitudes to corporal punishment. At Oxford he regretted that one of the prefects at his old school had to resort to beating as a means of maintaining discipline. He voiced disapproval when he saw an African being kicked by a European in South Africa. Then in his first tour he personally, and without doubt utterly unlawfully, whipped two drummers who had disturbed his night's sleep. Now he seems to be taking a detached, almost academic but close, interest in at least judicial corporal punishment. A few years later there was a further indication of his approach to corporal punishment – this time one of practical, not academic, interest. In the course of a tour of his district when he was district commissioner of Mongu, he visited a Roman Catholic mission station, where the priest in charge recalled:

On one occasion a boy in the school on the mission station attacked another boy and slightly injured him with a knife. I reported the matter to [Jones] and that afternoon he held a court. When evidence was taken and witnesses examined, he gave the verdict that the guilty boy should receive six lashes of the cane. The boy was brought into a classroom that evening, stripped, put lying on a table and had his bottom covered with a wet cloth. [Jones] got a cane and gave him six of the strongest lashes that he could.[22]

We do not know what Jones's reaction was to personally strongly lashing a young person, but it is clear that, at least in this case, he approved of fairly severe punishment for a quite minor offence, since, in this very remote mission station, he could readily have avoided passing a sentence of corporal punishment. He may well have had in mind supporting the priests in securing good behaviour in the school. But he ran the risk of the high court raising its appelate eyebrows if it learned of such a hastily prepared 'prosecution' and trial of a juvenile, followed by the sentence being promptly carried out by the magistrate himself.

MacDonnell, not the secretary, drafted the report and its contents were kept secret. Jones kept his copy of the report in the safe in his office. One night when he was asleep, some Africans broke into his bedroom, removed the office and safe keys from his trousers pocket, opened his office and the safe, took out the report, read it and returned it to the safe and the keys to Jones's pocket. Those who did this did not appear to make any public use of it and were presumably Lovale in whose favour MacDonnell had made his recommendations.[23]

It is clear that MacDonnell much appreciated Jones's work as secretary of the commission and he thanked him both privately and publicly. In a letter of 13 May he wrote effusively:

> Your too kind letter of yesterday anticipated [mine] as I wanted to write to you. Please understand that I cannot thank you enough for all the kind, unfailing and unwearied and always competent help I got from you ... what you did made my work a pleasure. I do hope, too, that you will get some official recognition [for] such invariably competent work as yours – you deserve anything good the administration can give you, and you will be capable of any responsibility – I trust the administration realizes that. Once again my best thanks – you have made this work of the Balovale Commission what will be, to me anyway, one of the happiest memories I possess.[24]

In the published report he repeated his thanks and admiration, adding that Jones was prompt, unwearied, accurate, instructed, willing, full of resource and at all times of unfailing help to the commissioner. His mastery of the Lunda dialect was of the greatest value.[25]

It was often the case that chairmen of commissions hoped that their secretary would be suitably recognized, and indeed might make discreet recommendations to this effect. However, the 'official recognition' which MacDonnell so openly advocated in this case did not materialize, since Jones was not decorated until 1944, some five years later. After such delay it is unlikely that the award was in recognition of his work as secretary of the commission.

The final months of the commission's work, April and May 1939, were spent in Lusaka. Here MacDonnell heard more evidence, had discussions in the secretariat and with the Governor, and began to write his report. Lusaka was on the line of rail, and this pleased Jones because he could visit Nancy Featherstone, a thirty-year-old nurse, at Broken Hill.[26] Finding she had not been particularly well paid in South Africa (her home country) she had decided to take a nursing job on the Copperbelt in Northern Rhodesia. Almost immediately after she arrived, about Christmas 1937, she was taken to a party and there met, and became friendly with, Jones.[27] He had then gone on leave. On his return, they renewed their friendship. During January, February and March 1939 he received frequent letters from her, which pleased him greatly, noting in his diary: 'Afternoon mail – a good one – letters from Nancy.' Then when he got to Lusaka they were able to phone each other frequently:

'Nancy phoned. Good', 'Phoned Nancy. Good'. And he was able to visit her, sometimes enduring uncomfortable train journeys. He was worried when she was not well and soon realized how much she meant to him:

> Train left Lusaka 12.30 a.m. and arrived Broken Hill 4 a.m. [I went] straight to the hospital where I saw Nancy in bed with tonsillitis, looking not very well but very brave and pleased to see me. As for me I was happy as soon as I saw her and realized that I had been wanting to see her terribly badly for a long time ... Spent the [next] day with Nancy who is much better and says that I am the cause. Gave each other a lot of back chat and ragged each other unmercifully. It was a good day and I found out many things I didn't know before and realized a lot of things I hadn't realized before. [The next weekend I] phoned Nancy 10 o'clock and told her [I was] going to Broken Hill on Goods train leaving [Lusaka] 3.30 [am.] arriving Broken Hill about 9 ... Arrived about 8.45 and walked to hospital ... Nancy looking better. Good. [On Monday morning] left Broken Hill at 7 o'clock on Kaffir mail. Arrived Lusaka 11.40 ... phoned Nancy 9. Afterwards drank in the bar. [The next weekend] left Broken Hill 3.45 am. Goods train. No compartment on it – just the luggage van. Sat on my box the whole way and froze. But it was quite good fun. Arrived Lusaka 9 ... Nancy phoned 7 and I phoned her 11. Good ... [The following weekend] met Nancy at station ... and picnicked in the fields for the day. We had a grand time.

During May he received almost daily letters from her, much to his delight. He was concerned about the position with his wife and, presumably, about the effect of this on his developing relationship with Miss Featherstone. He had told only a small number of colleagues about Margaret and had said to them that he did not know when she would be coming out.

By early July 1939 his work as secretary to the commission was at an end and he returned to his district work in Balovale where he was appointed district commissioner. He was soon on tour, walking up to 25 miles a day, often through thick sand, checking censuses and collecting tax. Conditions were not always comfortable: on one occasion he had to dig a water hole for water which was 'filthy' but which had to suffice since the next camping spot was 15 miles further on and he had already walked 20 miles that day. He sometimes travelled with the doctor who performed a number of operations *en route* while Jones heard court cases. He watched, intrigued and at close quarters, a boys' initiation ceremony and their circumcision. He played football with African schoolboys, loving the game and sometimes cycling 25 miles to to play with them.[28]

His official life continued to involve a good deal of touring, and he took whatever opportunity he could to visit Nancy with whom he corresponded frequently. On one occasion he found himself 'very irritable, and let loose at the messengers for bad arrangements: they were not much to blame – in fact I was a lot to blame myself. The mail boy did not arrive until 2 and he got ticked off for not reaching us yesterday. The mail was good, however, and soothed me. Two grand letters from Nancy.'

As the likelihood of war in Europe increased, the Northern Rhodesia government asked if its officers wished to register to be released for service. On 2 August Jones wrote to the manpower committee asking if he could give them his reasons for wishing to be released for active service with a fighting unit.[29] Just before war was declared, too, he applied to join the Northern Rhodesia Regiment European Reserve, and the commanding officer recommended to the Governor that he be appointed with the rank of sergeant.[30] His provincial commissioner, however, advised the chief secretary to reject the recommendation: 'Jones has unique knowledge of the dispute between the Marozi and the Malunda Malovale, and I think he should be kept at Balovale until Government policy has been decided upon and put into effect. I submit that he will be of much more service to the country in his present position as District Commissioner, Balovale, than as a sergeant in the Northern Rhodesia Regiment Reserve.'[31]

Jones also wrote to the chief secretary saying that if the government felt able to release officers currently in charge of stations, he would be 'very willing to join one of the fighting services either in Africa or overseas'. Shortly afterwards he applied to have his name placed on the register for service with a combatant unit. He added that his wife was in England and provided for.[32]

His applications to join the forces were all turned down, but he persisted, and at the beginning of June 1940 wrote to tell the provincial commissioner he was 'still anxious to proceed on active service, should Government find it possible to release' him. He would prefer to join the navy and, failing this, the air force, with the army coming last on his list of preferences. He preferred, too, to join a combatant unit overseas, but in the event of hostilities in Africa he would be willing to join a colonial unit operating in Africa. Indeed, seeming to reverse his preferences, his definite desire was 'to join a fighting service overseas, should it not be possible for [him] to join one in Africa'.[33] Again the provincial commissioner would not accept his application and there was further disappointment for him because, despite the provincial commissioner's protestations, he was not only kept at Balovale but another officer – one re-engaged for war service – was posted over him as district commissioner while he himself reverted to be district officer.[34]

Jones continued to press his claim and immediately wrote to the provincial commissioner who replied, with a touch of irritation and more firmly than previously: 'Your duty is to stay at Balovale as District Officer for the time being and until the political question has been settled ... It may be hard on you but it's your war job and there's nothing much to be said about it.'[35]

His keenness to join the armed forces would mean that Jones would not be able to see much of Nancy, but this did not seem to dampen his strong desire to leave Northern Rhodesia and fight overseas. Perhaps he was feeling somewhat disillusioned: the recognition of his work as secretary of the MacDonnell commission was not forthcoming, he was placed under a 'dugout' district commissioner after having been district commissioner himself, he may have felt that the provincial commissioner was not being completely open with him. Importantly, too, he may have felt uncomfortable as a recently married man developing a close relationship with another woman. Currently there was no significant prospect of his relationship with Nancy resulting in marriage, since he was already married, though there was no realistic prospect that his wife would join him, or desire on his part that she should. Maybe a spell away from Northern Rhodesia in the armed services would provide time during which this particular problem could be sorted out.

It became clear, however, that he would not be joining the forces. Late in 1941 he petitioned for divorce on the grounds that Margaret had deserted him without cause three years earlier. This step was taken at the earliest time permitted by law. Margaret did not defend the action and the decree nisi was granted on 3 June 1942. She did not enter an appearance and the decree was made absolute on 26 October 1942, notwithstanding that six months had not elapsed since the decree nisi was granted.[36] He was now free to marry Nancy and this he did without delay. They decided that the marriage should take place halfway between the places where they were living, Balovale and Broken Hill. On the last day of October, less than a week after the decree absolute was signed in London, he left Balovale in the early afternoon and walked four and a half hours before camping for the night.[37] The next day he continued walking eastwards for seven hours. He had travelled quite a distance before he remembered that he had not brought the wedding ring with him. Undaunted, he sent a messenger back to Balovale to fetch the wooden box in which he had concealed the ring. The messenger, carrying the large and heavy box, eventually caught up with Jones and all was well.[38] After the first two days, having walked about 40 miles, he travelled the remaining 140 miles by lorry and reached Kasempa on 5 November.

Nancy in the meantime had travelled westwards, 180 miles from Broken Hill to Kasempa in a lorry owned and driven by a Plymouth Brethren missionary, accompanied by 'his henchmen and a small child': 'They prayed incessantly; they prayed before breakfast; they prayed during breakfast; they prayed on the way to the truck; they prayed before morning coffee; they prayed at every stop; knowing that she was going to marry a district commissioner they prayed for him that he should make the right decisions.'[39]

The ceremony had been arranged for early the following morning but the district commissioner, who officiated at the marriage, was on tour dealing with an outbreak of bubonic plague, and was late in returning[40] – someone had to go out and find him – so the marriage took place at 11.30 a.m. The provincial commissioner, who gave the bride away, had made the arrangements for the wedding and the reception, the provisions coming from Fortnum and Mason in London. After the ceremony and the reception Jones played football with two teams of Africans. They spent the rest of the afternoon swimming. The following morning they swam again and Jones played soccer in the afternoon.

The next day, 9 November, he and Nancy started back for Balovale. This journey, of 180 miles in a direct line, took them exactly a month. For the first few miles each day Nancy walked and then was usually carried in a *machila* despite finding it uncomfortable. Much of the journey was made in the rain because the wet season had started. Jones, anxious to show his bride his district and the countryside in which he worked, combined his honeymoon with his normal district touring work, visiting villages on the way, checking censuses, collecting tax, hunting and shooting crocodiles. They reached Balovale on 9 December 1942.[41]

Within a year Jones was posted from Balovale to the Eastern Province – from one side of the country to the other. He was first posted to Feira, an unhealthy site in the Luangwa valley but not without its charms:

> The District Commissioner's house ... stood at the confluence of the Zambezi and Luangwa rivers on a small bluff. The privy was situated some 25 yards upstream on top of a low cliff. It had no door. The seated occupant looked out over the Zambezi, which at that point was about half a mile wide. Hippo in mid-stream were habitual while game of many varieties, including elephant and on one occasion a lion, would frequently be seen watering on the other side. When one took up residence (which often lasted longer than was strictly necessary), one pulled a cord which raised a small flag, thus indicating the premises were occupied and, in case he were needed, the district commissioner's whereabouts.[42]

Jones's predecessor at Feira had been very ill and had killed himself. Partly as a consequence of this it was decided to move the *boma* from its low-lying position to a new site and this task fell to Jones. About the middle of 1944, he began to move the *boma* and housing to a healthier, higher location at Petauke near the Great East Road, which was not only a more comfortable site but also was more central and enabled him better to coordinate the work of the district team. Petauke was a rural district but, unlike Gwembe, Mwinilunga and Balovale, it was not isolated. It was a busy staging post for traffic travelling from Lusaka to Fort Jameson and thence eastwards to Nyasaland. There were a few Asian and African stores which provided some of the local European needs, but otherwise provisions were ordered from Lusaka and came by road. For a rural station there were a fair number of other officers and their families. There were Catholic and Anglican mission stations in the district and a few European and Coloured planters.

Setting up a completely new station inevitably had its difficulties and involved a certain amount of discomfort. Temporary houses were erected while the more permanent buildings were put up, and for a while the station was 'a sprawling cluster of temporary pole and mud huts, pending construction of permanent quarters. The District Commissioner's residence was the only one with the semblance of a house.' This, too, was primitive, but the pole and mud walls were roughly plastered and whitewashed and 'Mrs. Jones [gave the rooms] a homely touch with bright curtains and reed mats'. The lighting in their house was by oil lamp though they used candles at table which were 'as much functional as ornamental in the circumstances'. There was the constant 'faint rumble of termites tunnelling a way to somewhere in the walls [and it was] just as well that the building was temporary, with nature's own demolition squad already moving in'. The bathroom was 'a hut at the back of the house, which had an uneven floor, causing the zinc tub to tilt to and fro in concert with one's movements'. Visitors were accommodated in the Jones's house since there was no official guest house.[43] Many years later, Jones's wife recalled:

> When we went to the new site, there was nothing there. We first of all lived in tents and then built ourselves rondavels and lived in them. We next built 'basket houses' made of split bamboos the walls of which could be pushed in or out like a basket. Over a period of time the walls either bulged in or they bulged out and a lot of dust from the wood weevils in the ceilings of the bamboo house came down and some of it fell on Elisabeth [their first child], who was only three months old, and covered her. She got a very bad skin rash as a result. Later we built permanent houses of brick.[44]

Jones was involved with the agricultural department in the development of cash crop production, the formation of the Petauke producers' association, a cooperative for marketing these crops, and the resettlement of a large area of empty land in the Fort Jameson and Petauke districts acquired by the government in 1941 for resettlement from the overcrowded African reserves.[45]

While they were stationed at Petauke, the Jones's two children were born: a daughter, Elisabeth, in 1944 and a son, Timothy, in 1946. A new member of the provincial team arrived at the provincial headquarters, Fort Jameson, where the hospital provided the nearest maternity facilities, at the time of Timothy's birth and recalled the occasion well: 'The Provincial Commissioner told us that the District Commissioner, Petauke, would be sharing the guest house with us. It was unlikely, however, that we would see him for some time as he was recovering from celebrating with his many friends the birth of his son on the previous day. But he made a rapid recovery and insisted that we join the continuing celebrations.'[46]

In September 1946, Jones was asked if he would accept transfer to Palestine as an assistant district commissioner. His response was immediate: he turned it down, giving as his reasons that the conditions, especially the salary, retirement and pension, were less favourable than those which he currently enjoyed. This, coupled with the high cost of living and the fact that he had 'a young and increasing family' – which may suggest that they intended to have more than two children – led him to believe that, having no private means, he could not afford the transfer.[47]

After nearly four years in Petauke, Jones returned to the Barotse province, this time as district commissioner of the Mongu district. Mongu was not only the district headquarters but also the provincial headquarters and the largest settlement in the province.

Mongu means 'promontory', and its site jutted out from the western edge of the slightly higher plateau into the great flood plain of the Zambezi. This flood plain, 80–120 miles long and 20–25 miles wide, is inundated each year from February to July as the Zambezi waters rise. It is 220 miles from the early capital, Livingstone, and 300 miles from the later capital, Lusaka, both by direct line, but in practice much further by the routes which had to be followed because of the rivers and the terrain.[48] It was not inconveniently cut off by the flooding of the Zambezi which lay to the west of it rather than between it and the other administrative and commercial centres. There was only one centre to the west of the Zambezi which the administration usually visited and which was cut off by the flooding: Lukulu Roman Catholic mission station. The road to the east, through bush and Kalahari sands, to Lusaka was difficult but passable even in the wet season although the journey by motor vehicle took three days and was not often used. The road south to Livingstone was in parts swampy and generally very poor, but passable although, again, the trip took several days. Local travelling was on foot or on bicycle or 'in a one-wheel bush cart with one man pulling and the other pushing' it through the sand.[49]

Because of the distances involved, there was a regular air service from Lusaka to Mongu which visited all the major district centres. Provisions were brought by the monthly barge service from Livingstone by the Zambezi River Transport Service manned by sixteen paddlers, up the Zambezi as far as Sheshele and then by lorries, or were brought all the way over appalling roads by lorries. Because of the large amount of damage caused to the goods and the losses of them, the prices were high. There were occasional other difficulties, too. Colleagues downstream who were 'lax in ordering, or had been too indulgent' would from time to time borrow from supplies being taken upriver and enclose an IOU with their thanks.[50] Generally, Europeans living in Mongu ordered their provisions – flour, sugar and other groceries, drinks and also paraffin for lighting and the refrigerators – in bulk quarterly, and in some cases half-yearly, direct from Livingstone and simply used the local stores to 'plug the gaps' in their lists. Most Europeans received a weekly parcel of perishable goods such as butter, bacon and cheese, flown in on the thrice-weekly air service, and the cost of this was high. From local sources they procured beef, 'wonderful' bream, maize, eggs, chickens, tomatoes, paw-paws, mangoes, bananas and oranges. Supplies of this local produce were seasonal and somewhat uncertain. Bread was made by each household, hops or yeast being used to leaven it. The administration also had a flourishing garden which provided fruit and vegetables. Most people grew flowers in the gardens of their houses: roses, Barbeton daisies, hibiscus, frangipani, bougainvillaea and poinsettia.

In later life, Jones looked back on his time in Mongu with great fondness and a sense of fulfilment. How did he react to, and operate in, the conditions which prevailed there? There are three aspects: the social, the private and the official.

First, the social. The main social activities of the Europeans centred on the 'tiny and intimate' club, private dinner parties ending with charades, Saturday curry lunches, fishing in the non-flood season and tennis. Golf was difficult in the sand but there was 'a very sporting dust-bowl of a nine hole golf course', the 'greens' consisting of sand, and before the players could putt they had to use a scraper to make a smooth path between the ball and the hole. There were weekly dances – on the 'minuscule but much used dance floor' – tennis courts, occasional cinema shows, play readings and a library at the club. At the foot of the Mongu bluff there was a small swimming pool. Football was played all the year round and once a year a team of farmers from Kalomo on the line of rail in the Southern Province flew in to play cricket against Mongu and to enjoy a long social weekend. Other matches were played when sufficient players could be rustled up.

Family groups spent Sundays on the flood plain or on the Little River in eight- or ten-paddle barges, fishing, picnicking (with iced beers), listening to the gramophone, relaxing and 'returning after dark with a hurricane lamp hanging on a pole'. These were peaceful, happy days which those who, like the Joneses, enjoyed them long remembered with great pleasure. Of Jones it was recalled:

> He used to play the organ, on festivals and occasional Sundays for services at the little church ... The organ was a foot pedal variety and very much in its last days, its bellows being very leaky. He was playing one day when the organ finally gave up the ghost. And the hymn being played? 'Our blest Redeemer e'er He breathed His tender last farewell'! His dancing was great to watch. He would hold his partner in a very formal way and determinedly steer straight ahead round the confines of the floor, turning right handed at each corner, never reversing, never trying anything exciting and taking little account of the tempo of the music or the feet of his partner.

He played cricket whenever matches could be arranged and although, as at school, he was 'not a great cricketer' he entered fully into the game and 'batted a bit'.[51] He was described as being as enthusiastic as any of the players 'with a fairly wild harvester's swing at the wicket'. The Joneses entertained regularly and this often took the form of dinner parties at their home. They were frequently invited to other people's dinner parties, 'mostly as two good people and not on account of their positions'. 'He was never stuffy at parties and always moved easily among the guests.' 'At our dinner parties, always followed by charades, he was openly inspired with his acting [and Nancy was] on these occasions extremely enthusiastic.' He took a full part in the life of the Mongu club, lending, as did others, some of his gramophone records for functions there and always being 'ready to be picked for a darts team' and being quite good at it.[52]

Next, in his private life he vastly enjoyed shooting and fishing. This enabled him to indulge the other side of his personality: 'he was both gregarious – parties, informal gatherings, sport – and liked to be on his own when shooting or fishing, without European company, although not always.' 'The plains were full of birds mainly a type of partridge, but Jones stopped over-killing. He was a great conservationist.'[53] This was expressed by another officer in different terms: 'He enjoyed shooting and during his time it was found necessary to protect the shooting of *kwale!!*'[54] So much did he and his family enjoy the rural life of Barotseland that they took some of their local leaves in the more distant parts of the province. For example, after an official visit to Sheshcke, which he much enjoyed, he spent a number of his local leaves there with his family:

> [They] travelled by Land Rover down the river from Mongu, spending

the night at Senanga, the district between Mongu and Shesheke, a total journey of over 200 miles, over a dreadful road ... a four wheel drive vehicle was essential. They stayed with [the DC] at Shesheke for three or four days. During the day [they] visited the Sioma falls, rapids 15 miles upstream, which were very scenic, and the children paddled; visited the forest officer's camp in the teak forests 30 miles away; went to see Chief Lubinda at Mwandi; and crossed the river by a pontoon propelled by paddlers to visit ... the [recruiting agency's] representative. Jones fished, for tiger fish, a fierce fighter and predator, each morning and evening with [the DC's] wife. [They] called out the prisoners from the gaol, who paddled the *boma* barge on the river. [They] played a little tennis. Their children played with the DC's two young children in the small paddling pool and in the garden. One evening [the DC] gave a dinner party ... Other evenings [they] chatted and played canasta.[55]

Finally, his official life. Mongu was the administrative headquarters of both the province and the district and was close to the Lozi capitals – Lealui and Limulunga. Government of the African people by the Litunga and the Barotse Native Government (BNG) was an all-pervasive feature of administration since it was in the Mongu district that the central BNG, the Litunga and the leading social and political personalities were to be found. '[The] DC Mongu, like any DC, was technically the chief central government representative in the district, ultimately responsible in it for any governmental activity, departmental as well as administrative. He was also the chief adviser to the local traditional authority, in this case the BNG.' The district commissioner fulfilled these responsibilities through his routine office work but particularly through various meetings: committee meetings with the BNG, other meetings covering specific issues as they arose and frequent meetings with villagers, dealing with a great variety of problems. It was through his regular touring and that of his assistants, however, that on-going close contact was maintained throughout the district. This was not easy because of the very extensive sandy and flooded areas which forced nearly all travelling to be done on foot or in barges.

It was in Mongu that Jones spent the last few years of his first two decades in Northern Rhodesia. All his time so far had been spent in the districts. It was a life which he thoroughly enjoyed since it enabled him to stay in close contact with the African people and to live the sort of social and private life which he enjoyed. His reputation as a field administrative officer was high. He had, by whatever means, avoided being taken into the secretariat in Lusaka which was the calculated fate of most officers who were considered to have potential for advancement to the highest ranks in the service. There is no evidence that he deliberately avoided this, but it is likely that if it had been proposed during his first two decades in the service that he be drafted into what was generally referred to by field administrators as 'the biscuit factory', he would have done what he could to escape such a fate.

CHAPTER 3

Northern Rhodesia: the Provinces and Secretariat

AT THE very end of 1951 Jones was moved to Lusaka. He had been in the administration just over twenty years – quite a long time for a successful and promising administrative officer to spend in district work without a spell in the secretariat. He had been happily married for nine years and had two small children. Much as the family enjoyed their district life, especially in Mongu, the urban domestic and social facilities and style of life in Lusaka held many attractions. Lusaka was over 4000 feet above sea-level and consequently the climate was pleasant. The European population was 4300. New shops had sprung up in the commercial area, there were three modern hotels, a 'fine European hospital' and three schools for expatriate children, each with boarding facilities. There was a modern airport with regular air services both internally and to East Africa and Southern Rhodesia. The recreational facilities for expatriates were excellent: golf, tennis, squash, cricket, soccer, rugby, hockey, swimming, billiards, horse riding, Saturday night dances and a modern cinema. Private entertaining in dinner and cocktail parties was common. It was not at all a bad place in which to live.[1]

Jones's new post was as commissioner for native development,[2] created after the war to oversee the country's ten-year African development plan. His tasks were extensive and varied: to 'secure coordination of effort throughout the wide field of African development in rural areas' and to maintain liaison between, on the one side, the provincial teams and the development authority, and, on the other, the central departments in Lusaka. His method of handling this responsibility was often 'by summoning meetings to discuss and remove difficulties and frustrations which [were] being experienced by the men in the field'. Another part of his work was to help provincial teams by guiding their applications for funds through the development authority. He did a great deal of touring throughout the country, to stimulate the staff, especially in the more remote areas, to check on development schemes in progress and advise on proposed schemes.

All this work required him to be a member or chairman of a large number of boards and committees. His headquarters staff consisted of a seconded district officer as his assistant, an accountant and a woman clerk-stenographer. He had no field staff. Instead, his work in the field was carried out by the administration and technical departments.

He agreed to accept the post on the understanding that its worth should be adequately recognized. He did this 'as a progressive district officer [who] believed in the importance of the post'[3] but no doubt he recognized its career advantages. Although graded as provincial commissioner the post was generally recognized as not being as senior as a provincial commissioner. It may have been to alter this recognition that he insisted on the post not being downgraded: 'There was, perhaps, a little prejudice against the post from other administrative officers, most of whom considered themselves line managers and generalists whereas the commissioner for native development was a specialist.'

His strengths were seen by his colleagues to include 'enthusiasm and the will to improve the lot of the rural African; the ability to get on with district commissioners, whose cooperation was needed and not always enthusiastically given.' He also had the skills of getting on well with technical officers – 'he never patronised and was well respected and liked'.

The strengths which he brought to the job were recalled many years later by a colleague:

> As a good administrator and organizer with a wide experience of rural conditions in Northern Rhodesia and a sympathetic appreciation of the needs of African people, he could be relied upon to seek ways of meeting these needs and to encourage others to do so. He was pro-active, not just waiting for ideas to come in but proposing them himself ... He toured regularly – probably more than most heads of Departments would do.

Another officer recalled that the commissioner needed to be 'someone with a sharp sense of what was practicable in achieving the improvements in the various communities'. He felt that Jones fitted this requirement well because of his understanding of the conditions prevailing throughout the country.

> He was quite laid back when dealing with schemes and ... let those who may be initiating a proposal provide the substance of the idea and yet, by a quiet application of his knowledge, provide the spark which could set it alight. He was ideally suited for this post for his knowledge of Northern

Rhodesia and its residents was very deep. He also had a very easy manner when dealing with people.

Others, including technical officers, who worked with him recalled that he 'was one of the few top civil servants who could recognize ability in his subordinates and was willing to back his judgement in their decisions. His sporting instincts on the field were carried into his everyday life.' His clerk-stenographer recalled:

> [He] was a quiet man ... I remember he would get up from time to time to gather inspiration by standing with his legs apart, hands in pockets, looking out of the window, and then went back to his desk to write reams of stuff that I typed ... He drafted in pencil, but his rough drafts were not messed up with too many alterations. As a boss he was not a boss, but a kindly ... 'laid back', character. He was not smartly dressed, but comfortable. He had a rather sad expression, with long eyebrows growing over his eyes a bit.

In June 1955, the substantive development secretary went on leave and Jones acted in his place. He was also made a provisional nominated member of the legislative council and a temporary official member of the executive council.[4]

At the end of his period as acting development secretary Jones was promoted to be provincial commissioner, on 1 December 1955. He then went on home leave and on his return on 9 August 1956[5] he was told to fly from Cape Town and take over the Western Province with headquarters at Ndola. He acted as provincial commissioner while the substantive holder, J. Murray, was on leave. 'The term Western Province was somewhat of a misnomer as it conjured up a notion of responsibility for a goodly slice of the whole territory when in fact the bush hinterland of the Copperbelt was little larger than an average rural district.' The provincial commissioner was therefore able to concentrate on the problems of the industrialized Copperbelt and its distribution centre of Ndola which was his headquarters. This post very much involved 'a balancing act between the races, mining power and money, and sheer discrimination'.[6]

Ndola, at just over 4000 feet above sea-level, had an 'agreeable' climate and was set in well wooded and hilly countryside. With a European population of about 3000, it was one of the most important towns in Northern Rhodesia, since it was the commercial and distributing centre of the Copperbelt. There was a well used airport with internal flights and other services to Nairobi and the Congo. The town of Ndola was set out on modern, pleasant lines, its shops were modern, there were numerous important business houses and the provincial headquarters of government departments. There was a central sports club with excellent sporting, recreational and social facilities. There was a very active association life with flourishing branches of various societies.[7] Again, it was not at all a bad place in which to live.

Jones arrived in Ndola at a troubled time for the mining industry. To attract European mine-workers to the developing Copperbelt from the early 1930s onwards, the mining companies had been obliged to set wage and salary rates far higher than those for similar jobs in South Africa and Southern Rhodesia. Until 1955 a closed shop was operated, with the better-paid jobs confined to Europeans.

In September 1955, following a damaging strike by Africans, the European union reluctantly gave way to mounting pressure and transferred several categories of work to Africans. Nevertheless, the Europeans resisted the implementation of the transfer and doggedly dragged their feet. The following June, a three-day strike of Africans took place at Nkana mine and similar 'rolling strikes' followed at the other mines. These went on throughout June, July, August (when Jones arrived) and into early September despite the strenuous efforts of the government labour officers and others to get successful talks started.

The government had a number of major fears: the loss of government revenue from copper should the strikes continue; the loss of life should clashes escalate; the danger of the mining companies failing to meet delivery deadlines and losing overseas markets; and the vulnerability of the railway line.

Eventually, after intense discussions involving the Governor, the labour commissioner and Jones, a state of emergency was declared. The government strategy, to which Jones was a central party, was to use the president of the African union, 'a pragmatist and cooler of hot heads', who was at the time out of the country, bring him back and persuade him to sway the masses to resume work, while the extreme leaders were in gaol under the emergency regulations. Many years later Jones wrote privately: 'over 50 political and trade union officials including Kenneth Kaunda ... were arrested and committed to prison without trial. The signature on the warrants of committal was mine.'[8] The plan was successful, the workers returned to work and the detainees were released fairly soon afterwards.

The senior government labour officer on the Copperbelt, a former district commissioner, who worked closely with Jones at the time said of him:

> In physical stature he was only of moderate height; but he was of very solid build and this was reflected in his strong personality and determination of mind. He had a slight tinge of red or rust in his hair with

noticeable eyebrows which might at first glance suggest a possibility of a fiery temperament! Not a bit of it. Jones was most patient and a very good listener, noting carefully and summarising well all valid points made ... Once he had summarised the points of a meeting and secured agreement from all present, he backed us all to the hilt and we could rely on him completely.[9]

When he left the Copperbelt, on Murray's return from leave at the end of February 1957,[10] he was posted to Mongu again, this time as resident commissioner of Barotseland, a post he held for ten months.

Barotseland Province enjoyed the status of a 'protectorate within a protectorate', reflecting the special relationship struck up with the British crown during the reign of Queen Victoria. As a consequence, the administrative officer in charge of the province was known as the resident commissioner – seen by some as a question of 'one-up-manship' – instead of, as in other provinces, provincial commissioner. Mongu was the headquarters of both the province – covering nearly 50,000 square miles – and one of its five districts.

Jones and his family knew Mongu well from his earlier service and they were extremely happy there. They lived in the new residency, the building of which he now completed. This was a dwelling of magnificent proportions, 'rambling, very spacious, and splendidly cool in the hottest weather'. It had the best site on the top of the hill with a splendid view of the plain in the dry season and of the lake which it became in the wet season. It had a good garden and was quiet and secluded.[11] They were able, individually and as a family, to enjoy all the social and recreational activities which they had so much appreciated when he was district commissioner at Mongu, and now he was able to travel widely – and in many cases in a more relaxed fashion – through the whole province.

The district commissioner of Sesheke recalled an official visit which Jones made to his district in 1957.[12] As on previous visits, he drove by Land Rover, crossing the Zambezi twice by pontoon, manually operated. During his visit he inspected a guard of honour of district messengers and met the *boma* staff – the district officer, the district assistant and the four African clerks. He inspected the *boma* buildings, the school, new houses for European and African staff and a number of other new buildings. He discussed with the district commissioner relationships with the chiefs, the effectiveness of the local *kutas* (councils) in administering justice, collecting tax and helping their people. He inquired into the state of missionary schooling and problems facing the district commissioner with neighbouring territories. He was keen to learn about progress in building new bridges, roads and clinics and the district commissioner's plans for continuing these works in the coming year, so as to make sure that the necessary capital budget requests were made to the public works and health departments. He asked about plans for future touring. He inspected the nearby leprosy camp.

It is clear that he brought to bear on the work of the whole of Barotseland his experience as a district administrator extending over the previous quarter of a century. Despite his very close attention to detail, district commissioners did not feel that he interfered with their work. Indeed, he let them run their districts virtually unimpeded – as he himself would have wished, and had been able to do when a district commissioner. District commissioners tended to admire his attention to detail although some instances of minute detail were found 'aggravating'. One district commissioner 'received a memo from him pointing out that on one of his many budgets which required monthly returns he had overspent by six shillings four and a half pence and unless he could provide a good reason for this he would have it deducted from his salary.'

Jones was able to enjoy his favourite relaxations when on official visits to the various districts. He would 'indicate that an afternoon's quiet fishing would be much appreciated' and he would often be left alone in a shady spot by the river to fish by himself. On other occasions he indulged in more active pursuits, even in the hot weather. A district commissioner recalled:

> [He] wrote to tell me that he and the Secretary for Native Affairs ... would be paying us an official visit and asked me to draw up a programme ... The formal business was completed by lunch time and I suggested that as the temperature was about 105°F, it was too hot to play tennis which I had foolishly included in the programme. To this [Jones] replied somewhat peevishly that 'we've brought our whites' and the game had to go ahead.

There was a particularly notable occasion when he was able to combine the love and skills of fishing with his official duties: an extended tour by the Governor, Sir Arthur Benson.[13] This tour, which lasted three weeks, was to the North Western Province and Barotseland late in August 1957. It was 'very much tailored to the old fashioned and conservative ideas' of the Governor who had himself been a district officer in Northern Rhodesia before the war. It was 'especially designed to include a high content of rural pursuits'. Benson and his private secretary, Michael Priestley, flew from Lusaka to Solwezi where they were met by the provincial commissioner of the North Western Province 'and a whole fleet of cars from Government House which had been driven up from Lusaka'. There was the usual round of official receptions and visits to schools and mission stations and they took a trip to the source of the Zambezi before driving on to Kabompo and then Balovale. In the meantime their kit from Government House was loaded on to barges and preceded them to the confluence of the Kabompo and the Zambezi rivers at Kakalunda on the border between the North Western Province and Barotseland. Here they were met by Jones with his district officer, Ian Mackinson, and a number of the Litunga's representatives.

> It was an idyllic spot with a camp site on the top of a hill with excellent views up the Kabompo river and both up and down the Zambezi ... It was all superbly and elegantly arranged. We spent at least one night at Kakalunda, and then proceeded in a fleet of barges by way of Silonga Palms, Lukulu, Libonda and Lealui to Mongu. At each of our night stops we stayed in riverside camps built in traditional grass compounds by the Paramount Chief's followers. At Lealui the Paramount Chief arranged a regatta of royal barges with all the crews and VIPs in traditional garb. There were also innumerable traditional events, drummers etc., organised by the Paramount Chief at each of our night stops.

Benson's private secretary had never known the Governor, 'a compulsive workaholic', more relaxed and at ease than he was on this occasion.

When Jones was told of the impending visit he immediately recalled his district officer from a tour he was making with some of the Barotseland chiefs to development schemes in the Eastern Province. As Mackinson recalled:

> Benson was entering Barotseland at one of the remotest points ... So, there we all had to be, on parade ... The whole party included Benson and team, Jones, myself and our team, the Paramount Chief and his entourage, the chiefs and village headmen through whose area we were travelling, 48 paddlers for three barges. We would paddle our way slowly downstream towards Lealui and thence to Mongu. Extensive and indeed extravagant camps were constructed on chosen sites along the Zambezi by local villagers. Perhaps there were four or five such camps to accommodate our five-day journey. Everyone had to be fed, perhaps eighty of us! I delegated the shooting of impala, waterbuck, kudu etc., to my head messenger ... He dare not come back empty handed, and to purchase a domestic cow or two in the event of failure would have led to immense loss of face. Meanwhile, back on the river I had a similar problem with the fish – what sort of fish, where they were, how far from the camp, could we find sufficient for at least Benson and the ten or twelve of us who would eat with him that evening? [Jones's] prowess as a fisherman was indispensable to me, but he didn't know the river this far north of Mongu that well. Out went the messages and the fish intelligence network was activated. Back came the information about noon and I would endeavour to position Governor Benson and dedicate the last two hours

before dusk to catching enough of the right kind of fish for our supper. As if that wasn't enough responsibility, [Jones] kindly reminded me that Governor Benson was, so to speak, on a fishing holiday and it was proper for him to catch the fish, not us, although we all had our lines out! I could see my career ... folding, before my two seniors, Resident Jones and Governor Benson, on the slender possibility of His Excellency catching sufficient bream to feed twelve of us before 8 pm. that evening. Jones's skill – sort of leading from the back – as he gently positioned the Governor, for catch after catch, was supreme.

The resident commissioner of Barotseland had close, ongoing, dealings with the paramount chief, the clearly acknowledged leader of his people, and with the highly organized indigenous system of government of the Barotse. He visited the Litunga on average every five days. These dealings had to follow a protocol and required significant skills of diplomacy, advising, persuading and guiding by argument and influence. The difference between dealing with the Barotse leaders and dealing with the leaders of other tribes in Northern Rhodesia was described by one senior officer:

With other tribes he would tell them what he wanted done and they would reply that if that was what the government required, of course they agreed and would make the necessary orders. They would then do nothing whatever to enforce those orders. With the Barotse it was quite different. He would have to spend a whole day with the *kuta*, arguing his case against constant and very apposite questions. At the end of the day, if he had made his case, the *kuta* would make the order, and would then enforce it most strictly.[14]

Part of the general atmosphere was captured by Lord Hastings who stayed at the residency in Mongu with the Joneses in April 1957 and who was regaled by the resident commissioner with stories – varying in credibility – of some of the more unusual aspects of African life. He described the visit as 'one of the most fascinating of my many tours in colonial Africa'. He met the Litunga and attended one of his audiences. The Litunga wore a top hat and long tail-coat given to his grandfather by Queen Victoria. His subjects entered the throne room ('more like a village hall') on hands and knees, and when they retired they had to crawl backwards.

It was also the time of a famous trial of two old women for cannibalism. They had eaten a baby, probably a grandchild who had died a natural death, so murder was not involved. When Glyn Jones questioned them in the first place, they left him with this parting line, 'But, bwana, you have no idea how delicious it was'! ... Jones had also been DC for a district to the north-west of Barotseland [and] he arranged for me to go there ... and I was met by a cortege of Africans ... who carried me in a *machila* shoulder high, while chanting, into the presence of their chief. He told me I was the first white man to visit his tribe, apart from the DCs, since the reign of Queen Victoria, and presented me with a witchdoctor's doll, which I still have ... When used it was covered with feathers stuck on with blood and was a gruesome sight. The only other people to have one were Alan Lennox-Boyd and the Queen Mother![15]

Jones's time at Mongu was extremely happy and fulfilling. In later years he and his wife looked back on it with profound fondness. In his personal life great contentment came from his happy marriage and from his children. He took great pride in his son, Timothy, recording in his diary his physical development and his accomplishments in sport and fishing. In his official work he was able to tour the five districts in his province, remain in close touch with the Africans – a feature of life which many administrators were obliged, with deep regret, to forgo as they rose to senior rank – and to indulge the pleasures of rural African life with its walking, shooting and fishing. In much of this he was able to involve his family who accompanied him either on tour or on local leave. It was rather like the life of a country squire, of a landed gentleman.

Professionally, he now occupied a very senior post in the administration. He took pains to develop his provincial team of administrators and specialists, demonstrating his own leadership qualities. In his relationships with the Litunga he dealt with an influential African leader, a traditionalist commanding the respect of his many followers.

The tour that he organized for Governor Benson was professionally and, for his future career prospects, of considerable importance. They were almost exactly the same age – a fortnight separated them – and they had been at Oxford at the same time, Benson graduating a year before Jones. Jones had joined the colonial service as a cadet the year before Benson. In 1931 they had both been members of the Adelphi Club which had only twenty members.[16] Later, after retirement, they both became honorary fellows of Oxford colleges. They both loved fishing and shooting. Of the 1957 Barotseland tour, Benson's private secretary recalled that, in addition to the superb fishing and other arrangements Benson clearly regarded the whole experience as 'justification of all his pet theories about indirect rule and the vital importance of the chiefs in British colonial rule'. Equally clearly, he saw Jones as 'the epitome of a relaxed colonial paladin, in complete and comfortable control of his province and on excellent terms with the traditional chiefs'. Political agitation was unknown in Barotseland at that time and, although none of them realized it, they were seeing 'the last few years of successful indirect rule in Northern Rhodesia'.[17]

So good had been the arrangements for the tour and so impressed was the Governor with the resident commissioner's competence and particularly his sympathy with his own views on African administration that he moved quickly to make sure that Jones's support and advice were brought directly to bear in the secretariat as secretary for native affairs (SNA). The private secretary saw a direct connection between the tour and Jones's transfer to Lusaka:

> His very success was his undoing. I am quite sure at that time that he had achieved his own career nirvana – Commissioner of the most remote, interesting and well organised native administration in Africa, with a great variety of hunting, shooting and fishing available according to season at his whim. Minimum interference from Lusaka was ensured by the special status of Barotseland and by the remoteness and poor communications. He must have thought that he could stay there until his retirement ... and avoid all the hassle and unpleasantness of a final Lusaka posting. I was not privy to the nature of the pressure applied by His Excellency to persuade Jones to accept the SNA job in Lusaka but imagine it was totally overwhelming!!

Priestley believed that Benson saw Jones as a mirror-image of himself and a person who 'would wholeheartedly support his traditional views in an Executive Council increasingly dominated by federalist politicians wishing to curb the traditional role of the chiefs'. In the event he was not disappointed and in Lusaka Jones became 'perhaps his closest friend and certainly his most trusted lieutenant and confidant'.

> Sir Arthur felt a real need for a soul-mate in Lusaka. He was widely seen, in political circles at least, as very old fashioned in his respect for the chiefly system and its longer term significance. Many of his senior colonial service colleagues were sceptical at that stage, and it was clearly a great help to him to have an SNA to dampen this tendency down in whom he could place complete trust. Jones shared his convictions totally and could be relied on to implement his policies without question.

Jones stayed as resident commissioner for a relatively short time. Benson's Barotseland tour started on 21 August 1957 and on 5 December – only nine months after he had taken up the post – Jones was told by Douglas Hall, who was shortly to become Governor of Somaliland, that he was to succeed him as secretary for native affairs.[18] Very early in January 1958 he moved to Lusaka. Benson had asked Hall to recommend who should be the next two secretaries for native affairs and he had advised that the post should go to Jones and thereafter to Robin Foster, another of the provincial commissioners. Benson agreed and Hall called Jones into the secretariat to fill the post of seconded provincial commissioner 'to get used to the idea of taking over' from him.[19] When Hall left, Jones succeeded him as secretary for native affairs.

As secretary for native affairs, Jones's responsibilities were for African administration and included the control of the provincial and district administration.[20] He exercised this control through the provincial commissioners and was directly responsible to the Governor. He was also responsible for rural and community development and the traditional courts. He was a member of both legislative and executive councils, and of most of the inter-departmental committees and the security and intelligence committee.

It was necessary for the secretary for native affairs to tour in the provinces and districts and Jones took full advantage of this. It enabled him to remain in close contact with the rural areas and people. 'So much of his service had been involved with rural African communities that they were an important part of his life' and one which he was reluctant to forgo more than he was obliged to.[21]

In the office he was reckoned by those who worked closely with him to be:

> a good rather than an easy man to work for. Good in the sense that he left his officers to get on with the job within the guidelines he had laid down, but demanding in the standards he required. He expected officers to accept responsibility and take decisive action as the situation required; and he would support them when he considered they were being subjected to unreasonable criticism or unfair attack.

Jones was reckoned by his colleagues to be a good administrator at headquarters, not wasting his own time or that of his officers. Unless the subject was complex, he took quick decisions. In the case of decisions on practical problems his field experience enabled him to propose ready solutions. In more complex matters which might lead to committee discussions, 'he was not patient with unduly involved and unnecessarily prolonged arguments or unreasonable personal commitment to a particular solution'.[22]

During Jones's period of office as secretary for native affairs there were a number of serious problems which came to the fore, with which he had to contend and on which he had to advise the Governor. The most important of these was the displacement of the Gwembe valley Tonga villagers. In the Gwembe valley, where Jones had served during his earliest days in Northern Rhodesia, the Tonga were much aggrieved by the decision to flood the Zambezi valley and consequently remove the inhabitants from the lower-lying areas when the Kariba dam was being built by the federal government. The district officer locally had spent a long period trying to explain to the Tonga why it was necessary to move out of the valley which would shortly be flooded. His explanations, and those of the district and provincial commissioners, fell on deaf ears. The people flatly and consistently refused to move and it was clear to the administrators on the spot that only by the use of force could they be moved. A native authority order instructed the people to move and authorized the use of force if they refused. Benson, Jones and others at headquarters were deeply reluctant to use force. They felt that the Tonga people were not really to blame but were being used by Congress politicians – opposed to federation and all its manifestations – to defy government and the law.

Benson decided that Jones should go to the Gwembe valley to assess things for himself.[23]

> Accordingly, he set off before dawn the next morning on the road to Gwembe. The police ... sent an escort to bring him through the last few miles towards the river, because the track passed close to [where several hundred Tonga had gathered with traditional weapons and were behaving in a very warlike, provocative and defiant fashion].
>
> [Jones] was well experienced with rural Africans; and it only took [the provincial and district commissioners and the district officer] a matter of hours to convince him that they were right [that only force would work]. Late that night, Jones told the senior officer of police that the plan [to force removal] was approved, subject only to the sanction of the Governor. The next morning Jones returned to [Lusaka with the provincial commissioner. The district commissioner and the district officer] and the police waited for the final order. But thirty-six hours later [the provincial commissioner] came back to say that the Governor had not agreed, but was coming in person, with full ceremony and a military band, to see if he could make the Tonga move.

Fellow officers felt that Benson 'could not refrain from concerning himself with the detail of events', and that he ' must have been a trial to Jones'. They 'raised a metaphorical eyebrow' when they learned of Benson's tactics.

The Governor arrived in the Gwembe valley on 6 September with the band of the 1st Northern Rhodesia Regiment, two hundred policemen, several vehicles, full camping equipment and a large union flag.[24] Over the course of the next three days he held a number of meetings of various sizes. He wore full gubernatorial white uniform with regalia, plumed hat and sword. The provincial and district commissioners, the district officer and the Governor's private secretary were also in white colonial uniform with swords. The band played selections from comic opera before dinner while the Governor was bathing. Much of the ceremonial and what the Governor had to say to the Tonga – some of the most primitive people in Africa – was, to modern minds, Gilbertian: 'Greeting. I am the Governor. I have been told there is something troubling your hearts, and I have come to find out what it is.' 'These are the Queen's words: "So that you shall not suffer you will move now before the water starts to rise."' Benson none the less showed great courage in the face of considerable hostility and physical threats, and attempted by simple logic, appeals to loyalty and accusations of shameful behaviour to win over the headmen. He failed.

Two days after the Governor left the Gwembe valley, the police moved in and a pitched battle ensued – shotguns, tear gas and rifles against large numbers of spears. At least six Tonga were killed and a much larger number wounded. Within a few days the village people began voluntarily to leave their old home for new ones on higher land.

In 1959 there were constitutional changes in Northern Rhodesia in which elected members of the legislature were made ministers and placed in charge of some government departments. Other departments remained in the charge of officials and one of these was native affairs. Consequently, Jones's post was retitled minister of native affairs and chief commissioner.[25]

Jones's relationships with the Governor, Benson, are interesting. We have already seen the care with which he prepared for and carried out Benson's tour of Barotseland in 1957. He was also at pains to convey kind, understanding and sympathetic personal messages to the Governor at times of worry and unhappiness. Two examples will suffice to illustrate this kindness. In 1955 when one of the Bensons' daughters fell from a horse and was badly injured,[26] Jones wrote to him to express his deep concern and thankfulness at the child's survival. Benson was touched and profoundly grateful:

> My dear Jonas, Bless you for your letter and thank you very much indeed for writing it. Both Daphne and I have been quite overwhelmed by the wonderful kindness shown to us since that very dreadful Saturday night when Anna's chances of coming through seemed nil, and the next couple of days when she made so splendid a climb back ... thank you and all of you for all the help which your sympathy and kindness has given to us. Yours ever, Arthur Benson.[27]

Then again, at the time of the Gwembe troubles, knowing that the Governor was distressed at the outcome, Jones – notwithstanding his private feeling that the Governor had not acted wisely – telephoned to commiserate with and to comfort him. Benson was again deeply touched: 'My very dear Jonas, I want you to know that your telephone call to me yesterday about the Gwembe trouble was worth my pension to me, and lightened the blackness of the day very much. And it was because you knew that it would do just that, that you did it ... God bless you and thank you. Arthur.'[28]

Other officers, some mildly critical, were aware of how well Jones got on with Benson: 'I have always had the impression that he was ... somewhat sychophantic towards Sir Arthur. But then so were a lot of others ... those who were not so close to him regarded him as slightly pontifical and very slightly "bogus".' Others, too, felt that when Jones moved into the secretariat he became more remote from his fellow officers and less sympathetic towards their needs and problems.[29] Such criticisms were not unusual, and may have been inevitable, when officers moved from the provinces and districts to the secretariat. We have already noted the tendency, mild as it was, when he was commissioner for native development, for his post, though formally equivalent to that of a provincial commissioner, not to be so regarded by others; for generalist field officers displaying 'a little prejudice'; and for district commissioners 'not always enthusiastically' cooperating with him.

Jones went on leave in August 1959. He could have retired at the age of fifty, in January 1958, and it is possible that Benson offered him promotion to be secretary for native affairs at that time in order to retain him. Compulsory retirement was at 55 years and he would reach this age in January 1963. Given that he had a fair amount of accumulated leave due to him which would have to be taken before he retired, his anticipated final tour would be somewhat less than three years.

CHAPTER 4

Nyasaland: Chief Secretary

JONES spent most of his leave visiting his family and friends in Britain. On 15 September he was asked by Hilton Poynton, permanent secretary at the Colonial Office, to visit the office, and this he shortly did.[1] This sort of visit was not unusual, and officials would have been keen to be brought up to date with affairs in Northern Rhodesia, since a general election was shortly to be held in Britain which would result in a new secretary of state for the colonies being appointed.

At some stage – almost certainly during this visit – his opinion was sought on Robin Foster's suitability for the post of chief secretary of Nyasaland, which, much against the will of the Africans, had joined Northern and Southern Rhodesia in the Central Africa Federation when it was created in 1953. Foster, a provincial commissioner in Northern Rhodesia, and a close friend of Jones, was acting in his stead while he was on leave. About a year earlier, the question arose of whether the current Nyasaland chief secretary, Charles Footman, should extend his service beyond the normal retiring age, as he wished, or whether a new chief secretary should be appointed. The secretary of state fairly rapidly decided on the latter, and a wide trawl quickly resulted in narrowing consideration to only two officers: John Ingham, secretary for African affairs in Nyasaland, and Foster. Armitage, Governor of Nyasaland, favoured the former and the Colonial Office the latter. Poynton felt there was advantage in bringing in new blood from outside Nyasaland and in doing so 'from the sister territory of Northern Rhodesia.'[2] Had Armitage not persisted in his view that Ingham was the better candidate, Foster would have been offered the job about the middle of 1959 and would then have accepted it, although a year later, when again offered the post, he initially turned it down because he had eight years left before retirement and was sure Nyasaland would not last that long.[3]

Since then, circumstances in Nyasaland had changed substantially. Dr Banda had returned to the country to lead the Nyasaland African Congress, after an absence of over forty years, with the avowed determination to achieve the protectorate's secession from the Federation and its independence from Britain. Nationalist political activity had violently accelerated and constitutional advance had been held up as a result. A state of emergency had been declared under which some 1300 Congress members had been detained. Banda, his principal lieutenants and many of his followers were still in prison. The Devlin commission of inquiry had found the declaration justified but there had been some illegal activity in effecting the arrests of those detained.

Although the government had largely rejected Devlin's report and had supported Armitage's actions, he had in fact written it in a way intended to assist them. The essence of his political message – though he claimed to eschew politics generally and in this particular case repeatedly claimed so – was that there was an impasse in Nyasaland and unless the government was to govern indefinitely by force it had to extricate itself. This necessitated dealing with Banda and ending the state of emergency. Of great importance was his distinction between Banda, whom he found 'charming' and not violent, and his principal lieutenants, particularly Henry Chipembere, whom he found to be men of violence. Without this distinction, the government would find it difficult to justify dealing with Banda.[4]

So, events had considerably altered the position in Nyasaland. Soon after the October 1959 British general election, in which the Conservatives were returned with an increased majority, Macmillan began to prepare for a major tour of Africa in which his 'wind of change' speeches were to symbolize the changes taking place – and others which he believed should take place. He decided the impasse had to be broken and conditions created for orderly constitutional progress in Nyasaland. This would involve considering the future form and scope of the Federation, and he realized that changes in Central Africa would have repercussions elsewhere in Africa, but he felt changes generally were necessary. To effect these changes, he appointed Iain Macleod as colonial secretary.

One of Macleod's early steps was to see Devlin.[5] It is virtually certain that he sought Devlin's views on Nyasaland and was given, clearly, the message which was – through a last-minute deletion of the drafted final chapter – not clear in his report. Another step was to consider the top administration in Nyasaland where Devlin had found officers above provincial commissioner level unimpressive. That top level included Armitage, Footman and Ingham. This confirmed the decision to replace Footman and seriously reduced Ingham's chances of succeeding him. In mid-November the Colonial Office told Armitage that, among others, Jones was now being considered for the post. On 19 December Macleod told him he had decided Jones should be the next chief secretary. They agreed that he should take over on 30 June 1960. None of this was known to Jones.[6]

The Jones family were away skiing in Switzerland from 1 to 15 January 1960.[7] On their return a formal letter awaited him, dated 6 January, offering him the chief secretaryship of Nyasaland, starting 'towards the end of June'.[8] This, his first indication that he was even being considered for Nyasaland, was accompanied by a personal letter from Poynton:

> You will be receiving together with this, a formal offer of appointment as Chief Secretary, Nyasaland, and this will, I am sure, be a little puzzling to you as some time ago your view was sought informally on the suitability of Foster of Northern Rhodesia for this appointment.
>
> I am writing to explain that the Secretary of State himself has decided that this appointment is of such crucial importance now as to demand the appointment of a candidate of whose quality and experience he is in no doubt whatever. Hence, here is the offer to you. I realise that you may in your present post feel this is something of a sideways step rather than an obvious promotion, but ... the Secretary of State feels he is asking you to take a more important and more difficult post than that which you now hold. The Nyasaland appointment is indeed one which we all regard as a very key post in Colonial affairs at the present time. I believe it offers exceptional opportunities for worthwhile service.[9]

Jones arrived back from Switzerland on Friday 15 January, and on the Monday and Tuesday went to the Colonial Office to discuss the Nyasaland offer with Poynton. He then accepted – with some reluctance. He and his family were extremely happy in Northern Rhodesia where they had many friends. They were looking forward to a comfortable final tour there before retiring.[10] Life in Lusaka was very much more sophisticated than it was likely to be in Zomba, Nyasaland's capital. Additionally, the Nyasaland salary was very little higher than his present salary, and Armitage had refused to increase it.[11] There may have seemed few advantages in this late transfer to a smaller and poorer country, even on promotion. Furthermore, since he knew others had been seriously considered, he may have wondered if, and why, they had rejected it. Yet the offer of a chief secretaryship must have been very tempting since it carried the opportunity to act as Governor when the substantive incumbent was away from Nyasaland. No doubt, too, he considered Armitage's probable future and would be well aware that while his predecessor in Nyasaland, Governor Colby, had been reappointed for an extra three years, Benson in Northern Rhodesia had not and indeed had recently been succeeded by Hone, his chief secretary. Whatever considerations he may have had in mind, he accepted the post and continued to enjoy the last few weeks of his leave.

On 23 January he saw his children off at London airport since they were returning to school. He then went to Chester for the last week of his leave to stay with his mother while his wife made the final arrangements for their departure, scheduled for 3 February.[12]

Circumstances in Nyasaland were again changing swiftly. Macleod had seen Armitage in Dar es Salaam on 18 and 19 December 1959 and had made it clear the emergency would have to be lifted at an early date and the detainees, other than a small hard core, released. Armitage, on security grounds, had argued forcefully against the fast rate of release Macleod proposed and against ending the emergency in the absence of any clear, or indeed unclear, policy on Nyasaland's future. They had eventually agreed on a programme of accelerated releases and on Banda being treated as other detainees – staying in detention so long as Armitage considered him a threat to security – rather than, as Macleod wished, given special treatment.[13] In the event, Macleod immediately reneged on this agreement and advised the cabinet on an even faster rate of releases and on freeing Banda at a very early date, irrespective of the Governor's assessment of the security dangers.[14]

Additionally, Macmillan had undertaken his Africa tour, in the course of which he fleetingly visited Nyasaland on 25 and 26 January. The visit, short as it was, was significant on two grounds. First, Macmillan and Armitage had a distasteful altercation over the date of Banda's release and the place – Britain or Nyasaland – to which he should be released. Second – and most important, as it transpired, for Jones's future – during a civic luncheon in Blantyre, the prime minister witnessed a minor disturbance and formed the view, or more likely pretended to have formed it, that the Nyasaland police had over-reacted.

Using these grounds – the row with Armitage and the disturbance – Macmillan wrote to Macleod on 28 January, saying he would feel very much happier if Macleod could take immediate steps to strengthen the administration in Nyasaland. He added: 'I understand, for example, that Footman is due to retire in a few months' time. Could you not send a good man there to replace him now?'[15] Macleod agreed. Macmillan's words suggest that he did not know the chief secretaryship had been offered to Jones.

While Jones was returning from Chester on 1 February his wife took a call asking him to go immediately to the Colonial Office for urgent discussions. She met him at the railway station and gave him the message. He went quickly to the office and was told he would probably be required to take up the post of chief secretary in Nyasaland immediately rather than at the end of June as expected. He returned to the Colonial Office the following day 'to see if [there was] any change of plan [but found that there was] none'. This 'bombshell', as he described it, caused the

Joneses radically to rearrange their departure for Africa. They decided that while he should fly back within a very few days, she would return by sea, as they had both intended, on the *City of Port Elizabeth* the next day, 3 February.[16] This was the very day that Macmillan delivered his 'wind of change' speech in Cape Town.

Jones then spent two days at the Colonial Office and on the second of these he met the secretary of state. Macleod spoke to him about the possibility of ending the Federation and of releasing Banda. He spent one more day in London, buying clothes and a fishing rod and watching Wales beat Scotland at rugby, on television.[17]

The following afternoon he left by air for Lusaka. He stayed at Government House as the guest of Hone and spent the next ten days working and attending farewell parties. On Friday 19 February, he flew to Zomba. He lunched with the Footmans and dined with the Armitages. He spent the weekend at Government House, devoting the mornings to working in the office with Footman. Each afternoon he accompanied Armitage on his habitual walk round the gardens of Government House. He attended evensong at the Anglican church on Sunday evening.

Within his first ten days in Nyasaland he met all members of the executive council, the three provincial commissioners, the commissioner of police, half the district commissioners, a number of their assistants, some of the chiefs and the detainees in Kanjedza camp.

He had a few days of relative ease when his wife arrived on 3 March though it took them a while to settle into the chief secretary's house. The Footmans had been required to move out at short notice and stay at the small hotel on Zomba plateau, which occasioned their distress and incurred criticism among the Zomba residents. They were guests of the Zomba club for the opening of the new cinema and attended a performance of *King Richard II* at the African teachers' training college, which he found 'inaudible, unintelligible and deadly'.

Jones was asked to visit Banda in gaol in Gwelo, Southern Rhodesia, by Armitage who thought it would 'help a bit' with his arrangements for Macleod's proposed visit. He wished to know 'what Banda is now thinking'. During the flight on 10 March

> [He] tried to imagine what might happen at a meeting with a man he had never met before and whom [he] had seen only on a television screen where he was subjected to questioning which he clearly considered was disagreeable and to which he responded sharply, earning himself the undying disapproval of many members of the media and of right-wing politicians in Britain and Central Africa who were being embarrassed by the Conservative Government's wind of change policy.[18]

At Gwelo he was given a small room – he believed it was the prison telephone exchange – for his interviews. The telephone machinery constantly clattered and made conversation difficult. Later he was to say, 'If our conversation was not bugged by the federal prison staff [as he believed it was][19] then Welensky was not the man I thought he was!'[20] The venue is surprising because when Dingle Foot and others interviewed Banda it was in the doctor's fairly well furnished and comfortable room. It is unlikely the conversation was bugged – though Foot's had been – because the federal government would have been entitled to assume that if they needed to know what transpired they had simply to ask Jones, a senior officer of one of the constituent territories of the Federation.

As Jones recalled:[21]

> I was struck by his bright alert appearance and immaculate clothing, from spotless white shirt and smart necktie, his well-cut dark suit, down to his brightly polished black leather shoes. He looked what he was – a respectable general practitioner with a successful city practice ... He was clean shaven. He had a deep voice for a small man and spoke in what I regarded as correct English, grammatically and syntactically perfect with the breadth of vocabulary and flavour of a cultured Scot.

He thought Banda was astutely sizing him up and sensing that they would see a great deal of each other in the future. He also had much shorter meetings with Chipembere and the Chisiza brothers, and was 'greatly impressed by the earnest sincerity of Dunduzu.'

Jones's discussions with Banda took place on two days for a total of four hours. So confident was the doctor of his ultimate leadership of a sovereign Nyasaland, that he spoke in detail of his plans for the country's development. He was clear that either the Federation had to be abandoned before Nyasaland received its independence, or Nyasaland's secession would bring about the collapse of the remainder of the Federation. He seemed supremely confident that the British government would release him and allow him to mount a political campaign. He was emphatic his methods would be peaceful. He could not conceive of any need for violence, provided he was permitted to operate freely as a political leader pursuing a legitimate policy. Violence, if it came, would not be of his making, and he was sure he could control his 'young men'. He was equally confident that his personal dedication, his influence over his people and the outstanding organization of the Malawi Congress Party would win the day for him in the not too distant future.

Notwithstanding Banda's supreme confidence in his personal ability and in the inevitability of his ultimate success, and his likening himself to Nehru, Gandhi and Nkrumah, Jones was impressed by his humility.

The following day Jones returned to Salisbury, visited the eleven detainees in Marandellas prison, and met the federal officials who would be involved in the event of Banda's release from gaol. He saw George Loft – of the American Friends Service Committee, who had frequently met with Banda and acted as an intermediary – and handed him a letter to give the doctor. On 14 March he flew back to Nyasaland and spent the evening telling the Governor about his Gwelo and other discussions.[22]

Jones's impression was that Banda was a dedicated, somewhat ascetic, man without racial prejudice, confident of his destiny, anxious for peace and, above all, a man with whom he could work. This, he said, was vitally important for one who, he claimed a decade later – possibly with the cataractal blurring that sometimes occurs with retrospection – already knew he was probably to be the next, and possibly the last, Governor of Nyasaland. It was, of course, more immediately important that as chief secretary he should be able to work with him. Like Devlin a few months earlier, Jones found Banda charming.[23]

Banda's reaction to Jones was revealed in a letter he wrote to him less than a week after the visit.[24] Written on prison paper, it was passed by a prison officer who, consequently, was aware of its contents:

> On Monday morning, Mr George Loft handed me a letter you had written to me on Saturday, March 12th. I greatly appreciated your letter. Once again the letter showed to me the difference between you and the others with whom I have been dealing. You did not have to write, just as you did not have to come and see us, so soon after your appointment. I was deeply and greatly touched by the letter ... because it shows how thoughtful and considerate you are of others. As I mentioned it in our conversation, when you were here, whatever my faults – and they may be many – lack of appreciation of others' good deeds to me and good intentions towards me and my people and my country, is not one of them.

He continued, saying he also very much enjoyed their meeting, which was a good opportunity for them to begin to know each other. He realized they had a long way to go, but he was looking forward, very much, to the time when they would see more of each other. 'If I may be permitted to say so ... releasing detainees will not mean disturbances in Nyasaland. Just the opposite. It will mean joy and happiness for the people [and] the end of present tension and distrust.'

There are a number of interesting points in this letter. It confirms that Loft was openly used as an intermediary. Banda and Jones each wrote to the other very shortly after the visit and the doctor was deeply and greatly touched by Jones doing so; Footman probably had not. Banda saw Jones as being different – thoughtful and considerate – from others with whom he had dealings in the past. They both saw the visit as an opportunity to get to know each other and Banda had high hopes that he would soon see more of Jones, to the benefit of Nyasaland and its people. He was confident that, far from causing unrest, the release of the remaining detainees would end the existing tension and mistrust and would greatly help race relations. This first meeting greatly impressed Jones and he referred to it from time to time over the succeeding years as, less frequently, did Banda.

The second half of March passed with the Joneses settling into their house, the usual round of social activities and some first attempts at fishing on Zomba plateau. In the office there were meetings with the Governor and the attorney-general, dealing with precautions against disturbances when Banda was released.[25] The date for this and the details of how it was to be accomplished had been fixed in direct negotiations between Armitage, who secured several postponements, and Macleod. Jones played little part because the operation had been largely worked out before he arrived.

Macleod arrived in Nyasaland on 29 March and Jones went with the Governor to meet him at Chileka. Meetings with the secretary of state, involving Jones, were held that evening and during the next two days. Banda was collected from Gwelo goal by Youens, the deputy chief secretary, flown back to Zomba early in the morning of Friday 1 April and delivered at Government House a few minutes after 9 a.m. He was taken in to meet Macleod and Armitage at 10.15 a.m. Jones played no part in the morning's activities until he brought Orton Chirwa and Aleke Banda – who together had founded the Malawi Congress Party during Banda's incarceration – to meet Macleod, Armitage and Banda. They had no idea why they had been asked to Zomba. Shortly, the doctor recorded a message asking for peace and calm, and then left with Chirwa and Aleke Banda to recuperate at his house in Limbe.[26] Jones stayed on at Government House and 'had gins' there. In the evening he went to police headquarters with Richard Kettlewell, staff officer to the Nyasaland operations committtee during the state of emergency, to monitor reaction to Banda's release and then 'drank with him at his house'.[27]

Jones gave a dinner party for the secretary of state at their house on the evening of 4 April. He invited the acting provincial commissioner and the officer in charge of police in the Southern Province over from Blantyre to join them for dinner and made it clear they were expected to attend. Since the Governor himself was at an official function in Blantyre, and was not told about the invitation, they thought it their duty to stay in attendance on him. They consequently declined the invitation and long considered it improper and embarrassing for the invitation to have been extended. It may also have been the case that they did not wish to spend another evening in Macleod's company, since five evenings previously they had been present when he had been gratuitously and grossly offensive, extremely rude and downright unpleasant at a meeting with the Governor, the provincial commissioners and senior police officers. They would have known, too, of the occasion the following day when Macleod lost control of himself, shouted at the non-official members of executive council and told one of them to 'mind his own bloody business'.[28]

On 6 April, Banda left to visit Britain and the United States. The following day, Macleod also left. Everyone was much relieved that Banda's release had been effected without disturbances, and once he and Macleod had left, Armitage, Jones and others looked forward to a period of peace and quiet.

With Banda's successful release, Macleod arranged a conference at Lancaster House to agree constitutional advance for Nyasaland, and the emergency was lifted on 16 June, leaving only a score in detention. Soon after Banda returned from his overseas trip in the middle of June he met with Jones.[29] Originally he had intended to talk only about delegates to the conference but,

> since the 'phoney' termination of the emergency he had been given another compelling reason for the interview. Why was the Government continuing to detain twenty people at Kanjedza? He wished the Governor to know that he was profoundly dissatisfied with ... this matter. He had been led to understand by both Mr Macleod and the Governor that if, after his release from detention, the situation remained peaceful, there would be a reasonable chance that all people would be released from detention. He was astounded and violently disappointed that the Governor had decided to retain twenty people in detention.

Jones responded that Armitage had reason to believe those still in detention had not given up their idea of securing political change by violence and consequently he was justified in continuing their detention so that they could not 'exert their malign influence on other members of the MCP and on the public at large'. They particularly discussed Chipembere whose continued detention Banda said was 'stupid ... since it would only make him more bitter. He should be released and Banda could vouch for his good behaviour.' Jones could not possibly agree with this: 'Chipembere was a violent young man whose behaviour in detention showed that he was resolved to be as bitter and difficult as he could be.' He showed Banda a recent letter from Chipembere in which 'he expressed himself in immoderate terms and displayed his contempt for established authority'.[30]

Armitage attended the Lancaster House conference from 20 July to 5 August, and Jones was Acting Governor during his absence. The conference's unanimous agreement provided for a legislature of five officials, eight higher roll and twenty lower roll elected members; and an executive of five officials – three *ex officio* and two nominated – with three lower roll and two upper roll elected members, all to be styled ministers. The two nominated official executive councillors were replaceable by elected members at the Governor's discretion. Up to three parliamentary secretaries could be appointed.[31]

Shortly after the conference, Armitage went on leave (on 10 August) and Jones was again appointed Acting Governor. Macleod's approach towards Banda was shortly given to Jones by Monson at the Colonial Office.[32] The basic tactic – and consequently that required of the Governor and, in his absence, Jones – was so to handle Banda that he in particular, but also other African politicians, would become involved in the work of government – become a member of the executive council – and thereby learn that federation had distinct benefits for Nyasaland. To achieve this they had to be patient, give Banda a fair chance of settling down and strive to create an environment in which he could gradually move further towards the centre – politically by a non-violent, more moderate approach, and constitutionally by a more balanced approach to continuing association with the Rhodesias, in particular being prepared to consider the Monckton report on the Federation's future and attend the federal review conference. Such was Jones's confidence in the secretary of state's ability that he believed 'it was by no means impossible that [Macleod] could sell the federal concept, even to Banda'. Jones told the senior non-official member of executive council he 'believed in the federal concept and would do all [he] could to further it in Nyasaland'.[33] Macleod expected Banda to find an issue which would divert his followers' attention from his failure at Lancaster House to secure more than he had, so as to re-establish his personal power and leadership.

When he returned to Nyasaland from the conference, Banda lost no time in verbally attacking those of his political opponents who had attended the conference. The results included physical attacks by rioting crowds of four to five hundred which could be dispersed only by the police using tear gas. Though Jones believed that others would be similarly attacked he none the less told Monson he did 'not detect any signs of a serious threat to law and order' and he thought things would go smoothly for a while. He told Armitage: 'We continue to play this game from day to day and feel reasonably satisfied if by the time the evening comes we have had no crisis.' He intended to issue a statement about violence, saying the Lancaster House agreement was 'based on the fundamental freedom of all people to express political views according to their conscience and without fear of molestation'. This statement does not seem to have been issued. Jones was fairly certain the incidents occurred without Banda's knowledge and consent but felt the doctor's failure to control his people might be because of disinclination, rather than necessarily inability.[34]

Jones did not have to wait long to deal with the question of Banda joining the executive council because the doctor himself raised it with Youens, and then Jones, only two days after Armitage left.[35] Banda said he was 'willing, indeed anxious' to accept nomination, but neither he nor his colleagues could possibly accept appointment or 'sit in the same room' with the current 'nominated stooges' so long as they remained in either the legislative or executive council. If the government really desired peace and cooperation it would immediately remove these men and give the seats to Chipembere, who was still in detention, and Chiume, from whom they had been taken early in the emergency, together with one of the Chisiza brothers. If it did not do this then it was clear it lacked good intentions and was 'intent on persevering with its role of lackey to Sir Roy Welensky'. Youens explained their difficulty: on the one hand they would be pleased to have him as a colleague on the councils, but, on the other, the nominated members had 'cooperated at some considerable inconvenience to themselves by accepting office in the first place – they had given good and loyal service under exceedingly difficult conditions and in the face of personal abuse from some quarters'. In these circumstances, Youens found it difficult to see how the government could arbitrarily dismiss them. Banda repeated his demands with some force:

> The time had now come for the Government to declare a general amnesty in respect of all those presently detained, to restore Chiume and Chipembere to their rightful places in Legislative Council and thereby to demonstrate to all concerned that it was the Government's intention to seek to cooperate with the peoples of the territory and to endeavour to lead them, without further delay or procrastination, towards the goal of fully responsible government. If the present nominees were not dispensed with he certainly would not take a seat on either council, nor could Government hope to get the cooperation from him which he was willing to accord except on the terms which he had stated and which must surely be seen to be eminently reasonable. If the Government would not act reasonably in this way, then he foresaw that the former pattern of events would be repeated. The Government would be 'pig-headed' and he would be 'pig-headed'. Tension would increase and stability would not be achieved.

Youens and Banda talked the matter over for a considerable time but made no progress. 'The matter was eventually shelved by the appearance of tea and toast, and the conversation turned to less contentious subjects.' They parted amicably; they had always got on well together and continued to do so.

Meanwhile, Jones was in Salisbury visiting Welensky, who was surprised Macleod had decided to offer Banda and possibly one or two other MCP members seats on the legislative and executive councils before the constitutional changes came into effect, without having consulted him. Some of his colleagues would claim the appointments meant prematurely introducing the new constitution, and would take a very poor view of it. Jones replied: 'it was indeed Sir Robert's intention ... to bring Banda into the Government about October. The reason for this was to get Banda involved in some responsible work so that he would have less time for irresponsible speechifying.'[36] It is strange he should have used reducing Banda's 'speechifying' as the reason for bringing him into government, rather than the true reason – as Monson had indicated – of hoping to bring him to realize the advantages of the federal concept. This latter explanation would undoubtedly have appealed to Welensky, would have been more accurate and would have helped them to get off to a better start in their new relationship.

Four days later, Jones invited the doctor to lunch, followed by a cordial discussion on membership of the executive council.[37] Banda repeated his position but less lengthily than he had stated it to Youens and was quite adamant that the existing nominated African members would have to be removed before he would consider taking a seat himself. Jones knew Macleod claimed it 'unthinkable' that he should accede to this demand.[38] Consequently, he simply told Banda he would find it difficult and asked him to think about it carefully and then discuss it with him again. The doctor agreed but could hold out no hope of changing his mind. He could, of course, afford to dig his toes in and use to his own advantage Jones's keenness to secure his cooperation.

When Jones reported these meetings to Macleod, he balanced the arguments.[39] On the one hand, getting the doctor into the executive council could significantly affect talks on the Monckton report and the federal review due to take place in December. On the other hand, he was exacting a very high price for his cooperation – abandoning people who had stood by the government during a very difficult period. Jones did not advise on the course to be steered between these two considerations, possibly because he knew both that Macleod thought – or more likely purported to think – that sacking the nominated members was unthinkable, and also that it was a matter Armitage intended to pursue. Armitage had shifted Banda from his insistence that all detainees be released before he would attend the Lancaster House conference. He might succeed again.

Macleod had foreseen that Banda would try to find a diverting issue after the London conference. Again Jones was not kept waiting long. The issue was the continued detention of the remaining detainees, now in Kanjedza camp near Blantyre. Among them were Chipembere and the Chisiza brothers. Banda had raised this question with Jones in June but it had rested there. A few days before going on leave Armitage had discussed with Jones and Youens a query from Macleod about how to deal with those still in detention. Armitage recorded their conclusion: 'We want to play the game as slowly as possible; not easy, as Macleod hates nothing so much as to defend in the House of Commons, a policy of this sort where he gets political blame instead of kudos. We don't yet know what Banda really wants.'[40]

The doctor, however, very soon made abundantly clear to Jones precisely what he really wanted. It is possible that when he refused to work with the 'stooges' his primary purpose was the release of the detainees. If Chipembere were appointed he would have to be released, and if he were released, the others would almost certainly have to be set free also. Similarly it is possible that the British government insisted on not ditching the 'stooges', so as to prevent this happening. It may have been that when Banda failed in his indirect approach he put pressure directly on releasing the detainees, including Chipembere. He had indirectly indicated what he was after in his meeting with Youens two days after Armitage left to go on leave – 'declare a general amnesty in respect of all those presently detained [and] restore Chiume and Chipembere to their rightful places' – but had not pressed the point.

On 5 September, at separate meetings with Youens and Jones, Banda directly raised the question of releasing the remaining detainees. This matter had been made extremely difficult for the government by Banda's own verbal attacks on his opponents, their intimidation and vilification by his followers and the physical attacks on them by large rioting gangs. The first meeting ('an uncomfortable interview') was with Youens.[41] Twice the doctor 'evinced an intention of abandoning it but though he got near the door, in the event he never actually went through it.' Banda was 'utterly dismayed' at the government's 'entirely unreasonable' attitude which showed a complete lack of appreciation of the difficulties he had to overcome and the compromises he had to make, both in going to the Lancaster House conference and in accepting the agreement there. Did they seriously think he could come on to the executive council and cooperate with a government intent on keeping his followers 'rotting indefinitely in gaol without trial'? If the government failed to see sense he would have no option but to abandon any plans for cooperating with them. Instead, he would organize the MCP and put their differences to a 'final test'. 'It will be back to March 3rd 1959 all over again.'

Youens, unfazed, said such threats would do no good to anyone's cause. The Governor could not release the detainees unless he was sure that to do so would not endanger public security. The present situation, he continued, was far from normal, and given the personalities and records of at least some of them, their release might bring about a further deterioration of the situation rather than the reverse. To Banda, by keeping even a single person in detention, the government was deliberately creating a situation which rendered normality impossible.

Youens then deftly, but deliberately and firmly, placed on Banda the responsibility and initiative for creating an atmosphere in which the detainees could be released. He believed it was in the doctor's power to improve the situation to an extent which would justify further releases. Indeed, he showed him how to do it. He could, for example, consistently and clearly condemn all violence and intimidation. He could require his followers to respect the freedom of belief and expression of all, and he could explicitly prohibit acts of violence, molestation and intimidation against political opponents. 'This theme', Youens told Jones, 'was played to the accompaniment of numerous expostulations by the Doctor and a sally towards the door.' Youens none the less pressed on. Banda had expressed disappointment with the government, but they also were disappointed in him. It seemed he had no inclination to act as Youens suggested. The doctor's responses to these points were weak and Youens readily countered them. They got no further, and at 4 p.m. Banda left for Government House to see Jones. They parted reasonably amicably, having regard to their set-to over the preceding hour: Youens's hard-hitting and frank approach and Banda's inability either by argument or bluster, to counter his points.

Jones's meeting lasted half an hour. His object was 'to keep contact with Banda and to try and make headway with him to change his policy of vilification of his political opponents'. The doctor would not listen to any argument that 'tranquillity should be established as a condition precedent to the release of all the detainees'. He was still steamed up after his meeting with the acting chief secretary. Although Youens had driven Banda into a corner and drawn much of the sting from his attack, there was still a good deal left, and the doctor gave the Acting Governor a rough ride. He may have used the earlier interview as a rehearsal for the second. In any event, he knew the advantages of shouting at and denouncing those who opposed him: '[To those] who are ... quiet and are not shouting at them, they give very little. But [to] those who shout and denounce them, they give [what they want].'[42] Jones recorded the course of the interview:

> Banda went into the attack immediately and reproached me for having issued a statement saying that it would hardly be possible for a general election [under the Lancaster House agreement] to be held under eight to nine months. He said that this was nonsense and a deliberate applica-

tion of delaying tactics on my part ... It was time civil servants woke up and did a job in reasonable time ... Finally he launched an attack against the Government and against me personally for continuing to detain people in Kanjedza. He said that he was disappointed to see that I was becoming infected with the Zomba virus; he had hoped to see a new policy initiated by me with a total release of people detained for political reasons without trial but he was sorry to see that I was the same as all other civil servants in Zomba and was intent on saving the face of Sir Robert Armitage. He displayed considerable emotion at this stage and I formed the opinion that it was genuine although I do not entirely rule out the possibility that it might have been a display of histrionics.

Jones, faced with this bluntness verging on rudeness, would have been justified in wondering if his earlier, and speedily formed, assessments of Banda as 'charming' and a man with whom he could work ought to be revised. Banda, on his side, seemed to think he may have been too hasty in seeing him as thoughtful, considerate and different from those with whom he had previously dealt, and this would have disturbed Jones.

Jones had arranged for Banda to take tea with him, his wife and daughter, but the doctor was very reluctant to accept the invitation, saying he could not drink tea with them when he was so distresed by Jones's refusal to see his point of view and his complacency in thinking there could ever be peace while any of his followers remained in detention. While any remained in detention his people were bound to cause trouble and it was not possible for him to persuade them to respect law and order. 'Their continued detention made a mockery of the Lancaster House agreements and he would not participate in the new constitution if they were not released.' He did not say so but, having told Jones in his letter after their Gwelo meeting that releasing the detainees would end tension and distrust and improve race relations, it may have seemed to him that Jones was trusting neither his judgment nor, possibly, his bona fides.

Jones eventually concluded that continuing the meeting could only lead to their parting with very hard feelings and this might prejudice their future relationship. It is surprising he did not deploy the same arguments as Youens had used about Banda creating the conditions in which all detainees could properly be released – and how to do it. The opportunity to do so was there but – startled and worried by the doctor's adamant and outspoken stance, injured by his strictures against himself, and fearful of their relationship deteriorating – he drew back and brought the discussion to an end. With great difficulty he managed to entice Banda into the drawing room where he had tea with him, his wife and daughter 'and went off the boil'.[43]

Jones had just managed to secure part of the object of the meeting ('to keep contact with Banda') but the doctor would not listen to him on the major part of it ('to try and make headway with him to change his policy of vilification of his political opponents'). On this latter part, Jones had made no progress at all. Immediately after Banda left, Jones received reports from Nkata Bay that two more political opponents had been attacked, one had escaped into the bush but the other had been 'beaten into insensibility and [was] unlikely to recover [and] their motor vehicle was completely burned out'.[44]

Jones reported the meetings of 5 September to Macleod:

> [Banda] was in a very angry mood ... Youens and I have never found him more difficult and it was impossible to get anything across to him. Patience and self-control on our part just, but only just, ensured that we parted on speaking terms. I think you should know of strained atmosphere here and Banda's attitude that there can never be respect for law and order in Nyasaland while any of his followers remain in detention without trial.[45]

This was the first occasion that Jones told the secretary of state he was only just able, and with great difficulty, to hold on to Banda. It was to happen repeatedly in the future.

Two days later Banda asked to see Youens urgently.[46] This time, in an entirely different mood, he acted reasonably and quietly. There were no explosions and they parted, after tea and toast together, on amicable terms. It is likely that in the intervening period he realized he had got nowhere with Jones and had not even received, as he had with Youens, advice on how he might get his own way. Bluster and threat had not worked with Youens and he was uncertain at this stage whether they, and rudeness, would work with Jones, who had not responded save to prevail upon him to have tea with his family. Consequently he may have decided on a different approach by showing that he was able to reason with his followers on this occasion, albeit with difficulty.

He told Youens his position with his supporters was becoming daily more impossible. When he told them he had made no progress over releasing the detainees, they responded violently and vowed to organize a large crowd to release them by force. Only after a very heated discussion in which he said their proposed action would probably lead to bloodshed and would not have the effect they desired, was he able to dissuade them. Maybe Youens's point that threats of a return to emergency conditions would not help anyone's cause had found its mark. Banda now pleaded with Youens and Jones to see things from his point of view. He was keen to cooperate but from their own experience of 'the African mentality' they should realize the impossibility of his effectively advocating co-

Nyasaland: Chief Secretary · 77

operation unless he was able to show something tangible for it. He begged them to see sense and if they did not, they must accept an inevitable regression to emergency conditions. There would be nothing he could do to prevent it. He implored them to consider the end-product of such a situation: 'In the long run [would] anything ... be gained by precipitating a further emergency, with the arrival of Federal and, he imagined, UK troops, with attendant deaths and bloodshed? Was the price worth paying for the remaining fifteen detainees and the removal of restriction orders? Could any reasonable Government say that it was?' Youens again made the point that Banda could himself do a great deal to justify releases. This argument no more swayed Banda than it had previously, and he 'hoped to be spared a further reiteration of the formula' which Youens had already rehearsed with him. If they were released, he was confident he could ensure their good behaviour. Of the related factors – release and control of his followers – Youens was after control first and release second, whereas Banda wanted it the other way round. The real *quid pro quo* the government sought – a more cooperative attitude to federation – was not mentioned.

Jones accepted Youen's conclusion that Banda had decided to make one last and reasoned appeal to release the detainees; if this failed he would break contact with the government, bloodshed would follow, Banda would be 'returned to Gwelo' and the Lancaster House agreement would be at an end. He had a long discussion with his other official advisers and decided to think in terms of very early releases. He would impress on Banda that he would expect him to cooperate and control his followers. He hoped that by acting in this way he could produce an atmosphere in which Banda would consider some form of continued federal association – as indeed were Macleod's instructions. He told the Colonial Office:

> If we act as proposed I do not rule out the possibility of further demands ... But we might feel better able to resist some if not all [of] his subsequent demands having met him on the question of the detainees and restrictees. If we do not do this we must face the distinct possibility that Banda will break contact with us ... will do nothing to control his followers and thus bring us to where we were in March 1959, with the Lancaster House agreement in tatters. This may happen anyway but is less likely if we wipe the slate clean.[47]

He did not consider this a surrender to threats, although he realized others would think so, but 'an endeavour to face up to the realities of the situation'. These realities, although he did not say so, undoubtedly included Banda's warnings – or threats. He found releasing the detainees a rather unpalatable step and realized it would incur criticism of himself and probably Macleod. If there were a serious security deterioration and they had to reimpose controls or declare a state of emergency, at least they could do so knowing they had given Banda 'the maximum of consideration'.[48]

Macleod had not expected Banda to raise the detainees question to crisis point, but now that he had, he agreed on balance with Jones's proposals, so long as there was any prospect of 'securing reasonable reception on Banda's part of Monckton Report'.[49] This was an important qualification. In fact, Banda had said nothing which might suggest that his cooperation would extend to federation, nor had Jones mentioned this hope to him. He had not even agreed to join the council, save under conditions which he knew to be unacceptable. The furthest the doctor had gone was to say he would control his followers. Macleod expected that with the release of the final detainees, especially Chipembere and the Chisiza brothers, there would be increased pressure on Banda to raise his demands to implement the new constitutional arrangements before the federal review conference and to insist on his conditions for accepting a seat on the executive council. Releasing the detainees would significantly damage the chances of working on Banda on the federal issue before the review.[50]

To minimize the effect of these setbacks Macleod prepared a message to be given to Banda when all the preliminary steps had been taken to agree on the releases.[51] In it he emphasized 'with all seriousness' that the recent physical attacks on Banda's political opponents made the Governor's task of releasing the detainees much more difficult. Banda had said publicly that political opponents should not be molested, but Macleod believed he could do a great deal more to create conditions in which the last detainees could be released. He repeated Youens's ways in which this could be done, which had still not been put to him directly by Jones.

Macleod went further and warned Banda of the risk that some of the detainees, if released, might use their influence 'to work against peaceable evolution on the basis of the agreement reached at the conference', and thereby 'recreate conditions of tension' and upset the political stability they had worked so hard to secure. He was determined to extract from Banda a clear undertaking in exchange for releasing the remaining detainees, rather than simply giving in to his threats. Whereas Jones had intended to make it clear to Banda that he would *expect* full cooperation if he were to release the detainees, Macleod, following Youens's line of reasoning, intended to *demand* cooperation as a condition precedent to releases. He concluded his message: 'If you could [indicate] your readiness to cooperate with the Nyasaland Government and myself ... together with a promise of your full further influence in preventing any further disorder or molestation of individuals, I believe ... the acting Governor could without further delay consider the release of the remaining detainees.'

Jones explained to the non-official members of the executive council, Dixon and Blackwood, his proposal and the reasons for it on 14 September and was surprised they were less horrified than he expected. Although they could not support the releases, they agreed not to make any public criticism provided Banda made a public statement denouncing intimidation and violence and enjoining his followers to respect law and order and freedom of speech. They also asked that Macleod should say there could be no elections until intimidation had ended. Jones was confident, though not certain, Banda would make the statement they sought but he could not commit Macleod to that asked of him. It is very unlikely that any of them believed Macleod would make such a statement, and in the event he did not.[52]

Jones arranged see Banda the following day, expecting him to be 'sour and hostile'. He intended to give him a short but encouraging statement and then meet him the following week to try and secure the promises Macleod sought and, if secured, tell him he would immediately release the remaining detainees. He needed this slight delay to assess Welensky's reaction and to confide in his provincial commissioners so that they could prepare for the releases.[53]

At the meeting Banda was indeed hostile to start with but once Jones had convinced him that he was in close discussion with Macleod and his representations were being taken seriously he quietened down. He was grateful to Jones for consulting Macleod on this vital matter which currently made it 'impossible for peaceful conditions to emerge'. He understood the consultations would not be completed until the following week, and gave a 'solemn assurance' that in the interim there would be no demonstrations or statements demanding the releases. He would publicly call for peace and denounce violence once he received an unequivocal assurance that all detentions and restrictions would be lifted. He guaranteed that Chipembere and the Chisiza brothers would be amenable to his influence and cause no trouble. Jones told Macleod: 'One would have to accept that for what it was worth': it appears he was not confident of Banda being able, or possibly inclined, to fulfil his guarantee.

> He declined to take tea with me but the interview throughout was a good deal more cordial than I had expected ... I gave him no indication that the result of my thoughts and discussions ... would necessarily result in the detainees being released, and it is quite clear that the situation is no less serious than it was and if we do not release them we shall have serious trouble on our hands and Banda will break contact with us.[54]

In fact, the situation, at least in the immediate future, was significantly less serious than it had been. Ten days earlier Banda's followers were threatening to march on Kanjedza, he was threatening to break off discussions, he was angry, rude and considered Jones unreasonable and as reactionary as the general run of Zomba civil servants. Now he was cordial, polite, undertook that there would be no march on Kanjedza or other demonstrations and was prepared to wait a week for a decision not guaranteed to be in his favour. Jones, taking the point that Banda had solemnly assured peaceful conditions only for a week, recognized that if the detainees were not then released he would have 'serious trouble' on his hands. Although he had, he thought, given Banda no indication that his discussions would necessarily lead to the detainees' release, he, Macleod and Banda must have recognized that it was the only option really open to him.

The ground had now been cleared with the secretary of state, Jones's advisers, including his provincial commissioners, and, partially, with Banda. Only Welensky remained, though Jones was clear that if the federal prime minister would not accept the releases, the step would none the less have to be taken. Welensky phoned him on 20 September and had a long and friendly conversation. The federal cabinet strongly objected to the releases. Jones told Macleod about the conversation:

> If I did not take [action] now I might have to yield to force or withstand it and risk serious trouble. I did not conceal ... the possibility that releases might of themselves lead in due course to serious trouble, but I genuinely felt that in the interests of [security] and of enlisting Banda's understanding of the need for Nyasaland to move peacefully into its new constitution and for him to attend the review conference in cooperative mood, I should carry on with my intention to remove all restrictions. Welensky accepted my reasoning ... although he had misgivings.[55]

Jones told Welensky that Macleod agreed with the decision but did not impose it. Similarly, Banda had made entreaties but had not 'given an ultimatum'. Many would have considered that Banda's blustering, threats and general stance had precisely amounted to an ultimatum: release or declare a state of emergency. Indeed, Jones had told Macleod this was the choice. He, as Banda no doubt calculated, could not afford to let this happen. To do so would amount to a colossal, extremely dangerous, humiliating and career-threatening failure at the very first hurdle he encountered as Acting Governor.

On 19 September Jones told Dixon and Blackwood that he intended to effect the releases during the current week to 'try and remove the bitterness of the past so that we can move forward to the implementation of the Lancaster House agreement in a more cordial atmosphere than exists at present'. Blackwood's response was formally and totally to disagree with the action proposed and to treat it as a breach of the undertakings given at Lancaster House. He felt 'extremely bitter' about it.[56]

The last step before finally making the releases was to meet Banda on 22 September.[57] Jones started by saying that, if the discussion proceeded satisfactorily, he had great hopes the doctor would leave satisfied that the government was doing all it could to ease his situation and remove all bitterness that remained in MCP minds In the course of the next two and a quarter hours he explained his difficulties: repeated and continuing violence and intimidation by members of the MCP; articles in the *Malawi News* attacking Europeans and the government in bitter, hostile and inflammatory terms; embittered verbal attacks on district commissioners and chiefs; European fears that individual liberties were threatened; concentration of large and volatile crowds in the urban areas and placing their control in the hands of MCP stewards rather than the police; and great anxiety that if Chipembere and the Chisizas were released, they would revert to their known bitter and violent tendencies. This was a formidable list of difficulties.

> If I was to revoke the detention and control orders, I must be given a very solemn assurance that this would not lead either in the immediate future or later on to disturbances in Nyasaland. If it did, I would be discredited and my action would be considered to have been reckless and unjustified. What I was proposing to do was an act of faith in Banda and I relied on him to be insistent that all his followers ... should keep the peace. He gave me his solemn assurance on this point.

Jones then read Macleod's message and Banda said he would generally operate within its spirit, using 'all his influence' to ensure that law, order and freedom of speech and association were maintained. He reserved his position on the timing of the elections. He was undecided, too, whether to attend the federal review conference, which was the very basis upon which Macleod had agreed on the releases. When Jones raised the question of his membership of the executive council before the elections, Banda said membership was not an important issue for him. He would still be acting contrary to his ideals if he sat with the current nominated African members. The price Macleod and Jones had been bent on exacting in exchange for the releases included the timing of the elections, Banda's attendance at the review conference and his becoming a member of the executive council. The doctor had acceeded to none of these. His saying that membership of council was unimportant reinforced the view that his demands to have Chipembere released were a subterfuge for securing his and others' release.

Jones showed Banda a statement he proposed to issue explaining his actions, which the latter read carefully and accepted. The doctor then composed a message for publication and as a consequence Jones told him he would release the remaining detainees and revoke all control orders. Banda asked particularly that the two statements should be issued simultaneously so that his own, if issued first, should not appear in a vacuum but should be directly related to the releases. Jones agreed. It passed without comment – and possibly without being noticed – that the effect of this request could be said to be that Banda was not condemning violence as a matter of principle but specifically as a means of securing the releases.

In reporting the meeting to Macleod, Jones said:

> I made it clear to Banda that ... if he or his party let us down over this, not only would my present action come in for strong criticism but my belief in his good faith might be shaken. We were wiping the slate clean in the hope that the difficulties in his path might be removed and in the expectation that the removal of this remaining cause of bitterness would enable him to play his part with us in the difficult months that lie ahead in a spirit of mutual confidence and good will.

Banda kept the secret of the releases – codenamed 'Operation Stunt' – to himself and there was no leaking of information about the operation. In the early hours of 27 September the remaining detainees were taken from Kanjedza camp and driven to Kota Kota, where the annual MCP conference was being held. There Banda produced them to the assembled but unsuspecting conference, wearing the red gowns of the 'prison graduate' and 'camp finalist'.[58] This was a major political coup for Banda and further strengthened his standing as leader of the party. The conference elected him as life president, Chipembere was reinstated in his former post of treasurer-general, Dunduzu Chisiza was made secretary-general and Yatuta Chisiza became administrative secretary of the party.[59]

Despite the statements by Jones and Banda calling for law, order and tolerance, the violence and intimidation continued. Jones tackled Banda about this a month after the detainees were released.[60] He reminded him that he had said that if law and order were not maintained he, Jones, would be discredited, but he did not refer to the harmful effect which such discredit might have on his ability to help Banda further. He did not mention the 'very solemn assurance' he had sought – and presumably thought he had secured – from Banda in exchange for the releases, or the possibility of his faith in the doctor being shaken. Nor did he mention the ineffectiveness of any steps the doctor might have taken over the previous month, despite his confidence in being able to control the released detainees that he had expressed from the very first day they met and had since repeated periodically. Jones said the attacks on political opponents could not help but damage Banda's cause and play into the hands of his enemies. They also embarrassed the government at a time when they were anxious to see the MCP get fair play. Banda responded with 'the old arguments about provocation' but said he was most anxious the incidents should not continue and he was doing what he could to stop them.

Jones turned to the *Malawi News* attacks on the Roman Catholic church. The recently formed Christian Democratic Party (CDP), supported by the church, had set itself up in opposition to the MCP. Banda said the attacks were not against the church as a whole but only against the political activities of parts of it. He was convinced the archbishop was using his spiritual influence for political purposes. He 'would fight tooth and nail against that'. It was not pointed out to him, as it could justifiably, though possibly not prudently, have been, that he had not complained when over a long period the Church of Scotland had involved itself in the country's politics, but then their involvement was overwhelmingly in his favour and he was a member of that church. The CDP would not, in Banda's view, get anywhere but he had no wish to stifle it: he welcomed the existence of opposition parties.

Jones wrote to Macleod the same day as he had this discussion with Banda:

> The Malawi Youth League is ebullient and causing us some anxieties by its attacks, both verbal and physical, on its political opponents ... Although I am satisfied that the incidents which occur are not in any way inspired by Dr. Banda or any of his party leaders, they damage his credit both at home and abroad.
>
> Generally speaking, there seems to have been a relaxation of tension during the past few weeks and Dr. Banda has played very fairly with me over the question of the release of the detainees ... One is chiefly unhappy at his political attacks on Chiefs and District Commissioners and I hope that he can be persuaded to lay off now that he realizes, as he must, that he is bound to win the vast majority of the lower roll seats at the elections.[61]

Throughout the three months of Armitage's absence, Jones kept him informed of events in Nyasaland by writing a series of letters. The Governor supported the detainee releases but asked if Banda could really control his people and could Jones strike a deal with him. The real significance in Armitage's questions was that if Banda could, or would, not control his people, there was no point in striking a deal with him, but the significance was not pursued. Jones thanked him for his support and added:

You certainly posed the two [crucial] questions – can Banda control his people and can I make a deal with him? I don't think one can answer the first with certainty. So far as the second is concerned, I have made a deal with him to the extent that he has agreed to the publication of a statement in which he denounced violence and intimidation ... He has given me an undertaking that he will control the detainees, particularly the Chisizas and Chipembere and will let me know immediately they get out of hand ...

There was a distinct danger that Banda would give up any pretence of holding his extreme elements in check and let things take their course – which in his view meant a return to Gwelo and all that. On the other hand, one could [wipe] the slate clean and have at one's back the argument that Government had done all in its power to create a cordial atmosphere in which the preparations for the elections could take place. If the ex-detainees cause trouble, Government might have to take firm action and could do so with a clear conscience.[62]

Jones took two further steps to try and create an atmosphere in which peaceful progress could be made. The first was to resign as patron of the Zomba gymkhana club, of which no African could be a member. He, as many others, found this exclusion 'a measure reacting against the best interests of the commmunities [and] an offence against the dignity of people whose goodwill is necessary for the happy and peaceful development' of the country. He had forbidden his children to attend functions at the club, whose social and sporting facilities were regularly enjoyed by their friends. Before he resigned he discussed the matter with Banda who was not particularly bothered one way or the other. Indeed, and probably to Jones's surprise, on the whole the doctor was not in favour of this sort of social mixing. He thought exclusion was old-fashioned and perhaps ought to be removed but he believed it unlikely that many Africans would wish to be members. None, it seems, had raised the question. The proffered step did not have much of an impression on Banda. Jones none the less resigned and this had the effect he desired: the rule was removed six months later and he accepted the honorary membership then offered to him.[63]

The other step was to try and get the members of the provincial and district administration (P&DA) to adapt quickly and fully to the changed circumstances in the country. Two days after Armitage went on leave, Youens visited Banda who immediately opened the discussion by referring to the attitude of the administration:

He said that it was essential, if peace and stability were to prevail, for the P&DA to adopt a different attitude to his Party. Hitherto District Commissioners had treated his Party as 'the enemy'. They had adopted a deliberate policy of doing everything they could to frustrate its legitimate political activities ... In doing this they had produced a climate of acute tension and mistrust between the Government and the governed ... It was necessary for Government officers to appreciate the realities of the situation and to act in accordance with them.

Youens assured him the government was anxious to secure his and his party's cooperation and friendship, but 'the position of District Commissioners in relation to his Party had been made very difficult by widespread acts of intimidation. Many of the perpetrators were members of his party, acting – they claimed – in the name of his party.' Banda replied with 'the usual disclaimer': intimidation was no part of the MCP's policy and for them it was an unnecessary weapon.[64]

Four days later Jones himself saw Banda, agreed that it was necessary for MCP leaders at all levels to keep in contact with government officers and hoped that he and his followers would 'meet officers half way'. Banda responded by going over what Jones found to be the 'familiar ground' covered with Youens. The discussion did not move things forward and added nothing to what Youens had said. So far, this step, too, did not have much impression on Banda.[65]

Nevertheless, Jones recognized that the relationship between the administration and the MCP was agitating Banda, and although he believed most of the fault was the MCP's the matter was sufficiently worrying for him to send a directive to administrative officers, guiding them in the changed political circumstances. This directive was sent to provincial commissioners on 22 September 1960. Though issued over the signature of the chief secretary, it set out Jones's current thinking and instructions.[66]

He had the directive issued in great secrecy. Provincial commissioners were ordered to make no copies and to keep the letter in their safes for their own personal reference only. They were required to read it to all their district commissioners and ensure that any new district commissioners in the future were made aware of its contents. The directive began: 'The achievement of responsible government in Nyasaland ... remains a primary object of Her Majesty's Government. The Lancaster House agreement when implemented will mean that a substantial move has been made in this direction and ... the elected members of the Legislature, some of whom will be functioning as ministers, will have a substantial and ever increasing say in the policies and activities of Government.'

Having dealt with the broad Nyasaland scene, he turned to the Federation where he was significantly less clear, largely – although he did not say so – because Britain was saddled with a policy that manifestly was not working but did not know with what to replace it. It 'appeared likely' that the central aim of the British government would be to retain a constitutional association between Nyasaland and the Rhodesias. Because the continued imposition of a federal association appeared unlikely, officers should be 'strictly neutral on the federal issue'.

The territorial position, the directive continued, was different because the Lancaster House result was achieved by the agreement of all the parties attending.

> A guiding object determining the actions of the Government and its Administration during the next few months is that the people at the date of the election should be in a reasonable and tolerant frame of mind ... No Government should instruct its agents not to enforce the law, but ... a discretion exists and political judgment must be exercised in furtherance of those political solutions on which the ultimate peace of the country must depend ... The overriding factor in deciding whether to enforce a law in any given circumstances is governed by the need to serve the public interest in its widest sense. It will, however, remain the Government's policy to prosecute with the utmost vigour offences against the person and property and also such offences as riot and intimidation.

District commissioners were asked to advise their chiefs in similar terms. As in the past, chiefs should stand outside party politics. The government could not protect them if they used their position to further the cause of any particular political party. As the country moved rapidly towards African party political control of the Government, 'an increasing measure of circumspection must be exercised by ... Government servants, not to take courses of action which will precipitate political strife and prevent peaceful progress towards the end [sic] of responsible government, which Her Majesty's Government is determined to achieve in Nyasaland.'[67]

In this frank but extremely carefully – although not always abundantly clearly, unambiguously and succinctly – worded top-secret directive, Jones was pointing out how greatly circumstances had changed and how essential it was for provincial and district commissioners to adjust the approach to their jobs. He was deeply anxious that they should do everything possible to avoid rocking the political boat even if this meant turning a blind eye to aspects of law enforcement other than in cases of the most serious kind, and failing to give the virtually unqualified support they had in the past given to their chiefs. His was a pragmatic approach and he was relying upon the commissioners to accept that a special position had to be conferred upon the MCP in the wider public interest, as he saw it.

During the week following the issue of this directive, Jones saw every district commissioner in the country and, on 28 September, the day after the detainees were released, wrote to Macleod: 'I think that all [district commissioners] now understand what is behind present Government policy. They appreciate the need to play the situation along as gently as possible to the elections, even if it means having to appear to condone certain political offences committed by Banda and other leaders in the rashness of the moment, and to accept personal insults and misrepresentations of their actions and words.'[68] Commissioners could perhaps be forgiven if they thought their instructions were *actually* to condone (in the sense of overlooking) 'certain political offences' rather than simply *appearing* to condone them, and if they suspected that some such offences were committed with deliberation rather than 'in the rashness of the moment'.

Jones's three months as Acting Governor were very full, with a number of deeply worrying and potentially dangerous elements. These included the wish to have Banda on the executive council and the price he demanded for it; Banda's extremely forceful demands for the remaining detainees to be released and his dire threats if Jones did not comply; violence and intimidation against opponents of the MCP and the unsuccessful attempts to get Banda to stop them; verbal attacks on the Roman Catholic church; similar attacks on district commissioners and the extraordinary steps taken to meet Banda at least half way in improving relationships between them and the MCP; undermining the authority of the chiefs and the steps taken, through instructions to district commissioners, to lessen the effect of this.

The Lancaster House agreement had set the pattern of the next constitutional steps in Nyasaland. Banda had achieved substantially less than he set out to accomplish, particularly in respect of the executive, and was anxious as quickly as possible to secure firmly what he had gained. He was, he successfully claimed, under extreme pressure from his colleagues in the MCP, especially Chiume.

Even without this pressure, Banda may have calculated that he was more likely to get his way quickly while Jones was in the chair rather than await Armitage's return. This was not simply that he may have thought Jones more amenable to his cause than was Armitage, but that on the Governor's return there would inevitably be a handing-over period in which Armitage could be expected himself to go over the ground again, with full knowledge of all the arguments and threats Banda had deployed. He may also have believed – although to have done so would have been a serious miscalculation – that Armitage, feeling badly treated by Macleod, having so many policies of the past reversed by the British government, with only five months of his governorship remaining, would take things easy and see no cause to give in to Banda's demands. Maybe Armitage would risk violence breaking out, respond by reimposing the emergency and ordering detentions, and would play for time, of which art he was a master, knowing he would shortly be safely back in Britain, when Macleod and his own successor could do what they liked but by which time, also, Banda would have lost a great deal of ground with his supporters and particularly his lieutenants.

These may have been some of the thoughts persuading Banda, and Chiume, to press for the release of the remaining detainees so forcefully, urgently and immediately after Armitage departed on leave. It was the one thing the doctor wanted. All others were matters the government wanted: membership of the executive council, a reasonable approach to the Monckton report, attendance at the federal review conference, cessation of intimidation of political opponents and other acts of lawlessness, an end to the verbal attacks on the district commissioners, the chiefs and the Roman Catholic church, and cooperation between the MCP and government officers. Since it was the one thing he wanted, he was prepared to make a dangerously threatening issue of it. He succeeded – and without the government getting much if anything of what it, on its side, wanted. At this stage, he was manifestly the clear winner in the deal Jones thought he had struck with him.

In the generally overcast and turbulent skies hanging over Jones during much of August, September and October 1960 there was a double shaft of sunshine. On 5 September Poynton wrote that the Queen had informally approved his appointment as Governor in succession to Armitage and his promotion to be a Knight Commander of the Order of Saint Michael and Saint George. Formal approval was given on 7 October.[69]

On 26 July, during the Lancaster House conference, Macleod had told Armitage that his present term of office, due to expire in April 1961, was not to be extended. 'The idea was for Jones to take over from [him] as Governor. [Armitage] would stay on until the [federal] Conference was over ... They were thinking of starting the Conference in the Autumn.'[70] Presumably, it was about this time that an offer of appointment was made to Jones, who accepted it. On his return from the conference early in August, Armitage publicly announced that he would retire the following April. On 18 September, Armitage wrote to congratulate Jones and said there were times when he had found it difficult to conceal from him that he knew of the proposed appointment; he had, of course, known for almost two months.[71] Jones replied on 28 September to thank him for his congratulations: 'I have accepted the appointment with somewhat mixed feelings – I already know enough about the job to realize that it is no sinecure: the kicks come from all sides and the situation is as difficult as any I have had to face and will, it seems to me, remain so for some considerable time.'[72]

On 11 October, Jones's appointment to succeed Armitage and his knighthood were formally announced. There was a mixed reception in Nyasaland. Banda was delighted.[73] Aleke Banda, assistant secretary-general of the MCP, welcomed the appointment and only hoped he would be as good as he had been so far. 'As long as he keeps that up, he can rest assured of our cooperation.' The president of the Congress Liberation Party congratulated him and wished him to hold his appointment 'with wisdom and courage for the benefit of all sections of the community'. In his view, what was needed was 'not personality but effective control of law and order ... and impartiality'. His statements about the benefit of all, effective control and impartiality were clear references to the feeling that the MCP was being supported by the government, and Jones in particular, at the expense of law and order and other parties. Blackwood, although pleased with the appointment, thought it was done in 'the most discourteous way the Colonial Office could have found'.[74] He probably had in mind that it was extremely unusual for a person to be knighted before they became Governor, that the more usual knighthood for a chief secretary, if any, was the Knight Bachelor, that the announcement was made in Armitage's absence and that it so closely followed, as if a reward for, the detainee releases.

In his retirement Jones gave accounts of his appointment as Governor which conflict with the account given here. The first is an undated typescript note – probably an obituary draft written in July 1970, when he was sixty-two years of age – in Jones's private papers headed 'Iain Macleod': 'I first met him at the Colonial Office in January 1960: he asked me to transfer from Northern Rhodesia where I was Minister of Native Affairs to Nyasaland as Chief Secretary. "The most difficult job in the Colonial Service at the present time" is how he described the Nyasaland post ... I accepted Macleod's offer.'[75] The discrepancy in dates is small but it is clear from Jones's diary and other papers that he first met Macleod on 5 February 1960 at the Colonial Office, rather than in January. More importantly, by then he had already been offered and had accepted the chief secretaryship of Nyasaland. Jones was away skiing until 15 January and could hardly have received the letter offering him the appointment, dated 6 January, before then. It is true that he visited the Colonial Office on 18 and 19 January but this was to discuss with officials, rather than the secretary of state, the offer of the post and taking it up in June 1960. The interview with Macleod on 5 February was not to ask him to transfer to Nyasaland, which was already agreed, but to do so at an earlier date than originally planned. It is significant that Jones did not claim in this document that Macleod said that when Armitage retired he would succeed him as Governor. Macmillan and Macleod saw Nyasaland as the most difficult of their colonial problems at that time and it may be that when this was said, Jones gained the impression that Macleod was saying the chief secretaryship was the most difficult job in the colonial service. In any event, Jones, at least much later, thought this was what Macleod said.

The second account comes from John McCracken who wrote an appreciation of Jones in *The Times* in 1992:

> In an interview with me in 1982, Jones [then aged seventy-four] revealed that while minister of native affairs in Northern Rhodesia in 1959, he was called to a meeting in London with the recently appointed colonial secretary, Ian [sic] Macleod, who offered him 'the most difficult job in the Empire'. This was to go out to Nyasaland ostensibly as chief secretary but in fact as heir designate to the governor, Sir Robert Armitage, whose tour of duty was not due to end until April 1961 ... Macleod gave strict instructions that Armitage was not to be informed of the identity of his successor, with the result that Jones, to his acute embarrassment, had to endure several months during which his immediate superior speculated on whether he, Armitage, would be reappointed and who else might be in the running for the job.[76]

In his interview with McCracken, Jones said that Armitage on a number of occasions discussed with him 'his plans for the next few years in Nyasaland, saying he was quite prepared to work with Banda, and then, when it became apparent that he was not going to be reappointed, speculating on who among his contemporaries would replace him'. Jones was obviously concerned that anything of this episode should come out while Armitage was still alive and for that reason McCracken did not write directly about it until after the death of both Armitage and Jones.[77]

Jones's personal papers show that he did indeed go to the Colonial Office in 1959 but he saw only officials and not the secretary of state. Indeed, the visit was almost certainly just before Macleod was appointed. At that time he was being consulted about Foster filling the chief secretaryship of Nyasaland, and his own name was not even being considered. Jones himself wrote that he first met Macleod early in 1960 rather than, as he told McCracken, in 1959. The papers also show that Macleod did not go so far as to tell Jones he was being appointed 'heir designate' to Armitage. There would have been no need to tempt Jones to accept the chief secretaryship by such means because he had already accepted it. He was at that time untried as chief secretary, had not served in Nyasaland and had never met any of its leading politicians. Macleod was adept at keeping as many options open as possible and not revealing his hand sooner than necessary. It is extremely unlikely that he told Jones he would succeed Armitage, though he may have had this possibility in mind. He may have been content that Jones should think it a possibility. Both their minds may have been influenced by the press about this time beginning to report that Armitage was threatening to resign because of disagreements with Macleod over Banda's release.[78] There had been an expectation in the Colonial Office for some eight months that if the secretary of state insisted on the Governor withdrawing detention orders before he, the Governor, felt it safe to do so, Armitage would resign.[79]

A third account is slightly later still: that given by Jones, now seventy-five years of age, in an interview with Brian Lapping and Sarah Curtis at the end of May 1984:

> In November 1959 I met Iain Macleod in London and he offered me the job. He did most of the talking. He began by saying 'I'm going to ask you to take over the most difficult job in the colonial empire'. He explained that Armitage was due to go in about a year's time. Meanwhile I was to be Chief Secretary with a view to taking over when Armitage left. Armitage must not be told.'
>
> [Lapping's notes continue:] Macleod did not appoint Jones because of his evolving view that African politicians were the men who had to be dealt with. Jones *thinks* he was chosen because he had been a successful trouble-shooter in Northern Rhodesia, particularly on the Copper Belt. Macleod said he wanted someone in the job who would keep a closer contact with the African leaders than had been done before. Armitage thought he would be appointed for a second five-year term ... He merely thought that he was going on leave. When he left the airport white settlers sang 'Will ye no come back again.'[80]

Again, for the reasons given previously, Jones was almost certainly mistaken in recalling that he met Macleod in November 1959 and was then offered, by the secretary of state, the chief secretaryship of Nyasaland and eventually the governorship. The letter offering him the chief secretaryship was written on 6 January by Poynton who anticipated that it would come as a surprise. It is inconceivable that the permanent secretary would not have known if Jones had already been offered the post.[81] Furthermore, Macleod's reference to Armitage – due to retire in April 1961 – leaving in about a year's time would fit in much better with him saying this in February 1960 than in November 1959. If Jones was at some stage told not to reveal to Armitage that he, Jones, was to succeed him as Governor, it is much more likely that this was immediately after Armitage was told by Macleod (in late July 1960) when, for some reason, he may not have wanted Jones to know that Armitage already knew. There is no evidence in any of Armitage's large collection of private papers, diaries and personal letters that he did speculate as to who might succeed him, and it may then be that any such speculation was a subterfuge to conceal that he already knew Jones was to succeed. If, as Jones claimed, Armitage thought he was to be reappointed for a further term of office he could not have speculated on his successor until he knew he was not to be so reappointed, and it was precisely at this point that he was told Jones would succeed him. Consequently, the two points Jones alleged – belief in reappointment and speculation as to successor – are logically inconsistent

Jones's reputation as a 'trouble-shooter'[82] on the Copperbelt would have been well known in the Colonial Office for over two years and during a time when Foster and Ingham, but not Jones, were being considered for the chief secretaryship of Nyasaland. Consequently, it is unlikely that this was the reason for promoting him and, of the two possibilities mentioned by Jones, the other was the more likely: his evolving view that African politicians were the men who had to be dealt with. Even this does not ring entirely true because, not long before, he personally had detained a number of such men in Northern Rhodesia, apparently with no regret but with some pride, and it was well known that he strongly shared Benson's belief in supporting the position of the traditional chiefs rather than the politicians.

Armitage's private papers contain no indication that he thought he would be appointed for a further five years. Such reappointments were exceptional. On the contrary, there were times when he expected he would be sacked, and from July 1960 he knew he was not to stay in Nyasaland after April 1961. It is true that he made arrangements for the administration of the country beyond April 1961 but he did so not because he expected to be there himself – he knew he would not be – but because he could not responsibly do otherwise. Most Governors worked up to the very last moment before their departure and inevitably dealt with future matters. It would have been irresponsible, and quite unlike him, if Armitage had not devoted his final five months, as we shall see, so diligently working for the benefit of Nyasaland, Banda and Jones.

It was true that when the Armitages left from Chileka airport, those seeing them off indeed sang 'Will ye no come back again'. This, however, was not the occasion of the Armitages going on leave – which was by rail and not air – as Jones said, expecting to return. Rather, it was the occasion of their final departure on retirement, knowing, and having known for over eight months – the public had known for six months – that he would not be returning as Governor. Jones and his wife were present at Chileka airport to see them off and walked to the plane with them. Indeed, within minutes of their departure, Jones sent a message to him on the aircraft wishing him Godspeed and a happy retirement. On this point, too, Jones's memory was not serving him well.

Whatever the facts surrounding Jones's appointment as Governor, it was announced before Armitage returned from leave on 2 November. Jones was confirmed in the Anglican church by the Bishop of Nyasaland in November.

November was taken up with discussions on the federal review conference, the forthcoming elections and the continuing intimidation by MCP members, which was unlikely to be dampened down, given Jones's instructions to district commissioners about condoning 'certain political offences'. Indeed, the violence and intimidation worsened as soon as Banda left in mid-November for the Nigeria independence celebrations and the federal review. Following a speech by Chipembere, a crowd stoned the police and two officers were injured. They were dispersed by tear gas but a large mob stormed the house of Chester Katsonga, the founder of the CDP, and burnt it to the ground. Katsonga, his wife, father and three children were only just able to escape with their lives.[83]

On 30 November Jones left with Ingham and Phillips to attend the federal review in London. The conference was in many respects a 'non-event', but Jones kept Armitage regularly informed by cable of what was happening. It started on 5 December and was adjourned twelve days later, to be resumed at a date to be arranged. It never was arranged. Banda walked out twice – Macmillan says he 'stormed out in a rage' – and adopted a 'policy of private charm and public intransigence'. Macleod had agreed to Jones releasing the final detainees 'so long as there was any prospect of inducing a reasonable attitude towards federation'. Neither Macleod nor Jones had mentioned this hope to the doctor. As Jones had already discovered, Banda was not always charming in private and his intransigence was not confined to the public arena. These were traits with which he would become very familiar and have to contend in the coming years. Jones, Ingham and Phillips said nothing during any of the formal sessions of the conference. It was 'nothing more than an exercise in futility'.[84]

Soon after he arrived in London, Jones spoke with Macleod about the security deterioration in Nyasaland, and as a result the secretary of state saw Banda. The doctor agreed to make a firm statement denouncing violence and calling on his followers to behave themselves. He did indeed send a telegram but it had none of the soothing effect intended. Intimidation of opponents to Congress continued apace, and Europeans, including visiting British MPs, were shouted and jeered at.[85] Banda's 'solemn undertaking' to secure peace and good order and control his underlings was conspicuously ineffective.

When he left Nyasaland for London, Jones was seconded for special duties, and this period of secondment was extended beyond the end of the conference to enable him to stay in Britain to be close to his sick son. On 30 July Timothy had broken his leg while playing football at school in Southern Rhodesia. It was thought that he would have to stay in hospital for about two months and his parents hoped that after a short spell with them in Zomba, he would be able to return to school. A nasty break, it was expected to take six months to heal, but complications set in. He joined his family in Zomba in October and then went with them to Britain. His parents knew the injury was serious and they confided in Armitage, who frequently and gently inquired after him in his letters during their absence in Britain. They were somewhat reassured when Macmillan told them he had spoken with his own doctor, Sir John Richardson of St Thomas's Hospital, who was 'sure the treatment which is being given ... is the right one'. Macmillan was sure that everything was being done which could be done. Jones told Armitage that Timothy would have to undergo an amputation in the new year. The Governor immediately cabled: 'You have been much in our thoughts and we send you all ... our deepest prayers for early 1961.' He followed this with a letter on New Year's day hoping that Timothy's morale was high, and adding that those in Zomba who knew of the operation were thinking of them and sent their best wishes.[86]

Timothy spent several days in St Thomas' hospital where his parents and sister were able to visit him regularly. For a few days he was out of hospital and they took him for walks, went shopping and to a football match, watched television and lunched at Harrods. On the last day of January he was told about the amputation, which was carried out on 2 February. Jones, his wife and daughter visited him twice a day for the next several days. They took him out for short periods three weeks after the operation and then, on 25 February, now 'recovering well in health and heart', he stayed with them at the flat they had taken in Dolphin Square. They went for drives in the car, and watched rugby matches and the Oxford and Cambridge boat race. The surgeon advised against leaving Timothy in England and said they should all go out to Africa straight away 'to let Timothy get strong'. On 2 April, they flew back to Central Africa. Elisabeth returned to school in Southern Rhodesia while the other three flew on to Nyasaland, arriving on 4 April.[87]

The next few days were hectic, since Armitage was about to leave and Jones had been away for the past four months. Although they had kept closely in touch by letters and cables, there was much to discuss. Jones particularly asked that he should not formally resume the duties of chief secretary during the few remaining days, so Armitage readily agreed to extend his secondment for six days on 'special duties'.[88]

On 10 April the Armitages left Nyasaland.

CHAPTER 5

Nyasaland: Governor

JONES had been away from Nyasaland for four months when he was sworn in as Governor and took the oaths of allegiance and due execution of office on 10 April 1961.¹ The Royal Instructions to him included the requirement that: 'The Governor shall, to the utmost of his power ... especially take care to protect [the inhabitants of Nyasaland] in their persons and in the free enjoyment of their possessions and by all lawful means to prevent and restrain all violence and injustice which may in any way be practised or attempted against them.'² Fulfilling this instruction was, as he already knew, not going to be an easy task and might well prove impossible.

Timothy's illness had caused immense anxiety and Jones was grateful to Armitage for agreeing to his staying in Britain to be with his son. Three months after they returned together to Nyasaland, Timothy died.³

The period of taking over from Armitage was confined to less than a week and there were frequent interruptions to attend farewell functions for the Armitages.

Much had happened during the past year in Nyasaland to bring about a completely different political state of affairs and this was to have a dominating influence on Jones's governorship.⁴ Banda had been released from detention. The emergency had been lifted. The Lancaster House conference had provided for an African majority in the legislature and a significant African presence in the executive council. As Acting Governor he had released the remaining detainees and secured the doctor's public denunciation ('for what it was worth') of violence and his plea for peaceful behaviour. Monckton had recommended that after changes to federal responsibilities and a trial period of five years, territories should be permitted to secede. The federal review had fizzled out.

Moreover, Armitage had taken steps from December to April to clear the ground and smooth the path for his successor. He had reprimanded Banda for rabble-rousing speeches against the judiciary and the police. This was the only time Banda received a gubernatorial reprimand and it had the effect of showing that the Governor was still governing and the secretary of state was not beyond authorizing him to deliver reprimands. Taking advantage of Banda's denunciation of violence and agreement that the law should take its course, Armitage prosecuted a fairly large number of MCP branch leaders and activists for arson, assault and intimidation. He had Chipembere prosecuted for sedition, convicted and sentenced to three years' imprisonment. In these ways he ensured, as far as he was able, that the violent men among Banda's lieutenants and followers were out of circulation and unable to stand in the way of the doctor fulfilling his undertaking that the country would be peaceful, so that elections could be held that would lead to an African majority in the legislature and the appointment of African ministers in the executive council. Following the prosecutions, there was no more intimidation and violence during the remainder of Armitage's term of office. He had also ensured that the full registration of voters had been smoothly achieved, and the administrative arrangement for ministerial government had been completed.

On the personal relationships side, Armitage had successfully invited Banda, his lieutenants, leading figures from other parties – African, European, Asian and Coloured – to a sherry party at Government House on Palm Sunday. The party was a great success. Banda, in his turn, had gone out of his way to assist by having a large farewell dinner for the Armitages, with guests of all races and persuasions. He made a friendly speech, making a number of complimentary remarks about the retiring Governor. It was a generous and helpful gesture.

These were vast changes and they set the scene for at least the beginning of Jones's period of office as Governor. His first task was to implement the remaining parts of the new constitution: the election and forming a government based on its results.

By the end of May Banda had personally chosen the MCP election candidates: generally moderates, people such as headmasters and prominent businessmen. He had been under some pressure to nominate the imprisoned Chipembere but had instead, 'by something of a master stroke', chosen Chipembere's father.[5]

There were a number of minor problems, easily dealt with, and some surprises in the preparations for the election. For example, while the government, to counter intimidation, was emphasizing the secrecy of the ballot, there were many 'insurance-seeking' voters who were 'insistent that the MCP should see and know how they voted'.[6] There was, however, one extremely worrying and more difficult matter: the re-emergence of intimidation.[7]

There were several United Federal Party (UFP) claims that the elections should be postponed so long as intimidation and other attacks on political opponents continued. On the other hand, the MCP, confident of success and impatient to form a government of their own, was very keen that the elections should be held at the earliest possible date.

The difficulties arising from intimidation came to a head in late July and early August when houses, food stores and cattle kraals belonging to leading members of the UFP in the Kota Kota district were destroyed, mostly by fire. Jones, suspecting 'political arson by LMY [League of Malawi Youth] thugs', sent a police mobile force platoon and CID team to the area. Leading MCP officials at headquarters cooperated with the police and seemed as horrified as was Jones. Banda 'deeply regretted' all such incidents and repeated his appeal for peace and calm.[8] The Governor seemed prepared to take a tough line, yet was defensive of the MCP leaders:

> I regard [the arson attacks] as a most serious matter ... senseless cruelty which must be stopped if necessary by strong measures ... and if there is any further outbreak in the area I shall seriously consider ... the postponement of elections in the Kota Kota District.
>
> I am satisfied that [the burnings] were not acts of political intimidation inspired by Malawi [Congress Party] hierarchy against UFP. Quite apart from known veto by MCP leaders on violence and trouble making, the constituency is Malawi stronghold and intimidation of opponents would be pointless.

Although intimidation in this particular area might not be necessary for the MCP to win the seat, it might not be pointless, because it could induce less secure areas to vote for the MCP candidate. While overlooking this possible effect of MCP activities elsewhere, Jones pointed to the possible effect of UFP reaction in other areas. He was extremely reluctant to use his power of postponement lest it create a precedent which 'certain irresponsible elements in UFP' might be encouraged to follow in other constituencies to bring about a general delay in the elections.

The election was not postponed, and polling took place on 15 August. Jones spent the morning visiting polling stations in and around Zomba and stayed up late listening to the results as they came in. The MCP won all the lower roll seats and their supporters won three of the eight upper roll seats, the remaining five going to the UFP.[9] It was a massive victory for Banda and the MCP and a humiliation for Blackwood and the UFP.

The other major step, forming a government, could now be taken. There were two important sets of questions: which parties were entitled to how many seats on the executive council, and also how many and which ministries should be created and who should fill them. The first of these was potentially the more difficult: to how many of the five non-official seats on the executive council were the UFP and the MCP, respectively, entitled?

It had been anticipated that the upper roll election would result in a virtually complete UFP victory, and the lower roll in a similar MCP victory. This would have produced an executive council of five official, three MCP and two UFP ministers. It would have left control of the council largely in official hands, since the UFP ministers would on most issues vote with the officials. The election, however, had resulted in the MCP securing three of the eight upper roll seats.

The constitution obliged the Governor, in appointing non-official ministers, to have regard to the composition of the parties in the legislative council. This initially seemed to Jones to preclude him from treating the two rolls separately although he could offer the three lower roll seats and one of the upper to the MCP and the other upper roll seat to the UFP, notwithstanding that the UFP had won five of the eight upper roll seats. The Colonial Office was not much help to him, but it is likely that officials thought the seats should in some way be shared between the MCP and the UFP, as had been intended and anticipated.[10]

On 16 August, Youens separately saw Banda and Blackwood, the leaders respectively of the MCP and the UFP, and went over the ground he knew the Governor wished shortly to discuss with them.[11] Then on 19 August, four days after the elections, Jones saw them.[12] 'Banda ... took the line that there was nothing in [the constitution] which required upper and lower rolls to be regarded as separate entities and strongly represented that his overall majority entitled him to all Executive Council unofficial seats, although he would welcome Cameron [despite his being an independent].' Banda stuck to this position. He could not sit with members of the UFP; any of their members in council would be 'Welensky's Trojan Horse'. Rather, he declared, he would go into opposition.

Jones found this interview difficult because the doctor was elated and 'obviously considered that the election results gave him a hand full of aces'. He was in effect again faced with an ultimatum: 'give me all the non-official seats on the executive council or I will go into opposition.' This seems a reasonable and eminently practical view for Banda to take. The election had been fought on party lines and only a government of the majority party, with officials, could work. In view of their opposed views, especially on federation, it was unrealistic to believe that an MCP–UFP coalition would operate well. Given Banda's overwhelming majority in the legislature, the prospect of allowing him to boycott the executive council was unthinkable. In opposition he would be in a position immediately to defeat every measure the government brought forward. It would be a constitutional nightmare which could not possibly endure for long.

Yet Banda, knowing that he held 'a hand full of aces', was prepared to wait until the Governor gave him all the executive council non-official seats. Jones thought he might persuade him to accept one UFP member, especially if he could give him 'some limited satisfaction' on another point the doctor was pressing: ministerial control over the chiefs and native authorities. But he recognized that 'the possibility of no UFP seats on Executive Council as the price of Banda's cooperation may have to be contemplated as a last resort'. He was sure the doctor was 'definitely aware [they had] serious differences of opinion to sort out'. Since he could not conceivably have contemplated Banda going into opposition, he must have been hoping to persuade him to give Blackwood a seat.

The discussion with Blackwood was easier because his requests were simpler: two seats on the executive council and – although he was prepared to forgo it – a parliamentary secretaryship. He wanted the portfolio of works for one of his colleagues and a ministry without portfolio for himself, but was prepared to accept just one seat – that without portfolio but with special responsibility for liaison with the federal government – for himself. He seems to have lost a good deal of his punch, had not prepared himself well and was ready to concede too many points. He must have recognized that the two upper roll non-African MCP supporters – Cameron and Surtee – seriously weakened his chances of being offered any the executive council seats.

Soon after his meeting with the Governor, Banda wrote 'asking for the lot or nothing'.[13] Three days later, on 22 August, Jones again saw him and explained that 'it would make things extremely difficult for the Secretary of State and for [the Governor] if there were no seat offered to the UFP, and [he] rehearsed to him the mathematical arguments in favour of giving the UFP one seat. This seemed to appeal to him, though he said that in his view the only honourable thing for the UFP to do was to go into opposition.'[14] They talked over this point and Banda eventually agreed to serve on the executive council with one UFP member, preferably without portfolio. He hoped Blackwood would reject an offer of only one seat.

The day following this meeting, Jones told Macleod he would like to offer Blackwood one seat, hoping – following Banda's lead – he would reject it. This may well have been Banda's intention in digging in his toes over two seats from the very beginning. The secretary of state quickly agreed to the proposal, notwithstanding Jones's belief that it would be 'extremely difficult' for him.[15]

Macleod's ready agreement is puzzling. The most important part of his Lancaster House negotiations, from his point of view, was the retention of executive power in official hands. The Governor was now faced with the prospect of having to choose between any differing but numerically balanced advice coming from his officials and the non-officials, rather than, as had been expected, being generally able to accept majority advice coming from the UFP siding with the officials.

The next Monday, having been offered one seat, Blackwood said that nothing less than two seats was acceptable to him, and Jones refused to grant this. He protested vigorously and argued that Cameron – an independent and the likely appointee – represented only a small minority of Europeans and consequently the vast majority would remain unrepresented in the executive council. Jones was quick to point out that his offer of one seat had been designed to avoid this and Blackwood himself had turned it down. Privately, he believed Blackwood had been over-ruled by Welensky and that, left to himself, he would have accepted appointment as minister without portfolio.[16]

Later that same day, when Jones told Banda that Blackwood had turned down the offer of a single seat, he was very pleased and said this gave him the opportunity to demonstrate his ability to govern in co-operation with officials and Cameron.[17] The doctor, through obduracy and the calculated risk that the UFP would accept a single seat, had successfully taken the first step towards dominating the executive council: his supporters equalled the number of officials.

The way was now clear for Jones to decide, in consultation with Banda, the number of portfolios, their contents and who should be responsible for each of them. He had gathered some ideas during their earlier discussions.

Immediately after the elections, Jones had found Banda's views 'somewhat divergent' from his own, especially over the provincial and district administration, chiefs, native authorities, African courts and district councils. Banda strongly believed these responsibilities should be in the hands of an African minister, probably himself. Notwithstanding this potentially dangerous difference between them, Jones had contemplated giving Banda control of the chiefs and native authorities as a *quid pro quo* for accepting one UFP member of the executive council. At that time he must have been very keen on the UFP having a seat. Banda also thought of having a minister of justice as well as an attorney-general but Jones felt these ideas were 'woolly' and he could probably be dissuaded from them. He spoke, too, of wanting lands included with natural resources under an African minister, again probably himself, but Jones hoped to divert him from this combination because expatriate confidence in the security of tenure was essential if they, their skills and capital were to be retained.

Their views were not divergent on a number of other issues. For example, Banda wanted the current financial secretary to become the minister of finance, and Jones agreed. It was an unnecessary request, since the financial secretary was *ex officio* a member of the executive council. Jones also agreed with Banda's view that the minister of finance should have a parliamentary secretary attached to him. Somewhat to his surprise, Banda made no bid to control the police, law and order, which he was content to leave to the chief secretary.[18] This may have been because he believed he was unlikely at this stage to be granted that control, but it is also probable he was not yet confident that law and order would be maintained. If it deteriorated it would almost certainly be caused by MCP members, and he would then rather not be ministerially responsible for law and order. Additionally, he knew there would be a massive expatriate police exodus and he was not yet ready for this.

Jones and Banda had continued their deliberations and, on 22 August, had discussed the areas of possible disagreement.[19] The Governor had said he would find it difficult to allow any elected minister to control the provincial and district administration; at this stage of constitutional development this responsibility usually remained with the chief secretary. As a partially placating means, however, had he pointed out that district commissioners were the agents of all ministries and that within their own spheres each minister could deal directly with them. This would have surprised district commissioners but it seems to have satisfied the doctor, though, again, he knew there would otherwise be a massive exodus for which he was not yet ready.

They had then discussed having a minister of justice as well as an attorney-general, and eventually Banda agreed to drop this idea, provided the current attorney-general remained in post and had a parliamentary secretary attached to him.

There had remained only the question of lands. They had argued over this for some time and eventually Banda reluctantly agreed to lands being a separate ministry under Kettlewell. He was well aware, although he did not express it, that Kettlewell's was a nominated seat on council and the new constitution provided for its replacement by an elected member, so the question of Banda getting his own way was simply postponed, probably for but a short period.

Up to this point in their 22 August meeting, the only non-official individuals directly mentioned in connection with specific portfolios had been Chiume, as minister of education, and Dunduzu Chisiza, as parliamentary secretary for finance. They had gone on, however, to speak of Chirwa and Banda himself. Banda was reluctant to discuss Chirwa but admitted that, like Jones, he was anxious about taking him – the only African barrister in the country – out of private practice. He would speak with Chirwa and others and would then talk to Jones again. Although co-founder and caretaker of the MCP during Banda's detention, Chirwa may have been suspect politically because in 1953 he had forsaken Congress to join a new political party.

They had next turned to discuss Banda's own position and the portfolio he might hold. Jones had understood Banda's colleagues wanted his position recognized in some way, and he believed the title of leader of the majority party would satisfy them and him. The Governor and his officials thought this title should be conferred, 'if only because it is unobjectionable and so very much in accordance with facts'[20] and because it appealed to his vanity. Banda agreed, but his colleagues, whom it did not satisfy, were to return to this issue with some insistence a little later. As for the doctor's ministerial responsibilities:

> The biggest 'rub' arose over the question of his own portfolio ... He wants the joint portfolios of Natural Resources *and* Local Government ... I suggested to him that a portfolio comprising both ... would be too big. Banda replied that the cooperation of the people would not be forthcoming if he himself had a portfolio which comprised the same range of subjects as that formerly in the hands of Mr. Ingham [secretary for African affairs].

Jones thought there might be room for manoeuvre over Banda's wish to control the two portfolios, 'but not much'. In the course of the discussion, Banda had said that in addition to Kettlewell being minister for lands, the second nominated official minister (Ingham) should be responsible for the portfolio of works. He was, in effect, moving these two officials out of their previous responsibilities and taking them on himself. This may have been a pre-emptive step to avoid these important responsibilities – natural resources and African local government – being claimed by others when the nominated officials were replaced by elected members.

For the present, at their 22 August meeting, this is where matters rested, but towards the end of the meeting Banda made it 'quite clear' that he personally would decide which Africans would be available for appointment to the executive council. 'He was quite dictatorial about this' and said 'They either take what I say or go!' The Governor may have had some say in which posts were to exist but none in who among the Africans was to fill them. He detected that Banda was jealous of Chisiza who, in Jones's opinion, was 'better material for leadership'.

Jones met Banda again on 29 August.[21] It was at the preceding meeting earlier the same day that Blackwood had rejected the offer of a single seat, so the number of places available for the MCP was now known and discussion to that extent was better focused. They had, of course, discussed the issues over the preceding two weeks and had agreed all but one point. Jones was unable to deflect Banda from holding both the local government and the natural resources portfolios himself, and he now 'proposed to meet him on this'. The doctor wanted Cameron as minister of works and Mkandawire as minister without portfolio as the two upper roll members provided for by the Lancaster House agreement.

The secretary of state agreed to Jones's ideas on forming a government, and on 2 September the Governor individually saw the elected members he intended to appoint and offered them the seats, together with the two parliamentary secretaries. He made two points. First, the fact that all the elected seats on the executive council were held by the MCP or its supporters threw a heavy burden on them to show they were capable of helping him administer the country in a way which protected the interests of all, including minority groups. Second, they were backed by a fine civil service, keen to maintain standards of loyalty and efficiency, whose loyalty and respect they could not command unless they respected their rights and dignity. Though 'greatly pleased' by their reaction to these two points, he admitted that all they did was to make the right noises.[22]

So, less than three weeks after the elections, Jones appointed Banda, Bwanausi, Cameron, Chiume and Mkandawire as ministers, and Chirwa and Chisiza as parliamentary secretaries. They joined the five official ministers: Foster, Pine, Phillips, Kettlewell and Ingham.[23]

At the beginning of October Jones reported to Macleod the current situation in the country.[24] He first wrote of the 'almost unbelievable air of tranquillity' which characterized the elections, and of the 'very serious' way the MCP treated it, showing it 'placed reliance on our new constitution as a means of attaining their ends'. He attributed the MCP's overwhelming victory almost entirely to 'splendid organisation coupled with a genuinely enthusiastic belief in Dr. Banda and the MCP'. He did not mention the intimidation and violence which had begun almost as soon as he took over as Governor, preceded the elections and no doubt contributed to the genuinely enthusiastic belief in Banda and the MCP, nor the effect which intimidation and violence quite clearly had on the elections themselves. It is likely that he hoped, and possibly believed, that these were things of the past and Nyasaland would now move forwards peacefully under his governorship.

There had been two meetings of the new council, only the second of which was a business meeting.

> This was a protracted and difficult meeting in which Chiume tested the patience of us all. I fancy he will be a difficult customer to deal with ... Dr. Banda ... has admitted ... that he will do as much business as possible by means of informal discussions with me and his colleagues, leaving the minimum of essential stuff to formal meetings of Executive Council. He and the other elected Ministers are very anxious that as many decisions as possible will be taken by the ministers themselves without reference to Executive Council and of course I will do my best to meet them on this within the possible limits.

On several occasions Banda had emphasized to him and Foster that he was personally solely responsible for MCP policy and the policy to be adopted by the elected ministers. He laid down the policy without consulting any of them. 'If they do not like it they can either lump it or sack me but I have made it quite plain right from the start that I impose my own policy on the party.' Jones recognized that while this attitude contained the inherent dangers of any dictatorship it could nevertheless be advantageous, particularly when Banda was 'in a cooperative frame of mind and willing to "smack down" people like Chiume when they become particularly difficult.' He was, however, under no illusions as to where it might end, including the possibility that 'it could lead ultimately to Dr. Banda's downfall'. Banda's policy would be obeyed while it was popular with the people but once he tried to impose an unpopular policy 'his dictatorial methods could sink him'. The Governor's private secretary recalled how in the executive council, although Jones tried to give other members the opportunity to state their views and work towards a consensus, 'it was Dr Banda who did most of the talking'.[25] Jones's willingness to allow as much discussion and as many decisions as possible to be taken outside council was extremely dangerous since from the outset it deprived council of the moderating influence that official ministers could bring to bear and potentially exacerbated Banda's dictatorial tendencies. He concluded the letter by saying: 'I have no doubt that our ship will have to pass through very troubled waters during the next few months and I shall be very hard put to avoid sacking the crew or preventing mutiny. I will endeavour to steer as safe a course as I can and I will let you know pretty quickly if we are in danger of running aground or capsizing.'

Less than a week after this letter was written, and probably before it reached him, Macleod was replaced as secretary of state for the colonies by Reginald Maudling.[26]

In the busy five months Jones had been Governor, a good deal had been accomplished. If anyone thought the pace could now slacken they would have been mistaken. The new elected ministers were determined not only to throw themselves into their departmental work but also to keep up the pace of constitutional progress to show their followers they were capable of securing further, and rapid, advances. This they did by pressing two points on Jones. The first was an appropriate title for Banda. The second was replacing the two nominated official executive councillors by elected members.

As soon as they were appointed, the two parliamentary secretaries and the elected ministers, other than Banda, asked for an interview with Jones. Chiume opened the discussion by saying they wished to accord to Banda a title more appropriate to his position and the support he commanded among his people. The time had come for him to be recognized as chief minister, and he and his colleagues asked the Governor to convey this view to the British government. Chisiza emphasized that Banda himself was not keen on the idea because he was a modest man and had always made it clear he did not wish to press a claim of this nature. Jones pointed out that the custom elsewhere had been to accord the title at a slightly later stage than that currently reached in Nyasaland. The chief secretary was still the Governor's deputy when occasion demanded and thus had to take precedence over other ministers. Banda's position had been recognized by giving him special precedence immediately after the chief secretary. This, together with the title of leader of the majority party, had been given very careful thought and had Banda's agreement. Jones would carefully consider the matter but would require time and would need to consult the secretary of state. He was aware that some people in Nyasaland thought he was going too fast, and although he himself did not feel that this was necessarily so, the pace should be dignified.[27]

This same group of ministers, with Jones, met the new secretary of state during his visit at the end of November.[28] Chiume again opened the discusssion, saying they had now been in office three months and had amply demonstrated their preparedness to work within the constitution. As the key figure in this, Banda should be recogized by the title of chief minister. They needed to show the people they 'were still fighting and progress would be seen to be made'. Chirwa wanted the chief secretary to be made deputy Governor; he would take the place of the Governor in his absence but would otherwise move out of the political arena and have some of his responsibilities transferred to the doctor. This was the first time they had raised the responsibilities of chief minister – the substance as well as the form. The secretary of state said 'he was impressed with their arguments, which seemed to him to be absolutely right ... He hoped that they would not press him but give him time to think things over. He wanted to think in terms of the actual month. There were a number of dates in the coming months when such an appointment might be appropriate.'

Before he left London, Maudling's officials had briefed him to the effect that if Banda could not be 'kept in play on the federal issue' he was very likely at the best to demand an early advance to full internal self-government which 'in itself would give rise to great difficulty'. At the worst he would withdraw from the government and take up open opposition to the British government. This would almost certainly lead to widespread disorder, requiring external military forces to control the situation. Maudling's officials therefore concluded that they were faced with three interconnected questions. First, 'how to keep Dr. Banda in play until the federal review can be resumed, probably late in 1962'.

Second, 'how in the meantime to avoid a clash on specific issues of Nyasaland's relationship with the Federation'. Third, 'whether anything can be done by way of interim constitutional moves to ease Dr. Banda's position *vis-à-vis* his supporters' such as the chief ministership and the replacement of the two nominated official ministers.[29]

It is probable that Maudling went somewhat further at this stage than he should or need have done in making such an encouraging response to the chief minister request. No doubt he was trying to keep Banda 'in play', but so far Banda had not shown any signs of not being kept in play, or of being about to demand early self-government or to go into opposition, or of feeling he needed his position easing. Consequently, it is likely that his encouraging remarks were stimulated by Jones as a result of the lieutenants' representations.

Jones and Maudling do not seem to have coordinated their ideas particularly well. For a while they were unclear whether or not there were precedents for granting the title of chief minister at this stage. Jones thought it was somewhat too early and was inclined to find another acceptable title, and Maudling felt there was a strong case for granting the title at an early date. Maudling thought the change of title would not materially affect Banda, while Jones hoped it would lead to a lessening of the subjects in his portfolio. Maudling did not think the title would confer authority over other ministers, while Jones thought they should represent the change as conferring the right on Banda to control the work of all the unofficial ministers. Neither appeared to have a solution to the problem – if there was one – of the relations between the chief secretary and the chief minister.

With very little real pressure from the elected ministers, Maudling seemed anxious to accede to the request, and Jones did not voice a contrary or alternative view, despite the difficulties they foresaw. They paid little regard to the fact that Banda himself was not particularly keen on the idea. Furthermore, notwithstanding Jones's awareness of the dangers in the doctor's dictatorial tendencies, including ultimately the possibility of his downfall, he, Maudling and the elected ministers seem not to have been concerned about the significantly increased personal dominance which granting the title would bring to Banda, and the exacerbation of those tendencies. This would especially be so if Jones's suggestion were adopted: that as chief minister he would have the right to control the work of the other ministers. It may be that Jones was prepared to risk these dangers in order, should the occasion arise, to avoid being placed in a position of having to arbitrate between Banda and his ministers. He had already recognized the advantage of the doctor 'smacking down' difficult colleagues. He may also have felt that if he gave the ministers what they wanted they might be less inclined to push

Banda into making further, less acceptable, demands. By February 1962 Maudling was quite prepared to grant the title, and he had in mind 14 February, which he believed was Banda's birthday, for doing so.[30]

The second point the elected ministers pressed was the replacement of the two nominated official ministers by elected members. During Maudling's meeting with them on 30 November, they reminded him that at the Lancaster House conference they had been strongly opposed to including nominated members but had compromised. Jones said their inclusion was to preserve a balance of power but the elections had thrown up a balance quite different from that which had been anticipated. This was correct but the different balance ought to have made it even more important to retain the nominated offficials, because the balance of power Macleod had in mind was one which kept executive power in official hands. In the event, the MCP commanded all five elected seats and the officials were now numerically matched by a united band of elected members, not a divided group part of which would support them. Maudling simply said that when the Governor was satisfied the right time had arrived to replace the nominated ministers, he would find the secretary of state sympathetic.[31]

When Maudling met the official ministers the following day and they too discussed the replacement of the nominated members, he and Jones met a certain amount of opposition.[32] Phillips felt strongly that the replacement should be dependent on the smooth running of the government machine and should be used as a bargaining point to secure two ends. First, to make sure the elected ministers cooperated with civil servants in the smooth running of government which, presumably, he thought was not currently the case. Second, to ensure the elected ministers adopted at least a neutral stance and not frustrate the necessary dealings of government in the federal sphere. These were shrewd, important observations and sound political tactics.

Foster made the point that the replacement would be a far greater gain for the majority party than they could reasonably expect. It sounds as if he thought the demand should, and might successfully, be resisted. He did not expand on it but his point was shrewd and profoundly important. If the replacement took place – and the Lancaster House agreement had provided for it to happen but left its timing to the Governor – it would be a major constitutional step, for it would alter the balance in the executive from the parity of five official and five elected councillors to three official and seven elected councillors. Not only would this give Banda a substantial majority in the executive but it would also give him significantly increased scope to arrange the overwhelmingly greater part of the subject matter of government as he wished and to distribute it to whom he wished. It not only further increased the MCP's power in government but it also very considerably increased Banda's personal power both in the MCP and in the government. It also completely undid what Macleod was aiming at, and which he had considered vital: the retention of real power in official hands.

The advice of Jones's official executive councillors was clear. They should not rush into the replacements, though they could not long be delayed; they should extract a *quid pro quo* which would greatly improve the efficiency of the government both internally and in relation to the federation; and they should recognize that they were overturning the fundamental basis on which the Lancaster House agreement had been negotiated.

Maudling also had 'a most cordial discussion' with Banda. The secretary of state and the Governor made three points. One was concerned with the secession issue but the other two arose from Phillips's pleas. Addressing Banda, Jones

> asked him to ensure that the machinery of Government, including unavoidable cooperation with the Federal Government, was kept moving. He pointed out that this would not commit elected Ministers personally; but that it was essential that the functions of Government continued to operate and in particular he referred to the problem of obtaining and repaying loan funds. He went so far as to say that even if Dr. Banda felt it necessary to disown His Excellency on this question of cooperation with the Federal Government, he would not mind so long as he did not disassociate himself from Government.[33]

Presumably, Jones felt the financial arguments were those most likely to persuade Banda. What in effect he was asking him to do was not to make federal government operations in Nyasaland unworkable – as he had the Nyasaland government in 1959 – and, if necessary, to put the blame on the Governor, but not to withdraw from the government. Banda did not respond clearly, but both the secretary of state and the Governor felt 'that this plea had seemed not to be unfavourably heard'. Nevertheless, Maudling, less convinced and optimistic than Jones, felt that too much reliance ought not to be placed on Banda's acquiescence 'as his impression was that the financial arguments used by [Jones] had gone over the Doctor's head'.[34] It is more likely that, rather than them going over, he had at this stage allowed them to go through, his head – in one ear and out of the other.

Despite the clear reservations of his official advisers and Maudling's non-committal approach to the matter, and notwithstanding his awareness of the ultimate dangers of increasing the doctor's personal power, Jones told Banda on 6 December that the two nominated official members of the executive council were to be replaced within the next three months.

It was a decision which he made by himself, as he explained: 'The initiative was taken by the Governor after consultations with both the official members of the Executive Council and the secretary of state ... Their replacement was mooted in the absence of pressure from Dr Banda and his colleagues.'[35] It was true that the doctor had not pressed him, but his colleagues had. Banda, who said he had been 'under much pressure' from his party to find out when this would happen, was pleased. While not insisting on the points, Jones added that he was relying on Banda to make this constitutional change easier by ensuring that the elected ministers and members of the legislature behaved more pleasantly towards the civil service and by allowing him and the government to 'cooperate with the Federal Government at all points where such cooperation was necessary either under the constitution or for the purpose of furthering the interests of Nyasaland'. Banda promised he would do his best in both these matters. Perhaps Jones had learned that insisting on conditions prior to granting concessions was pointless. His attempts to do so when releasing the final detainees in 1960 had not brought about the end of physical attacks on political opponents and verbal attacks on the civil service, despite Banda's 'solemn undertakings'. He was convinced Banda sincerely wanted to help him but realized he could do so only in so far as his followers could be persuaded to agree. 'There [was] also the question of his own irascible temperament: when his blood pressure rises tact goes to the winds.'[36]

When Jones told the elected members that inclusion of nominated officials in the executive council was designed to preserve a balance of power, but the elections had resulted in a quite different balance from that expected, he seems almost to have been saying that since the election results did not yield the balance hoped for, a balance of any sort was no longer desirable. This interpretation would support the view expressed later by Foster, that Jones believed that once the British government had decided a colony should be given self-government, the quicker this was done the better, and it was the job of the Governor to see it done as swiftly as was decently possible.[37]

Jones found the timing of replacing the nominated officials 'not an easy matter'. Notwithstanding the worries about ministers not co-operating in Nyasaland government relations with the federal government and about MCP–civil service relationships, he believed the constitution was working well. He believed, too, that there were additional members of the legislature available to assume ministerial office. He was clear in his own mind that his timing 'only just anticipated the chimes of the clock' and had he delayed he would have been 'subject to heavy pressures'. He thought they had 'bought an appreciable measure of extra good-will which [might] stand [them] in good stead on other issues'.[38] In effect, he was saying that it was wise not to wait for heavy pressure but to make concessions at the prospect of it, hoping to gain some goodwill for future use.

Banda had successfully, and with very little effort, taken the second step towards dominating the executive council: against three officials he now had seven seats, to be filled by individuals of his personal choosing.

In considering what changes to make when Ingham and Kettlewell left, Jones did not assume that the current parliamentary secretaries would necessarily become full ministers. He envisaged 'a fair degree of reshuffling' of subjects and thought Chisiza, but not Chirwa, would be a good choice for one of the new ministries. He would then have the opportunity to appoint a new parliamentary secretary to a ministry other than the treasury, probably Banda's ministry 'which covers a wide field and lacks adequate ministerial attention due to Dr. Banda's other preoccupations'. The breadth of the doctor's ministerial responsibilities was a perpetual concern to Jones. At no stage did he or anyone else suggest that a third parliamentary secretary should be appointed, as provided for in the Lancaster House agreement. Nor did he seem concerned that if Chisiza were made a minister, the vital ministry of finance would be left without an understudy. He probably felt there was time to remedy this later. Banda disagreed with his reasoning and was keen to keep both Chisiza and Chirwa as parliamentary secretaries 'in training for the two most important, difficult ministries that he would hope to take over, at the appropriate time'. He did not say so, but if he could show, at the appropriate time, that there were well trained elected colleagues to take over it would strengthen his case for removing the *ex officio* members. Alternatively, it may be that Banda preferred Chisiza not to be a full minister and therefore also a member of the executive council where he could shine, possibly dent Banda's personal domination and influence the course of government policy. Chisiza and Chirwa stayed as parliamentary secretaries. The doctor had Willie Chokani, or Gwanda Chakuamba, and John Msonthi in mind as the new ministers. When Jones floated the idea that one of them should be a second minister without portfolio, Banda made it clear that he disagreed, though he would turn it over in his mind. He wished to take Kettlewell's and Ingham's portfolios himself and give the two new ministers development, and trade, commerce and industry. This is what happened.[39]

The replacement of the nominated official members marked a major turning point, as Foster had predicted. Banda was now in a position of extraordinary power. The MCP had already conferred wide autocratic powers on him in controlling the party. Within government he decided the line which the elected MCP ministers adopted in the executive council, and since he now had a considerable majority in council it followed that, whatever the *de jure* position, in practice he decided the policy of the government, backed up by his overwhelming majority in the legislature, nearly all of whose members he had personally nominated as candidates. The change can be seen in the way in which decisions were reached concerning which ministries should exist and who, of those selected by Banda, should fill each of them. Whereas the previous August there had been the appearance of collaboration and Jones had had some say in which ministries should exist, though not in which African elected members should head them, now it was Banda alone who made the decisions on both counts, and did so with scarcely any discussion with the Governor and certainly none with anyone else. From this point onwards – in advance of self-government – it was Banda and not Jones who was to govern Nyasaland. If he met any resistance from within the Nyasaland government or from the British government, he had the Gwelo card ready to play. Whether he produced it in the form of 'You will have to send me back to prison', or 'I will resign and go into opposition', or 'I can no longer control my followers', or 'You will have to bring in the army', it was a card of extraordinarily great potency.

Of the original seven elected the executive council and junior ministers, four were from the north (Chiume, Mkandawire, Chirwa and Chisiza) one was from the centre (Banda) another was from the south (Bwanausi) and one was a European (Cameron). Banda now increased the number from the centre by one (Msonthi) and from the south also by one (Chokani). Jones was aware of the southerners' jealousy of the northerners and the part which Chipembere – still in gaol – could play as a focus for southern discontent.[40] Banda's appointments now went some way to even up the balance.

We have noted how a major and worrying issue discussed during the secretary of state's visit was that of Banda and his fellow elected ministers not cooperating in the Nyasaland government's working relations with the federal government. This was not surprising since their deep loathing of all things federal was well known and of long standing. It would have been politically dangerous to risk the opprobrium of their followers and the ridicule of their opponents by being seen to cooperate in any way with the federal government. Although non-cooperation manifested itself in a number of ways, one was particularly disturbing and persistent: the Nkula Falls hydro-electricity scheme on the Shire river.

The British government's position on the Federation – and consequently their instruction to Jones – was that they still were committed to it but realized that changes, probably substantial, in the allocation of power between the federal and the territorial governments were inevitable. Basically, they were keen that a form of association involving all three territories should be maintained. It was their hope that, given time and experience of governing, with the Governor's guidance, the African politicians in Nyasaland would come to accept that a continuation of the Federation, albeit with changes, was in the country's best interests. This was why they were so keen to have Banda, and possibly others, join the executive council soon after the Lancaster House conference. In the meantime, the Governor, as he made clear to Banda after the elections, considered the matter *sub judice* and would support the federal government in the fields where it had sovereignty so long as the British government required him to.[41]

Banda's position was quite different. Although he intended to conduct his campaign against the Federation peacefully, the elections had given him a mandate to press for secession. Jones's view, given to officials, at this stage was:

> I fear that [Banda] will resent most bitterly even oblique approaches from either myself or from officials designed to persuade him there is any good at all in any kind of federal association that includes Southern Rhodesia, and any attempt on our part overtly to commend a continuation of the Federation to the people of Nyasaland would lead to a critical situation. I expect officials to be neutral on this.[42]

There is no evidence that this means of handling the question was on the instructions of the secretary of state. It is more likely to have been Jones's personal method of handling it: to tell Banda it was *sub judice* and should therefore not be discussed, which neatly avoided incurring the doctor's wrath, and to expect his officers to be neutral so that they did not provoke that wrath. This was a clancular reversal of policy from his predecessor's time when every step was expected to be taken to win over the Nyasaland Africans to federation. His motive was to avoid the boat being rocked until Britain had made up its mind how the future of the Federation was to be handled. To rock the boat over federation would seriously endanger the operation of government in Nyasaland and the relations between Banda and Jones and between ministers and civil servants. The future of the Federation was a subject best avoided, despite the British government's wish that some form of association be retained.

In June 1961, Banda refused to agree to the Nkula Falls scheme and told the Governor, 'If you sign, I will resign.'[43] Shortly after this, and no doubt as a consequence of it, Jones advised the secretary of state:

> I am naturally concerned that we have now reached a stage where, unless a miracle happens, the Nkula Falls scheme is to be put in cold storage for so long as the Federal Government has the constitutional power to construct it. Moreover, the announcement will more or less coincide with

the publication of our rather ambitious development plan which will demonstrate the need for electricity without making any provision therefore. [The] only person who can save the situation is Banda himself ... I fear that there is now little hope of a compromise.[44]

Soon after Banda and his colleagues were appointed to the executive council, notwithstanding that he considered the matter *sub judice*, Jones asked him to 'lay his cards on the table with regard to his thoughts on the Federation'. The doctor assured him he had no intention of embarrassing either him or Macleod. He respected Jones's position and realized he, Jones, must support the Federation until Britain changed its policy. However,

> He is dedicated on behalf of his people to get Nyasaland out of the Federation. He will try to do this by peaceful negotiations with [Macleod] ... I fear that Banda and his colleagues are going to make our relations with the Federal Government very difficult indeed. We have already had evidence of their determination to have nothing whatsoever to do with the Federal Government if they can possibly avoid it ... Banda said to me that inordinate delay in the resumption of the Federal talks would make things very difficult for him and in this case he might be unable to resist the demands of his followers that he take some overt and perhaps unconstitutional action to end federation so far as Nyasaland is concerned. But he would contemplate such a course of action only in the very last resort.[45]

So wary was he of rocking the boat in any way, that the Governor did not, as perhaps he should, react to the warning of possible unconstitutional means to end federation. This must have heartened Banda. To threaten unconstitutional action, even as a last resort, and receive no reaction from the Governor was a considerable achievement. To have made the point, albeit gently, that unconstitutional actions would not be in Banda's best interests, would not be tolerated and would if necessary be met by force, both British and federal, would undoubtedly have risked rocking the boat, but it might have induced Banda to think twice about taking unconstitutional action, and have encouraged him to persuade his followers of the unwisdom of doing so and of the futility of creating another impasse. It might also have had an effect on the frequency with which he played the Gwelo card.

Three weeks after Banda assumed office, the Governor spoke with him specifically about Nkula Falls. Jones felt he had at one point almost got the doctor to agree to the scheme going ahead, but he had changed his mind 'as a result of pressure from some of his leading supporters'.[46] Chiume later confirmed that he had put pressure on Banda and Chisiza to delay implementing the project until the country was independent.[47] Banda's response now was quite clear: 'He greatly regretted that he could not possibly agree to the Federal Government's providing funds for [the Nkula Falls scheme.] He feels so strongly about this that if [Jones] decided to carry it through in the face of his opposition, he would feel that it would be necessary for him to resign from the government.'[48]

By the middle of October Banda's intractability was fast becoming alarming. Allowing the majority party to go into opposition was unthinkable, since this would immediately bring the process of government to a halt and would result in large-scale disturbances; moreover, it would return the country to the impasse which, the secretary of state had been hoping, had been broken by Banda's release from detention and the Lancaster House agreement. There was, in Jones's and Maudling's minds, the 'danger of an early constitutional crisis ... arising from the unwillingness of Banda and his ministers to cooperate with the federal authorities'. This was especially so because Welensky was thought to be using the scheme 'as the ground for the coming struggle with Banda'.[49] So worrying was this danger that Jones and Phillips immediately flew to London to discuss the matter. Face-to-face discussions between Maudling, his officials, Jones, Phillips and Welensky might, they hoped, produce some new, workable ideas.[50] They were not able to come up with any helpful ideas save to 'play down' the numerous points of friction which cropped up daily and to ensure that approaches from the federal government to the Nyasaland government should be through the chief secretary 'wherever possible in order not to court rebuff'.[51]

Banda soon made his position quite clear. At a press conference on 26 November, in reply to a question on what he intended to do about the Nkula Falls scheme, he said: 'Who is going to build it? You can't build a thing here unless I sign a piece of paper. I would rather see the whole of Nyasaland starve to death than take charity from Welensky.'[52] Chisiza, on the other hand, was conscious of the extent to which the development plan depended on additional power supplies and was 'very upset' by the prospect of the Nkula scheme being rejected.[53]

In July 1962 the secretary of state 'made a final effort to bring Banda round'. The doctor was still quite adamant: 'He [again] made it quite plain that it would be a matter involving his resignation from the government if the issue were forced through.' The secretary of state concluded that he had 'to accept the Governor's advice that he must decline to provide the Federal Government with the necessary authorization to proceed with the project'.[54] It was to be some years, and in different political circumstances, before the Nkula project went ahead.[55]

The major motivations driving Banda during the first three years after his return to Nyasaland in 1958 were attaining independence from Britain and withdrawing from the Federation. This was why he was so keen on securing a majority in the legislature and a significant proportion of the seats in the executive council. Now that he had secured these, the main emphasis of his political activities became directly focused on secession. Given secession, Nyasaland could rapidly move to independence without the Federation holding it back or subsequently restricting its sovereignty. He was keen that the federal review conference should be reconvened at an early date in order to agree secession.

The British government, however, was keen to delay reconvening the review conference. They hoped that, with time, experience and guidance, the elected ministers would come to appreciate the benefits of a continued association of the Central Africa territories. Delay, too, gave them a better chance of persuading Welensky to accept internal constitutional changes in Nyasaland. They, Jones and his officials were anxious also to establish a *modus vivendi* between the elected ministers in Nyasaland and the federal government so that day-to-day Federal operations should not be hampered or thwarted. As a means to these ends, Jones tried to persuade Banda to meet Welensky.

In London, Welensky had said he 'was not unfavourably disposed to the idea' that the first part of the Nkula scheme should be in Nyasaland's control, but he would want to discuss it with Banda first. Soon after his return, in November 1961, Jones put the idea of a private meeting, as tactfully and persuasively as he could, to the doctor. Banda said he would think it over, though he had 'grave doubt as to the wisdom of such a meeting'.[56]

The following week, Banda told him he was prepared to meet Welensky either alone or, preferably, with the Governor present. The meeting would have to be known to his followers because the risk of a private meeting, news of which leaked, would be too great. He would await a letter from Welensky: 'If it seems that Welensky is prepared to talk secession with me I will meet him. He is a charming man, but can be vicious – but then, I also can be vicious, I suppose.'[57]

During his late 1961 visit to Nyasaland, Maudling, with Jones, saw Banda and raised again the question of his meeting Welensky. They still felt the meeting would be desirable but the matter hung 'slightly in the balance'. In fact it hung more than slightly in the balance because Banda would now meet the federal premier only if the *main* subject was secession. He would be prepared to discuss other matters after that.[58]

A week before Christmas, Banda received a letter from Sir Godfrey Nicholson, a senior member of the Conservative Party, in which he said: 'I know that I can give you ... a definite pledge, that no one in this country would dream of trying to coerce Nyasaland into remaining in the Federation ... I am absolutely definite about this.'[59] This letter was written about the same time as Banda was meeting the commonwealth secretary, Duncan Sandys, in Dar es Salaam. Very shortly, too, Nigel Fisher, a close friend of both Macleod and Nicholson, wrote to tell Banda that Maudling had told him in confidence: 'He could not refute the logic of your argument ... that you had been elected by an overwhelming majority to secede from the Federation as at present constituted. He thought this was a perfectly reasonable attitude for you to take'.[60] Banda showed Jones both these letters.[61]

When Banda returned to Nyasaland from Dar es Salaam he was in a belligerent mood and Jones found a meeting with him 'fairly difficult'.[62] Banda now said he would not meet Welensky. Jones did not pursue the matter but went on to discuss the exercise, with which Banda had agreed earlier, of examining the implications of secession for Nyasaland and the possibility of association after secession, possibly based on common services. At this point, 'he blew up' and said this was now not necessary and he would be under grave suspicion from his followers were he known to be taking part in it. He 'got very emotional on the subject of Federation, and said "I hate Salisbury and its politicians. I want to cut Nyasaland away from them for ever. I do not want any common services with Southern Rhodesia."' When the Governor tried to point out the merits of retaining some of the common services he ran into further trouble:

> He waved this aside saying that all these services had existed before Federation and could continue to exist after Federation ... When I pointed out how much we depend upon Salisbury for the carriage of mails and the passing of telegrams and telephone calls, he became very wild and said that we would have to direct all our traffic through East Africa. He was clearly in a very belligerent mood and the very mention of Salisbury produced a tirade. We parted on very friendly terms but clearly I have lost ground with him on the subject of a meeting with Welensky and also on the subject of a working party to consider the implications of secession.[63]

Three days later Jones found Banda much calmer. He agreed once more to meet Welensky, provided the federal premier made the approach and agreed to secession being the main topic of conversation. Banda still maintained that secession must be an established fact before he would turn his mind to any future association, but he was less vehement than at their previous meeting. Jones thought that in the doctor's present mood he would be able to get him talking 'more and more about what lies ahead but the possibility of him agreeing to a working party [on the implications of secession seemed] now seems to be remote'.[64]

Alport, British high commissioner to the Federation, visited Nyasaland for a few days early in January 1962 for one of his periodic meetings with the northern governors.[65] Jones explained that since Maudling's visit Banda was convinced the British government had accepted that his policy was founded on secession and that Nyasaland would not, therefore, be forced to stay in the Federation against the will of its people. Similarly, although Banda's meeting with Sandys in Dar es Salaam 'had its difficult moments', he had again come away with the view that Sandys also accepted that his policy was secession.

Jones was disappointed by the elected ministers' failure to recognize the financial realities of the country's budgetary position, and by the MCP's attitude to the civil service. Banda was constantly needled by those of his followers who would not forget the past and wanted unpopular officers moved or dismissed. It was indeed the case that a number of officers were moved at the simple behest of the MCP.[66] This led to despondency, and if attitudes did not change many expatriates would leave at the earliest possible moment. He turned finally to security, law and order:

> There was no present threat to law and order ... so long as Dr. Banda stayed in the Government and pursued a peaceful policy. This situation could change overnight particularly if Dr. Banda's aim on secession from the present federation were not achieved by constitutional means in what he considered to be a reasonable time (a period he had never defined). If Dr. Banda left the Government and provoked a crisis, massive security forces could be needed to contain the situation – at least six battalions of troops.

Alport spoke also with Banda, who found it 'very interesting' and indeed wrote 'a friendly letter' to him after his return to Salisbury. As Alport told Sandys:

> Banda, with whom I had quite a long and friendly interview said that he was determined to obtain acceptance of the principle of secession before committing himself in any way to any future association between the territories and before he would examine the consequences which would flow from it. I did not, however, get the impression that this provides us with an insuperable problem, though, of course, it will be extremely difficult to handle from the federal point of view.[67]

Jones, who was not present at their meeting, and possibly fearing that the high commissioner might have the impression – and, worse, pass it on to those in London, where it might be shared – that handling Banda was not as difficult as he was making out, uttered 'one note of warning':

Banda was in a good mood when you saw him and I understand that you raised no contentious subject with him. I feel it is dangerous to infer from one short and peaceful contact that pressures are not imminent ... we here are continuing to be subject to day to day pressures which are not relaxing in any way ... Maudling's opinion that the situation here was potentially explosive was the correct one and is still valid today.[68]

A little later in January 1962, during 'a friendly discussion' and without having discussed the matter with him, Banda told Jones he was going to London to arrange with the secretary of state a dissolution conference, since he did not now think there was any need for a general review conference with the other territories present. His talks with Maudling, Sandys and Alport had convinced him that the British government would not oppose his policy of secession. Banda stressed that he was 'under unceasing pressure' from his party to raise the secession issue, and in this case, Jones felt, he might demand the substance as well as the title of chief minister as the price for buying time until the federal review was resumed.[69]

Sandys visited Nyasaland from 10 to 13 February. He and Jones had three meetings with Banda, in none of which was the Dar es Salaam discussion mentioned. At the first two meetings Banda 'explained with great clarity and vigour [his] inflexible opposition to Federation with Southern Rhodesia'. He 'expressed himself bluntly and forcibly [and] put his case clearly and unequivocally'. He implored Sandys to tell Macmillan and the cabinet that they must be allowed to secede from the Federation at the earliest possible opportunity. 'If the British Government wished to maintain the Federation as constituted at present it would have to send an army to Nyasaland to deal with the revolt that would ensue ... and send me to prison again.'[70] 'Dr. Banda could not listen to any suggestion that the present Federation should be modified ... What he hoped to get by April this year was a decision by the British Government that Nyasaland could secede from the Federation: thereafter a Commission of Enquiry could be appointed to advise how the details of secession could be worked out.'

Sandys was left in no possible doubt as to Banda's adamant position. He hoped he would pursue his objective peacefully and with as little recrimination as possible. He could not commit the British government one way or the other on secession. Possibly thrown off guard by the doctor's references to an army being needed to keep Nyasaland in the federation, he none the less undertook that the British government would tell Banda 'within one month from 12th February, one way or the other, what it proposed to do about Nyasaland and the Federation'. If they could not release Nyasaland, they would tell him so. If they felt Nyasaland's secession could be pursued, they would say so and arrange for him to visit London in April. Banda quickly agreed to this proposition and the two men 'shook hands on it'.[71]

Sandys's undertaking is astonishing and seems to have come completely out of the blue. No wonder Banda shook hands on it: it was the most significant advance he had made in his campaign for secession.

Sandys reported to the cabinet his first two meetings with Banda as soon as they were completed, making it clear that whatever was said was without commitment on either side. He wished to receive the cabinet's authority for the action he proposed to take: to tell Welensky there was no prospect of keeping Nyasaland in the Federation except by force. If Welensky attempted forceful action, he would fail, would alienate any remaining African sympathy for the Federation in Northern Rhodesia and would gravely prejudice Britain's relations with other African states. If Britain and Welensky accepted that Nyasaland must be allowed to secede, the 'best and most dignified' procedure would be for Welensky to take the initiative by announcing that he had no wish to retain an unwilling partner and he was therefore asking the British government to arrange for Nyasaland's secession. If Welensky was to be persuaded along these lines and avoid a humiliating formal demand for secession by Banda, there was no time to be lost. He therefore asked for authorization to bring matters to a head at once and strongly advise Welensky to follow the course he was now suggesting. Sandys was quite confident he could persuade Welensky to agree to Nyasaland's secession, but Jones 'was sufficiently doubtful about this to accept his wager of an even pound that he could bring it off'.[72]

At Sandys's third meeting with Banda and Jones[73] before he went on to Salisbury to see Welensky, he retracted his promise – 'got himself off the hook' as he told Jones – that the British government would tell Banda before 12 March whether or not it was going to allow secession. Instead, he undertook that the decision would be given 'some time during March'. Banda, presumably confident the decision would be in his favour, agreed to this. In securing a little more time, Sandys had eased himself into a slightly more comfortable position on the hook but had certainly not got himself off it. The amount of time available to consult others – particularly the British cabinet, Welensky, Whitehead and Hone – let alone win them over to a decision by the end of March, was patently and woefully inadequate.

On the question of the title of chief minister, Sandys – unlike Maudling a few weeks earlier – said that raising this issue at present would embarrass the British government. It 'might complicate consideration of the larger issue of federation', and he advised that it should rest while that issue was pursued. Banda, who naturally did not want the federal issue complicated, readily agreed, saying he was not at the moment interested in his own title and status. The urgent matter was secession, which he wished to pursue to the exclusion of other matters. This discussion took place only two days before Maudling was proposing to confer the title on the doctor. Shortly, Jones told the Nyasaland ministers that the question had been deferred and they agreed to drop it for the time being. The real reason for the change of mind was that having played the delaying-tactic card of replacing the nominated official ministers, the British government wanted to postpone using the other card – the title of chief minister – so that when they disappointed Banda by not agreeing to an early resumption of the federal review conference the title 'would be some trophy for him to return home with'.[74]

Sandys also talked about the financial implications of secession: an annual shortfall on recurrent account of some £6 million. It would be impossible for the British government to shoulder this responsibility and consequently it would be necessary for Nyasaland to reduce expenditure, increase taxation and obtain external assistance. This was an early reference to a matter which was to be taken up much more fully a year later and which contributed to a great deal of trouble eighteen months after that.

On 13 February, in a press conference, Banda said he would accept an invitation to meet Welensky 'if secession were on the agenda'. Sandys, who had just arrived in Salisbury, immediately phoned Jones and told him he and Welensky were keen to take advantage of this. So highly did the British government and the Governor value the possibility of a meeting that, in the course of the next seven hours, Jones talked to Banda three times about it.[75]

At the first meeting Banda would not see Welensky unless he gave an assurance that he agreed to Nyasaland's secession. When Jones telephoned him, Sandys asked him to press Banda further, on the basis that he had publicly volunteered to meet if secession were on the agenda. Welensky was keen to meet on this understanding, but the condition now imposed – an assurance that he agreed to secession – was unacceptable.

At the second meeting, although Banda 'remained extremely reluctant', he was prepared to accept provided Welensky clearly understood he would do so only to discuss ways and means of seceding. 'He would walk out if any bargaining were attempted or if any effort were made to get him to change his mind.' Sandys was fairly confident he could persuade Welensky to go along with this. In the event, the federal premier would not accept Banda's terms which he considered unreasonable. Instead, he asked that a formula be put to the doctor to the effect that he was fully aware of Banda's conviction that Nyasaland should secede and was prepared to meet him for a general discussion of the problem with this awareness in mind. This preparedness did not imply acceptance of the principle of secession.

Jones saw Banda for the third time, and this further approach 'exasperated him considerably'. For a while he entirely refused to entertain Welensky's formula. He did not want the meeting at any price and it could not possibly serve any useful purpose. After Jones had 'exerted considerable pressure on him and advanced every argument in favour of the proposed meeting', Banda agreed to meet Welensky without insisting on his prior acceptance of the principle of secesssion. For his part, however, he would discuss nothing other than ways and means of effecting secession. Jones felt that 'no good and probably definite harm' would stem from a meeting on this basis, especially since Banda agreed to it with great reluctance and only out of deference to himself. He advised against it. In Banda's view, the only advantage to be gained would be to establish good relations between him and Welensky so that Nyasaland's secession could be dignified and peaceful. This would have been a very worthwhile objective, but neither Britain nor Welensky was yet prepared openly to contemplate secession.

Given this situation, Welensky would not agree to the meeting, provisionally scheduled for 15 February, under Banda's conditions. Jones's view was that on the whole it was good the meeting did not take place – he doubted if it would have lasted five minutes.[76]

Jones must have been getting at least a little fed up with Sandys involving him in federal matters. It was a dangerous area into which to be drawn. When he had returned from Dar es Salaam Banda had spoken to Jones about his meeting with Sandys, as the Governor then told Maudling: '[Sandys] accepted that there must be secession for Nyasaland. Banda favours proposal that he should have talks with [Colonial Secretary] and Commonwealth Secretary but hopes that I [Jones] may be present. He considers that these talks will do away with any need for talks with Welensky.'[77]

Jones told Foster that when he asked Banda how he had got on with Sandys in Dar es Salaam, he was 'somewhat evasive' and gave the impression the meeting had not gone well. Jones told Foster precisely what he had told Maudling: 'Sandys had accepted that there must be secession for Nyasaland.' It may be that Sandys *seemed* to be saying – though much less clearly than Nicholson or Fisher, who were not ministers – that Nyasaland would be allowed to secede, but the doctor could not tie him down. Perhaps whatever was said was said with no one else present and this would account for Banda wanting Jones there on future occasions. Possibly, too, Banda's evasiveness was because Sandys had told him not to say that he had agreed to secession, if indeed he did say so, or he would deny it – as he did.

The wording Jones used in reporting Banda's account of what Sandys had said in Dar es Salaam is confusing. His report to both Maudling and Foster was that Sandys accepted that Nyasaland must have secession. His account to Alport was that Sandys, and probably Maudling, accepted that Banda's policy was secession. This seems a pointless remark because everyone knew this was his policy. It is unlikely that either Sandys or Maudling confessed to accepting that Nyasaland must have secession. Indeed, Sandys's statement that the British government would tell Banda within a month what they proposed to do about secession, and if they could not release Nyasaland they would tell him so, is inconsistent with Britain having accepted the principle of secession. What Sandys, and probably Maudling, now accepted was more likely to have been Banda's unconquerable determination to succeed in that policy, regardless of the cost. If, as seems to have been the case, Sandys also accepted that Britain would not use military force to keep Nyasaland in the Federation, the matter resolved itself into a difference of interpretation of the acceptance, first, that Banda would not be shifted from secession and, second, that Britain would not use military force. To Banda, fortified by the support of senior Conservatives such as Nicholson and Fisher, the combination of these acceptances meant that Sandys accepted secession, but to Sandys they meant no more than that there was still a chance Banda could be brought round to accept some form of association between the Central African territories, it was hoped, short of secession. This explanation would account for Banda suddenly saying that talks with Welensky and a resumption of the review conference were no longer necessary and should be replaced by direct talks with Sandys and Maudling. It would also explain his now bluntly saying he was off to London to arrange a dissolution conference without consulting Jones about it or seeking his involvement. It would account, too, for Sandys denying he had said Banda could have secession. It would explain why Jones, presumably sharing Banda's personal but unvoiced interpretation, believed Sandys to be lying when he denied telling Banda he accepted that Nyasaland must have secession.[78] Finally, it would explain why from this point onwards Jones took a very firm and more openly pro-Banda stance in dealings with British ministers. It is unclear why Jones never asked Banda to tell him precisely what it was that Sandys had said.

Almost a month after Sandys's visit to Nyasaland, Jones wrote to Monson, on 9 March, enclosing a copy of the typed record he had made of the meetings, written immediately after they were held and sent to the Colonial Office on 17 February.[79] He explained that in that record he had 'left out one rather important point':

Towards the end of the second meeting Mr Sandys said 'I cannot of course commit the British Government but I am sure Dr Banda that you can read between the lines, you can read between the lines.' That is the basis of the statement in my letter of 17 February that 'I am pretty certain that Dr Banda has been left with the impression that the answer will be favourable to him.' I may add that I also am under the same impression.[80]

Jones's explanation of what happened was that 'Sandys repeatedly said he could not commit the British Government one way or the other, but the discussion was such that I am pretty certain that Banda has been left with the impression that the answer will be favourable to him.' This degree of certainty was based on the alleged 'between the lines' comment which possibly reinforced in Jones's mind what Banda had said on his return from Dar es Salaam: that Sandys accepted there must be secession for Nyasaland.

Jones's second letter to Monson, that of 9 March, arrived in London at precisely the time R. A. Butler was taking over Central African affairs from Maudling at the Colonial Office and Sandys at the Commonwealth Relations Office. This letter was handed to Butler on 21 March with a minute saying that a copy of the first letter (that of 17 February) had been sent by Maudling to Sandys on 23 February, but not a copy of the second. It is almost certain, therefore, that Sandys did not know at this stage about Jones's allegation. When Butler received the second letter he immediately minuted, 'I shall keep this for suitable talk with P[rime] M[inister]. It will be news to the Cabinet.'[81]

Jones became most anxious that the British government should honour what he saw as a pledge given by Sandys to Banda. Perhaps he was doubtful about Sandys keeping his word, or the cabinet honouring it. Time was passing, they were well into March and there were no signs of the British government giving Banda a decision. Maybe in his anxiety he was linking too closely the clear undertaking that a decision would be reached and given, and the far from clear possible words between the lines to which he had belatedly – and some would think suspiciously – drawn attention. No one challenged, or doubted, that the undertaking to reach and communicate a decision had been given. What was challenged and denied vigorously by Sandys was that he had told Banda he accepted secession, either expressly in Dar es Salaam – as Jones understood and told both Maudling and Foster – or by clear implication in Zomba, as Jones alleged to Monson. In speaking to Alport, who was responsible to Sandys rather than Maudling, Jones said of the Dar es Salaam conversation not what he had told Maudling and Foster but that Sandys had said he accepted that Banda's policy was secession. At the very most this could have meant a personal, rather than a governmental, acceptance. At no stage did Banda repeat or subsequently rely on what Jones understood him to say about this – a statement which would have been enormously to his advantage – despite numerous opportunities for him to do so. It was an allegation to which Jones adhered for very many years. One of his closest friends and colleagues, both in Northern Rhodesia and in Nyasaland, recalled how Jones later, at least in private, 'relentlessly pursued' Sandys and accused him of lying when he returned to London and denied telling Banda he would give him secession.[82] Indeed, Butler, who visited Nyasaland in the middle of May 1962, recalled: 'Hardly had we arrived at Government House than [Jones] informed me that Dr. Banda had already had a governmental assurance that the right of secession would be granted to his country. Neither the Governor nor I subsequently mentioned this to Banda.'[83] Jones, it seems from this, was still convinced Sandys had assured Banda that Nyasaland would be allowed to secede and was stating it as a fact. Butler knew that while Sandys may, deliberately or otherwise, have left Banda and Jones with the impression that secession would be allowed, he had not said so.

Banda planned to visit London in April, and Jones wrote to Maudling on 9 March to say that the most important fact was Sandys's 'solemn undertaking' that a decision on secession would be reached and communicated to him during March. The visit could be considered only in the light of that undertaking. It was 'important to understand that the good faith of the British Government [was] involved in this and [he] would hope nothing [would] be done to destroy Banda's trust at the beginning of what must inevitably be a fairly lengthy process of negotiations'.[84]

The British government was at a loss as to what best to do, and the situation was not helped by the division of responsibilities between the Colonial Office, responsible for Nyasaland and Northern Rhodesia, and the Commonwealth Relations Office, responsible for the Federation and Southern Rhodesia. Sandys's visit had exposed some of the weaknesses and emphasized the need for change. On 15 March responsibility for all Central African affairs passed to Butler, first secretary of state, deputy prime minister and home secretary. His appointment had a mixed reception in Central Africa. It came as a 'very great shock' and a 'very considerable blow' to Hone who 'deeply regretted' it. Welensky received it with 'initial surprise' but 'gratitude' and he thought it would be 'of great value'. Whitehead 'was even more astonished' but thought it would have 'great advantage'. Jones welcomed Butler's apppointment.[85]

Butler did not start with a clean slate and he told Alport he had little room for manoeuvre over Nyasaland. 'You will know from what I inherited that things had gone quite far.'[86] This was almost certainly a reference to Sandys's statements which, while probably not telling Banda that he accepted the right to secede, certainly told him the British government would very shortly reach a decision on it and tell him. This major step, taken without prior consultation with the cabinet, at least partially explains why Butler was brought in.

Although Butler was not overly keen to take the Central Africa job, he lost no time in getting to grips with it, and called Jones, Hone and Alport to London for discussions. It was not simply that he took over control of Central African affairs; he restored control. Jones travelled on 26 March and stayed in Britain until 4 April, during which time there were eight lengthy meetings.[87] At the first meeting Jones outlined the position in Nyasaland: 'Dr. Banda['s] position was unassailable. It could only be shaken if he was seen to be wavering in insisting on secession ... He was unlikely to demand further constitutional advance before secession unless secession were in his view likely to be unreasonably delayed ... He had a poignant interest in the economic consequences but would not allow this to sway the argument.'

Butler said the British government realized the Federation could not continue without consent, which the present leaders had failed to win. Even so, he did not want to desert the federal idea straight away; that would be a betrayal. He was keen to be advised whether or not he should bring matters to a head now. It was important that whatever was done in the immediate future should not adversely effect the ultimate prospect of the Federation's survival. He could not look at Nyasaland in isolation if a decision on it frustrated hopes of retaining economic links.

Butler asked Jones if, while saying Britain would give an early answer in principle, Sandys had told Banda that the reply would be favourable. Having seen the two letters, Butler had almost certainly concluded, and the cabinet had concurred – probably with the commonwealth secretary present – that what Sandys had said fell well short of saying secession would be conceded. The Governor's reply, whatever his intention, by implication confirmed this. Asked what Sandys had actually said, Jones went no further than to say: 'the conversation had been such that Dr. Banda had been given reason to think that the reply would be favourable.'

Butler wished to reach an understanding with Banda on both secession and future viability, and asked if it was possible for him to delay a decision on secession. Jones, presumably fearing a damaging or even irreparable row if he mentioned this to the doctor, replied that he personally could not do it; only Macmillan or Butler might be able to do so. While Banda accepted that a de-federation commission might take nine months to complete its work, he was unlikely to accept that this might delay the fundamental decision. Thereafter he would expect independence within two years. He must be able to tell his people quite soon that the decision in principle had been irrevocably taken.

When Alport wondered whether the commission's terms of reference should be qualified by a phrase such as 'if secession takes place', Jones interjected that any attempt to do this would lead to trouble, Banda would probably withdraw from the government and this would lead to widespread disorder. The ideal solution would be for Britain to dissolve the Federation and then get the territorial governments round a table to discuss their future association, but he realized this was unacceptable to the British government; the removal of Nyasaland would inevitably mean the withdrawal of Northern Rhodesia and the collapse of the Federation.

When Butler asked if Banda could be kept in Nyasaland until May or June, Jones replied that this would be difficult unless he was empowered to give Banda the assurances he expected as a result of Sandys's visit.

Jones was taking an open and markedly pro-Banda stance. He declined to attempt to get Banda's agreement to postpone a decision on secession. He warned of the dire consequences of using words such as 'if secession takes place'. He preferred to have the Federation abandoned immediately – and probably not replaced by any form of association – and pushed to have Sandys's between-the-lines hint converted into *en clair* actuality. In taking this stance he advocated that dithering and qualification should be avoided lest Banda withdraw and military intervention become inevitable. It is likely that this firm, almost impatient, strongly expressed and newly displayed approach was based on a belief that Sandys had in fact given an assurance that secession would be granted, on a feeling that Britain felt unable to renege on the assurance, and on a conviction that Butler had been brought in to confirm it and sort out the problems involved.

Butler opened their second meeting the following morning by saying there were two options:

> [First] a unilateral decision to allow Nyasaland to withdraw from the Federation which could be justified on Dr. Banda's landslide election victory and the fact that it was generally accepted now (even by Welensky) that Nyasaland would have to be allowed to go ... There would be an immediate reaction in Northern Rhodesia. Logically this would lead to ultimate erosion of the Federation.
>
> [Alternatively] a 'composite solution' ... would be both more difficult and more sensible. We should have to hold Banda off for a month and use this time to convince Welensky that a piecemeal approach would inevitably erode his Federation's foundations ... This approach would also ease the position in regard to Northern Rhodesia. We should have to try and ensure that this was presented as an effort to try and find a suitable alternative to the present form of Federation.

Jones and Hone, while much preferring to dissolve the Federation and make a fresh start, accepted the alternative option.

The composite solution would tackle the problems of the future of the Federation and its current constituent territories by an integrated rather than a piecemeal approach. Although apparently simple in retrospect, it was a remarkable concept and one which could be originated and implemented only by a single minister in charge of the whole of Central African affairs.

Subsequent meetings over the next three days refined the composite solution and developed the way it should be put to Banda, Welensky and Whitehead. Jones felt that Banda's cooperation would depend on whether an assurance of his eventual right to secede could be read into the formula and on what was said when it was put to him. He was still pushing for some positive advance towards secession. He believed that a commission to examine the economic consequences of secession, an important element in the composite approach, was 'the only hope of getting Nyasaland politicians to face the facts and was also the last chance of retaining a willing Nyasaland in some form of association'.

Butler was in a quandary:

> The question of secession would be an extremely difficult one for him to carry [with his cabinet colleagues] since it would be opposed by the majority of his party. The difficulty was that there was little else that could be done ... The Conservative party were not prepared for an announcement on secession and there would be inevitable criticism that it was too soon. [He] had not yet had time to consult the Cabinet or his supporters, and this proposal would come as a shock.

When Butler again asked if he could defer a decision on secession, this time until he received the commission's report on the economic consequences, Jones thought it most unlikely. Butler, however, was clear that the doctor would have to be told that Britain could not allow Nyasaland to secede without ascertaining whether there was any possibility of a continuing association in examining the implications for Nyasaland's economic future. To Jones, it would be 'touch and go'.

Enormous care was taken over drafting the commission's terms of reference, an explanatory passage for Butler to use in the Commons and a note of guidance for Jones. This last note was:

> In ... answer to the expected question from Dr. Banda whether ... the right of secession is recognised, the answer should be that HMG certainly accept in principle that Nyasaland should be permitted to withdraw from the present Federation, if its people so wish. They believe, however, that it is in the best interests of the people that when and in what way an actual withdrawal should come about should depend on careful consideration of the results of the proposed enquiries into the consequences of such a move for Nyasaland as well as the possibilities of other acceptable forms of association.[88]

Thus, within a fortnight of Butler taking over Central African affairs, a good deal of progress had been made and the British government was significantly less at a loss as to what best to do.

During his stay in London, Jones went with Butler to see Macmillan, had meetings with Roger Hollis, head of MI5, Godfrey Nicholson and Nigel Fisher, spent the weekend with the Butlers at Stanstead and an evening with the Macleods at Sloane Court. He flew from London on 4 April.

The following evening, in Salisbury, he received a telegram from Butler, indicating the cabinet's consent to the composite solution.[89] Bulter intended to announce it in the Commons on 8 May. It was 'most important', therefore, that they 'should aim to hold the situation for the time being'. This disturbed Jones. No doubt he was bearing in mind that Banda had been promised a decision during March, it was already April and Butler was proposing not to announce the decision until May; even then it would not say Nyasaland would secede. Continuing to push on Banda's behalf, he told Butler:

> If you withhold making the statement for a month from now, Banda will indeed begin to feel that we are merely trying to gain time. These proposals are designed to give the initiative to HMG. Much of it will be lost if we now have to suffer a month's delay. I therefore advise most strongly that you make your statement at the very earliest moment, if possible at the end of this week [14 April].[90]

He now had the task of telling Banda about the composite proposals, getting his reaction and, he hoped, securing his agreement or at least his acquiescence. A few days after he returned to Nyasaland, he and Banda had a long discussion on the proposals.[91] The doctor accepted them in the faith that they would not be used as delaying tactics. He was 'very impatient to see the mission [examining the implications of secession] begin and complete its task with the greatest despatch'.[92] He would be in great difficulty if its appointment were not very soon announced.

At the close of their meeting, Banda asked for, and received, Jones's assurance that he was personally satisfied the proposals were made in good faith and not as a delaying tactic. Cameron told the Governor about this time that Banda was 'passing through an extremely difficult time'; his apparent reluctance to push the British government 'urgently and openly' was not favoured by his immediate advisers and was causing 'rumblings' among the more extreme of the MCP rank and file. This may have contributed to Jones pressing for an early announcement of Butler's proposals.[93]

Jones did not want Butler to think Banda was enthusiastic about the prospect of examining the consequences of secession and of other forms of association. Rather, he saw the operations as a means of achieving secession and as a means whereby the British government 'could concede this peacefully and without creating for itself embarrassing opposition in Britain'.

Jones fared much better with Banda than Alport did with Welensky who was in the process of fighting an election on the basis of preserving the Federation. To Welensky it 'seemed inconceivable that any man aiming to be reasonable would refuse to accept a delay of two to three weeks [when the election would take place] in making an announcement of such importance'.[94]

In these circumstances Butler asked Jones to do his 'utmost to hold Banda until after the Easter recess'. This would increase Jones's difficulties but he was keen that what he proposed to do should be seen as part of a constructive approach to the whole problem rather than as making a concession.[95]

Postponing the announcement put Jones in a difficult position because one of Banda's few reservations about accepting the proposals was that there should be no delay in announcing and implementing them. It was a matter on which he felt strongly and about which Jones was much concerned. Jones was not hopeful of success and would have to adopt an extremely delicate approach because there was a real danger that Banda would believe Butler was having second thoughts, and consequently might withdraw his agreement. The Governor proposed not to try and persuade Banda to accept Butler's position but merely to ask for his comments on the proposed delay and to note his response. If it was unfavourable he would hold the position by saying he would report it to Butler and it might then be necessary for him to ask for a statement confined to Nyasaland. He did not say so, but this would, of course, wreck the basis of the composite approach.[96]

It so happened that Banda had asked to see Jones the day after Butler's request that he be 'held off'.[97] In the event, at this meeting, Banda himself brought up the question, and Jones spoke of Butler's wish to delay the announcement until after the recess but before leaving London to visit Central Africa early in May. As Butler had suggested, he explained that parliament was about to recess. To Jones's considerable surprise, but relief, Banda immediately said he understood Butler's difficulties. He particularly emphasized that if he thought there were delaying tactics he would withdraw his cooperation. Once more, at Banda's request, the Governor gave as his 'firm private opinion that the good faith of the British Government was not to be doubted in all this so far as Nyasaland was concerned'. Butler thanked Jones for his 'skilful handling' of Banda in the 'present tricky situation'. The secretary of state's relief is understandable, but, in fact, it had been a simple interview, requiring little skill from the Governor, though a good deal of trust from the doctor.

Jones had another long discussion with Banda on 26 April at which the doctor 'quite unexpectedly raised the question of further constitutional advance for Nyasaland within the territorial field'.[98] Jones had recently told Butler he did not think Banda would raise this issue. It is likely that Banda now felt certain of securing secession and consequently was keen to turn his mind, and the minds of others, to the next step in fulfilling the aims for which he had returned to Nyasaland. Even more likely, these were his lieutenants' thoughts and they were pressing him to move on this other front. He intended to raise the question with Butler and would like to secure agreement on a programme taking Nyasaland through self-government by September 1962 to independence in April 1963. He asked Jones to 'give the question some thought', discuss it further with him before Butler's visit and in the meantime 'sound' the secretary of state and discover his reactions. Jones told Butler:

> I confined myself ... to saying that resolution of the Federal problem which it was proposed to tackle without delay seemed essential before anyone could begin to think about independence. The progress towards self-government should be made at a rate that was within the competence of the country's leaders ... I know how much you would wish to avoid further territorial changes while the work of the Mission is taking place. Nevertheless it would be difficult to avoid discussion of the subject. I and my official advisers think that you should agree to discuss it with him and that you should authorise me to say so in non-committal terms.

Four days later, Jones had another meeting with Banda during which there was 'a short and unpleasant outburst' from the doctor who 'became most impassioned'.[99] Dissatisfied, it seems, with Jones's response at their last meeting, he insisted there must be no delay in allowing secession and in agreeing a programme for self-government and independence. It is likely that, in the meantime, Banda's lieutenants had been angered by the Governor's response. Jones sensed that pressure was building up on Banda to secure these constitutional advances. The doctor was transmitting the pressure to Jones.

On 1 May, the Governor met the elected ministers at their request. They 'very forcefully represented' that Banda should within the next few days be made chief minister, with the chief secretary becoming the deputy Governor. They wanted Banda to be recognized as a national and not simply a political leader in order that his status as a negotiator in constitutional matters should be clear. They pressed for Butler to give them his views before he arrived in Nyasaland, but Jones told them this was not possible, and explained that Banda himself had agreed during

Sandys's visit to let the matter drop. The Governor again sensed that pressures were building up after 'successive visits of Maudling, Alport and Sandys had produced no tangible results' so far as they were concerned.[100] It may be that they were prepared to let Banda handle the major constitutional developments – provided he was successful in his demands and did not take too long about it – rather than intervene themselves, but they still had to show their followers that some progress was being made. It is possible, too, that Banda deliberately allowed them to pursue this matter of the chief ministership directly with the Governor so as to reduce their pressure on him concerning the major issues. In this way they would feel they were being active and taking things forward during a period when he himself was unable to move the British government as quickly as they wished.

In response to Jones's 'sounding', on Banda's behalf, Butler wrote to him on 5 May:

> It is only too clear that our problems in the coming months are going to be further complicated by pressure from Banda on the internal constitutional front as well as the general Federal front. We shall have to face this although ideally what we want is to put the internal constitutional question on one side, at least until the autumn, by which time we may be able to see what progress we are making with the Federal problem.
>
> I entirely agree ... it is not possible to begin thinking about independence in advance of the resolution of the Federal problem and, of course, the kind of programme he has suggested is completely unrealistic ... It is hardly less difficult to contemplate a move to self-government until we can see our way to a solution of the Federal issue ... All this leads to the conclusion that somehow or other we shall have to try and keep Banda in play on this for the next few months at least.

He asked if, in the meantime, Jones would give further thought to giving Banda the title, but definitely not the substance, of chief minister fairly soon as 'it might still help us to hold off the demand for further constitutional change for the time being'.[101]

Butler arrived in Nyasaland on 15 May. In the course of his four-day visit, the secretary of state, with Jones, had three meetings with Banda.[102] Early in the first Banda told Butler that whatever the results of the mission to examine the implications of possible secession, he and his people were determined to secede from the Federation.

> This was his declared policy and his patience ... to attain his object by peaceful and constitutional means was not being very well understood by many of his adherents ... Sandys had promised him [a] decision one way or another during the month of March. He was surprised and dis-

appointed that nothing had happened during March or April, and now there was this examination by expert advisers. How long would this take and when would the British Government make its decision about Nyasaland's secession?

Butler's reply was not encouraging. The advisers could not start until June and might take several months to complete their work. Though frank and firm, he did not provoke the outburst from Banda which might have been expected and against which Jones had warned him.

At their second meeting, Banda repeated what he had told Jones three weeks earlier about constitutional development, but added more detail. He now altered the target date for full self-government from September to after the budget session in July – two months ahead. The chief secretary should become the deputy Governor, and the minister of finance and the attorney-general should be replaced by elected ministers. Immediately thereafter he hoped the British government would announce that Nyasaland should secede from the Federation, though he realized this could be only after the advisers had reported. Then a commission should be appointed for the complicated task of detaching Nyasaland from the Federation. Although this would take some months, he hoped the country could become independent within the Commonwealth by April 1963 – a year ahead.

Butler bluntly told Banda this programme was much too fast. He would not commit himself to a timetable and he would need to discuss the matter with his colleagues in London. The following day he said he would have great difficulty with Banda's proposed timetable and so far as independence was concerned he would have to await the report of the advisers he was to appoint to look into the implications of secession on Nyasaland's viability thereafter. Banda reacted with 'considerable heat' and insisted he must have independence in April 1963. Butler was not to be bullied, and his response was firm: he could not possibly go any further at present and suggested, on Jones's advice, that they resume their talks when Banda went to London in June. This the doctor accepted. Although Jones's advice was based on the view that Butler 'could not do less unless [he] wanted to arouse [the country] to a state of rebellion',[103] the secretary of state told Jones a few days later that during Banda's imminent visit to London he would not concede the right to secede nor would he fix a date for independence. He was, in fact, calling Banda's – and maybe Jones's – bluff.

The secretary of state then brought about an explosion from Banda who 'violently disagreed' with, and 'vigorously opposed', his saying there should be a conference before Nyasaland's constitution could be amended to 'provide for a measure of self-government'. In particular Butler had in mind 'the need to introduce, for the protection of minority interests, a Bill of Rights and a Council of State'.[104] Eventually the doctor said he would accept a conference on condition that it also gave a date for Nyasaland's independence. Butler, again standing firm, said he would need to consult his colleagues. He would think about it but would not commit himself at least until they discussed the matter further in London.

Banda 'strongly represented' that Butler's advisers need take no longer than two months to complete their work and he expected a decision on secession not later than September. If the inquiry could not be finished quickly and if Britain did not rapidly thereafter grant secession to Nyasaland, he would have to go to his people and say, 'I must now resign because my methods have failed the aims for which you chose me. You must now choose somebody else who may have to adopt different methods.'[105] This sort of threat by Banda, successful as it may have been with others, did not unduly worry Butler, but it did reinforce his awareness of the strength of feeling in the country and the pressure to which Banda himself, and probably Jones, was being subjected.

Before Butler left Central Africa he asked Jones to meet with him, Alport and Hone in Salisbury – where he had gone after Nyasaland – to review the progress made during his visit.

> Nyasaland was likely to prove an increasing political embarrassment, particularly as African politicians in Northern Rhodesia would regard any public admission of her right to secede as a precedent. It should be made clear to Dr. Banda, however, that secession from the Federation would not entail independence from Britain ... Recognition of Nyasaland's right to secede should if possible [and Jones said it might not be possible] be delayed until after the Northern Rhodesia elections. [This might] prolong until at least mid-December the period during which it was desirable to hold Dr. Banda.[106]

Soon after Butler left Nyasaland, Jones wrote to give him 'the first reactions to [his] visit': 'African leaders are thoroughly satisfied because they consider you to be a person whom they can trust and also to be a wise administrator. We understand that you have been referred to as *Njobvu Yeikuru*. This literally means "large elephant" but the implied meaning is "sagacious beast". Here the title is definitely an honourable one.'[107] Butler was physically a large man, especially when compared with Jones and Banda, and it may be that Nyasaland politicians perceived him as being as difficult to frighten and move as is an elephant.

Jones believed Butler had no cause to worry that he had not been tough enough with Banda. He and his advisers believed that there was only one course Britain could take if bloodshed was to be avoided. 'That course must be orderly although the brakes can be only lightly applied.'

Butler was pleased with this 'first round', as he termed it, and any doubts he may have had about not being firm enough may have been the result of his discovering that he could get away with the degree of firmness which he had applied and his wondering why it had not been attempted before.

On his return to London, Butler told the cabinet that the elected ministers paid little or no regard to the 'practical issues which condition the desirable and possible pace of advance'.[108] Although 'it would be unwise to underestimate the strength of the political pressures at work in Nyasaland', there was 'a grave risk, if the pace of advance is unduly forced, of financial and economic recession, leading to a catastrophic setback in the territory's progress, and of a breakdown in the governmental machine, with a large and rapid exodus of expatriate officials'. Butler was taking a rational view of the pace of progress which could responsibly be allowed, notwithstanding the pressures to hasten the pace and Jones's view that the brakes could be applied only lightly if bloodshed was to be avoided. Perhaps he felt that this depended on who was applying the brakes.

Jones left Chileka for London on 28 June. In correspondence, Butler had outlined how he planned to tackle their meetings with Banda.[109] He hoped to hold the line where he had left it in Zomba. He would try to convince Banda that secession and independence were not the same thing and that the latter 'must be subject to realistic consideration of all the usual factors on which the ability of a country to stand on its own feet depends'. He hoped to 'keep Banda on the rails' until his advisers reported, by offering him a constitutional conference as late in the autumn as he could manage.

Jones spent the early part of the following week in meetings with Butler and Banda.[110] They first discussed the advisory mission with which Banda had agreed.

> However, and he must be blunt, while he had agreed to the appointment of this group of advisers with the intention of cooperating with the Secretary of State ... he and his people regarded the exercise as academic since whatever the advisers might report, he and his people were determined to secede. Either secession would be granted amicably and without further delay or he and his followers would be forced to resign from the Nyasaland Government and leave the field to 'Blackwood and the UFP.' HMG would then have to impose its will by force of arms. There was no other way.

Butler repeated what he had told him earlier: 'there was no intention whatever of imposing a solution by force of arms.'

Banda strongly pressed that secession and independence should be granted together. He had failed in his hopes that secession would be gained in 1961. Now, in mid-1962, under constant pressure from his followers, he had still not achieved it. He had contained them 'thanks to his standing with them, but this could not go on indefinitely. He must have a firm answer. There must be an end to delay. Secession and independence must come now.' Butler calmly stuck to his view that he must first receive and consider the advisers' report. Only then could the government decide on secession and arrange a conference 'to discuss a substantial measure of self-government and possibly draw up a programme in broad terms for advance to full independence'. The doctor pressed for a date for the conference and accepted that some time in November would be 'all right' – especially if it were in the first week of the month.

At the beginning of a subsequent meeting, Banda was in 'one of his more emotional moods [and] his nervous tic was in evidence'. With Butler's skilful handling, however, he eventually calmed down and even accepted that he should await a decision on secession until after the advisers had reported, provided the decision was reached and announced before the constitutional conference – now, it was hoped, not later than the end of October.

The meetings were primarily between Butler and Banda. Jones was present, as Banda would have wished, but he was required to say very little at any of them. The results were summed up by the Central Africa Office:

> From HMG's point of view the talks would seem to represent a remarkably sucessful piece of negotiation. Dr. Banda could never be described as a particularly amenable national leader. He came to London with a demand for 'secession and independence now'. In the event a decision on secession has been held off until early November ... No date has been given for independence. What has been given is an indication that a decision on secession would be taken before the territorial constitutional conference in November, and that the conference would provide a substantial constitutional advance and ... be asked to consider arrangements which would make it possible for Nyasaland to achieve independence at a later date without the need to convene a further conference; again ... no commitment was entered into.

The Governor thought they were lucky to hold Banda to their policy but thought he deserved 'credit for being both wise enough and decent enough to want to attain his ends by reasonable constitutional means'. In his opinion, as he told the secretary of state, Butler's handling of Banda had a great deal to do with the success of their efforts in London.[111] It did, of course, have virtually everything to do with it.

Jones left London by air on 7 July and arrived in Nyasaland three days later. His next few weeks – save for one ominous happening – were full but not too pressurized. He opened an international economics symposium, dealt with the budget session of the legislature and had frequent discussions with Butler's team of advisers. Indeed, in many ways these weeks were relaxing. He spent a week touring the Central Province, shot duck at Port Herald, enjoyed a great deal of fishing and shooting during a visit by the Governor-General of the Federation, shot clay pigeons, visited Northern Rhodesia 'for a magnificent camp' and more fishing and, as so often, back in the capital, enjoyed the relaxation, peace and solitude of fishing on Zomba plateau, climbing up from Government House on foot.[112]

Butler's advisers, under Stevens, their chairman, met the elected ministers who listened carefully but 'tended for the most part to produce ready answers which made light of [the financial and economic] difficulties. Chisiza in particular said that a deficit which they reckoned in the order of £3 million could be met half by higher taxation and half by retrenchment.' The point was not made but the political implications of such measure could be severe. They then saw Banda who asked that Jones should also be present. On the question of future association with the Rhodesias, 'Dr. Banda repeated his absolute refusal to discuss anything bearing on this subject before secession had been granted ... On the other hand he fully recognised the need for a negotiation to unscramble the existing Federal structure in Nyasaland and said that he attached importance to this being done as quickly as possible.'[113]

The ominous happening which interrupted this otherwise relatively unpressurized few weeks following Jones's return from London concerned most of the elected ministers and one of the parliamentary secretaries.[114] The difficulty surfaced late in July 1962 as a 'feud' between Cameron, minister of works and transport, and Chiume, minister of education, over implementing the schools building programme in the development plan.[115] Shortly, Cameron, Chisiza, Bwanausi, Chokani, Msonthi and Mkandawire met and discussed their dissatisfaction over the behaviour of Chiume with whom they were thoroughly fed up because he was interfering with the work of their ministries and undermining Banda's trust in them. He was 'virtually decrying the other Ministers' efforts [and] lauding Dr. Banda even more than others were doing'.[116]

That evening Cameron, Mkandawire and Chisiza (but not Bwanausi, Chokani and Msonthi who declined to accompany them)[117] went to see Banda and told him about Chiume's behaviour and the dangers of allowing it to continue. They alleged he was using his good standing with the doctor to frustrate their schemes and to influence him against them. They felt he was 'gradually obtaining for himself the position of chief adviser and crony to Dr. Banda'.[118] The meeting was 'heated and all three ... took part but there is no doubt that Dunduzu Chisiza was the most powerful of the speakers but nevertheless what [all three] said fell on deaf ears'. Banda seemed not to believe what they told him and refused to do anything about it. They did not take any further action at this stage because they wanted to preserve government and party unity. They told Banda that for this reason they would support him until independence but made it clear that once independence was achieved they would not automatically support him.[119]

There was a second meeting of the ministers with Banda, as Chiume, who was also present, recalled:

> When I got to Banda's house I found there Cameron, Dunduzu Chisiza, Mkandawire, Bwanausi, Chokani and, representing the MCP, Yatuta Chisiza. Banda told me that the others present had made complaints against me, and, in his usual confrontational way, asked them to repeat their complaints in my presence. This they did, and Dunduzu took the leading part, accusing me of overly influencing Banda and being responsible for him and Orton Chirwa not being made full ministers but only parliamentary secretaries. Yatuta was vicious and said I was very unpopular in many areas ... Yatuta was angry because he had not been given a ministerial post and blamed me for this. Banda did not decide who was right and who was wrong. Neither Chirwa nor Chipembere – who was in prison – was present.[120]

It may have been this meeting which Chipembere had in mind when he recalled that Banda 'after listening carefully to each side ... walked away from both groups, uttering not a word aimed at bringing about a reconciliation.'[121] This disconcerting technique of walking away from an interview was one which Banda used to considerable effect on other occasions.[122]

Following this meeting, Cameron, Mkandawire, Bwanausi and Chisiza went to see the Governor to complain that they 'had not received a very sympathetic hearing' from the doctor. Chokani did not accompany them. Cameron, Mkandawire and Chisiza – but not Bwanausi – tendered their resignations from the legislative council and, in the case of the first two, from the executive council. Jones declined to accept the resignations and had a meeting with Banda: 'I was able to convince him that the complainants appeared to me to have reasonable grounds for complaint and ... while Cabinet changes did not necessarily imply that the Majority Party was experiencing serious internal disorders, nevertheless a change at this point of time would make it difficult for Dr. Banda to represent [at the forthcoming conference] that all had gone well since the election last year.'[123] He also told Banda 'in no uncertain terms' that Chiume was also making things difficult for him, Jones. Banda took this in good part and was pleased that all the complainants had 'expressed their complete loyalty and devotion to [him] personally'. He agreed that Jones should see them again and ask them to reconsider their resignations in the interests of party unity.

The Governor then saw the complainants and after a long and frank discussion they agreed to withdraw their resignations and accept Jones's advice that they should show more courage in future dealings with Chiume and insist on Banda taking them more into his confidence. He did not think that any of them really wanted to resign but thought the threat of resignation would bring things satisfactorily to a head.

Dunduzu Chisiza – one of the most able and promising, many thought *the* most able and promising, of African politicians in Nyasaland – did not let matters rest where Banda and Jones had left them. He, unlike the others, was not a member of the executive council and was therefore unable to make his points directly in council. In a letter to the Governor on 4 August he set out the grounds and nature of his concerns, and repeated that Chiume was making the work and life of his elected colleagues impossible.

> I am satisfied that [Banda] is for some inexplicable reason not prepared to see that Mr. Chiume is engaging in activities which are harmful to teamwork on the Ministerial level, dangerous to the morale and cohesion of the Party (MCP), and unfortunate for the country ... Mr. Chiume has launched a campaign of undermining the confidence which the Doctor has in other Malawi Ministers and Members of Legislative Council. He is casting suspicion on innocent people; he is questioning the integrity and loyalty of men who have willingly suffered for the Doctor, the Party, and the Country; and he is subjecting his colleagues to a feeling of alienation. Further, he is subjecting the Doctor to a feeling of insecurity by making the Doctor believe that some of his followers and aides are undermining his prestige and authority ... He is also making the Doctor believe that other elected Ministers are being run by the permanent officials and that only he is able to control his Permanent Secretary. He would have the Doctor believe that the judgement of everyone except Mr. Chiume must be held in serious doubt. And most unfortunate of all, he has established such a relationship with the Doctor, that he is able to kill out of sheer jealousy schemes and proposals from other Elected Ministers by setting the Doctor against the proposals.[124]

The remainder of his letter was taken up in emphasizing his admiration of, and loyalty to, Banda: 'Without Dr. Banda's leadership this country would go to the dogs. It is no exaggeration to say that Doctor Banda is the most important asset of this country.' He ended with what was a thinly veiled offer to oust Chiume if Banda wished him to do so: 'I would like to assure the Doctor also that if there is anyone who poses serious opposition to him and the Party ... he has only to send for me and in collaboration with his other soldiers I will make sure that his opponents are defeated.'

It is extremely unlikely that Banda was ever told of Chisiza's offer to oust Chiume and that he would have accepted the offer had it been made known to him. Even if Chisiza was in effect asking Jones to tell Banda of the offer, the Governor would have believed that this was no time to allow a split to appear in the party. Banda would have shared this view.

A possibly related matter surfaced at about this time, the second half of August 1962. At Banda's request, Jones asked the secretary of state to agree to Yatuta Chisiza being sent to the Bramshill Police College 'A' course in Britain in order to prepare him to take over the commissionership of police. Butler's official advisers were alarmed by the request and pointed out that he was not qualified for the course. They also asked Jones for an assessment of Yatuta Chisiza's personal temperament and asked, 'Is he likely to turn out a "Dunduzu" rather than a "Chiume"?' Jones's precise reply is not known but it was 'encouraging'. It appears that he continued his advocacy, because the matter was taken up personally by the secretary of state who said that his entry into the police force would involve him, Butler, in tacitly endorsing Banda's selection of him as a potential future commissioner of police and he naturally had doubts about doing this in view of his political record and because of the effect it would have on other serving officers. Jones did not pass on to Banda the reservations of Butler and his police advisers. Eventually the secretary of state agreed with Jones's point that if they did not accede to Banda's request, the doctor might take other steps to groom him for the post. Butler therefore agreed that they should accept the situation and do their best to 'turn Chisiza into a capable policeman in the time likely to be available' to them. In the event the matter was not pursued because Yatuta shortly entered the legislature and a police service career became irrelevant.[125]

One other matter about which a number of the elected members of government approached the Governor at this time was the release of Chipembere from gaol. Bwanausi, Chokani, Dunduzu Chisiza and possibly others claimed that if Chipembere were released fairly soon, before the November 1962 constitutional conference, 'he would be bound to break the present influence being exerted by Chiume over Dr. Banda'. Jones received this argument with some reserve because all his Special Branch reports showed that in the past Chipembere and Chiume had been close friends and each had supported the other's extremism.[126]

After the elected members of government spoke to him at the beginning of August, Jones intended to take an early opportunity to see Chiume and tell him 'in no uncertain terms' that his conduct could lead to a political crisis in Nyasaland. He hoped that what he had to say would 'persuade him that he must be a good deal more cooperative with us all in the future'. He told Banda that he intended to speak in this manner. The doctor did not attempt to dissuade him. Jones told him that Chiume's colleagues were very angry and he did not think they would 'put up with any more nonsense from him', though they stressed that they recognized his competence and did not wish to see him leave the government. Jones hoped that on the whole 'this letting-off of steam' would have done some good.[127]

The Central Africa Office was pleased with the way Jones handled this affair 'which while avoiding open breach may temper Chiume and should have strengthened his colleagues'.[128] Banda, in fact, had a very high regard for Chiume and was impressed by the sense and industry of both him and Mrs Chiume, dating from the time he stayed with them at Nkata Bay during the August 1958 Congress conference.[129]

Jones did not speak to Chiume about his behaviour, because a tragedy intervened. On Monday 3 September, in the very early hours of the morning while returning from Limbe to Zomba, Dunduzu Chisiza was killed in a car crash some ten miles south of the capital. He was known to be 'in the habit of driving at excessive speeds.' He had been working at high pressure. He was alone in the car and no other vehicle was involved. Special Branch found nothing sinister in his death, knew he was fatigued and believed that he probably fell asleep at the wheel while travelling at a speed 'reliably estimated at 80 miles per hour'. The coroner returned a verdict of accidental death.[130]

The crash occurred just over a year after a very similar accident in which Chisiza had been seriously injured and hospitalized at Ncheu. He had recovered from those injuries.[131] Following his death, the vacated legislative council seat at Karonga was filled, unopposed, by his brother, Yatuta. The parliamentary secretaryship to the ministry of finance was, after a while, filled by John Tembo, the uncle of Cecilia Kadzamira, for many decades Banda's nurse and his official hostess.[132]

In addition to his worries about Chiume, Jones was concerned about the relationships between the MCP and the civil service. Indeed, there may have been a connection between the two: Dunduzu Chisiza had told him how Chiume had reported to Banda that the other ministers were being controlled by their permanent secretaries, and this would not have led to improved relations. On 25 August, Jones wrote a long, detailed letter to Banda, which he hoped he could soon discuss with him.[133] This was a matter which had concerned Phillips in the meetings with Maudling the previous December.

Jones reminded Banda that there was a period of less than three months before the Marlborough House conference. It was his 'earnest wish and determination' that they should, during this period, make 'a very special effort' to improve relationships between the party and the service. He appreciated that many civil servants had been involved in the 1959 state of emergency and some members of the MCP found it difficult to forget what happened at that time. He knew, he said, that some officers were marked men and he understood there was a blacklist of those who might be victimized when the country attained independence. Although he did not tell Banda, he knew from his Special Branch reports over several months not only that there were blacklists but also that they were compiled at the behest of the most senior officers of the MCP below Banda, and were checked at MCP headquarters.[134]

Jones went on to say that some civil servants found it difficult to settle to the new regime because, in their view, the changes were too rapid and too radical. However, he believed these to be few, and the vast majority of expatriates were dedicated to serving Nyasaland and its people, were loyal and were proud of their service. They could easily be influenced to adjust to the new conditions, especially if they were encouraged and shown confidence by Banda and his followers.

> We are both aware that some MLCs and party members are making complaints to you continually about the attitude and conduct of civil servants. You receive your information from them: I receive information from the other side, from civil servants who feel that their motives and actions are being wilfully misunderstood and misreported. You and I ... must do all that we can to ensure that on the one hand the members of the service give loyal support to the Government, and on the other, that their work and position are not undermined by frivolous or spiteful complaints.

He was particularly concerned about specialists who were internationally in short supply and could easily find work elsewhere. It was true that people could be acquired from 'other countries throughout the world, but a civil service composed of people collected from the highways and byways' would, in his view, not provide Banda with the required loyalty and *esprit de corps* that he could command from the present civil service. He did not say so, but whatever else he did to keep Banda in power, and Nyasaland peaceful, his efforts would count for little if there were a mass exodus of expatriate civil servants and their replacement by insufficiently trained and inadequately experienced Nyasalanders and by other nationals with less loyalty to the country than to a do-good ideology for whom Banda would have to pay a *quid pro quo*. He reminded Banda that in return for wiping the slate clean when releasing the final detainees in

1960, the doctor had undertaken that animosity towards the civil service because of past differences of opinion would be forgotten. He could have added that Banda's subsequent promise to do his best to ensure that the elected ministers and members of the legislature behaved more pleasantly towards the civil service had been ineffective and that his own attempts to get the civil service to meet the MCP more than half way in this matter had not been reciprocated. He had at his command a devoted body of civil servants in whom he was convinced Banda and he must repose their trust and confidence and against whose integrity they should not permit themselves to make any damaging statement either in public or in private.

Although Jones was directing his attention to improving relationships between the MCP and the civil service whose 'morale [was] deteriorating because they [felt] they [were] not being trusted', and he was seeking Banda's and the MCP's help in putting matters right, there was another aspect of morale which must have concerned him deeply, especially since it related to the provincial and district administration, a service to which, in Northern Rhodesia, he had devoted almost the whole of his adult life and of which he was proud. Whereas he was looking outwards, to Banda and the MCP, for the solution to the problem of service morale, others suggested that he should also look inwards to what he himself could do.

In about September 1962 there was prepared in the chief secretary's office a paper about the provincial and district administration.[135] This paper was drafted by senior officials in the office, it was intended for the Governor and it is virtually certain that its contents were conveyed to him. The officer preparing the initial draft of the document was working on the security desk in the chief secretary's office and recalled that he 'thus saw many reports of political pressures brought to bear on individuals ... All too often it appeared that the Governor took the line of least resistance.' Although it was not widely known, Chiume had proudly told Maudling of 'His Excellency's cooperation in transferring certain District Commissioners' who were not popular with the MCP.[136]

The draft opened by saying that the morale of administrative officers had sunk to a point never before experienced by serving members of the administration. There were a number of reasons for this prevailing discontent. First, there was federation whose cause between 1953 and 1960 they had been required as a matter of government policy to further by every possible means and on all suitable occasions. Although 'most of them [knew] in their hearts that they were faced with an impossible task' and most were as opposed to federation as were the Africans under their care, they carried out their instructions faithfully. The official policy of supporting the Federation, which culminated in the state of emergency being declared in 1959, resulted in a widening gulf between the administration and the nationalist politicians. The frequent verbal, personal, attacks by politicians on the commissioners 'were allowed to pass largely unanswered; there was no retaliation by Government, and it came to be generally believed that such speeches and insults could be delivered with impunity'.

> [After the 1959 general election in Britain] decisions were quickly made and new men, untainted by the events of recent years, were brought in to fill the top positions in the Nyasaland Government; but the District Commissioners remained, and it was not possible [for them] so quickly to restore on a personal plane relationships which nearly a decade of suspicion and finally animosity and hostility had effectively destroyed ... Official policy changed so quickly ... that many district officers were left bewildered.[137]

It appears from this that when, two years earlier, Jones told Macleod every distict commissioner in the country now understood what was behind government policy he may have been over-stating the extent to which he had made that policy – as opposed to what was behind it – clear. It seems, too, that this was so, notwithstanding the secret directive issued to provincial commissioners a few days earlier. What may have been made very clear to him by Macleod had not, it seems, been made clear by him to his district commissioners, who were consequently left to discover many of the changes required of them by unhappy experience over the course of time. The September 1960 directive had inevitably been couched in cautious generalized terms, since it directed on political grounds the turning of a blind eye to some breaches of the law rather than the prosecution of offenders. As a consequence of this cautious and generalized wording, of the secrecy with which the directive was issued, of the possibility that it was taken to apply only until the August 1961 elections and of its communication to district commissioners by word of mouth only, its message seems to have been lost.

> Whilst, therefore, senior civil servants, free from close association with the events of recent years, have been able to establish and maintain good relations with the top African politicians, the same has not been the case at District level. This has led many district officers to feel that their seniors in Zomba, not fully understanding the differing circumstances, expect more of them in this respect than is possible. Thus there is resentment; there is also the belief that this resentment may to some extent be mutual.

This last remark suggests that administrative officers felt it was not only by the MCP that their 'motives and actions [were] being ... misunderstood', whether wilfully or otherwise, but also by the Governor and chief secretary.

The document then turned to the second main reason for the existing discontent. District commissioners recognized that it might not be expedient for political reasons to start criminal proceedings against politicians for alleged offences – which had increasingly become the case since the final detainees were released. This state of affairs had inevitably strained relationships between officers serving in the field, who had to decide on the spot on a practical basis precisely when and in respect of whom the law should take its course, and senior officers in Zomba who could express themselves from a distance in generalized, imprecise and ambiguous terms. As a result, many officers had their personal reputations attacked and all of them had been openly insulted and their authority progressively undermined. 'Yet they can not escape from the belief that Government is prepared to sacrifice them and their reputations on any occasion when political considerations so demand.'

Finally, the document claimed that there was a general feeling in the administration that there was no officer at the top of government prepared to further their interests: 'Senior officers in Zomba do not do enough travelling to establish mutual relations of friendship and trust with their juniors in the field.'[138] Although it was not said, in the past the secretary for African affairs had been the officer in Zomba responsible for the provincial and district administration, but his post had now been abolished and district officers, it seems, felt those responsibilities had not been adequately taken over by anyone else.

> In short, the administrative officer of today feels that he has been let down. He charges his seniors with four failings: lack of contact, lack of trust, lack of candour, lack of support ... A District Commissioner literally does not know whether he will be supported if he takes firm action on previously authorised lines. At present there is very grave suspicion that Government is making District Commissioners the scapegoats for the events of the last few years ... District Commissioners have battled for years to the best of their abilities and loyalties to promote Government policies. Most of them feel that they have now had enough.

When Jones told Banda that the majority of expatriate civil servants could be influenced to adjust to the new circumstances if they were encouraged and shown confidence by the doctor and his followers, he ought perhaps to have realized that he and his most senior colleagues could do well by themselves showing the same encouragement and confidence to administrative officers. Jones had been correct in telling Banda that their morale was deteriorating because they felt they were not being sufficiently trusted. What perhaps he did not appreciate was their feeling that they were not being trusted by Jones himself and that he had done very little to show that he understood the 'differing circumstances'; that is, in respect of relations with the MCP, how very much more difficult it was for officers, who as a result of carrying out unpopular government policy had incurred the displeasure of the politicians, than it was for him and others who had not been required to carry out that policy in Nyasaland but were required only to carry out a new and popular policy. He attributed the difficulty in settling which a few officers were experiencing to their feeling that the changes were too rapid and too radical. While this was undoubtedly true, it overlooked the other factors unsettling officers, including the gap which had opened up between the Governor and his district officers. He was placing on Banda and the MCP the responsibility to improve working relations between the party and the civil service but neglecting to play the very considerable part which it was within his power to play in respect of contact, trust, candour and support. It is not clear what, if anything, Jones did about this document prepared in the chief secretary's office, but the message which it conveyed to him must have caused him considerable distress.

Jones's pleas to Banda to lay off the civil service had little immediate effect and victimization and abuse of expatriate officers continued, as the MCP sought greater and greater effective control of the service. Armitage had created a Public Service Commission before he left office, and the Lancaster House conference, welcoming this move, had agreed that 'security and non-discrimination should be assured to the Civil Service'. Although the commission was advisory to the Governor, it was envisaged that, as in other territories, it should be given constitutional or legal status and independent executive authority. Indeed, the subsequent Marlborough House constitution provided that the commission should have independent executive powers. The commission was formally set up in May 1961. Its membership was a chairman – a European, recently retired civil servant from Tanganyika where he had been an official minister and member of Nyerere's cabinet; two Africans – one of whom was a much respected former long-standing civil servant; and one European – a businessman. Its functions covered recruitment, promotions, transfers, confirmation of appointments and compulsory retirements. It was required, in the case of appointments and promotions, to 'have regard to the maintenance of the high standards of efficiency which are necessary in the public service', to 'give due consideration, without regard to race, to the claims of [applicants] to appointment or promotion to vacancies in the public service'; and in the case of promotions to 'take into account qualifications, experience and merit as well as seniority'. It was created in order to safeguard the standards of the public service and the rights of individuals in it. All these matters had Jones's approval. At a time when it was to be expected that the MCP would wish to demonstrate its supremacy, to reap the rewards of electoral victory and to force the pace of Africanization, the Public Services Commission had an important and delicate role to play. In a worrying number of cases, where the MCP, for party or personal reasons, took an interest, Jones felt unable to accept the commission's recommendations. The chairman understood the difficult position in which the Governor found himself, but felt that, having regard to the clear intentions in setting up his office, he could not with propriety adjust the recommendations. He had the right of direct access to the Governor and when he found his representations being rejected and it became clear that he was not going to be able to alter Jones's stance, he eventually said to him 'Play it that way if you must but I'm afraid you'll have to play it without me!' He discreetly declined to continue in office beyond the two years for which he had originally been appointed. Expatriate and many longer serving African civil servants found this turn of events disturbing.[139]

Jones's pleas to Banda to lay off the civil service had little immediate effect in the case of the police, as Bryan Roberts, the new attorney-general, was soon to discover.[140] In mid-October Banda expressed to Chirwa, his 'gravest concern' over the police's handling of prosecutions and their pursuing a deliberate policy of political discrimination by encouraging prosecutions against the MCP and suppressing those against opposition parties. When Chirwa told Roberts of Banda's concern, the attorney-general immediately wrote to the doctor and asked for an interview.

At their meeting two days later, Banda reiterated his general claim that there was widespread dissatisfaction with the police's attitude towards preserving law and order and enforcing the criminal law. The police, he alleged, were most partisan, were actively hostile to MCP members, initiating unjustified prosecutions against them and minimizing the importance of cases against members of minority parties. Roberts asked if he thought this state of affairs was the result of the police generally being reluctant to accept the authority of the political party in power. This was precisely Banda's view: 'In his view the police and the District Commissioners were vitiating the whole atmosphere of the country by adhering to past loyalties and to factions which were unworthy of respect.'

Roberts asked Banda if he had brought these criticisms to the attention of the chief secretary, the minister responsible for the police and the administration. Banda replied that he had not raised the matter formally as he was waiting his time, which Roberts thought would be the Marlborough House conference and thereafter. Roberts explained that while the police investigated cases, it was the attorney-general, Roberts himself, who controlled the decisions whether or not to prosecute. This led to a discussion of specific cases, particularly one at Kota Kota about which

Banda had very strong views. Roberts thereupon pointed out that he had written three letters to the doctor about this case and had received no reply.

The case was one of wrongful assumption of judicial powers by the local MCP chairman. Roberts asked Banda what factors he felt justified his view that a prosecution would be contrary to the public interest, and received the reply that it would arouse general resentment in the area and lead to disturbances. To this Roberts said that, assuming the law was being fairly and properly enforced, hostile local reaction did not justify a failure to prosecute. He was surprised the doctor had raised this point, since the matter had been fully discussed by Msonthi, a minister and the local member of legislative council. He had confined his objection to the grounds that a prosecution and conviction would be a grave embarrassment to the MCP and might bring forth hostile criticism by the UFP. Banda agreed this was not a ground which could be pursued with propriety. In his account to Jones, Roberts said:

> I stressed to Dr. Banda the danger, particularly in cases involving the deprivation of the liberty of the subject, of trying to inhibit the normal processes of justice on such general grounds, and in particular underlined the mischievous consequences of asking the Attoney-General to usurp in advance the functions of the Courts in deciding whether a particular accused was guilty or not guilty. Dr. Banda replied by criticising 'Colonial Office lawyers', who he claimed were frequently unrealistic and obsessed with legal technicalities. I informed Dr. Banda that both as a member of the Bar and as a public servant I could never concede that the liberty of the subject or the impartial administration of justice were matters of mere legal technicality.

Banda said that if the Governor, the chief secretary and the attorney-general were determined to proceed in this case regardless of his warnings as to public reaction, they must take responsibility for the consequences, and he would have his say later. Roberts responded that it was wrong to impute responsibilities to the Governor or the chief secretary: 'the decision whether to prosecute or not in a particular case was ultimately entirely a matter for the Attorney-General.' He emphasized that in reaching a decision the final criterion was the public interest, and it was on this that the views of ministers were of great value.

Roberts's interview with Banda was a rare example of a senior civil servant standing up to the doctor, refusing to be browbeaten and, by correctness, skill, courage and firmness, demonstrating that Banda's views could be challenged on grounds of principle rather than conceding on grounds of immediate pragmatism – even by the most pragmatic of men.

A month before the London conference was scheduled to begin,

Youens returned from leave and called on Banda.[141] It was ostensibly a social occasion on which the doctor was amiable and relaxed and Youens was non-committal. Banda knew, and probably intended, that Youens would tell Jones about their conversation. It was, over a very long period, part of their way of doing things. He maintained that he had been led to believe during the July discussions in London that he would receive a decision on secession before the conference started and said, 'I will resign if I do not get it.'

Turning to the civil service, he indicated that he would press for full control over it immediately after the conference. He was keen to retain the services of 'all' expatriate officers with a very few exceptions but he would not continue to operate under a system where they had divided allegiances and where Britain still had ultimate responsibility for them. For Banda, this was 'a politically impossible situation and ... to perpetuate it would make a mockery of any form of self-government'. Given Jones's concerns about the relationships between the MCP and the civil service, the district commissioners' criticisms of the lack of support and understanding from officials at the very top of government, and Banda's run-in with Roberts about the police and administration, it is not surprising that Youens saw the doctor's stance as a 'tough nut'.

The doctor was presumably drawing the battlelines – the issues they would need to discuss behind the scenes – stating them in a somewhat extreme, dogmatic fashion (as he could afford to in private with Youens) and getting a reaction upon which he could base his tactics.

The discussion was indeed reported by Youens to Jones, and by Jones to Butler.[142] Saying that Banda was definitely expecting to be told Britain's decision on secession before the conference, Jones thought it would be helpful if Butler could give him a private assurance on his arrival in the United Kingdom. He was apprehensive of what might happen if Banda could not be satisfied on this point, and gave the now very familiar warning: 'There is a real danger that he may not attend the conference at all unless he gets such an assurance ... a breaking of contact with Banda at this stage would almost certainly lead to a security situation involving dangers particularly to Europeans which ... I could not possibly hope to contain without outside help.'

Stevens submitted his report to the secretary of state during the second half of October, only a month before the conference. Having read the report, Butler, without reference to the Governors, reached a number of conclusions in his own mind which he shared with the Governors and the high commissioner on 25 October, some four days before they received their own copy.[143] His first and major conclusion was: 'As regards Nyasaland I am sure that we can now win no more time on secession unless we are prepared to see Nyasaland held within the

Nyasaland: Governor · 149

Federation by force.' The report confirmed that of which Butler, Jones and many others had been convinced for some considerable time. He then turned to the consequences of the country's secession, both economic and political:

> The economic and financial consequences of secession for Nyasaland are serious, and a claim upon HMG for substantially increased assistance over the next few years at least is to be expected. We have gained something in bringing Malawi ministers broadly to accept the hard financial facts and to indicate their readiness to meet their own problems in a practical way. They believe that given a sympathetic attitude by HMG over the next few years they can succeed. They may well be over optimistic ...
>
> There is, however, at least a prospect of launching Nyasaland into independence on a reasonably stable basis and of negotiating a 'tapered off' financial settlement which in the circumstances is the best solution we can hope for. Moreover, the financial considerations clearly cannot over-ride the political pressures nor have they in the least shaken Malawi Ministers in their determination to secede.

Butler thought, therefore, that he should announce, before the conference opened, that the British government accepted in principle that Nyasaland should be allowed to secede. A little later, he changed his mind on the date of the announcement because both Welensky and Whitehead argued, he believed with justice, that it would seriously affect the outcome of the Southern and Northern Rhodesia elections and because he found Banda less impatient than the Governor's advice led him to expect. Consequently, despite Jones's dire warning about the security dangers he decided to delay the announcement until after those elections and just before the Commons rose in December.

Butler went on to say that he would couple the announcement with an intimation that Nyasaland would be expected 'to shoulder to the full extent that may be equitable all the consequent commitments and obligations', for example concerning the federal debt and absorbing federal civil servants. He expected to get Banda to agree to the negotiations to implement the move taking about nine months. He hoped that during this period they might be able to 'bring other Federal issues to a point where the possibility of some new form of association between Nyasaland and the Rhodesias might be reopened with him'. He realized this would not be easy. It is surprising that he even entertained the possibility.

There were related matters with which Butler had to deal once the decision on secesssion had been taken: self-government, independence and future association between the states in Central Africa. He thought they must be ready at the conference to move to internal self-government early in 1963 provided they could limit the powers to be given to the new government, especially over the civil service and finance. He intended to try and avoid committing himself to a specific date for independence because this would be premature and unrealistic before they had worked out the main consequences of Nyasaland's secession and because of its inevitable repercussions on the Rhodesias. If pressed hard, he might have to give a private assurance to Banda indicating that the whole process might be completed by the middle of 1964.[144]

On 5 November Jones left Chileka and flew to London for the Marlborough House conference which lasted from 12 to 23 November. Just before the conference, Butler received a general briefing by his officials in which their advice was clear. Independence should not be considered until the detailed financial consequences of secession had been worked out, particularly the burden that would fall on Britain. Even in the case of self-government, control of finance should remain in official hands, constitutional provision should be made to ensure financial and economic stability, and a compensation scheme for voluntary retirement, sufficiently attractive to retain expatriate officers, must be worked out and agreed.[145]

On 9 November Jones attended two meetings between Butler and Banda. The morning meeting consisted mainly of an exchange of pleasantries, with Banda in a cheerful and confident mood. Secession was mentioned only obliquely and Banda said he would resign if he did not receive an unequivocal decision before he left London, 'and let his people choose another leader who could perhaps more easily obtain for the people the object which he had been put into power to achieve'. This was a step back from the position he had adopted with Youens a month earlier. Jones had warned that failure to give a decision *before* the conference would run the risk of Banda not attending and a security situation developing which would require outside military help. Fortunately, his fears proved to be misplaced. Now, in the absence of an unequivocal decision by the *end* of the conference, Banda would resign from the government while he was still in London. 'There must be no quibbling or beating about the bush.'[146]

During the luncheon interval Butler had a discussion with Macmillan as a result of which he asked Banda to see him during the afternoon. In his private diary Jones described the afternoon meeting as 'a bit of a crisis'.[147] Again, Banda was relaxed and cheerful as they started the meeting. Butler began by saying that he was under pressure both in Britain and in Salisbury to delay a decision on secession until the following year, 1963. At this point Banda immediately became gravely agitated and began to rise from his seat as if to leave. Butler, watching the doctor closely, quickly saw the danger signs of his opening bid having failed, as he almost certainly anticipated. With scarcely a break in his delivery, he calmed the doctor by adding, 'but that would be wrong' and clearly it would be unfair to ask him to wait for a decision on secession until next year. Instead, what he had in mind was to make an announcement in the Commons before the House rose in the week beginning 17 December. Banda, relieved that Butler was not going to keep him waiting until 1963, said this was agreeable to him since he was confident he could contain his people, who trusted him, until then. Butler then told the doctor, in confidence, that the government had decided Nyasaland could withdraw from the Federation. Banda was delighted.[148]

Sandys had put the British government on the hook when he told Banda a decision would be reached, first in mid-March, then by the end of March. Notwithstanding Jones's fears and repeated warnings of alarming consequences, Butler, by successive steps, had successfully delayed this until well into November – with a further delay of six weeks before publicly announcing it – but the decision was the one that Banda wanted: Nyasaland could secede from the Federation. He had fought a long and determined battle. Sandys had significantly muddied the waters, which Butler had then skilfully clarified. Butler had engaged in a series of delaying manoeuvres. Banda had feinted with his threats to resign and bring about a situation in which military force would have to be brought in. Now the gladiators had reached agreement without fighting breaking out, for which they both, and Jones, must have been thankful.

The remainder of this second meeting on 9 November was taken up in fairly brief discussions on a number of points. Banda, flushed but not softened by his success in securing a favourable decision on secession, was not to be swayed from his adamant position on any future association in Central Africa. He refused to discuss the matter until the instrument allowing Nyasaland to withdraw from the Federation had passed through the Commons. When Butler said he intended under the new constitution that Banda should be called chief minister, the doctor said the time for this had passed and he should be called prime minister. Again, he was not to be softened by the 'gift' of secession and seems to have taken the sensible view that when one is advancing one should keep going. Next, he wanted all officials to leave the executive council except the minister of finance who should stay, possibly until the end of 1963. Finally, he asked for full self-government immediately and independence within the year. Butler had his doubts about this but said that within a year of the new constitution being agreed Banda would be consulted on a date for independence. The doctor did not oppose this but was violently opposed to another conference being held before independence was granted: 'surely [this could] be the subject of negotiations between himself and the Prime Minister or the First Secretary of State.'

Jones was able to relax over the weekend. On Saturday he watched Arsenal beat Sheffield United at football and then went to the theatre in the evening. The following day he went to Holy Communion at Saint James's, Piccadilly, had a meeting with Cameron at his club and then went to the Remembrance Day service at Westminster Abbey. In the afternoon he travelled to Stanstead to spend the remainder of the weekend with the Butlers.[149]

Jones returned to London on the Monday morning, 12 November, and attended the formal opening of the conference at Marlborough House.[150] In his opening address, immediately following Butler's introductory remarks, he said:

> We in Nyasaland have travelled hopefully since 1960 and have now arrived at this important point in the territory's history. Many sitting round this table must feel a sense of achievement. It is right that they should. At the same time, all of us here are, I think, keenly aware of the problems, particularly the economic and financial problems, which face Nyasaland at this stage of her development. We shall not rest until we have solved those problems. We wholeheartedly acknowledge how we shall need help to do this and we are all grateful ... that Her Majesty's Government are prepared to do everything possible to assist us.[151]

When the Governor sat down, Banda rose. Glowing inwardly from his success in being assured of secession, he paid tribute to 'our beloved Governor, Sir Glyn Jones, and to the civil servants under him'. No one, Banda said, knew better than he that without Jones's wise understanding and sympathetic guidance Nyasaland would not have made the progress that it had. He added that because Jones himself understood Nyasaland's problems he had been able to transmit his feelings to the civil service under him. He anticipated no great exodus of expatriate officers as Nyasaland advanced: 'The relationships between the British civil servants and the elected ministers can only be described as excellent.' In fact, of course, it was not those limited relationships – which, despite Chiume's allegations, were indeed very good – but the general attitude of the MCP, particularly the youth league, the level of violence and victimization in the country and, at least in the case of the administration, the degree of understanding and support of the Governor, which so far they felt had not been forthcoming, that would determine the extent of any exodus.

Between them, Jones and Banda had touched, albeit briefly, on Britain's two main worries about Nyasaland's future: finance and the civil service.

The next day Jones met with Banda in the morning before the conference session. The doctor did not intend to say much himself during the sessions, but his 'boys' had a lot to say and it would be advisable to let them say it.

So far as he was concerned he [was grateful for what had been promised to him – agreement on secession – but] he needed to take home with him more than that. For instance, he wished to know the date when secession would be implemented [and] the date for full independence within the Commonwealth. The Governor said ... he felt sure that both matters could be raised by Dr. Banda in private discussion.[152]

If he could be given firm undertakings on all points, Banda said he would feel confident in being able to hold his people. If, however, Britain appeared to be procrastinating he might have difficulty in handling them. Even at this stage he was prepared to use the same old warning, or threat. He had in mind that Nyasaland's secession would take place in July 1963, and independence be granted in April 1964.[153]

The following day Jones attended a meeting with Butler and Banda at which the secretary of state was extremely firm and made it clear that it was impracticable to give a firm date for independence until the secession issue was out of the way, the decision announced and the problems stemming from it resolved sufficiently for Nyasaland to stand on its own feet and the country's financial position could be be cleared. He bluntly continued:

> With the best will in the world it was not practicable for HMG to divest itself of its responsibilities until these problems had been solved ... he proposed to appoint a Commission to assist him in these matters ... the Commission's work would take at least nine months which would mean that it could be anticipated that consultations leading to arrangements for independence could be entered upon some time in the autumn of 1963. He believed that Dr. Banda had some date like April 1964 in his mind for independence and, if all went well, this date might not be far out – but he could not offer an undertaking on a definite date at this stage.[154]

Banda reacted favourably to this frank and straightforward approach, but having regard to his own position and difficulties he was most anxious to secure from Butler 'a firm undertaking on this matter' and would be content with a date given to him on a personal and confidential basis. Butler wanted to help Banda as much as he could and, while he could not offer a definite date, he accepted that some reference to independence should be included in the White Paper emerging from the conference.

Having declined to give Banda a firm date for independence, even in confidence, Butler turned to a point to which he could agree. He did not intend to arrange a further constitutional conference despite the pressures the UFP was likely to raise. He envisaged personal consultations with Banda, of which Blackwood would be kept informed. This form of consultation was precisely the way Banda preferred to operate.

They then turned to the limitations on full self-government on which Britain would insist, particularly in respect of finance and the civil service. Banda intended to 'put in a person who would train under Mr. Phillips with a view to his ultimately taking over the portfolio' of finance. He wanted to know why Butler wished the Governor to retain reserved powers over finance and was told they were designed to ensure that monies provided by Britain were properly utilized. He accepted this on the assumption that the Governor continued to be Jones.

The question of the Governor's continued responsibility for the civil service was more difficult to resolve: 'Dr. Banda expiated on the difficulties which he saw in such an arrangement ... a number of officers had made [the position] intolerable by the attitudes which they had taken up, viz. that they were, in fact, Her Majesty's Government's men and not servants of the elected Nyasaland Government.' Jones suggested that such attitudes could be corrected by himself in consultation with Banda. There was no question but that officers worked under and served the elected ministers. They wished to preserve the present system of appointments, promotions, discipline and conditions of service only for a limited period. Banda was not entirely satisfied, and he reserved his position so as to consult his colleagues. In the event, the stance taken by Butler in respect of the Governor's control of the public services until the voluntary retirement scheme was introduced was maintained in the new constitution.

Butler, Banda and Jones met again two days later when Banda took up a number of questions not settled in their earlier meetings.[155] Between the introduction of the self-government constitution and full independence, he would accept an independent director of public prosecutions provided that in matters involving the public interest he would be obliged to consult the attorney-general who would also be the minister of justice, a politician. As soon as independence was achieved he would see that the direction of public prosecutions was entirely in the hands of the attorney-general. It is likely that Banda had been able to get his colleagues to agree to this by arguing that in view of the strong position taken by Butler they should allow him to say he would put up with it for now because as soon as they were independent he would alter it. Privately, Jones told Butler he was opposed to Roberts becoming solicitor-general and director of public prosecutions at the same time. In addition to the objections in principle, he doubted 'from the point of view of personalities ... whether this arrangement would be acceptable to Banda'. This judgement turned out to be significantly erroneous. Jones knew Roberts would stand up to Banda and feared he might rock the boat, but he underestimated both Roberts's ability to stand up without rocking the boat, and Banda's appreciation of frankness in his advisers.[156]

Banda made a particular point of saying he hoped he could have Youens as secretary to the prime minister and cabinet. In this position, Youens would be the official head of the civil service under the prime minister. This may have been Banda's way of acquiring some control of the service while reassuring officers that on a day-to-day basis the official head of the service would be in control. Jones 'could see no objection to this on the face of it but would like to have time to consider the matter further'.[157] Banda had told Armitage in 1960 that he wanted Youens as chief secretary when Jones was to become Governor, but Jones had preferred to bring in Foster from Northern Rhodesia. Banda no doubt sensed Jones's opposition at the time, and was now returning to the point and making it directly to the secretary of state. Youens had worked with Banda longer and knew him better than did any other official, including the Governor, and they had always got on well together. In the event, on 1 February 1963, Foster became deputy Governor and, as Banda had requested, Youens became secretary to the prime minister and cabinet and head of the civil service.

The pattern of private meetings and formal sessions lasted throughout the first week of the conference but Jones was able to escape for the weekend by spending it at Grantham with an old friend from Northern Rhodesia. On the Saturday they shot pheasants, partridges and hares. On Sunday he went for a 6-mile walk before returning to London where he attended evensong at Saint James's, Piccadilly. He went to the same church for Holy Communion the following morning. The pattern of meetings and sessions continued through the second week of the conference, with the addition of rather more luncheons.[158]

The morning after his return from Grantham, Jones attended another meeting between Butler and Banda to deal with points which, in the formal sessions, the doctor had reserved for private discussion.[159] Where it had not been possible to come to quick agreement, Butler suggested that Banda meet separately with Jones and see if they could sufficiently agree to bring a recommendation back to him.

The first point Banda reserved for further discussion was that the prime minister should be consulted before a new Governor was appointed. Jones and the doctor agreed the matter could be dealt with informally by his being given a private assurance on it. In the event, the constitution was silent on the point and the occasion for private consultation never arose.[160]

The second reserved point concerned the prerogative of mercy. Banda asked that in respect of non-capital punishments the prime minister should have the right to make representations, especially in sentences for political offences. In discussing this together, Jones agreed that he should give Banda a private assurance without including it formally. This was unsatisfactory, and in the constitution as finally introduced the Governor was formally required to exercise the prerogative on his own judgement but in capital cases to consult a special committee of the cabinet.

One further point persistently bothered Banda: the division of responsibilities for the police force between the Governor and the prime minister. He felt this was insufficiently clear and repeatedly returned to it. He was particularly keen to gain whatever control he could over the police. The outcome was that the constitution gave the Governor responsibility for public order and public safety, including the operational control of the police force, but he was empowered to delegate these responsibilities to the prime minister – which he did.

Banda had secured agreement on secession, the nature of the new self-government constitution was virtually decided – and was as close to what he wanted as he was going to get at this stage – and he now immediately pushed for the final and culminating point of everything he had been aiming at since his return to Nyasaland four and a half years earlier: independence. The Governor had two meetings on the day preceding the end of the conference, both about independence. The first of these was with both Butler and Banda and the second was with Banda alone. At the first Butler explained very carefully that the British Cabinet was unable to permit him to give a date for independence. Nyasaland was not yet out of the Federation and there were very grave financial and economic problems to be looked at. 'The most he could say, therefore, was that there would be further consultations on the subject towards the end of next year.'

Banda fully understood the position but made it quite clear that 'his date was the 3rd March, 1964, and if Nyasaland had not reached Independence by that date there would be disorders in the country and another State of Emergency would have to be declared'. Making this threat, it seems, had become something of a habit but it stood no chance of swaying Butler.

The second meeting on 22 November, when Jones met Banda by himself, took place in the evening. They particularly discussed Banda's wish that, in order to minimize any delay between self-government and independence, the new constitution should be implemented in two stages. Butler had mentioned this possibility earlier and now Banda asked that it be implemented. The official report of the conference, prepared at its conclusion, said the constitution would be introduced in two stages. In the first the existing constitution would be amended to cater for changes in the executive and legislative councils, leaving the other provisions, including the Governor's powers, unchanged. This would be done not later than the beginning of February 1963. In the second, the complete new constitution would replace the existing constitution. This would be done as soon as administratively possible. In the meantime, negotiations would be concluded to introduce a compensation scheme for expatriate civil servants.

The Marlborough House conference closed the following day, Friday 23 November. In his concluding remarks, Jones – no doubt conscious of the fact that since his short opening address on the first day of the conference he had said nothing during any of the thirteen formal sessions – said the role of a Governor in the plenary sessions of a conference was 'largely to be seen and not heard. Such influence as he may exercise on the proceedings is for the most part appropriately confined to raising the eyebrow or a kick under the table'.[161] The raising of Jones's eyebrow would not have passed unnoticed although his kick under the table might have, for his eyebrows were several inches long and his legs were short!

Over the weekend Jones escaped once more, spending Saturday again with old Northern Rhodesia friends, this time at Cambridge shooting partridges, pheasants and hares, and Sunday with his sister and her family in Hull. Back in London he had a meeting with Butler and Banda the day before leaving for Nyasaland. Butler said the announcement on secession would be made on 17 or 18 December. It would include reference to Nyasaland meeting a fair share of the costs of dismantling the Federation. The exercise would require close dealings with the federal government, and Banda accepted that the Governor, official ministers and other civil servants would need to be involved, but the elected ministers, including himself, would take no part. When Butler said he intended to put an enabling Bill for secession through parliament early in the summer, the doctor – ever a man to squeeze the utmost advantage even out of a favourable situation – said he very much hoped this meant early May.[162]

Jones flew from London on 29 November and arrived back in Zomba two days later.[163] The Nyasaland constitutional wrangles were now largely over, though its future relationships with either or both of the Rhodesias had yet to be decided. There still remained, however, the actual introduction of the new constitution and the detailed working out of how the federal link was to be finally severed. There remained, too, the introduction of a scheme entitling expatriate civil servants to retire from the service and be compensated for loss of career. The scheme needed to allow officers freely to depart, but also to be so devised as to encourage those who wished to remain in the Nyasaland service to do so. There was much anxiety that there would be a damaging mass exodus if the scheme was not sufficiently attractive and if working, living, social and political conditions – especially the maintenance of law and order – were such as to persuade officers and their families no longer to live in the country. Nyasaland was going to have enough trouble managing without federal financial and service support, without having to worry about major and sudden shortages of staff. It was these considerations which occupied much of Jones's thought, energy and time in the months following the Marlborough House conference.

The new year, 1963, opened with a busy though not troublesome month. At the final meeting of the executive council, on 23 January, the Governor said his greatest ambition over his many years of service had been achieved by contributing to the advancement of the people of the country in which he served to a point where they could take over the government themselves. From now on the duties of the Governor-in-council would be taken over by the prime minister and cabinet. It was, as Jones said, a momentous step forward.[164] Butler visited Nyasaland from 27 to 30 January and discussed with Jones and Banda the machinery of secession: a working party of members of the Nyasaland and federal governments chaired by a senior British civil servant. Banda agreed to cooperate fully with this working party.[165]

We have noted how a number of elected ministers had approached Jones to release Chipembere from prison before the London conference. Banda had not pressed the Governor on this nor mentioned it to the secretary of state,[166] but when Butler raised it privately, the doctor said he hoped the Governor would curtail the sentence and release him after the conference. Jones already had in mind releasing him about Christmas time. Butler, however, was markedly doubtful about this: 'I cannot help feeling some doubt about an early release ... and I should be grateful if you would let me know how you see the advantages of this course so that I can offset them against my general anxieties.' These anxieties existed notwithstanding Banda's expressed confidence that he could control Chipembere. Possibly because of them, Jones changed his proposed date of release to 31 January 1963, but Butler was still doubtful about an early release, especially close to his proposed visit to Nyasaland: 'If release is to take place, it seems to me that the best time might be while I am in Lusaka, say 25 January.'[167]

It so happened that the day before Butler expressed these views to Jones, Banda had told the Governor that he hoped Chipembere could be released before the secretary of state's visit and he suggested 15 January.[168] The opinions of Butler and Banda, especially the latter, induced Jones to change his mind again:

> [15 January] would allow Chipembere to go to his home in the Fort Johnston District before attending Dr. Banda's swearing in [as prime minister] ... In all the circumstances, and having regard to the fact that I have staved this one off for a long time I feel inclined to release him on the 15th thus hoping to gain from him some good will for the future when he becomes a minister.[169]

Jones was overdoing the 'staving off' argument, because Banda had not in fact pressed him or Butler except late in the day and then only gently. The pressure, such as it was, had come five months previously from some of the ministers who hoped Chipembere would be a counterbalance to Chiume. Thereafter Chisiza had been killed and the others had not pursued it. Nevertheless, Banda was grateful and later said that Jones, 'being a good man, a sympathetic man, an understanding man, in the British tradition of fair play, listened to me and released Chipembere'.[170]

The reason for wanting Chipembere freed before the end of January was that Jones could cancel the normal period of licence after early release for good conduct, thereby removing the restrictions on membership of the legislature and the cabinet and enabling him to become a minister as soon as the new government took office. He released him from prison and cancelled his period on licence during the late evening of 15 January but did not announce it until the following day.[171] Chipembere had served just under two years of his three-year sentence and would have been due for release on licence on 9 February.

CHAPTER 6

Nyasaland: Self-Government

ON 1 February 1963 Jones administered the oath to Banda as the first – and, as it turned out, the only – prime minister of Nyasaland, and the members of his cabinet: Chiume, Chipembere, Bwanausi, Cameron, Mkandawire, Chokani, Msonthi, Chirwa and Norman-Walker (acting for Phillips who was on leave) with Tembo as parliamentary secretary to the ministry of finance. He had them all to lunch together with Kaunda, Kapwepwe and other nationalist politicians from Northern Rhodesia.[1]

The festivities to celebrate self-government took place during a generally peaceful period, save in Nkata Bay where there were cases of arson, crop damage, assault and intimidation. Towards the end of the month, an article in the *Malawi News* warning Africans not to trust Europeans caused alarm among expatriates and fears of deteriorating race relations. In a letter to ministers and permanent secretaries, a month later, Banda dealt with this article, saying it applied only to a limited category of white people and 'only those whom the cap fits should seek to wear it'. The letter, copies of which were sent to all expatriate civil servants, included attempts to reassure them also about medical facilities and schooling for expatriates. It does not seem to have been particularly reassuring.[2]

Even less reassuring were the renewed outbreaks of violence in June, stimulated by Chipembere. He visited the Lower river and

> made speeches in Port Herald and Chikwawa districts at which he ... said that Capricorns and 'stooges' could not be tolerated and that action should be taken against them. Following this visit a number of incidents [of assault, boycott and closure of shops] were reported, together with 'sweeps' checking MCP cards, an assault on the [Portuguese] stationmaster at Port Herald, and other cases of assault on individuals. A number of youths [marched] up and down [outside] the police station at Port Herald shouting abuse at the police ... In Chikwawa district a local court clerk was beaten up and dismissed when he complained to the police.

[Chipembere said] at a meeting in Chikwawa that he is to be regarded as 'Minister of Violence' and that the activities of 'stooges' and Capricorns are to be reported to him so that he could issue orders for dealing with them.

In June, too, leading members of political parties opposed to the MCP were assaulted. One was beaten and left unconscious beside his car which his assailants burnt out. Youth leaguers assaulted four others, one of whom was stoned.[3]

Banda visited the Lower river twice towards the end of July – a month or more after the unlawful events took place – and called for peace and calm. After this, the situation in the area quietened down. Trouble, however, broke out in Nkata Bay with renewed cases of assault and malicious damage. There were confrontations between the MCP and the Congress Liberation Party, and a strong police unit was sent to disperse 'two opposing groups, numbering some 300 each, and armed with traditional weapons ... facing each other', ready to fight.[4]

Banda continued adamantly and consistently to refuse to contemplate any future links with neighbouring countries until dates for secession and independence had been decided. He was naturally keen that they should be as early as possible and, unusually, he found apparent and partial allies in Welensky and Blackwood.[5] Just before he became prime minister he was told by Blackwood that the federal government entirely endorsed his date of 1 July 1963 for secession, and any delay beyond that date would be the fault of the British government wishing to avoid paying the bill.

Banda was 'rather excitable and clearly very much impressed' when he told the Governor about this conversation the following day. Without consulting Jones, he had set up his own defederalization committee of his ministers to meet federal ministers, and Jones was unable to dislodge him from this. This was a major change from his previoius attitude of having nothing to do with federal ministers. He assured the Governor there would be no question of going behind the back of the working party Butler intended to set up to deal with the mechanics of leaving the Federation, and there would be no agreement with federal ministers 'on the side'. He simply wished to hear what they had to say.

Jones, in his turn, assured Banda there would be no delay on the grounds of not wanting to pay the bill. The doctor was not satisfied with this assurance, and sought others. The Governor told Butler: 'Clearly these cunning tactics on the Federal Government's part have had a considerable effect on Banda, and [he] has asked for an interview with Alport when he is here, early in March [to get] more assurances about unnecessary delay. He is clearly in a very suspicious mood at the moment.' Jones went on to describe to Banda the considerable amount of work required before the date could be fixed, but Banda was 'so set on [1 July] that he tend[ed] to brush all argument aside'. Jones made three other points: the secession exercise must be handled as a whole and not, as Welensky wished, piecemeal – the composite solution must be adhered to; Nyasaland must not be saddled with more than a just portion of the federal debt; and the takeover must be orderly. He was pleased that Banda agreed with him on all these points.

Butler was inclined categorically to tell Banda and Welensky that secession on 1 July was out of the question. Jones, aware that this might rock the boat, argued that if the British claimed it was not yet possible to fix a date they were on weak ground if they categorically rejected any particular date. Rather, they should emphasize, as he had recently, the need to reach agreement through the working party proposed by Butler to resolve the complex problems involved. He was sure the most effective way of handling this matter was to show willing about the date but let events demonstrate what date would be practicable. These events would be determined by the attitude of the governments in Central Africa towards helping the working party achieve agreement. Only in this way would the financial realities be brought home to Banda. If they fixed a date now, Banda and Welensky would lose interest in the working party. These were sound arguments.[6]

The secretary of state visited Nyasaland from 27 to 30 January 1963. He and Jones had a number of very cordial meetings with Banda, who made it clear that he wanted a date for secession and a date for independence which, so far as he was concerned, had to be 3 March 1964. These were the two matters unresolved from the Marlborough House conference. Butler was not yet prepared to discuss a date for independence, but in respect of secession he outlined the machinery he had in mind: a working party of members of the Nyasaland and federal governments chaired by a senior British civil servant and assisted by treasury and technical cooperation experts. He would finalize arrangements for this as soon as he got back to London. Banda agreed to this machinery, which rendered his own ministerial committee unnecessary, and said he would cooperate fully with it. Butler hoped the Bill enabling Nyasaland to secede would pass through parliament in June and this would enable Banda to tell his people that secession was an irrevocable fact, though its implementation might not be completed until the end of the year. He hoped Banda could come to London for talks later in June, and the doctor agreed.[7]

A fortnight after Butler's visit, Jones went on leave to Britain. Two weeks later the federal government formally requested that the date of secession should be 1 July 1963 and that if thereafter they were required to provide services in Nyasaland, Britain should make good the difference between the federal government's Nyasaland expenditure and revenue.[8] Butler – contrary to Jones's advice about not rejecting a particular date – responded that the date proposed was 'completely impracticable' if the transfer was to be orderly, and they must wait until Curtis, heading the de-federalization working party, arrived and discussed the matter.[9]

In a conversation with Foster on 25 February, Banda repeated Blackwood's allegation that Britain, reluctant to meet the financial liabilities of secession, was dragging its feet.[10] This 'completely unwarranted suggestion' distressed Butler. He asked Foster to pass on a personal message, saying the British government wanted to see Nyasaland's withdrawal implemented as early as practicable but if the transfer was to be orderly they could not believe it would be possible by 1 July, only four months away:

> As soon as the Working Party has achieved the necessary agreement among the Governments concerned to a mutually satisfactory resolution of the complex problems involved HMG will be ready to consider what date might be determined having regard to the administrative and legal processes which will then require to be completed before the formal secession can take place.
>
> You will appreciate that it is not until the financial consequences of withdrawal for Nyasaland have been worked out and it is possible to take stock of the new situation which Nyasaland then faces that HMG will be in a position to consider with Nyasaland Ministers to what extent and over what period the Nyasaland Government may need financial help in their own efforts to bridge the budgetary gap (which secession will of course increase substantially). I have said publicly ... that we shall approach this question with sympathy though I cannot of course give an advance commitment.[11]

The question of Nyasaland's future financial position had now come to the surface of discussions, and Jones spent a great deal of his time on leave discussing it with the secretary of state and his officials. He returned to Nyasaland on 17 May and met Banda straight away. He explained that Butler had asked him to let the doctor have his views on the country's finances. Since this was a crucially important matter and their talks were bound to be lengthy, they decided to start immediately and spread them over several days.[12]

> [He] began by telling Dr. Banda that Nyasaland's shortfall of finance for the ensuing year was far greater than [they] had realized. [The] unpleasant fact had to be faced that Nyasaland's internal resources failed to meet the level of recurrent expenditure by something like 6.5 million pounds, and of development expenditure by over 4 million pounds.[12]

The secretary of state, Jones continued, was gravely anxious about this difficult situation, for a number of reasons. First, Britain was already subsidizing a large number of developing countries. The thought of subsidizing Nyasaland to the tune of 60 per cent of its annual budget was alarming. Once it became known how heavily Britain was supporting Nyasaland, other countries would demand similar treatment. Second, some Conservatives believed Nyasaland's financial troubles stemmed from Banda's and his colleagues' determination to secede from the Federation against British government advice. Consequently, these people thought, Nyasaland should be left 'to stew in its own juice', and the very large sum of money required to balance the budget at the current level of expenditure might seem to support their arguments. Third, with taxation in Britain already very high, no minister could contemplate with equanimity additional taxation to subsidize such territories as Nyasaland. Butler regarded this financial position as 'extremely serious'.

Notwithstanding these profoundly disturbing worries, Butler had asked Jones to tell Banda the British government were most anxious to help Nyasaland overcome its financial difficulties so that it could eventually move to independence. He very much hoped he could persuade his cabinet colleagues to be sympathetic in the years ahead, but it would be necessary for Nyasaland to 'take the sternest and most painful measures to help itself' if he was to be able to overcome their reluctance to incur expenditure in keeping Nyasaland afloat.

Jones then gave Butler's views on the sort of measures the Nyasaland government should take. They should urgently find ways to increase taxation and retrench services – as Sandys had told Banda fifteen months earlier – although he recognized there was a limit beyond which it would be politically unwise to go. Just before federation was imposed, he pointed out, Nyasaland had become self-supporting albeit at a low level and it might be that it would have to revert to that level for a few years. The proposed increase in the education estimates, especially for primary education, was difficult to justify and he hoped it would be scrutinized and reduced.

The Governor then turned to the development plan, compiled under Dunduzu Chisiza rather hurriedly, which Butler hoped would be revised because there were so few local resources to finance it. He very much hoped Nyasaland would do everything possible to attract outside development financing. Whereas the possibilities for external financing of recurrent expenditure were gravely limited, those for development were more favourable, provided the applications were detailed and attractively presented.

In essence Butler was teaching the brutal facts which elected ministers had brushed aside till now. If they would not learn by themselves or with Jones's help then he would teach them. He was relying, too, on Banda taking a responsible stance on Nyasaland's future and as realistic a view of its finances as he himself was, and inducing his ministers to follow his lead.

Jones spoke at this meeting for three-quarters of an hour, uninterrupted by Banda who indeed took the subject 'very seriously indeed'. He was grateful to Butler for his obvious desire to help Nyasaland, and to Jones for speaking to him so frankly on the secretary of state's behalf. In the past, and had it not come from Butler, remarks such as that about leaving Nyasaland to stew in its own juice would have provoked an explosion from the doctor. Not so on this occasion. Banda had achieved all that he set out to accomplish except a date for independence and the factors that would first have to be tackled. He paid very close attention to what needed to be done to tackle them. The Governor ended the meeting by saying the basic reason for Butler's anxiety about finance was that 'Nyasaland might never become viable and thus never completely independent ... This would be a great sorrow to Britain not only because the people of Britain felt a real affection for the people of Nyasaland, but also because it might appear to be a sign of the complete failure of [their] policy towards the Protectorate.'

Jones had two further meetings about finance with Banda the following day so that the whole ground could be covered before the cabinet met to discuss the coming year's estimates.[13] He told Banda that Butler approved the draft budget for the first six months of the 1963-64 fiscal year, subject only to details, but hoped that for the 1964 year the cabinet would strive earnestly to reduce expenditure.[14] He referred again to the education budget and the balance between primary and secondary education expenditure. In the interval between the meeting the previous day and the present meeting Banda had 'already had Chiume up and given him instructions to try and find ways and means of cutting the Education account'. Clearly, the doctor was treating the finances of the country as put to him by Butler and Jones seriously and with an acute sense of urgency.

The Governor then turned, as Butler had asked, to the development estimates. These he also approved for the first six months but thereafter very much hoped they would look closely at their development plan. This projected £4.7 million expenditure in its third year with only £1 million to cover it. Jones urged Banda to undertake an early revision of the plan and give priority to schemes of direct benefit to the country which would stimulate greater revenue so as to balance the recurrent budget as soon as possible. He advised, too, that education, health and social service schemes, which would not yield early returns, should be the subject of early applications for aid from non-British government sources.

Banda again listened carefully and quietly, and undertook to heed Butler's advice, for which he was grateful. Whatever view one might take of Banda's statesmanship and sense of responsibility during his fight for secession, there can be no doubt that he acted in a statesmanlike and responsible fashion once the right to secede was secured.

Finance, then, occupied a great deal of Jones's time and attention during the months following the Marlborough House conference, both on leave and on his return. Although the problems were not solved during this period the ways in which they could best be tackled were worked out and made clear to Banda and his colleagues.

The two years since Jones became Governor had been extremely busy and worrying. The pressure of work and the stress involved inevitably had an effect on his health. In his mid-fifties, he normally enjoyed good health and he was an unusually active man. On 9 and 10 June, only three weeks after returning from leave, he felt that he 'was not really on form' and retired to bed. The following day his doctor examined him and sent him to Blantyre hospital by ambulance, suffering from 'a cardiac indisposition': rapid and irregular action of the heart. His condition turned out to be not as serious as was first feared and after a few days the heart rhythm and residual electrical changes reverted spontaneously to normal. The provincial commissioner, who visited him daily and was briefed by the director of medical services in Zomba, understood that the indisposition was a 'nervous breakdown'.[15] Jones was discharged after a week to begin convalescence and did not return to work until the end of June. At the end of July his doctor examined him again, found no evidence of permanent damage, his blood pressure was normal, his pulse rhythm regular and his heart not enlarged. He was now 'medically fit and in good health' and was able to spend a week at the lake, resting. His doctors would not allow him to travel to Salibury to see Butler during the dissolution conference there at the end of June, and two months later, although he had taken up his full duties, he had 'still not yet quite got [himself] into condition', for example, for walking up flights of stairs.[16]

Part of the financial discussions was directed at evolving a scheme encouraging expatriate civil servants to stay after the country attained independence, allowing others to retire, and compensating officers for loss of career. It was commonly accepted that, given the overall level of education, training and experience of local officers and the vast amount of important work independence would demand, it was vital that experienced and skilled expatriate officers should be retained in fairly large numbers. It was unlikely, however, that, regardless of the generosity of the inducements offered, many would stay if the state of law and order in the country caused them concern. Questions of law and order, then, assumed critical importance in the period leading up to independence, and worries on these grounds, like concerns over finance, took up a good deal of the Governor's time and thoughts.

There had been previous occasions when politically motivated and other more general breaches of the law incurred criticism and caused Jones and his officials concern. There had been worrying deteriorations of law and order, for example, at the time of the 1960 federal review conference and during the lead up to the 1961 elections. Now, however, the implications of lawlessness were different. While violence as a means of applying pressure to secure constitutional advance was no longer necessary, it was likely that intimidation and physical attacks would continue in order to reduce still further opposition to the MCP. Moreover, there was now a different form of lawlessness which began to be of considerable concern: intimidating and roughly treating non-Africans.

Although secession had been agreed, the date for its actually coming about had not yet been fixed, and this was a source of irritation to some less patient Nyasaland Africans, who selected senior European staff at a variety of federal institutions on whom to vent their impatience by way of intimidation and threats of dismissal. In a number of these incidents Welensky and his minister of justice took up the matter personally.[17] Reporting developments to Butler, Jones said:

> No sources of information available to us indicate a purpose on the part of the MCP to pursue any general course of action designed to molest and humiliate Federal officials. There is however on the one side an increasing impatience on the part of the MCP for the visible severance of all ties and on the other an edginess on the part of many Federal officials largely occasioned by uncertainty as to their future. These circumstances combine to make a potential source of friction which could result in sporadic incidents.[18]

Ministers and officials in the Central Africa Office, however, took a less narrow view and were troubled by much more than Jones's simple 'edginess', 'potential source of friction' and 'sporadic incidents'. They were deeply worried about the effect the incidents were having on Nyasaland's reputation and the probable damaging repercussions on staffing the civil service. Although generally concerned about retaining expatriate territorial officers after independence, their immediate anxiety was about retaining federal officers after the imminent dissolution. It was the manifest fact of intimidation and threats which disturbed individual federal officers, and they were unlikely to be comforted by the knowledge – even if they had believed it – that the MCP was not pursuing a 'general course of action designed to molest and humiliate' them. In mid-July, Duncan Watson wrote to the Governor and expressed the Central Africa Office concerns:

The real trouble is that, however slight such incidents may be in themselves, it is the image of Nyasaland which is thus built up and the repercussions of that which do the damage ... it does seem to us, sitting outside, that there is a real danger that, if the sort of thing that has been happening in recent weeks continued to happen, Nyasaland could (no matter how undeservedly) get such a reputation that very few people would be willing to serve in the territory.

If you start with very few Federal officers willing to come over (as seems to be likely), and if your own expatriates were to catch the bug [and leave under the early retirement and compensation scheme] then presumably Nyasaland would be asking us to recruit a substantial number of overseas officers on contract, if the machine were to be kept ticking over. You will realise that in that event the kind of image of the territory that was making chaps on the spot leave would also constitute a serious bar to successful recruitment here, and that we should have to be quite sure of our ground ourselves before we could genuinely and wholeheartedly press candidates to accept employment in Nyasaland ... It would be most unfortunate if Nyasaland were to develop an image which might cause the good faith of the British Government in recruiting for the territory to be brought into question.[19]

Watson said that his purpose in writing this very pointed letter to Jones was to give him ammunition which he could use in talking to Banda, 'at the right moment'. The trouble, he added, was that there was so little time left. He was, in essence, concerned about a breakdown in the machinery of government in Nyasaland before independence and the clear implications of this for the British government. Although he did not say so, he was less concerned about retaining officers after independence, because experience elsewhere suggested that sufficient would stay on.[20]

In replying some three weeks later, Jones said he appreciated the feelings prompting Watson's letter.[21] He entirely shared the views on the need to project an attractive image of Nyasaland and he agreed that the present picture painted by the press was 'indeed far from pleasant'. He would continue to take every opportunity to impress the need on Banda and he hoped Butler would do so in September (a month away) when he met the doctor in London.

The Governor was, however, chary of rocking the boat by suggesting to Banda that Britain might be reluctant to undertake recruitment for Nyasaland unless the present image was improved. No matter how tactfully such a suggestion might be deployed, he felt 'it would certainly produce the rejoinder that in that case he would look elsewhere for his needs'. Banda had recently been successful in obtaining doctors from Israel and this would reinforce the likelihood of such a rejoinder.

Jones may have thought he detected a feeling in the Central Africa Office that he and his colleagues were not being as firm with Banda as they should be. In a rare revealing of his personal feelings, he told Watson, defensively:

> In my experience of [Banda], for what it is worth, appeals to sentiment are likely to be more effective than suggestions of unpleasant consequences. Indeed, I fear that, so far as ammunition goes, threats, whether veiled or otherwise, are unlikely to produce the sort of results which we would wish ... I do hope that all people concerned with us both in the Central Africa Office and in the Department of Technical Cooperation believe that I and my official colleagues are doing the best we can to carry out HMG's policy in Nyasaland. I do not think that any of us are shirking unpleasant tasks in order to secure an easy life. But we believe that unless the security situation should get very seriously out of hand – and it would be ludicrous to suggest that this has yet happened – we should do everything possible to stay with Banda, knowing that the alternative could be a very unpleasant situation in which we should have to ask your help to get military assistance from outside.
>
> We like to think that we are showing that we are on the same side as HMG. Sometimes we wonder if this is accepted ...
>
> Please believe that I fully understand your difficulties when unpleasant (and of course highly unneccessary) incidents occur here leading to unfavourable publicity. Please believe also that these incidents cause me great personal distress because my aim is to persuade Dr. Banda and his boys that no country can achieve civilised status unless and until the Rule of Law is normally observed.

Jones concluded by saying that the general atmosphere in Nyasaland was presently 'reasonably peaceful'. He could not, however, guarantee that there would be no further incidents.

It is surprising that Jones did not use his knowledge of Banda's admiration for things British, to make the appeal to sentiment – in which he rightly placed confidence – not to turn too readily to other countries for staff. Also, Banda was not always averse to having unpleasant consequences mentioned, as Jones knew from their recent discussions on Nyasaland's finances after secession, when the doctor had been grateful for his frankness. It ought not to have been difficult to express the unpleasant consequences in terms of a genuinely helpful and sympathetic warning rather than, as Jones seemed to think, a threat. Again, it probably was the case that Whitehall officials and ministers occasionally wondered if the Governor was on their side or on Banda's. They may have found it significant that he was doing 'everything possible to stay with Banda' rather than to have Banda stay with him. It is interesting, too, that while

Watson made no mention of 'a security situation' and calling in military aid, Jones should on this occasion still use the technique so frequently used by Banda and vicariously, to a lesser extent, himself, especially since it was clear that Butler was not easily impressed by such warnings – or threats. Privately, Whitehall officials understood that Jones would inevitably appear on occasions to take the Nyasaland position rather than the British, but were clear, at least in retrospect, that 'he would never have agreed that there was any essential diference in objectives or interests – the long run criteria he would have seen as coinciding'.[22]

Concerns were not confined simply to ruffled relations between the MCP and federal officers, as a worrying incident against European civilians on 30 June, and the reactions of Jones, Banda and expatriate civil servants illustrated. On this occasion Banda attended a football match in Blantyre and his personal bodyguard, his 'Malawi police', intercepted a car and assaulted the Austrian driver and his two Portuguese passengers, a seventeen-year-old girl and a twelve-year-old boy. All three subsequently received hospital treatment. The incident was quickly linked by the press to a warning Banda had given four days earlier to 'arrogant Europeans' who would risk beatings from Malawi police if they adopted 'incorrect attitudes'.[23]

The actions of the Malawi police were a worrying recent innovation. Jones, presumably seeking to justify, and to minimize the significance of, their existence, though not their actions, explained to Butler: 'The so called Malawi Police are a body approximately 42 strong employed by the Malawi Congress Party to guard the house and person of Banda and to escort him on his travels. There are of course, in the context of African tradition and custom, numerous precedents for the attachments of such retinues to important African leaders.'[24] He explained that they did not operate under any legislative authority, enjoyed no special immunity under the law and had no legal powers not enjoyed by ordinary citizens. They wore 'a uniform of boots, black trousers with a red stripe, white jacket, shirt and tie, and a black beret'. Then, again presumably to justify and to play down the significance of this uniform, he continued: 'There is no more legal impediment to the wearing by these people of uniform than there is by a number of other bodies, including Boys' Brigade and Scouts so long as the uniform does not simulate that worn by the Nyasaland Police.' Some may have found likening the bodyguard to the retinue of traditional chiefs and their uniform to that of boy scouts offensive. It was not, of course, the retinue aspects nor the uniform which many people found objectionable but the extra-legal powers and immunities which the Malawi police did in fact enjoy. So far as the assaults in Blantyre were concerned, Jones told the secretary of state that the injuries were 'of a very minor character' and the incident 'though regrettable, unnecessary, and intensely irritating at the present time, [was] being inflated out of all proportion by persons seemingly intent on discrediting Banda'. Again, it is likely that some would have been offended by the use of the words 'very minor' in relation to teenage children receiving hospital treatment, and by the assumption that those who took exception to the violence and bullying of the Malawi police were simply intent on discrediting Banda. Jones emphasized that the incident took place without Banda's consent or – notwithstanding that the bodyguard was closely accompanying the prime minister – knowledge. He then sought to attribute the incident and, presumably, the blame for it to someone else:

> As to his reported statement on the arrogance of Europeans, this was the subject of an 'off the cuff' speech of which no authoritative record exists. It is known, however, that it immediately followed an incident in which a young European subaltern in the KAR [King's African Rifles] in a high-powered sports car displayed impatience and brusqueness in an attempt to force his way through a crowd congregated in the road to pay respects to Banda. If the youth had displayed tact a way would have been made for him through the crowd – as it was subsequently after members of the Nyasaland Police had spoken to him; the incident would not have occurred and the speech would not have been made.

The matter was not, however, to be disposed of so readily. When Jones had objected to Roberts being the director of public prosecutions as well as solicitor-general, a new director, Colonel R. F. L. Gulliver, had been appointed. He and the police were seeking statements with a view to establishing a case for prosecution against Banda's bodyguard. This presented Jones with a delicate and worrying problem. If the police were obstructed in this work it might be necessary to make arrests 'without further ado' but, since Banda's personal position in relation to the party was involved, the arrests would almost certainly provoke strong reaction from him and his followers. Jones sought to minimize Banda's responsibility by diverting blame on to the KAR subaltern and by telling the secretary of state that the doctor had to some extent been let down by his entourage. 'Rumour and emotion' were exaggerating the incident 'beyond all proportion' and, while he did not condone it, it was important to keep it in perspective. Raising yet again the security spectre he explained: 'There is a danger that if this is clumsily handled by us Banda might be provoked into renouncing any responsibility for the control of the Police. [If I had] to resume direct control of the Police and [had] to administer them over the head of the government ... a security situation might well be precipitated.'[25]

The police were hampered by Banda's entourage not cooperating with them. The doctor knew the identity of the occupants of the Land Rover in which the men involved had been travelling but 'this information [was] not forthcoming from him or others'. Jones told the secretary of state he might have to make a personal approach to Banda for the information but this would 'be disagreeable and could only be done as a last resort'.

Over a period of two days, Youens saw Banda three times and urged on him the need for the law to take its course. Eventually, Banda, 'with considerable ill-humour', acceded to the police continuing their investigations, but made it clear they could expect no help from him. These were far from comfortable meetings. Banda delivered a diatribe against the police, convinced that they had no sympathy with, or loyalty to, his regime. He dismissed as hypocrisy the advice that the rule of law should be impartially imposed: 'How impartial', he inquired, 'were you and your people in 1959 when you killed and beat up many of my people and imprisoned hundreds of us without trials?' He asserted that the present case was being blown up to delay independence. He told Youens, with great force: 'You should know that if there is any attempt to frustrate us I shall declare my own independence. If I do, Ghana and the Afro-Asian states will sponsor me before the United Nations. If need be I shall do it whatever the financial and economic results.'

Later the following day the doctor received reports through his own intelligence machine of a meeting which the senior civil servants association had held the previous evening at the Zomba club, which still further exacerbated the situation.[26] While some expatriate officers working and living in Zomba were unaware, save possibly in broad terms, of the lawlessness and the difficulties the police were experiencing in bringing prosecutions, there was widespread concern among officers in other areas for the safety of their families. The association's committee had asked Jones for an interview but this had been refused.[27] There followed a meeting of the association, in which several police officers offered to demonstrate that Youens, who addressed them, was wrong in denying that prosecutions were being forbiddden and the law not being enforced. It seems that Youens then walked out of the meeting and the association sent a cable to Butler about the breakdown of law and order, as they saw it. Banda quickly became aware, in Jones's words to Butler, of 'the hysterical nature of some of the speeches and the high emotions which they generated [on an occasion when] the bar did exceptional business before, during and after the meeting', and the doctor was 'visibly shaken that as many as 300 European civil servants [almost a fifth of the whole expatriate service] should have indulged in such a display of hysteria and high emotion'. Jones must have been irate about the incident, for these were unworthy – indeed, some would say snide, unnecessary and disloyal

– remarks for the Governor to make, even in private, about the representative organization of his compatriate civil service. It must have escaped his memory that less than a year earlier he had pleaded with Banda that they both 'must repose [their] trust and confidence' in the civil service, against whom they 'should not ... make any damaging statement either in public or in private'.[28]

Jones suggested that the secretary of state should reply to the cable, saying the Governor, Banda and Butler himself had stated that law and order would be preserved and it was their intention to promote confidence and harmony between the races, an intention that would depend to a significant extent on the degree of understanding and goodwill which the civil servants themselves were able to demonstrate. He also suggested that Butler should indicate that he was not unmindful of the concern which prompted the telegram but it was vital that the expatriate civil service's conduct should be above criticism and therefore he hoped they would in future forward their views through the Governor 'in accordance with the normal procedure'.[29] It is likely that Jones was distressed and angered by the implication that the civil service association, in communicating directly with Butler, lacked confidence in himself and this may account for his lapse in using unworthy language regarding them. He may have been embarrassed, too, that notwithstanding his, Banda's and Butler's statements that law and order would be preserved, it manifestly was not being preserved, and possibly some of the chickens were coming home to roost two years after his first instructions that a blind eye be turned to some breaches of the law so as not to rock the political boat.

The following Sunday afternoon Banda made a public speech at a meeting of 8000 people in Zomba.[30] To Jones's relief the crowd was calm and peaceful and treated the small number of Europeans present in a friendly way. In dealing with Europeans Banda said:

> It was his belief that there were still a few Europeans ... who felt that they might induce a feeling of hysteria among Europeans and Asians which would lead Welensky to send troops to Nyasaland and thus delay the territory's independence ... he was convinced that the great majority of Europeans in Nyasaland were supporters of his government and he therefore impressed on those present the need for peace and calm. No-one was to be attacked or cursed, not even stooges.

He said he was satisfied that neither Butler nor Jones wished to impede Nyasaland's progress to independence and repeated that if any attempts were made to impede it he would declare Nyasaland independent and 'damn the consequences'.

For some time Jones had been urging Banda to absorb his bodyguard, the Malawi police, into the Nyasaland police. Now, although he would not do it while the heat was on them, the doctor told him that at a suitable moment he would do so. Jones regretted he could not use this in order to allay anxieties, but he was clear that the move when it came had to to be seen as Banda's own decision.[31] It is unlikely that it would have allayed many anxieties – since senior police officers were aware that the Malawi police 'did commit [even] vicious murders but arrest and prosecution were vetoed'[32] – but it would certainly have increased many more, especially in the police, where it could be seen as a politicization of the force and a bypassing of the normal channels of recruitment. In fact Banda never did incorporate his guard into the police.

The police difficulties in preparing a case for prosecuting members of the bodyguard were increased when the father of the assaulted teenagers, presumably fearful of the consequences, would not allow them to give evidence. Short of issuing a subpoena, only the Austrian driver, who was asked by the Austrian consul not to get involved, was left as a witness, but he was unable to identify the malefactors. Consequently, when the case file was submitted to the DPP, he decided that no prosecution should be brought. This decision could have done nothing to allay expatriate fears. Jones told the secretary of state that 'the outcome of the case might have been different had the Malawi party been more cooperative'.[33]

The attack on the three Europeans was not an isolated case, for the number of assaults at this time led to questions in the Commons. All these assaults, the Governor reported, were caused by the MCP or LMY against political opponents except for three cases: the three Europeans; the case of a Coloured who was beaten up after he had sought an interview with Banda, allegedly by members of the bodyguard in plain clothes who again could not be identified; and, as Jones belatedly revealed, a case two months previously when an African driver and two Asian schoolchildren were 'slapped' by the bodyguard because they failed to stop when Banda was passing. There was also a case in which a teenage English schoolgirl was in the garden of her father's house when Banda's motorcade passed. The girl was wearing a long T-shirt which covered her shorts, and the bodyguard took exception to this form of dress, broke away from the convoy, dragged the girl into her house and insisted that she leave the country within forty-eight hours. Her father, a civil servant, left soon after this incident.[34] There were other non-African cases reported to Jones by his Special Branch but since no complaints were made no action was taken. 'Some of these [had] the ring of truth, others [were] of doubtful validity but none of them involve[d] death or serious injury.'[35] This last remark gives the impression that attaching importance to an incident depended on whether death or serious injury had been caused. He no doubt made it because he was aware that the death or serious injury of a European or Asian, or possibly a Coloured, would have provoked such a reaction in Britain and elsewhere as fundamentally to question the way in which Nyasaland was being governed. The senior police officer investigating the Coloured's case reported how

> he was told to meet the bodyguard at a certain location, and at the appointed time and place he arrived. The bodyguard insisted that they drive his car and, explaining that they did not want him to see where they were heading, blindfolded him. Somewhere on the slopes of Mount Soche, they stopped, bundled him out and beat him up very seriously. A crime docket was opened and the investigation reached a stage where arrest warrants could be issued. It was a strong case with evidence sufficient to prosecute. Because the case involved Banda's bodyguard, it was submitted for scrutiny in Zomba, with the result that we were told to drop it. This instruction came from the Commissioner of Police.[36]

The pot in which this unfortunate brew was dangerously simmering was further stirred in the meeting of the legislature two days after Banda's public address in Zomba.[37] One of the MCP members proposed a motion deploring 'recent attempts to fabricate stories about the breakdown of law and order' designed to slow down progress to independence. Most of the African members criticized Europeans, especially civil servants, and the ministers did so in 'most vehement' terms, with Yatuta Chisiza (using such expressions as 'super-hypercritical, treacherous, dangerous and treasonous'), Chiume ('rude and rotten', 'rascals and dangerous characters') and Chipembere ('these robbers and confirmed buffoons', 'unprincipled robbers', 'mentally and emotionally retarded') being particularly vituperative. They all expressed 'the most fervent and emotional support for the Prime Minister'. They attacked the press, the civil servants who had cabled the secretary of state, the 'settler Europeans' and Welensky. Banda 'made much of the fact that no protest meetings, no telegrams to the Secretary of State and no press sympathy were noticeable at the time when he and his supporters were being knocked about in 1960 and 1961 [sic].' The enormities of the security forces and the civil servants were dwelt upon. The assault by the bodyguard on the three Europeans was not denied, but was reduced to insignificant proportions by being compared to other, much more serious, incidents occurring throughout the world and attracting less comment.

Nevertheless, Jones told Butler, despite the 'highly charged atmosphere', Banda's speech had much to commend it. The doctor repeated a number of the helpful things he had said publicly the previous Sunday about his confidence in Butler and Jones; about most Europeans supporting him, if only out of self-interest; and about observing peace and calm, not being violent and not taking reprisals against those who had cabled the secretary of state. Jones hoped the debate would not increase racial tension which indeed did seem to him to relax in the following day or so. He was fearful, however, that in letting off 'a good deal of steam', many unfortunate phrases were uttered that could be used against the speakers by a hostile press.[38]

Butler was not reassured. He was most gravely concerned about the adverse publicity Nyasaland was receiving in the British press, based mainly on 'the excesses of Malawi Youth and other extremists and the childishly intemperate pronouncements by Ministers'. Greenfield, federal minister of law, delivered a major speech in the federal assembly at the end of July on the erosion of the rule of law in Nyasaland, which he claimed would soon cease to be operative. He gave wide circulation to a pamphlet reiterating his claims. The Nyasaland government issued a rejoinder, and the exchanges became acrimonious.[39] Banda was indignant but took Jones's advice that he 'adopt a detached view of the matter'. Jones believed Greenfield's outbursts resulted from bitter disappointment over the impending dissolution of the Federation which caused him to suffer from 'a somewhat acute form of emotional disturbance'. Neither side came out of the exchanges with improved reputations.

Watson's warnings to Jones had had no effect, Nyasaland's reputation was very seriously endangered and the secretary of state personally pursued the matter.[40] He thought it only right to draw clearly to Jones's notice how a 'profoundly unfavourable image of Nyasaland' was steadily being built up, and – not confining himself to the more diplomatic phraseology of his officials – he did so in a frankly expressed and pointedly critical telegram of 16 August:

> Anxiety is being shown not only in the press but in Parliament and in numerous letters coming in from MPs and others. [The] basic misgivings concern dictatorial tendencies, [the] workings of [the] judicial system, and [the] maintenance of law and order. Critics not infrequently ask how we can contemplate independence for a country in this palpably immature and unstable condition. Moreover, the current tomfoolery about 'Messianism' etc, is creating for Banda a mixture of ridicule and contempt not merely in average European opinion but in more mature African opinion.

He acknowledged that those who were closely concerned appreciated the 'valuable qualities and generally sound intentions of Malawi Ministers' and could see in perspective many of the unfortunate incidents or statements as mere 'blowing off of steam' which would 'work itself out in due course'. The general public, however, and many well-informed and influential observers took a different view and it was becoming increasingly difficult for him and his colleaguesus effectively to counter

1. ABOVE. Agnes, Glyn, Nesta and Gwilym Jones, 1919.
2. BELOW. King's School Boat Crew, 1925. (Jones front row, left.)

3. Oxford, 1930.

4. Barotseland, 1950.

5. ABOVE. Northern Rhodesia, Provinical Commissioners, 1958. (Jones back row, second from right.)

6. RIGHT. Governor of Nyasaland, 1961.

7. ABOVE. Executive Council, Nyasaland, October 1961. (A. Bwanausi missing.)
8. BELOW. Lord Alport, Sir Evelyn Hone and Sir Glyn Jones, 1963.

9. Sir Glyn Jones, relaxing outdoors.

10. Sir Glyn Jones, relaxing indoors.

11. LEFT. London, 1963.

12. BELOW. Prime Minister and Governor, July 1964.

13. Sir Glyn Jones and the Duke of Edinburgh, Independence Day, 1964.

14. Sir Glyn and Lady Jones in Government House Grounds, Zomba.

15. LEFT. Departure from Malawi, July 1966.

16. BELOW. Sir Glyn and Lady Jones, 1992.

their 'sharp criticism'. They could shrug off the various incidents in isolation but the cumulative impression was 'getting definitely tiresome'. 'You will best be able to judge how far Messrs Banda and Co. are capable of hoisting aboard this side of the picture (i.e. the way they are damaging not merely their reputation but their economic prospects through intemperate excitement and allowing power to go to their heads); but certainly if they could hoist a little more and a little further it would be incalculably helpful.'

In this frank telegram, Butler seems to be indicating that he was tiring of Jones always justifying and playing down the severely damaging excesses of Banda and his leading followers. Perhaps he was wondering whether such appeasement as may have been shown over the past few years had yielded the results hoped for, or had made matters worse. He illustrated his concerns with clear examples of the sort of statements and actions by Banda and his ministers which concerned him. He instanced worries about the judicial system with examples of vindictive sentences for trivial 'offences' such as using insulting language against Banda and refusing to buy MCP membership cards. Although he did not say so, Butler's underlying concern was basically political. He had long since passed the point where independence could be denied or much delayed, and yet his critics repeatedly asked how he could possibly think of granting independence to such an immature and unstable country. For a man hoping to be Britain's next prime minister this was not a comfortable dilemma to be in. Jones, as Governor, must have had similar concerns.

In a letter, written the same day as he sent the telegram, Butler said quite frankly that Nyasaland's image was not being improved by the way the local courts were dealing with paternity cases against Europeans nor by the steps taken to clear the way for Banda's car as he drove around the country. These were matters about which he wanted to talk to Jones to seek advice on 'the extent to which and the manner in which [he] ought to raise these questions with Dr Banda himself'.[41]

In reply the Governor said he was pleased that the secretary of state contemplated talking to Banda.[42] Unusually, he did not warn him that by tackling Banda frankly on an issue such as this, which implied criticism of him and his party, they might 'lose ground' with the doctor, dangerously upset him and necessitate the bringing in of military forces from outside. He thought Banda took these things too lightly and was too inclined to talk about his 'thick skin' indifference to what the press said about him. He had done his best, he said, during the past month to impress on Banda that he could not both ignore the bad impression he was making and at the same time ask people for financial and staffing aid. The most Jones had been able to get out of him was that he would refuse to see the press when he was in England, at least until the

Governor himself arrived. Jones saw this as some, but presumably not a great deal of, comfort, because Banda was 'very bad at press conferences and interviews and invariably [lost] his temper'.

Jones then turned to the law obliging all vehicles and people to stop and get off the road whenever Banda's car with its retinue of Malawi police bodyguards passed. Surprisingly, he said, this was not creating much feeling locally. Indeed, the fact that the motorcade was now always led and followed by a Nyasaland police escort vehicle had 'pleased everyone'. The absence of local feeling to which he referred must have been in relation to the law being passed and not to the fact of being forced to get off the road, which continued to cause widespread resentment and considerable fear among all races. To Jones the worst feature of this law was the ridicule which it was inspiring in the press.

He concluded his reply to Butler's telegram with what amounted to an apologia:

> Although of course I use what influence I have to urge moderation, you will appreciate that we are not in a position to dictate or control what Chipembere, Chirwa and other similar African nationalists may say in the legislature or on the public platform. Their speeches are of a type, neither worse nor better, for which numerous precedents may be found in virtually every African state which has emerged into independence under British rule. It would, I suggest, be naive to expect anything else, particularly in such cases as that of Chipembere who was interned by the colonial government under emergency regulations without trial for some eighteen months and later imprisoned for a further two years for sedition. What however we could reasonably expect is that attention should also be given to the more reassuring side of the local picture ... Moreover, if the speeches of local politicians are to be given extensive publicity overseas, why must that publicity be confined to the wilder aspects of their utterances to the total exclusion of the more reassuring statements which they make?

So far as Nyasaland's general image was concerned, Jones accused *The Times* in particular but also a number of other newspapers, of taking on their face value the reports of local correspondents. 'If attention is to be focused on us, then surely it is reasonable that the whole picture should be painted, not just the black spots.'

There are a number of intriguing aspects of this letter. In effect, Jones seems to be pleading his own impotence, the naïvety of others and the bias of the press. He seems to be critical of the actions of his predecessor and to be implying that Chipembere's incarcerations were wrong or unnecessary. Again, he may have considered it reasonable to expect the press to cover the more reassuring aspects of Nyasaland's activities, but reasonableness is not the same as realism, and he seems himself to display a naive appreciation of the role and character of the press.

The Governor felt the press was focusing far too much attention on the 'black spots'. Yet the 'black spots' of any situation could, naturally, be sufficiently worrying as genuinely to cast an obscuring shadow over praiseworthy aspects. Perhaps the press thought one should be able to take for granted that a government would ensure the rule of law, and that when they did not this failure should be highlighted.

The 'black spots' – threats to the rule of law and to the protection of persons and possessions, the prevention of violence and injustice and the path which it seemed to him Nyasaland was taking – deeply disturbed the chief justice, Unsworth, at this time, the middle months of 1963. He had discussed judicial matters with the Governor from time to time, and a week after Jones returned from leave, he wrote to him about his 'growing concerns for the future of the judiciary in Nyasaland'.[43] He asked that the contents of his letter be conveyed to Butler, and he recommended that a commission of inquiry into the local courts be established. The grounds of his concern were fourfold: the speed with which the government was seeking to implement a new judicial policy, the jurisdiction and composition of the local courts, the system of government being introduced and the increasing interference with the judiciary. These were worries not dissimilar from those expressed by Butler: the workings of the judicial system, Banda's dictatorial tendencies and the maintenance of law and order.

First, the chief justice was disturbed by the withdrawal of judicial powers from administrative officers, not because of withdrawal in itself, for this had much to commend it provided, as was not the case, they were replaced by trained and impartial people. Second, Unsworth turned to the local courts whose jurisdiction had recently been increased to cover cases previously tried only by professionally trained magistrates or by administrative officers of considerable judicial experience. In his view the local courts were not suitable for the exercise of this jurisdiction. 'The appointments are political and the members are inexperienced and incompetent.' In respect of this last point, a local court commissioner recalled:

> Orton Chirwa himself would come to each local court and announce the names of the new local court president and clerk at a public meeting. These of course were nominees of the local MCP. Chirwa himself no doubt influenced the choice but I know that some appointments were made in spite of his being aware that the chap was quite unsuitable ... illiterate and quite untrainable ... Presidents who listened to some trumped up charge against someone who failed to join the MCP [which

was not an offence] and found the man not guilty, were certainly liable to find they were no longer president, and the clerks who advised their presidents 'wrongly' were equally very quickly vulnerable.[44]

Next in his letter to Jones, Unsworth dealt with the system of government which was being introduced:

> It is apparent ... that the Malawi Congress Party are seeking to govern direct rather than through the normal constitutional channels ... There were a number of cases recently where ... Dr. Banda tried to intervene and has criticized the decisions on the ground that the [offenders, members of the LMY] were acting on the instructions of the Party ... I do not think that an independent judiciary could survive under a system of this kind and there are already indications of ministerial interference.

Further, he did not think the constitutional provisions relating to the judiciary would be effective after independence and he based this view on discussions with Banda and Chirwa, the minister of justice. These were 'stormy meetings and the Chief Justice did not mince his words'.[45] Finally, he was not prepared to continue responsibility for the administration of the judiciary after independence. In the meantime he would do his best, unless circumstances arose which left him with no alternative but to resign.

Three weeks after receiving this letter Jones forwarded it to Butler. He told the secretary of state that much of what Unsworth said was 'undoubtedly true' – indeed, he made no attempt to argue that any of it was untrue – and he had 'the very greatest sympathy' with him in the 'most embarrassing position' in which he found himself.[46] He explained that the aim of Banda's policy was to effect a break with the 'colonialist past' and establish a judiciary divorced from the administration, and operated by judicial officers acceptable to the people. Banda argued that it was essential for those holding judicial office to have direct knowledge of the thought processes and background of the people within their jurisdiction. Jones did not comment that this was precisely what the chiefs' courts had done but had now been replaced by political appointees, and he presented the position as people being judged by their peers. He confessed to not being able to dissent from Unsworth's view that Banda intended, as soon as he was able, to establish a one-party state and to rule direct as a party.

> In this context, a cause for present concern is the policy being adopted with regard to prosecutions. The dictum that the direction of public prosecutions should have regard to general considerations of public policy is, of course, written into the constitution. It seems apparent however that the Government is increasingly intent on equating public policy with

party interest ... It is possible therefore that even before independence we may have trouble, and the Chief Justice has told me that there are limits beyond which he is not prepared to go in cooperating with the present regime.

He did not think there was anything he could profitably ask Butler to do at this stage. He would himself do all he could to ensure that Banda and Chirwa did not make things too embarrassing for the chief justice, and he would try to bring home to Chirwa (he did not say also to Banda) 'the vital need to ensure that the Rule of Law [was] impartially imposed'.

During October, about four months after Jones sent him a copy of Unsworth's letter, and five months after it was written, the secretary of state wrote to the chief justice. The delay was not explained.

> I have considered with great care your proposal that a Commission of Inquiry should be appointed to examine the administration of justice in the Local Courts, and I can well understand the reasons which have prompted this. I have reached the conclusion, however, that, certainly at the present time, the advantages to be gained would be outweighed by the very grave political dangers which would certainly be incurred. The same would apply, in my view, to any present proposals to alter the jurisdiction of the Local Courts.
>
> With this in mind, and having regard to the Governor's advice that the working of the Local Courts is now improving, rather than deteriorating, I think that the wisest course for the time being will be simply to continue to keep a careful watch on the situation.[47]

Unsworth, especially after such a long delay, could hardly have found this a reassuring response to his concerns.

The brunt of the difficulties over lawlessness was borne by police officers, though those in other departments also felt that they were letting down the people of Nyasaland.[48] There may have been a feeling in the very top levels of government that some of the police officers were reactionary, disapproved of the effects of constitutional advances and were concerned about their personal careers. To apply this explanation to more than a very few officers would have been an error. What concerned most of them was the requirement that they should ignore offences when committed by MCP officials and members, especially the Malawi police who committed 'many near atrocities' and frequent serious assaults about which the police were repeatedly told to take no action.[49] Many of these officers had long experience in the police both in Nyasaland and in other countries, including Britain. They were required under the law to prevent and detect crime, apprehend offenders, preserve law and order, and protect property.[50] Their whole tradition and training was to fulfil these obligations regardless of the political or other allegience of the perpetrators. It was a tradition of which they were rightly proud, and was in accordance with Butler's words at the Marlborough House conference – which were given wide publicity – that officers 'within the framework of policy determined by Ministers ... are expected, without fear or favour, to perform their duties honestly and conscientiously'.[51] Butler publicly assumed that this was common ground, but in fact it conflicted directly with the Governor's policy of not rocking the boat, a policy which was probably pushed further by the commissioner of police and his most senior colleagues than Jones intended or hoped would be necessary. Like other officials who lived and worked outside the few larger urban centres, police officers were apprehensive for the safety of their wives and families, but they bore the additional professional burden of being required to ignore their fundamental duties. The matter was far worse than not being able to secure permission to prosecute cases which they had investigated, since they were on many occasions directed not to take even the preliminary steps in investigation, when the suspect was a member of the MCP, such as holding identification parades.[52] The penalty for resisting these directions was immediate compulsory retirement[53] or instant transfer to uncongenial posts.[54] For many the matter culminated in June 1963 when the commissioner of police held a meeting of all senior officers, presumably with Jones's approval:

> He told us flatly that no action was to be taken against party officials without express authority of Dr Banda. He said we were to lean over backwards to accommodate these people – his words. He acknowledged that these were difficult times and it might appear that the rule of law and order was being flouted, but said that this was the way it had to be ... We walked out in dismay and disgust.[55]

Many took the earliest opportunity to retire voluntarily and thereafter had sucessful careers in a variety of professions. In just a few cases, the scars of their experience lasted through the remainder of their lives.

Banda was scheduled to leave Malawi in August to visit Europe and the USA, and Jones was anxious to ensure that there was no continued widespread lawlessness during his absence. This was a most important matter for the Governor, not only in its own right but also because in Banda's absence responsibility for law and order reverted to himself unless he delegated it to another minister – to which Banda was unlikely to agree. If there were a breakdown he would be unable to appeal to Banda to tell his people to behave themselves. If things went radically wrong, outside forces might be needed to quell the troubles. He could well undo much of the progress made over the past two and a half years.

Such was the importance of maintaining law and order during Banda's absence that Jones wrote him a letter which was both pleading and flattering in its tone and phraseology, was heavily qualified so as to avoid any possibility of causing offence, but very clearly made the point that it was important to Jones that Banda should intervene to pre-empt the likelihood of disturbances.[56] He thought that of all the matters to be arranged before the prime minister left, this one needed special consideration. Banda, due to leave less than two weeks later and not wanting trouble in his absence, did as Jones asked. In a speech on 11 August at the inauguration of the Young Pioneers Movement, he made it clear that he wished the people to behave themselves while he was away.[57]

In the three weeks before Banda's departure Jones had a series of meetings with him to deal with a number of the issues which had exercised them over recent months, particularly, as we have just seen, the maintenance of law and order, but also powers of restriction, and independence.[58]

Jones was much disturbed by proposed legislation to restrict the movement of people known to be a danger to law and order but against whom a conviction could not be obtained under the ordinary law. He had seen the legislation in draft and been dismayed. He told Banda he did not wish to be hypocritical, and admitted that similar legislation had frequently been used by colonial governments in the past. Nevertheless, the old Nyasaland government, warmly supported by Banda, had repealed the legislation. It was clear that at present Banda had very little to fear from opposition movements. 'Why then run the risk of incurring hostile criticism by reintroducing legislation of a kind which he had always inveighed against in the past?'

Banda explained that all he wished was to get the legislation back on the statute book and 'of course it would be his intention to use it very sparingly, if at all'. His prime reason for this, he claimed, was to deal with a particularly difficult person, whom he named, against whom the police had been unable to obtain convictions. Jones undertook to talk with the commissioner of police to see if it was possible to take conventional action to restrain the man's activities. The prime minister then said he would not for the time being introduce the legislation.

At another meeting Banda raised two important points about independence. First, he had changed his mind about moving straight to republican status on independence. This had been an idea suggested to him by Blackwood which they had jointly put to the secretary of state without either of them consulting Jones. The idea had initially attracted Banda but he had later concluded that it would be better to delay republican status for 'a period of six or even nine or twelve months' during which period the country would have a Governor-General. He also changed his mind on the date for independence. Initially he had asked for 3 March 1964 – and warned of serious trouble if this were not granted – but he now wanted to 'go all out for' 6 July 1964. He asked Jones to secure Butler's agreement to this date before he, Banda, left Nyasaland for London. The Governor persuaded him to 'hold his horses' because it would be unfair on the secretary of state to ask him to give a definite decision without having been able to discuss it with Banda when he saw him in September.[59]

Banda's overseas tour from late August to mid-October 1963 took him to Ghana, Nigeria, Liberia, Germany, Britain and the USA. These visits were in most cases personal and were arranged privately. He was accompanied by Tembo, Cecilia Kadzamira and her sister, Mary. Most of the governments he visited knew little or nothing of his plans or the reason for the visits.[60]

The doctor's main purpose in going to London, where he was joined by Jones, was to settle the date for independence. He wanted this agreed and announced before he went on to the USA. Butler had been briefed by his officials that the date for independence in July 1964 should be made conditional on the satisfactory resolution of Nyasaland's financial problems. 'The financial card is the only one remaining in our hands and it should not be thrown away at this stage. On the other hand it does not seem feasible politically to use it in so direct a way.'[61]

Butler, in speaking with Banda on 23 September, said that of the two dates mentioned, March and July 1964, the British government preferred the latter. If Banda agreed, he would put that date to his colleagues that evening and confirm it the next day. Such firm progress induced Banda to say, as he had told Jones, he wished independence to be on 6 July and to move to republican status six to twelve months later. When Butler, toying with the 'financial card', asked if he could agree to a later date, Banda replied that he could not and any postponement beyond that date would involve his resignation. As for republican status, the secretary of state said some of his colleagues favoured this coinciding with independence although he personally preferred a period as a monarchy.[62]

Save that it was connected to the date of independence, Butler was more interested in Nyasaland's financial position. At their second meeting on 23 September Jones said his May discussions with Banda had been full and frank and he had received the greatest understanding and cooperation from him and his cabinet: 'the Nyasaland government and Dr. Banda in particular had faced up honestly and responsibly to their very serious financial problems.' They had agreed to make 'substantial economies so that Nyasaland could become independent not only politically but also financially in the shortest possible time' by retrenching services and increasing revenue and productivity.[63]

So anxious was Butler to maintain the momentum and increase the pressure on the Nyasaland cabinet to effect further economies, that he asked if Banda could retain Phillips as minister of finance until independence. 'What had been achieved was very encouraging but there was much difficulty ahead and he thought this would help everyone.' Banda had originally planned to replace Phillips in April but he now agreed to him staying until independence. Thereafter he planned to keep Phillips or Norman-Walker or someone else as a financial adviser. He had earlier told Jones that at independence he would have to have an African minister of finance but, since Tembo was comparatively inexperienced, it would be necessary to have a financial adviser.[64]

While in London in September, Jones was asked by Poynton if he would accept the governorship of British Guiana. On his return to Nyasaland, he discussed the offer with his wife and daughter, and although he generally felt that if asked to do a job he should do it, on this occasion he declined. He told Poynton that although the post would present a great challenge, he would very much like to stay in Nyasaland at least until independence and possibly thereafter, if he were wanted, as Governor-General. He thought it would be unfair on Nyasaland if both he and Foster left at about the same time. Although the country was proceeding reasonably peacefully towards independence there were still many problems needing the advice of someone at the top 'who is familiar with the conditions and people, and leaders of the country'. A few days later, he directly asked Watson to pursue the possibility of his becoming Governor-General. In the middle of November the Queen approved the extension of his term of office as Governor until 5 July 1964.[65]

November 1963 was generally a quiet month but in December the inteligence committee reported 'a disturbing manifestation of pre-election violence'. During the lead up to the previous general election in 1961 there had been similar politically motivated, but less violent, disturbances. Now the troubles focused on the main opposition party, Mbadwa, and were deeply worrying. Early in December Mbadwa announced they would contest all seats in the forthcoming general election. A few days later a petrol bomb destroyed the Blantyre house of Pondeponde, for many years a leading member of Congress. He had taken no active part in politics since 1961 but recently had been named, against his will, as Mbadwa's shadow parliamentary secretary. On 16 December Chief Chikowi – an able and outspoken chief who had for many years shown great loyalty to the colonial government but who had recently been deprived of his chiefdomship by the government – and a member of Mbadwa travelling with him were assaulted and the chief's car was badly damaged. The next day the Lilongwe house of another Mbadwa member was burned down, and that same night Kumbikano, a former African federal MP, was grievously assaulted with an axe and hospitalized with severe head wounds. There were attacks on individuals in the Port Herald area led, it was alleged, by the local member of the legislature, Chakuamba. Just before Christmas Pondeponde was attacked, had his skull fractured and died. His body was dumped at the entrance to the chief justice's official residence. Unsworth and Pondeponde both regularly attended the same Roman Catholic church in Blantyre. Two days after Christmas the house, maize mill and two cars belonging to a member of Mbadwa in Mlanje were severely damaged. On 28 December the house of yet another Mbadwa member was seriously damaged in Chikwawa.[66]

In every one of these cases, where evidence was available, the crimes were carried out by 'gangs of young men allegedly members of the League of Malawi Youth'. Jones saw them as part of a planned policy to prevent any African opposition party from contesting seats in the May election. There were reports of 'special action squads' of the LMY being formed to carry out the violent incidents in the belief that they had the tacit approval of the MCP. By early January the leaders of Mbadwa had left Nyasaland and were staying in Salisbury and Lusaka.[67]

Jones, who did not believe Banda to be a party to the incidents, told him on the last day of 1963 of his 'anxiety at this turn of affairs'.[68] As he recorded:

> I drew Dr. Banda's attention to the murder of Pondeponde and [another murder which arose from an LMY attack on a church congregation when demanding the purchase of MCP membership cards.] These and other incidents appeared to be caused by hooligans who were not obeying the Prime Minister's instructions for the observation of peace and calm. My information was that Dr. Banda still commanded 99% support throughout the territory and there was no need for his political opponents to be the subject of physical attack ... I asked him to speak to his party leaders to get them to do all that they could to put an end to violence and intimidation, and also to make another plea at some convenient time for people to observe peace and calm and to give no trouble to political opponents.
>
> Dr. Banda said that he could not understand why Pondeponde had been chosen for assassination as he was a very lowly member of the opposition and if the killing had been the work of any MCP member he would have expected the attack to be made on a much more prominent member of the opposition. However, he agreed to ... speak to his party leaders and make another appeal for peace and calm at some convenient opportunity.[69]

The police made very little progress with the Pondeponde case and were unable to gather any information which might lead to a prosecution. By February Jones felt their chances of making any further progress were remote.[70] No prosecution was made in respect of this murder.

The intelligence committee's reference to pre-election violence was accurate, and with the opening on 30 December of registrations for the forthcoming general election the country entered upon a further and particularly disturbing period of political violence. Already there had been two brutal murders and a worrying number of other cases of severe violence. During the early stages of registration there were incidents where members of parties in opposition to the MCP were prevented from registering. There were at least two more petrol-bomb attacks. Jones drew Banda's attention to these cases and the doctor reminded all those concerned that everyone should be allowed to register. Although he thought this reminder proved effective, Jones told Sandys – who, as commonwealth and colonial secretary, had resumed responsibility for Nyasaland affairs at the end of 1963 when the Central Africa Office closed – that as registration proceeded attacks on Jehovah's Witnesses increased. He explained that this sect had always been a problem and their behaviour exasperating to government. Although they refused to register on principle, there could be no excuse for 'the considerable number of incidents which took place'.[71]

> As time went on the number of incidents multiplied. They took the form of bands of young thugs usually identified with the Malawi Party going about slashing crops, burning houses, assaulting and threatening people, mainly Jehovah's Witnesses because they decline to register as voters. By the close of the [three week] period of registration on 19th January there had been some 420 such incidents reported to the police, including two more violent deaths.
>
> During the registration period, 1.9 million adults registered. This was an impressive response from a population of about three million.
>
> The period was marred, however, by the occurrence ... of an extraordinarily large number of incidents of a political nature. The incidents chiefly concerned, on the one side, groups of men and youths who appear to consider that they are interpreting government policy and, on the other, members of opposition parties and religious organisations. Some of the incidents involving members of opposition parties occured because they endeavoured to register, whereas the incidents involving members of a religious organisation, which were far greater in number, were because they failed or refused to register.
>
> Police are unfortunately receiving little cooperation from local people in investigating these incidents and indeed in some incidences ... are meeting with obstruction even from persons in responsible positions. [72]

Jones hoped that with the close of registration and thereby the removal of the cause of the incidents of violence, as he saw it, the country would quieten down, but this was not to be. In the last two weeks of January 1964 there were a further 369 reported cases of violence, mainly concerned with refusals to register, bringing the total for January to 789. Undoubtedly there were large numbers not reported. Jehovah's Witnesses were still the main targets of attack and although most were 'comparatively minor assaults and damage to property and growing crops' there was a sufficient number of serious cases, including murders, to cause the Governor considerable concern. Banda's recent visit to the Central Province had not resulted in any fall in offences.[73]

Jones was right to be considerably concerned. Although he never mentioned it, the royal instructions, coupled with his oaths of office, required him to the utmost of his power especially to take care to protect the inhabitants of Nyasaland in their persons and the free enjoyment of their possessions and by all lawful means to prevent and restrain all violence and injustice which might be practised or attempted against them. Clearly, over the past several years many Nyasaland inhabitants had not been protected in these ways, and in large numbers they were certainly not being protected now. Jones may have felt that his 'power', politically and prudentially, was insufficient to comply with the first part of these instructions – the protection of persons and property – but the 'lawful means', the legal powers, at his disposal were certainly available to comply with the second part – the prevention of violence and injustice. The instructions to the Governor had been designed for an age which had passed, but they remained a requirement, under oath, until the end of the colonial period.

The police kept Banda fully informed of what was happening. At the same time he received information from party sources which told him that 'general peace and calm prevailed'. When the Governor spoke with him at the end of January, the doctor admitted that there were assaults and destruction of crops but claimed the complaints were grossly exaggerated and in some cases fabricated. He had no objection to people refusing to register as a matter of religious principle but he did object to them persuading others who had registered to destroy their registration certificates; this was provocative, was anti-social and incensed local people. Jones told the secretary of state that he accepted there was some provocation but not nearly as much as Banda claimed and it certainly did not justify the many incidents that were occurring.[74]

The violence caused the Governor 'very serious disquiet indeed', and he followed up his late January meeting with Banda by another pleading letter written in flattering terms on 8 February:

> I know that this situation must be disturbing to you and you will understand how embarrassing it is both for the Secretary of State and for

myself, who have all along tried to give you every assistance in your march towards self-government and independence ... My object in writing this letter to you is to urge you once again to instruct your leaders throughout the country to ensure that peace and calm are maintained and that violence shall cease. I know well that your word is law in this country because of the respect in which you are held by the great majority of the people.[75]

Despite his protestations of exaggeration and fabrication in reports of violent breaches of the law, Banda took two steps following the talk he had with the Governor and the letter which he received from him.

First, he agreed to meet with Jerker Johannsen, the European representative of the Jehovah's Witnesses, and to tell him that if his adherents stopped being provocative he would ensure that his followers observed his instructions for peace and calm. Banda met Johannsen early in February, and while he did not receive much comfort, Johannsen was impressed by the doctor's sincerity and reasonableness. Although not a great success, Jones thought the meeting played a part in Banda sending instructions to all LMY groups that 'they must cease taking violent action against religious sects and opposition groups'. But, as Jones told Sandys, 'Unfortunately this lawlessness had been allowed to continue too long and it took time to subside completely.'[76]

Second, a fortnight after Jones's written plea and nearly two months after his oral request that Banda 'at some convenient time' appeal for peace and calm, the doctor addressed a large public meeting in Zomba, on 23 February, and said there should be no trouble for anyone, including Jehovah's Witnesses. This statement was given wide publicity in the media – there was a supportive editorial in the *Malawi News*. By this time the registration period was over and nomination day very close. Though from that point onwards violence began to decline, Banda's appeal was of limited effectiveness.

The intelligence committee's report for February made sorry reading. Particularly in the Mlanje district, where 80 per cent of the Southern Province offences occurred, gangs were slow to respond to the prime minister's instructions. The response of local party officials 'varied considerably'. In some cases the instructions were not obeyed and in other cases their colleagues, 'by contrary advice and activities, frustrated their efforts'.[77] Having given details of the number and distribution of politically motivated crimes, the report went on to say:

> On 19 February, Mr. Aleke Banda addressed gatherings [in the Dowa district] ... the people addressed understood him to indicate that they should carry on damaging the crops and taking offensive action against 'Capricorns' and Jehovah's Witnesses and that by doing so these people

must learn that the MCP demands cooperation. A particularly savage murder occurred in the Mponela area of the Dowa district on 19 February 1964 when a gang of youths ordered three families of Jehovah's Witnesses to leave the area. All the families left with the exception of three men who were not prepared to move. They were attacked in daylight by youths who hacked them to death with pangas. On 21 February ... in the Mlanje district a Jehovah's Witness was trussed up by youths and ... buried up to his neck. He was rescued by the village headman before his face was covered with earth.[78]

The report was, however, careful to point out that the prime minister's 'authoritative call' to cease violence, followed by the helpful editorial in the *Malawi News*, 'appeared by the end of the month to be effective in reducing the number of incidents in all areas'. This was the first monthly intelligence report which Banda had seen. The committee compiling the report, from this time onwards, used it not only to bring to his attention the degree and detail of violence prevailing, including reports about some of his most senior colleagues, but also to encourage his condemnation of the violence by praising the effectiveness of his appeals. It was a new experience for Banda to be officially confronted with details of the violence and the part played in it by senior leaders of the MCP. He was the only African to see these reports and although he was free to pass them on to his cabinet colleagues he did not do so.[79]

In the early days of February, Jones had told the secretary of state that in his view an instruction from Banda to observe peace and calm and to desist from violence would be 'completely effective'.[80] Nevertheless, in addition to the 789 cases reported in January, there were a further 1263 cases reported in February. Altogether there had been eight deaths. Jones took comfort in the fact that most cases occurred before Banda's speech and only forty-five in the last week of February.

There were a further 100 cases reported in the first two weeks of March and Jones again took comfort in being able to say, 'in the past seven days there have been 47 political cases only and it is clear that Dr. Banda's instructions are being obeyed'. In fact, they were far from being fully obeyed. During March 237 cases of violence were reported and by the end of May 404 more, by which time the number of reported cases of injury to persons and property since registration opened in December had risen to 2693, a third of them after Banda's appeal that violence should stop.[81]

In reporting the chain of events to Sandys towards the end of April, Jones wrote about the difficulties the police were having.[82] So far they had sent 322 cases – each usually involving several accused – to the director of public prosecutions, but he had authorized prosecutions in only nine cases and had rejected seven; the other 306 cases were still pending a decision. The March intelligence report had drawn attention, including Banda's, to this problem.

Jones still 'firmly believed' that Banda personally and his senior colleagues did not instigate, and thoroughly disapproved of, the incidents of violence which had occurred in recent months. Instead, he attributed the fault to 'the extremist members of the party in the lower echelons'. This attribution ignores or rejects the intelligence report allegations against senior members of the party. The situation caused him the gravest anxiety and he had on several occasions contemplated revoking his assignment to Banda of responsibility for law and order, though he did not mention this possibility to the doctor. He and his advisers had concluded that to revoke the assignment would lead to serious estrangement between him and the doctor and would thereby worsen the situation, and it 'could quite easily result in the declaration of another emergency'.[83] Consequently, and since – a little oddly in view of the many hundreds of cases of intimidation and violence including several political murders – he assured the secretary of state at the end of January that law and order had not broken down, he decided that his best course was to give Banda what he called 'robust and frequent advice' to instruct his party leaders and followers that violence must stop.[84] It seems, however, that his style of approaching Banda did not change from the pleading and flattering tones of the written requests of the past. Nevertheless, he felt his approach was having some success. He was having rather less success, however, with Chirwa, the minister of justice and attorney-general.

His problem with the attorney-general stemmed from the constitutional requirement that the DPP should consult him in cases where the public interest might be involved. This inevitably slowed down the pace at which the director could reach decisions on whether or not to prosecute. The situation was exacerbated by the director's difficulty in securing regular or early access to the attorney-general to consult him: he was 'very often away and [was] a highly evasive person when it [came] to something he [did] not care for'.[85] Banda had pressed hard to have the direction of public prosecutions placed in political hands and had agreed to forgo this, until independence, on condition that the director should consult the attorney-general in cases where a political element was involved. It was a subject on which Jones knew the prime minister had strong feelings.

Soon after Banda made his Zomba speech calling for an end to violence and intimidation, Jones wrote to Chirwa, referred to the speech and hoped that violence would now die down. Information about the large number of complaints of murder, serious assault, arson and crop destruction[86] were reaching Britain and he expected to receive many questions from the secretary of state about 'the number of prosecutions that are being conducted against the perpetrators of these atrocities'. It would help if he could say the government was taking active steps to seek out and punish those responsible for the more serious cases. The police had sent a number of case dockets to the director because they felt there might be a political flavour to them. He sincerely trusted that Chirwa would look upon cases of murder, serious assault, arson and crop destruction as being 'straightforward cases of unjustifiable violence which should be prosecuted with the utmost vigour regardless of whether they have political content or not'. He would be happy to discuss this with Chirwa if he wished.[87]

Receiving no reply, Jones wrote again a week and a half later. As he had anticipated, news of the wave of violence had now reached Britain and other countries friendly towards Nyasaland. It was essential to be able to reassure these countries, quite apart from the general principles involved, if their attempts to recruit specialist staff were not to be undermined – a point Watson had made strongly seven months earlier, but which Jones had been unwilling to pass on to Banda. Jones thought, too, that the constitution was being interpreted in such a way as to stifle prosecutions for certain classes of violence. He sincerely hoped this was not so, because it would cause 'extreme anxiety' to both the secretary of state and himself. He asked for an early reply and reiterated his willingness to discuss the matter with the attorney-general.[88]

This second letter secured the desired result. Chirwa replied two days later: he had been away and unable to reply to the first letter. He had discussed the matter with Banda and they both agreed that murder, serious assault, arson, crop destruction and 'other acts of violence' should be investigated and prosecuted regardless of any political ingredient. Each case had, however, to be dealt with on its individual merits. He denied that the constitution was being used in the stifling way Jones feared and he insisted on being fully consulted in all cases which in his opinion had a political flavour. He assured Jones that the director would authorize public prosecutions in appropriate cases, and he agreed to see him to discuss the issue a few days later.[89]

At their meeting on 17 March, Chirwa did not differ in principle from the Governor but repeated that each case had to be treated on its individual merits. He also repeated that some of the reports were exaggerated, fabricated or the outcome of provocation by Jehovah's Witnesses. Jones's retort to this was: 'Granted that many complaints were unjustifiable, there was still a hard core of ugly cases of violence which would be prosecuted with vigour in any civilized country. Corpses, badly injured people in hospital, burned-out houses and slashed crops provided abundant evidence that there had been in Nyasaland an ugly wave of violence during the past two months.' When Chirwa said the police were too ready to blame MCP members for all acts of violence, the Governor responded that in cases of violence the political affiliations of the offenders was of little relevance and violence must be punished from whatever quarter it came.[90]

On the whole Chirwa was amicable, accommodating and reassuring, but the problem persisted and Jones had to write to him again three weeks later. Banda was away and Jones expressed himself concisely and unequivocally. The police had told him earlier that day that there were still many cases in which the DPP had not received the attorney-general's opinion.

> This is extremely embarrassing and disturbing to me, not only in view of our recent exchange of correspondence and final discussion on the matter, but also because of the bad impression it is creating here in Nyasaland and inevitably must create in our relations with other countries.
>
> I have further been informed that in the last few days there has been a resurgence of crimes of violence, mainly in the Chiradzulu area, and it is even more difficult to cope with this latter outbreak when so many crimes remain outstanding and not dealt with over a period of months.
>
> Having regard to my overall [constitutional] responsibility for public order and public safety ... I shall have no alternative but to bring the whole matter to the attention of the Prime Minister immediately on his return.
>
> Meanwhile, however, I am addressing this urgent letter to you to ask you, as Attorney-General, to express your views ... so that the Director of Public Prosecutions can, without further delay, exercise his powers under the Constitution. With this in view, I am requesting the Director of Public Prosecutions to contact you in person as soon as possible so that he may, as agreed between you and me at our last meeting, go ahead with the prosecution of the serious offences involving violence.[91]

This letter provoked an irate and outspoken response from Chirwa on 17 April.[92] Quite recently, as he saw it, he had agreed to look into and expedite a decision on all outstanding cases, and political implications would not be considered in serious cases of violence. He repeated the insistence that as attorney-general he must be consulted on all cases having a political flavour. He again denied that the constitution was being interpreted to stifle prosecutions. He then rounded on Jones and vented two major resentments:

> What I have resented in this matter is that Your Excellency should avail yourself of advice either from the police or the Director of Public Prosecutions or from any person other than your Prime Minister or

myself or other Minister over matters for which we are fully responsible in a self-governing state. The Director of Public Prosecutions, whom I met at Kasungu on the 9th April, spoke about his powers under the Constitution to go ahead with the prosecution of political cases. Your Excellency knows that politics is the art of the possible, and in this country it is not yet possible for any person other than myself, as the representative of [Dr. Banda] and the Malawi Congress Party, to mount any major political arrests. I have, therefore told the Director of Public Prosecutions that if he persists with the prosecution of political cases without my knowledge and support he will not make the slightest progress, and such arrests will be vigorously resisted in every corner of this country.

May I also add that we resent being pushed around by any person, for we have been pushed about far too much in this country. Nor should we be hurried into doing foolish things because certain people within or without this country are clamouring for action. These may well be the same people who have given us little or no support throughout our political struggle.

I have since, however, received a letter from the Director of Public Prosecutions, in which, after a vehement attack on my professional and political integrity, he says he has no option but to resign his appointment. As he feels so strongly about me and my Government we have come to the conclusion that it is better for him to leave us in peace as soon as arrangements can be made for his repatriation. We would like to have someone who is not so wide-mouthed about his constitutional powers which, in our view, are non-existent. I say non-existent because we hold that the ultimate power belongs to the people of Malawi, of whom I have the honour to be one of their representatives.

Since Banda was away, it is likely that Chirwa's repeated use of the word 'we' refers to other lieutenants, probably Chiume and Chipembere, with whom he discussed the matter.

Jones was not to be cowed by Chirwa's letter. He continued, he told the secretary of state, to push Chirwa hard and did not intend to relax the pressure on him.[93] He wrote straight back to Chirwa. He first denied that he had received advice from the commissioner of police or from the DPP from whom he had simply sought information on the number and progress of cases pending in the DPP's office. He was aware that he had no powers in relation to mounting prosecutions although he could not escape his ultimate responsibility for public order and safety, notwithstanding that he had currently assigned responsibility to the prime minister. He would not exercise this responsibility in a way which overrode the opinions of the prime minister. Nevertheless, as Governor, he had the right to tender advice with the object of serving the best interests of Nyasaland and its people. He hoped that giving such advice would not be construed by Chirwa as pushing him about. He hoped, too, that arrangements could quickly be made to secure continuity in the functions of the DPP and that he could discuss this with Chirwa at an early date.[94]

For whatever reason, the position began to improve, and in May British ministers were briefed – presumably so that they should be better prepared to respond to the many parliamentary questions – that things had very much improved.[95] It is likely that in the meantime Banda had spoken to Chirwa about dealing with the outstanding cases. Independence was only two months away and he had made it clear that he would not put up with the present restrictions thereafter. By the end of May the police had sent 391 dockets to the DPP seeking permission to prosecute and this was given in 209 cases. He was still considering 164 cases. Prosecutions were now approved in all cases involving death where evidence was available, save in one case which was still being considered.[96]

Unsworth had told Jones that he was not prepared to stay as chief justice after independence, and the controversy over public prosecutions could have done nothing to persuade him otherwise. He left Nyasaland on 1 June 1964, a month before independence.[97] A senior colleague who knew the chief justice well commented, 'Sir Edgar Unsworth resigned as he could no longer stomach the apparent immunity of the MCP and the Young Pioneers [and I] knew of his mounting disgust at what was happening in Nyasaland.'[98]

Nomination day for the national assembly elections was 6 April and the day passed off quietly. The violence and intimidation over the past several months had its effect. None of the seats for either roll was contested and the MCP took all fifty general roll seats. Blackwood's new Nyasaland Constitutional Party took the three special roll seats.[99]

Banda now turned his mind to the cabinet he wished to form ready for independence. This was a matter on which Jones offered his advice. The ministry of finance was clearly crucial both because of its role in internal public finances and development and because of the budgetary support Britain would continue for some time to give. Special arrangements had been made to retain Phillips as minister of finance until independence. Banda had told Jones the previous August that he intended to make Tembo Phillips's sucessor. Notwithstanding this and his knowledge that Tembo was Cecilia Kadzamira's uncle, Jones now told the doctor:

> I know that you have been grooming young John Tembo to be Phillips' successor and I have no doubt that he has the intellectual qualities required for the job. I ask you however, with respect, to consider whether John is yet strong enough and mature enough to take on the onerous

task of Minister of Finance at the present time ... I communicate these thoughts to you in the full knowledge that you are in control of your party and that I have little knowledge of its working. I feel however that I would like to draw your attention to a possibility which you may already have examined – that is, that for the time being you should consider Bwanausi for the post of Minister of Finance and John Tembo for the post of Minister of Development where he will obtain further valuable training for the post of Minister of Finance in the future.

Please believe me when I say that I do not wish to interfere in your discretion in this matter. I merely tender advice which is not coloured by any personal feelings. I like both John Tembo and Bwanausi but above all, I want to see Malawi go ahead under your leadership.[100]

A few days later, and without any discussion, Banda told Jones that he had reached decisions on the ministers he wished to have appointed: Chirwa, justice; Chiume, independence and information, and after independence, external affairs; Chipembere, education; Chokani, labour; Msonthi, transport and communications; Bwanausi, development and housing; Cameron, public works; Phillips, finance, until independence when Tembo would take over; and Yatuta Chisiza, home affairs.[101] Jones had tried very hard to get the doctor to retain Cameron in transport and communications. He had tried, too, to get him to agree that Bwanausi should become minister of finance and Tembo minister of development. In all these cases Banda either ignored or rejected his advice.

The tribulations of the months preceding Nysaland's independence were not without their lighter side. There was much fluttering in the Commonwealth and Colonial Office dovecotes in February when a director of Rolls-Royce asked them to provide transport to get Banda's brand-new bright red Rolls-Royce car to Nyasaland in time for the independence celebrations. It was not that they could not do this which worried them so much as Banda's apparent extravagance. The Nyasaland treasury and independence office knew nothing about the car and Jones at first believed that it was a gift from the Asian community. Why, he inquired, did his London colleagues not ask the Rolls-Royce director who had placed the order, rather ask the Governor to make oblique inquiries in Nyasaland? Maybe, over the years they had become accustomed to not directly tackling Banda on issues which might irritate him. In any event, they asked Jones for an assurance that the car was not being paid for from government funds, which he gave, and after several more inquiries they proposed 'to let the question of this band wagon run into the sand'. The Rolls had in fact been ordered and paid for by the MCP.[102]

On 26 June the Queen approved Sandys's formal application that Jones be appointed Governor-General of Malawi when it became independent.[103] The previous July Banda and Blackwood, without consulting Jones,[104] had written a joint letter to Butler asking for a republic to declared at the moment Nyasaland became independent. Jones had ascertained that Banda might compromise on this, and Butler had asked him for his views. The Central Africa Office officials had not yet formed a view but thought that if the delay were for only a few months there would be little advantage in the delay.[105] Butler, however, said:

> I am sure that with his financial position Banda ought not to go too quickly ahead. He has already got himself all he wants and there are three ways in which I think his country might suffer. The first is through the decline of justice. The second is through quite stupidly menacing the few Europeans who still live there and the third is by a financial breakdown. On all these I am sure he would be wise to be constructive before we move too far to be able to have any control.[106]

He did not make it clear how any of these matters would be affected by the country being a republic rather than a monarchy. Even as a colony with a British Governor at its head Nyasaland had clearly not avoided a significant decline in justice or the menacing of Europeans. An independent monarchy with a Governor-General nominally at its head was less likely to help in these respects. In his reply, Jones said that if independence and republican status coincided, it would save the cost of two sets of celebrations and avoid 'having to undertake two adjustments to the government machine'. On the other hand,

> Early attainment of republican status might ... result in the loss of more senior expatriate officers who might otherwise digest independence by itself and thereafter be influenced to serve on for a period under the republic. The Queen's representative as head of state will have a sentimental influence and under the Crown could have advantageous effects on British businessmen and investors. Banda might value having someone to whom he could turn for advice and assistance but this must be balanced against the status he would gain in having the offices of head of state and head of government combined in him as President. The balance of advantage from HMG's point of view is slightly in favour of taking this in two stages. However, it seems quite certain that Banda would not agree to a period of independence under a Governor-General lasting longer than a year and possibly six months would be the maximum he would feel able to agree to.[107]

The machinery for appointing Jones as Governor-General had been set in motion in the middle of November 1963. A month earlier Jones had turned down the offer of the governorship of British Guiana. He took the initiative, said he was prepared to stay in Nyasaland after independence as Governor-General and asked Watson to pursue this possibility. Several minutes then crossed various desks in Whitehall. On 12 November an official in the Commonwealth Relations Office wrote to Sir Saville Garner, permanent under-secretary of state, to say he understood there was a school of thought opposed to the appointment of a Governor as the Governor-General at independence. On the other hand there were a number of precedents: Ceylon, Ghana, Nigeria, Tanganyika, Uganda and Sierra Leone. 'In the case of Nyasaland [he had] no doubt that the mutual confidence and respect that exist[ed] between Dr. Banda and the present Governor would be invaluable in the early days of independence.'[108]

Garner then discussed the matter with G. W. Chadwick, assistant under-secretary of state, and they both expressed themselves in terms of general principle before turning to the specific case of Nyasaland. To Garner the main objection was to a country retaining its monarchical status and then very shortly proclaiming itself a republic. If the change was to be made it was more 'dignified' to make it at the moment of independence. The same objection in principle did not apply, in his view, to the Governor staying on as Governor-General 'at least for a short time'. The danger, however, was that the transition from one post to the other was not an easy one to make and there was the risk, certainly if he stayed for any length of time, that he would 'find the constitutional limitations irksome and may seek to exceed his proper share, running the risk of his efforts being counter-productive'. Having said this, he saw no objection, if Nyasaland was to remain monarchical, to Jones staying on for a short time.[109] Chadwick's response to these views was:

> The question of Governors soldiering on after independence has of course been discussed many times in the past. As you say, it is far preferable to have a republic straightaway rather than have to make the change very soon after independence. But in view of Dr. Banda's desire for a monarchy I suggest that Sir Glyn Jones's future (and that of other Governors in similar circumstances) can only be decided against the following criteria: the personality of the individual Governor, the confidence the new Prime Minister has in him and his capacity for keeping the boat steady in the months following independence, and the availability or otherwise of an alternative local candidate.
>
> If without disrespect I may refer to earlier Governors-General in Africa, I would say that Sir Charles Arden Clarke did extremely well and attracted no criticism; this must have been due partly to his excellent personal relations with Dr. Nkrumah, but also to his capacity to make the change smoothly. Sir Maurice Dorman in Sierra Leone on the other hand showed

increasing signs as time went on of yearning for the old colonial days and before he left there were some embarrassing signs of friction between him and his Prime Minister. In Tanganyika, Sir Richard Turnbull started brilliantly and exerted useful influence on Tanganyika ministers but towards the end he was beginning to alarm us by the degree to which he lectured and hectored his Prime Minister. Sir Walter Coutts's tenure in Uganda was frankly undistinguished and he showed little ability to appreciate the difference in his status. That said, I would from all I have heard of Sir Glyn Jones and of his good relations with Dr. Banda, equate him with Sir Charles Arden Clarke rather than any other African Governors

This, coupled with the fact that there can hardly be a suitable local candidate in Nyasaland, leads to the conclusion that we should welcome his retention with perhaps the rider that it would be preferable that he should not stay longer than twelve months as Governor-General.[110]

In praising Arden Clarke and likening Jones to him, Chadwick must have forgottten that he was Governor-General of Ghana for only two months, which he devoted to travelling round the country and bidding the people goodbye. Similarly, in criticizing Dorman he must have forgotten that after Sierra Leone he was none the less appointed Governor of Malta; indeed, he then became Malta's Governor-General for seven years.[111]

On 13 November, Sandys 'entirely agreed' that Jones should be offered the appointment. No one told Banda, however, that it was for him to make the request, and Youens had to 'remind' him. The doctor 'had not realised that this appointment was a matter on which it was for him to advise the Queen'. He had assumed the Governor-General would be appointed by the British government in the same way they appointed the Governor. 'He seemed quite pleased to learn of his personal authority in the matter and said that he would of course be recommending Sir Glyn Jones ... He asked how soon his recommendation was required. He added somewhat ruefully, that he would not be able to do so immediately because of the constitutional matters then outstanding between him and the Secretary of State; he might be declaring his independence and the matter would not then arise!'[112]

Banda made his formal application that Jones's name be submitted to the Queen, on 13 January 1964. Macmillan agreed four weeks later. When approached towards the end of February, the Queen said she would be pleased in due course to approve the appointment but could not do so formally until the Nyasaland Independence Bill had received the royal assent. This she did on 26 June 1964, ten days before Nyasaland became independent.[113]

The last year of colonial government leading up to independence was a period of almost relentless worry for Jones. There was little that was not deeply concerning between his successful meetings in May 1963 with Banda about finance and the formal announcement late in June 1964 that he was to be Malawi's Governor-General – not that there had not been many previous causes for concern. It is when the events of that last year are concisely set out sequentially that their full impact is seen: his 'cardiac indisposition'; the intimidation of federal government employees; Watson's worries over Nyasaland's deteriorating reputation; the prime minister's bodyguards' attack on the European teenagers; the civil service association's cable to the secretary of state; the vitriolic attacks in the legislature on the European population; the federal government's allegations about the erosion of the rule of law; Butler's intervention to point out the dangers of the continuing decline in the country's reputation and its implications; Unsworth's representations about interference with the judiciary, the defects of the local courts system and the move towards a one-party state; the proposal to introduce legislation to restrict the movement of certain individuals; the widespread and appalling outrages leading to the elimination of all African contest for parliamentary seats in the early months of 1964; and the dispute with Chirwa over the prosecution of offences with a political flavour. What is surprising is that Jones did not have a heart attack or nervous breakdown at the end of, or in addition to, all this rather than just at the beginning.

CHAPTER 7

Malawi: Governor-General

THE political situation in Malawi at the time of independence was described by the British high commissioner, David Cole. He thought 'Dr. Banda's position in Malawi seemed beyond challenge ... The whole political system revolved around him. It was almost inconceivable that it could ever change.'[1] Again, 'Politically the country was under the firm paternally despotic control of Dr. Banda. Politics here had gained a certain monolithic appearance that suggested security and permanence. There was no real opposition ... Stability, moderation, realism and firm leadership seemed to be Malawi's distinguishing characteristics.'[2]

Banda left for London and the Commonwealth prime ministers' conference a week after independence day. He then travelled to Cairo for the OAU summit of heads of state. Before he left he dropped Msonthi from the cabinet without discussing the matter with Jones, or indeed even informing him or explaining his reasons.

While he was away, Chisiza spoke to Lomax, head of Special Branch.[3] He had already explained his concerns to Jones. He spoke first of Msonthi's unexplained 'dismissal' which was giving rise to speculation and making the other ministers fear they would also be dismissed. He complained of Banda's excessively wide range of responsibilities – 'he would kill himself running six Ministries and taking all the decisions.' Turning then to Banda's failure to delegate responsibilities to ministers, he said: 'Dr. Banda had promised that when independence came the Malawi people would run their own country. But in fact they were not [being allowed to do so]. If Dr. Banda tried to run six Ministries, the only possible consequence was that those Ministries were run, after independence, as they were before, by British civil servants.' Chisiza was also disturbed by the slow rate of Africanization and the recent promotions of many African clerical officers instead of 'some of the younger men of real quality whom the country needed'. He had broached this with Banda and 'got his head bitten off and been accused of disloyalty'. He felt Banda might lose touch with reality and be told only what was agreeable to him.

Meanwhile, at the OAU summit in Cairo, Banda dealt with Malawi's foreign policy:

> I share the view ... that all independent African states and all African leaders must do everything possible in their power to help those countries which are still under the imperial yoke. [But I] want to make it quite clear ... that the geographical position of Malawi makes it impossible for me and my country to sever all ties, diplomatic, economic and cultural, with a certain power still controlling great portions of our continent.

Banda's explanations were accepted and no one disputed his courage in stating these unpopular views or protested when he abstained from voting for a boycott of South Africa.[4]

When Chiume, who was with him in Cairo, tried to persuade Banda to be more positive in condemning the Portuguese in Moçambique, the doctor became angry.[5] Indeed, he was still angry when he arrived back in Malawi on 26 July and he told the crowd welcoming him at Chileka airport to 'Watch everybody! Even Ministers', and if they did things which the people thought were not good for the MCP they were to report them to him.

When Banda came down from the rostrum, Youens, who was present at Chileka, remarked to him, 'That was a very interesting but rather injudicious speech, wasn't it?' In reply he grinned and said, 'You know, Mr Youens, you are really rather naive. I know what I am doing.'[6]

Chiume saw the Chileka speech as the beginning of a 'bitter tussle', and recalled: 'My colleagues summoned an urgent meeting and each group — there were two factions in the cabinet — agreed to bury their differences; it had become a question of surviving or perishing together.'[7]

Two days after the Chileka speech, Jones swore-in Tembo as minister of finance, and was visited by Banda.[8] They spoke of Msonthi's recent expulsion from the cabinet because, it was thought, of disloyalty. The prime minister said it was 'not so much an expulsion as a suspension from duty'. He had received reports that Msonthi's behaviour was bringing the government into disrepute and he wished to have these reports thoroughly investigated.

Having dealt with the Msonthi matter, Jones then — probably following Chisiza's representations — raised the question of Banda's heavy responsibilities and asked if he could not shed some of them, especially in view of his external commitments in the Commonwealth, UN and OAU, now that Malawi was independent.

> However, I was not very successful in my approach because he told me what he has often told me before — that he finds it tolerably easy to manage his multifarious activities including the important functions of

being the controller and watchdog of the Party – and that he was quite happy to carry on provided he was served by efficient civil servants. Moreover, he could not contemplate at the present moment delegating portfolios such as agriculture, trade and industry [because] he could trust none of his Ministers to stand up to bribery.

Although he did not tell Banda, Jones did not agree with this point about ministers being unable to resist bribery: 'some undoubtedly could not, but there are others who are as full of integrity as the Prime Minister himself.'

The following day, 29 July, at the usual Wednesday cabinet meeting, Banda 'casually announced'[9] a proposal to re-introduce detention without trial in the absence of a state of emergency. Jones had spoken against this exactly a year previously and the doctor had then agreed to delay it. He now brought it forward again.

Cameron made it clear that he was not going to go along with that suggestion. He said that Banda was ... adopting the sort of worst practices taught him by the British and that he was not prepared to be associated with it, and he got up from his chair in the cabinet and took his leave and said he was off. After he had gone Banda said, 'Anybody else want to go?' At that stage there were no volunteers.[10]

In view of his remark a few days earlier about knowing what he was doing, this question of Banda's suggests that he was deliberately inviting, provoking or challenging his ministers openly to disagree with him. Although all the ministers disagreed with reintroducting preventive detention, only Cameron spoke out against it.[11]

Soon after the cabinet meeting ended, Cameron visited Jones and told him what had happened and that he had resigned. The Governor-General suggested that Cameron should call on Banda and see if there was any possibility of a compromise. They must both have known that the chances of a compromise were remote, but Jones thought that a visit and a 'quiet candid conversation' might be helpful in retaining good relations.[12]

The significance of this cabinet meeting was not so much Cameron's resignation, important though it was, but its emboldening effect on the other ministers. They secured a temporary withdrawal of the Bill, and this further encouraged them in their determination to get him to change the autocratic way he was running the government of the country.[13]

Two days later, on 31 July, Jones and Banda met.[14] Although the prime minister would not change his mind on detention without trial there was no ill feeling between Cameron and himself. He was keen to appoint another European to the cabinet in Cameron's place and suggested Major

Peter Moxon. He asked Jones to make inquiries. Jones saw Moxon on 1 August[15] and must have reported favourably on him, for Banda then asked that he be told he was being considered as a replacement for Cameron 'on the strict understanding that he would give loyal support to Government's policy in regard to changing the constitution to permit detention without trial without a declaration of a state of emergency'. If Moxon shared Cameron's objections there would be no point in offering him the post.[16] Jones saw Moxon on 12 August and he refused to accept an offer on the condition stipulated.[17] He had, incidentally, hoped to be made commander of the Malawi army.[18]

Jones then raised the question of African membership of social and sporting clubs, and the discussion reveals the attitudes of the two men to this question:

> I felt that the time was ripe for Africans who could afford to do so to join the various clubs with a view to participating in sports and cultural pursuits with the Europeans ... It seemed clear to me that those Europeans who had been responsible for the racial attitudes adopted by the clubs had now left the country and that the majority of the residual European population were very anxious to establish friendly social relations with Africans. The Prime Minister said that neither he nor the Government would raise any objections whatsoever to Africans joining European clubs but he would not expect to see a great movement among the Africans to join these clubs. He did not feel it was necessary for Africans and Europeans to mix together socially in order to maintain friendly relations with each other, although he admitted that there was no harm in such social mingling and it could lead to increased understanding between the races.

The explanation of Banda's attitude, given directly to a senior diplomat, was that 'Malawi needed expatriates [and] while they were in Malawi they must be allowed their clubs ... But Africans would not be paid expatriate salaries and should not try to enjoy a way of life they could not afford.' This seemed to the diplomat 'one of Banda's more rational attitudes'.[19] It is interesting that Banda did not give this explanation to Jones.

Several years later Chipembere, looking back on the Chileka speech and subsequent events, said: 'Banda had gone too far, and we decided to ... seek an immediate audience with' him.[20] Banda was extremely reluctant to see them as a group and suggested they come individually. Eventually he agreed to a meeting. This was held on 10 August and the ministers were 'frank and courageous'. They complained, first, about Banda's 'slighting references' to them in public. Second, they objected to his keeping too many government functions in his own hands. He initially gave vent to a display of anger but then gave the ministers a patient three-hour hearing. At the end of the meeting the ministers were left with the impression that he undertook to pay regard to their complaints and 'reform his ways'.[21]

There were various reasons for wanting Banda to reduce his responsibilities. Jones's concern was that he needed to be relieved in order to concentrate on key areas and to have time to devote to new responsibilities. Chipembere and Chisiza believed that looking after too many portfolios would affect Banda's health. Chisiza was additionally worried that by having too many portfolios he would inevitably entrust too much power to his European civil servants.

The prime minister and Governor-General met again on 11 August and Jones brought up the question of Banda's relationships with his ministers. The doctor 'was not very forthcoming on this subject. [He continued] to give every appearance of being quite relaxed and happy with the present situation.'[22]

Jones was away on a game-viewing visit to Gorongoza from 15 to 19 August. Five days after his return, Chirwa secretly visited him.[23] He told him about the meeting with Banda two weeks earlier and added that the ministers had decided they could no longer tolerate the prime minister's conduct. He was becoming increasingly dictatorial and was making important decisions without consulting his cabinet. A feeling of great insecurity had been created by Msonthi's unexplained expulsion from the cabinet. Moreover, Banda's acceptance of the Skinner report – which introduced severe restrictions on African civil servants' salaries and conditions of service – was deeply unpopular, and the continuing power of expatriate top civil servants was much criticized. The people were accusing the ministers of simply being 'yes men'. Their morale was 'rock bottom'.

Since their meeting with the prime minister, Chirwa continued, there had not, contrary to their expectations, been any reforming of Banda's ways. The ministers, now in a very determined mood, were about to tackle him again. The Governor-General should not be surprised if he received Banda's resignation during the next forty-eight hours. He asked Jones to take no action other than to give the doctor tactful 'Queen's advice' about delegating responsibilities to his ministers.

Jones told Chirwa he appreciated the ministers' feelings that they were being slighted, belittled and deprived of the opportunity to exercise their full responsibilities as ministers and members of the cabinet, where the principle of collective responsibility should be observed. In effect he was agreeing with their complaints. Indeed, Chipembere later said the Governor-General told Banda that, at least on the question of consultation, the ministers 'were quite right'.[24] Chiume, too, was told by

Chirwa that 'Jones felt some of the grievances [they] voiced against Banda were genuine and needed redress'. In this way Jones was encouraging the ministers to pursue their confrontation with Banda, but he told Chirwa he could not himself intervene. Strangely, in view of the possible resignation of his prime minister, he did not give any advice as to how Chirwa should proceed, save to see the prime minister, which he agreed to do that evening.[25] Chirwa added that he was worried about Malawi becoming a republic, and repeatedly said the country must not be allowed to become 'a dictatorship like Ghana'. He called on Jones again the following day and it may be that he reported either on a visit to Banda the previous evening or, more likely, that one had not taken place.

Jones was becoming increasingly concerned. Far from things having improved in the cabinet they were somewhat worse. He was less optimistic than he had been and feared that, at the very worst, Banda would at some stage declare a state of emergency, 'lock up all his Ministers and replace them with stooges.' All ministers except Tembo were opposing Banda on two fundamental points: his refusal to transfer authority and his public insults. He told Cole immediately after Chirwa's visit on 24 August about their meeting and, according to Cole, said that when all the ministers, except Tembo, went to see Banda on 10 August he had 'immediately offered to resign, warning them however that in that event all external aid to Malawi would cease'. The ministers said they had no wish for him to resign. Since their meeting Banda had been much more agreeable towards his ministers but was giving them no greater authority. Rather, the increasing authority of Aleke Banda outside the cabinet was deeply resented.[26] Jones's own notes on the meeting with Chirwa make no mention of Banda having offered to resign.

Chirwa's references to ministers being about to tackle Banda again and to a possible resignation during the coming forty-eight hours suggests they intended to provoke a situation at the latest at the cabinet meeting on 26 August, in which Banda would either agree to reform his ways or would offer to resign. Since Chirwa was addressing Jones in secrecy, the request that he do nothing except tender tactful advice implies that he wanted Jones not to tell Banda about their meeting and neither to accept nor to reject his resignation. If this is so, then the ministers probably hoped that, in the absence of being able themselves to persuade Banda to change his ways, they could provoke him to the point where he would feel he should go to Jones to offer his resignation, the Governor-General would express his view supporting the ministers – Chirwa already knew that he agreed with them – and advise him to reform his ways, whereupon he would withdraw his tendered resignation and all thereafter would be well, with the ministers enjoying more ministerial autonomy and greater collective cabinet responsibility. Had this occurred the ministers would have been well pleased and the outcome would have been much to Jones's satisfaction.

Two days after Chirwa's first meeting with Jones, there was a long meeting of the cabinet, from 9.30 a.m. to 2.45 p.m.[27] Banda, Chiume, Chirwa, Tembo, Bwanausi, Chokani and Chisiza were present. Cameron had resigned, Chipembere had left on 19 August for a conference in Canada and Msonthi was not currently a member of the cabinet. Youens, secretary to the cabinet, and David Ellams, clerk to the cabinet, were in attendance. The early items on the agenda were dealt with fairly amicably, although even in these there were signs of trouble.

The first item was a proposal to alter the constitution to allow for the appointment of non-cabinet ministers. Three regional ministers – McKinley Chibambo, Richard Chidzanja and Gomile Kumtumanji – had been appointed on 14 August in order to give them appropriate status in their regions.[28] Strictly speaking, they were already members of the cabinet.[29] This was not what Banda currently wished and consequently he sought to alter the constitution. Members hoped the regional ministers would not be allowed to interfere in the work of their ministries and said they should respect the seniority and superior status of cabinet ministers.

Possibly with the intention of drawing out the ministers, Banda went on to say that civil servants, too, especially Africans, should show proper respect to ministers. Many were inclined to take advantage of their earlier acquaintance with ministers and 'treat them with undue familiarity'. This gave Chirwa and Chiume the opportunity to say that European civil servants also were at fault. A number had inflated ideas of their importance and powers. The secretary to the prime minister, Youens, was particularly at fault, labouring under the delusion that he was the deputy prime minister. With this, albeit at this stage limited, airing of their grievances, the ministers then agreed to the constitutional amendment.

The cabinet turned to the second agenda item, a Bill to set up a provisional council for the proposed University of Malawi. Banda introduced it and said the post of vice-chancellor had been offered to a European academic. Chiume – a former minister of education – expressed concern about appointing an expatriate and he urged that a Malawian understudy be appointed. Banda, generally agreeing with appointing understudies, pointed to the ability of high-calibre expatriate staff to attract outside investment into the university. Chiume countered: 'Many countries of the world were not impressed by Europeans who purported to speak for African nations.' If they allowed themselves to be taken for granted by the western powers, they were likely to obtain less financial support from them. Banda's response, gentle and measured, was in general agreement with this view but 'those Europeans who had contacts with, and some influence over, sources of financial aid, were better placed than some to obtain such assistance'.

Banda rounded off the discussion by telling his colleagues that most of the money for their development plan was already secured from Britain, Germany and the World Bank. 'Thus already the greater proportion of the money needed for the Development Plan had been promised' and, although he did not highlight the point, promised from western sources. Ministers, seemingly diverted by this apparent *non sequitur*, then agreed that the Bill should be introduced into the next session of parliament.

So far, the criticisms of Banda's policies and methods of operating were veiled, though only thinly, and he had responded reasonably and patiently, explaining his rationale for his views and giving ministers somewhat fuller information than they already possessed. By giving these explanations, and to that extent sharing his views and taking his colleagues into his confidence rather more fully than previously, Banda may have hoped they would feel he had taken to heart the points they had made to him two weeks previously and was indeed beginning to reform his ways. Whether or not this was his intention, he had skilfully and fairly amicably brought discussion to a close and secured agreement to the two items so far dealt with. This was not to last.

After a minor item on factories subsidiary legislation, Chokani, minister of labour, introduced a paper about an agreement with the Witwatersrand Native Labour Association (WNLA), entered into by the colonial government some time previously. Many thousands of Malawians were recruited each year under this agreement for work in the South African mines. He thought this an appropriate time to negotiate a new agreement to 'reflect the constitutional changes which had recently taken place'. Chiume was ready to lead the attack and he did so in outspoken terms. Opposed in principle to the Malawi government having dealings with South Africa, his most immediate objection was to bringing the world's attention, especially the attention of African counties, to the matter by entering into a new agreement.

Chirwa had additional concerns. The Portuguese government had agreed that Mozambique Africans could be recruited in the association's offices in Malawi. He felt 'some concern' that ministers had not been told in advance that the prime minister was negotiating with, and intended to visit, Mozambique. Malawi's dealings with Portugal were earning the country 'a bad name throughout Africa'. Bwanausi thought it wrong to obtain more money from South Africa, and Tembo, while saying that the money involved was 'of considerable importance', believed the political costs of a new agreement were serious. Chokani, accepting the political objections, none the less said the country had a significant unemployment problem. Terminating the agreement would bring considerable internal labour unrest.

So far in this discussion, Banda had scarcely spoken, but now, probably with the intention of bringing discussion to a close as he had, successfully, with that on the university, he said he had allowed a long discussion on this subject because of the important matters of principle which it raised.

> He was aware that a campaign against Malawi was being mounted by her ill-wishers ... Nevertheless there was another side to the picture ... The indication was that [in Cairo] he had been able to convince African leaders that his policies were based on a realistic appreciation of certain inescapable factors. It would be to the country's ultimate advantage for its leaders to be seen as mature men who were prepared to face the realities which confronted them and to deal with them on the basis of what was in the best interests of the people as a whole.

He believed the annual financial grant from the association was less important than unemployment. 'The plain fact was that a decision to terminate the activities of WNLA must be expected to give rise to considerable labour unrest in Malawi.'

If Banda hoped these remarks would bring discussion to a close, he was mistaken. Chiume warned against too readily believing the assurance of people from African international organizations that they accepted his stance on external relations; many were 'political rejects in their own country'. Chirwa hoped ministers would be informed of proposed prime ministerial visits to Mozambique: it was difficult for ministers to defend the prime minister's action if they were not consulted in advance on what he intended to do. Chisiza, having so far said nothing, now intervened:

> In all sincerity he must speak out at this point. The Prime Minister had allowed him to travel extensively and hitherto he had been highly respected as one of the Prime Minister's men. On his recent visit to East Africa he had found this situation drastically changed. Whereas Malawi had ranked high in world esteem, the reverse was now true. It was said that Malawi was a traitor to the cause of Africa ... It appeared that the Prime Minister trusted his European civil servants more than his own Ministers ... The Prime Minister had too many ministries; he could not possibly devote sufficient time to the affairs of these Ministries, and it appeared that the Government was still controlled by expatriate European civil servants. These men came between the Prime Minister and his Ministers ... These officers, such as the Secretary to the Prime Minister, were the enemies of the country. It was a dangerous and disgraceful situation.

By this time the list of grievances had grown substantially from that reported to Jones by Chirwa: Banda's slighting references to ministers and his personal retention of too many portfolios. Finally returning to the specific agenda item, the cabinet agreed that the minister of labour should not for the time being negotiate a new agreement with the association and that he, with Tembo, Bwanausi and Chiume, should further consider whether an agreement would be in Malawi's best interests, and bring the matter back to the cabinet.

After the discussion on the WNLA agreement, Chiume – to be followed by his colleagues, except Chisiza – pursued the attack by reporting on a recent visit to Northern Rhodesia. The ministers added nothing new but repeated, emphasized and reinforced the points they had already made. Chiume said of his visit:

> Nationalists from Southern Rhodesia had alleged that Malawi was a friend of Portugal and a traitor to African nationalists in the southern part of the continent ... and throughout Tanganyika and Kenya he had found a mounting hostility towards Malawi. He was sure that the real friends of this country were the free African countries.
>
> [Chiume continued] that there was much criticism of European civil servants ... The Prime Minister had allowed himself to be dominated by his European Permanent Secretaries who had sought to persuade him that he could not trust his Ministers.

Bwanausi added that it was the duty of ministers to defend Malawi's foreign policy, in the formation of which, therefore, they must be consulted. The prime minister had failed to place confidence in his ministers and had 'forced through a number of measures which the Ministers had been unable to discuss fully and with which they were not always in agreement'. He particularly had in mind the Skinner report which, he said, 'had been bulldozed through the Cabinet'.

Chokani said the prime minister's dealings with Portugal and Southern Rhodesia were resulting in Malawians resident in Southern Rhodesia encountering bitter hostility from local Africans. Moreover, the Skinner report was having a most serious effect on the civil service, and his own ministry's representations had been rejected by the prime minister's office. He doubted whether Banda had been properly informed of these representations.

Chirwa emphasized that apathy and criticism of the Government were growing and one cause of this was Banda's failure to inform, consult and make proper use of his cabinet ministers. The principle of collective responsibility needed to be observed. Banda should place more trust in his ministers and rely less on expatriate civil servants.

Tembo also spoke critically. The people felt that there was no sign of the improvements they had expected to see once independence had been achieved. Africans in the civil service had suffered as a result of the Skinner recommendations. Most of them were prepared to accept the changes which were for the ultimate benefit of the country but they compared their own conditions with the recent rise in expatriate officers' salaries. They also complained bitterly of the promotions of European officers which had followed so soon after independence.

By this time, Youens, who had repeatedly been insulted, and Ellams 'felt they could take no more' and asked to be allowed to withdraw. Banda, possibly embarrassed by the criticisms voiced by his ministers in front of these two officials, including the most senior of all officials, and glad of a break in the spate of criticisms, permitted them to leave.[30]

After Youens and Ellams left, the cabinet members continued their discussion until 4 p.m. Banda listened patiently and 'in exceptional silence' to all the complaints which his ministers made and from time to time simply asked if anyone had other complaints to make. He now told them: 'This all amounts to a vote of no confidence in me as your Prime Minister. Therefore I feel that I should resign. I have achieved what I came here to do – secession from Federation, self-government and now Independence. If my present policies are disapproved by you I should go now.'[31]

The ministers were shocked at this and, although what he said began with the conditional 'if' and fell short of actually offering to do so, they begged him not to resign. Probably correct from the point of view of political practicalities, but not necessarily constitutionally accurate, he insisted that a prime minister could not continue in office if all his ministers disapproved of his policies. At this stage Chirwa intervened to say the meeting had probably gone on long enough and they should leave matters as they stood, take time to rest, reflect and then meet again the next day at 11 a.m.

A little later that day, Chirwa called on Jones to tell him there was a crisis in the cabinet and repeated what he had said two days previously, but now more imminently: the Governor-General might receive the prime minister's resignation 'at any moment'. He added that the ministers did not want Banda to resign but merely to mend his ways by delegating more to them. He said too much weight should not be attached to the attacks made in cabinet on senior civil servants, particularly Youens, since they were intended to let 'the Prime Minister down gently in the form of an oblique attack on him personally'. Jones thought the attacks grossly unfair and was sorry the ministers lacked sufficient courage to make their complaints in a forthright fashion. In his view the ministers had damaged what was probably a fairly legitimate case by 'such unpleasant remarks'.

When the Governor-General tried to see Banda in the evening of the cabinet meeting, he excused himself, saying he was very tired, but asked to see him the following evening at 6.15 p.m.

The next morning, Banda met his ministers, as Chirwa had suggested, and they covered the same ground as the previous day. In his subsequent account to Jones he said he again threatened to resign and contemplated sending Chiume or Chirwa to the Governor-General to be appointed prime minister. However, having listened once more to their 'earnest plea', he told them he would 'put the question to the Governor-General who would decide whether it was in Malawi's best interests that he should remain as Prime Minister'. The ministers agreed to this and asked him to tell Jones they unanimously wished him to remain in office. Banda and the ministers knew his question would be rhetorical and the answer a foregone conclusion. Jones could not have appointed Chiume or Chirwa unless he was sure one or other of them could command majority support in parliament. He, Banda and the ministers knew that no one else could command this support, save possibly Chipembere, who had a substantial personal following in the south of the country though much less so in parliament, but he was out of the country and scheduled to be away for at least another fortnight. Again, what Banda said fell well short of offering to resign and he said nothing about agreeing to accept Jones's advice.

A quarter of an hour before Banda arrived at Government House that evening, he was preceded, somewhat to the Governor-General's surprise, by Msonthi and his spiritual adviser, a priest. They said Banda had instructed them to await his arrival. Jones later recalled the odd proceedings which then took place. After the prime minister arrived and they had exchanged the usual courtesies he asked if he could bring in the priest and Msonthi.

> When they came he delivered a homily on the evils of drink, particularly its tongue-loosening effects, and hinted that Msonthi had been guilty of indiscreet talk on various occasions of a kind calculated to bring not only himself but the whole Government of Malawi into disrepute. He had decided to 'suspend' him from his duties and would have done so prior to 6th July but for Msonthi's earnest entreaties that he be allowed to be present at the celebrations as a Minister.

After the independence celebrations Msonthi went home to Visanza and had been 'living quietly and giving no information to his many questioners'. In the meantime, Banda had investigated allegations made against him, though he did not say what they were, and had come to the conclusion that Msonthi had been guilty of no more than 'indiscreet talk in his cups in mixed company'. He had decided to have a talk with Msonthi's priest friend and confessor, and had asked that Msonthi should be taken before the bishop at Lilongwe and 'admonished for his insobriety and indiscreet behaviour'. When this was done Msonthi was told that he should drink only in his own house and go to bed afterwards. The prime minister had then told the priest and Msonthi that he would, in their presence, ask Jones to offer Msonthi the ministry of transport and communications. Jones now 'had great pleasure in congratulating Msonthi and asking him to come to be sworn in at Government House the next day'. As Jones recalled: 'The priest with great difficulty concealed his mirth at this truly strange performance and I must confess to having to exercise considerable restraint myself.'

It is likely that Banda, having been attacked the previous day by everyone present in the cabinet, was anxious to secure the support of Msonthi, a leading colleague and a minister until recently, and to have that support in the cabinet itself. He was the only member of the cabinet, although temporarily 'suspended', who had not voiced criticism of him. Having been at home for the past several weeks, he was not part of any alliance of opposition into which his colleagues may have entered.

As soon as Msonthi and the priest left, Jones tackled Banda on his relationships with his ministers. He was possibly miffed that the prime minister had not mentioned to him before now the ministerial confrontation which was already well over two weeks old, had not been forthcoming when Jones raised the question the next day, and had declined to call on him the previous evening. No sooner had he begun than Banda cut him short and said that the purpose of coming to see him was to tell him 'frankly what [had] happened during the past two days'. Jones was, as so often before, impressed by the doctor's candour and truthfulness. His account differed very little in detail and not at all in general from that given by Youens covering the period while he and Ellams were present, and he went on to describe what had happened after they had left.

When he was told of Banda's reference to resigning and his colleagues' reaction to this, Jones 'told him without hesitation that he should retain the office of prime minister in the general interests of the people of Malawi'. Banda was very pleased with this response and, as Jones recalled, 'his tail rose appreciably'. There was no persuading on Jones's part nor need for it. Indeed, one of Jones's own accounts makes this clear: 'There was a stage when he felt inclined to resign ... I did not dissuade him from resigning, so much as give him advice as to why he need not resign.'[32] Furthermore, Cole's account, which must have come from Jones, was that Banda went to Jones and said 'he had come back to Malawi to lead the country out of federation and into independence. This had been achieved and if the people wanted him to go he would go. What did the Governor-General think? The Governor-General advised

Banda against resigning though he said he fully respected the principles on which Banda said he must stand.'[33] The emphasis had shifted from what the cabinet wanted to what the people wanted. The words 'What did the Governor-General think?' do not amount to specifically seeking his advice, as opposed to his opinion, on resigning, and, with the word 'inclined', are far removed from tendering his resignation or even threatening to resign. Jones's saying he 'fully respected the principles on which Banda said he must stand', could be taken to imply that if he stuck to those principles – rather than reform his ways which was what Jones and the ministers wanted – then maybe he should go.

With the question of Banda's immediate future out of the way, they talked of ways in which they could make the ministers feel happier than they had felt since independence day. Jones urged him to treat them with respect, not make important decisions without consulting them, not appear to repose more trust in expatriate civil servants than in the ministers, and delegate more responsibilities to them. In this way, without, save in one respect, giving specific examples or going into detailed recommendations, he gave precisely the advice which the ministers had, less amicably and helpfully, given him the previous day and, to some extent, a fortnight earlier. All his previous attempts to get Banda to reduce the scope of his ministerial responsibilities and allocate functions to particular individuals had completely and without exception failed. There was no reason to believe that a suggestion to do so at this stage would be accepted, unless he felt that the ministers had sufficiently softened up the doctor as to cause him to consider reforming his ways.

The one respect in which on this occasion Jones went further was to suggest that he shed the ministries of health and of natural resources and give Chisiza the latter. He should retain defence, law and order and the public service although later, 'as he saw a convenient opportunity', he might take external affairs and appoint a parliamentary secretary to do most of the travelling involved. The effect of these suggestions, if adopted, would have been that Chisiza was elevated, by taking over a vital ministry from the prime minister, and Chiume made less powerful, by losing a prestigious ministry to the prime minister. He did not go into his reasons for making the suggestions nor what effect, intended or otherwise, they might have on Chiume or Chisiza, both northerners, but it must have been clear that the political ramifications of such changes in their personal fortunes might well be considerable.

They next discussed the policy areas agitating the ministers. Banda would not alter his relationships with Portugal nor his policy of gradual Africanization and the retention of expatriates. Jones undoubtedly recognized, after four years of dealing with Banda, that these were points on which no amount of persuasion would shift him. His advice, therefore, was that, 'without being Machiavellian', the prime minister could concede some points to his ministers but not in fact alter his basic policy on important matters – which is precisely the sort of advice Niccolo would have given his Prince.

Jones moved on to talk about Banda's proposals on the future republican status of Malawi:

> I referred to his intention to announce [in the legislature the following week] his decision that Malawi should become a republic on 1st April 1965. This would come as a considerable surprise to the House, the Cabinet and the people since it was clear he had consulted no one about it except Blackwood. While I would not attempt to push him off 1st April 1965 I thought it inadvisable that the announcement should be made so soon.

Banda, probably feeling he already had enough trouble on his plate, agreed not to make the scheduled announcement. To have done so might well have provoked his ministers to flash point, and he was not yet ready to deal with them in public. He could bring the proposal forward later at a more propitious moment.

Just before their meeting ended, Jones gave the doctor 'a secret warning' about Chiume and his lack of loyalty to Banda. This was probably what he had in mind when he suggested that at some stage the prime minister might take over external affairs himself. Banda's reply was simply that he 'quite understood what [Jones] was getting at'.

It would not have escaped Banda's notice that, however he expressed it, Jones was in principle agreeing with the ministers and siding with them, while not withdrawing his support from the prime minister. Jones had made a similar response two years earlier when he had agreed with the ministers' complaints about Chiume. Then Banda had taken no overt action. Now, save for postponing the announcement of republican status, he ignored or rejected all of Jones's advice.

Later that evening the prime minister briefly met his ministers. He told them he had accepted Jones's view and would not resign. He did not say with what alacrity he had accepted this view, still less did he indicate the very high probability that he never intended actually resigning. He may, however, have left the impression with his ministers – shared by many others later – that the Governor-General had to press him hard and at length not to resign. This indeed may have been the impression he wished to leave with them. Being pressed hard may be interpreted not as a real intention to resign but as demonstrating strong support. The greater the pressure needed, the stronger that support. The impression that much time and energy had been expended, fortified Banda's position. It reinforced the belief, expressed by Jones on behalf of the people, in whose best interests he would have been acting, that the doctor's continuing in office was extremely important, even indispensable, to Malawi and its people. The impression also showed the ministers that they had a great battle on their hands if they wished to force Banda to alter his ways, since the Governor-General, who had indicated that he agreed with their complaints, now went to great lengths to support the prime minister in office.

The possibility that Banda wished to leave in the minds of his ministers and others the impression that he was seriously threatening to resign, and required energetic persuasion not to do so, is accompanied by the similar possibility that Jones was content that this impression was left, and for the same reason: to demonstrate a belief, held personally by the Governor-General, that Banda's continuing in office was very important indeed, to make clear how big the battle would be and to concentrate the minds of the ministers. Certainly the impression created in many minds was that Banda required great persuasion from Jones not to resign, but this is far from what Jones's own papers show to be the case. Youens was convinced that Banda never had any intention of resigning, firmly believing it would have been quite out of character for him to have done so, and consequently he would not have required persuading to stay in office.[34] Indeed, when the idea that Banda had sought Jones's advice on resigning and that Jones had 'strengthened him against it' was put to Youens some years later, he replied, 'I never knew that. I must admit I never knew. I find it hard to believe that he would ever think of resigning.'[35] Nowhere in his two speeches to parliament in which he gave detailed accounts of what happened did Banda mention having sought the advice of the Governor-General over resigning, still less that Jones had expended much energy in dissuading him. In one of those speeches he said: 'I wanted to make it quite clear to them that I would consider concessions, compromises, accommodation, only if I could do so with honesty to myself ... Otherwise I prefer to go, I prefer to resign.' Again there is the conditional 'if', and the words 'prefer to resign' once more fall well short of offering to resign and indeed of threaatening to resign.[36] Roberts's account mentions that Banda consulted Jones but does not say the Governor-General had any difficulty in persuading him to stay; indeed, he does not say that Jones gave him any advice.[37]

The ministers met again, on 28 August and were joined by Msonthi. They met at Chiume's house and then adjourned to the Kuchawe Inn on Zomba plateau where they compiled a document, which they called the Kuchawe manifesto, in which they set out their complaints and demands. They insisted that Banda should meet the full set of demands before the next session of parliament, scheduled for 3 September, only five days away.[38]

The Kuchawe manifesto was headed 'Matters on which ministers want immediate action'.[39] It was probably intended by the ministers to be the ultimate debilitating battery of blows in their contest with the prime minister. It contained eight major demands with numerous subsidiary demands.

It was a hurriedly prepared, poorly written and ill-considered document. In essence the ministers objected to the disregard of collective cabinet responsibility, and had three substantive policy areas of concern: foreign relations, the Skinner report and hospital charges. Two additional sections were personal attacks on Banda's style and practice of government but even these were separated and not put under a single heading – treating government as personal property, and favouritism and nepotism – though both were concerned with criticisms of Banda's support of the Tembo family, especially Cecilia Kadzamira, and Aleke Banda. There were good and telling points but they were not gathered together: the need for economy and careful planning, the politically dangerous hardship caused by the Skinner report and the hospital charges, and, particularly, the effects of Malawi's foreign policy. Not unnaturally, the counter-arguments were not put. It was an unsigned, jointly submitted paper. It was manifestly an ultimatum, ill-judged and, despite its prolixity, peremptory. Banda did not take kindly to it or to its authors.

At 5 p.m. that day Chirwa called on the doctor and handed him the list of demands, which they wished to discuss with him the following morning, Saturday. Chirwa told him the document was not complete because they wished to add something to it. He then began to read his own copy to Banda. It is unlikely that he was allowed to read much of the 'bill of indictment', as the doctor called it.[40] An hour and a half later, Banda went to see Jones. Initially, he was in an excitable mood – undoubtedly sorely shaken, and very likely immensely incensed, by the list of demands Chirwa had just handed him – but as their discussion proceeded he 'showed more confidence and became more his old self'. He said things had gone tolerably well the previous evening when he met the ministers and told them he was not going to resign. He had not asked the ministers to see Jones as he had intended because he wanted to keep the Governor-General out of the business. He felt confident he could handle it himself. He already knew from their conversations that Jones basically agreed with the ministers' complaints and he probably felt uncomfortable about it. When, a little later, he told parliament that this was a family affair in which no outsider should meddle, he may have had others than just the media in mind.[41] He continued that not only had the news of the conflict leaked in Blantyre but it was also known in the Central Province: ' If Chiume puts his head into Lilongwe he will be killed.' Although the prime minister himself did not raise the question at this meeting – indeed, he had already told the ministers that he did not intend to resign – Jones reiterated his opinion that Banda should stay in office. The doctor shared this view, but none the less added that it might not be a bad thing to let them 'run their own show themselves for a bit and see how they get on', probably by giving them some of the responsibility for which they asked, and letting this, and the consequences, be known to the public. He implied that they would make a dismal failure of it. Again, Jones, still leaning in the ministers' direction, advised restraint:

> I advised him to play it cool. He could agree to certain modifications to Skinner. He could delegate more responsibilities. He could play down his foreign policy so far as Portugal and Southern Rhodesia were concerned. In short, he could go some way with his ministers without having to go the whole way. He said the crucial thing for him [in his relations with Portugal] was the Nacala rail link ... He would resign rather than give way over this.

The prime minister did not mention the written list of demands at this meeting with Jones – another example of him not keeping the Governor-General up to date with what was going on. It may be that the allegations of treating government as private property, nepotism and favouritism so hurt and embarrassed him that he did not wish Jones to know of them yet. Although he could confidently explain and justify his policy decisions and his methods of operating, he may have felt it would be more difficult to explain, justify or, possibly, refute these more personal accusations, and certainly more uncomfortable, though he did so in parliament a little later. It was these particular complaints and allegations which seemed, and probably were intended, most to hurt him. Just before he left the Governor-General, he referred to their final comments the previous evening. He was fully aware that Chiume was 'the spearhead of the attack and was organizing the Africans in the civil service against [him]'. He thought Chirwa and Chisiza might follow him, Banda. Later Chipembere, was to say Chisiza and not Chiume was the leader of the revolt.[42]

The following evening, 29 August, Banda met the ministers yet again to discuss their written demands. He found a number of points 'very difficult', but he gave the impression that he was prepared, as Jones had suggested, to move on some issues while not basically changing his policy. He was willing to compromise on the Skinner report by helping existing civil servants. He would not make an announcement about republican status. He was prepared to play down the appointment of Jardim as Malawi's honorary consul in Beira. The allegations of nepotism and favouritism were not touched on. It is unlikely that the ministers were particularly satisfied with these responses but they thought they detected a shift in their direction, which may have been the lulling impression Banda intended to create.

The prime minister went straight from this meeting to visit the Governor-General for about half an hour. Not perhaps surprisingly, Jones found him 'still pensive and rather unwilling to talk. [He] had to drag information from him.' Clearly, the list of written demands had deeply disturbed him although he still did not mention it. He told Jones about the meeting and had made no arrangements to meet the ministers again. He thought nothing was likely to happen over the remainder of the weekend.

Banda's pensiveness and unwillingness to talk reflected his having much on his mind. During the previous afternoon he had began to receive anonymous letters saying his ministers were stirring up trouble against him and there was not the widespread unrest, resentment and bitterness which they claimed. Further, during the Saturday, a number of people called personally on him, concerned that he had not appeared in public for the past few days, and imploring him, as had the anonymous letters, not to resign. Long aware of the divisions and individual ambitions within the cabinet, he had not previously accepted the rumours he heard about the ministers conspiring against him. Now, however, he began to believe them.[43] He also had a number of meetings with 'Muwalo and other party stalwarts' who, 'for obvious reasons ... strongly advised him not to resign and instead to expel the ministers'.[44] Furthermore, rumours circulating in Blantyre – almost certainly originating from Chiume – claimed Banda had surrendered to his ministers, and this infuriated him.[45] These factors, coupled with the written list of demands, made him even more strongly determined not to resign, 'come what may', and notwithstanding any progress made in discussion with his ministers.[46]

Chirwa, Chiume and Bwanausi saw Banda's receipt of the anonymous letters as a fatal turning point in their discussions with him: 'At one stage we almost reached agreement, but [it was] spoiled by outside influence, when people started writing letters to the Prime Minister, telling him that we were plotting.'[47] Banda also indicated that 28 August was a turning point, though his explanation was that the Kuchawe manifesto determined him to reject their demands.

Already Banda's mind had turned to how he was to handle the crisis from now on – by himself. He had already decided not to give up the premiership. His tactic so far was to appear to shift marginally on a few points of difference without changing his basic policies. He was convinced now that the ministers were conspiring against him. He contemplated asking Jones to dissolve parliament so that he could tour the country to see what support he had. He told Jones: 'The ministers are getting no sleep and the thought of my possible resignation troubles them.' This suggests that he believed he was winning the battle and could afford to take the initiative himself.

Over the weekend, 29–30 August, Banda took further 'stock of his standing in the party', by consulting 'the strata of party leadership immediately below' the cabinet ministers.[48] These party colleagues, who included the administrative secretary and two of the regional ministers – the third was in Britain – assured him the party was solidly behind him. This consultation – Banda's parrying blow to the ministers' written attack – presumably was sufficiently reassuring as to do away with the need to dissolve parliament and undertake a nation-wide tour to assess his support. Certainly, no more was heard of the proposal.

After the weekend, on Monday 31 August, Chirwa asked to see Jones urgently. They spent an hour and a quarter together in the early afternoon. Chirwa explained that the purpose of the visit was for the ministers to 'maintain contact' with the Governor-General. He seemed 'quietly confident but not perky'. All the ministers, Chirwa said, were united in their determination to ensure that the principle of cabinet responsibility operated. He briefly summed up Saturday evening's meeting with Banda, which he referred to as 'round five', at which he and his colleagues felt they had made progress. 'Round six' would take place during the coming week and they all hoped it would be a 'hand-shaking meeting'. He said they would not rush into converting Malawi into a republic, and if Banda had not changed his mind about announcing his intentions in the legislature, the ministers would strongly have opposed him publicly. 'We do not want a Ghana here. We will not tolerate an executive president.' Finally, Jones warned Chirwa that the ministers should 'not go too far and drive the Prime Minister over the edge'. Still in sympathy with their complaints, though not with their presentation, he said they would do very well for the time being if they got Banda to agree to delegate more functions to them. Policy differences could then be thrashed out in detail.

A few hours after Chirwa saw the Governor-General, Banda also asked to see him.[49] He saw Youens in advance of this meeting and said 'he was going to teach a political lesson to the Cabinet that they would not forget'. Banda then went on to Government House. Gone was the reflectiveness and reticence of the previous Saturday evening. Now he was in a very excitable mood, his speech was staccato, he was 'rather breathless', he often repeated himself and he left sentences unfinished. He spoke of his weekend soundings. Confident now of his following in the country, he was 'not going to suffer the same fate as Nyerere at the hands of his Ministers'. Sweeping aside Jones's advice given three days earlier that he should 'play it cool', he was determined that now was 'the time to be firm, to be tough'. To clear the air, he proposed to resign, not for good but momentarily so that he could instantaneously be re-appointed and could then form a new cabinet without actually sacking anyone. Sacking the ministers would 'cause anxiety among the population, particularly Europeans'. His momentary resignation would, he said, mean that all present cabinet ministers would be out of office unless and until they were re-appointed. He intended to advise Jones to re-appoint all except Chiume, Chisiza and Chipembere and to appoint Chidzanja, Chakuamba and Muwalo to the cabinet. The present cabinet ministers had gone too far and his discussions with them could go no further.

As soon as Banda left, Jones asked Youens and Roberts to see him. Together they sought to devise a plan of action. Roberts's role in advising Jones, and thereby Banda, was crucial. Arriving at an agreed plan was not straightforward because although Youens and Roberts were clear and consistent, Jones was not, and inevitably so because, as he said, the prime minister was 'mad with rage' and consequently any solution needed to be acceptable to him. Such a solution was difficult to reach. Jones preferred Banda to sack those he termed 'the enemy ministers' and keep the rest. Youens believed the cabinet was united very solidly against the prime minister who would be ruthless with them 'once they came apart'. Banda was adamant that he should momentarily resign and instantaneously be re-appointed. He 'baulked at the idea of resignation without immediate re-appointment'. Although Jones thought Banda put the idea forward 'rather disingenuously', he was inclined to accept it, since it would give the doctor time to re-form his cabinet and give general confidence to the people. It is not clear that Banda was being disingenuous. His proposal would have kept the ministers somewhat in limbo while he decided how to re-form the cabinet and would be a public indication both that Banda was not going to give up office and that the Governor-General was supporting him. However, Roberts said that, given Banda's majority support in the Assembly, there were no grounds for him to resign; indeed, resignation was quite inconsistent with that majority.

Jones toyed with the idea of dissolving parliament and holding a general election, but Roberts pointed to the lack of constitutional guidance on who nominated candidates in, effectively, a one-party state. This was a significant point because if, as in the past, Banda personally made all the MCP nominations, the nominees would be certain to support him, and the process would be pointless. Jones tried to fall back on doing nothing: let things simmer for a month and then have the matter settled in parliament. Not only did this not overcome Roberts's objection based on Banda's majority – assuming it lasted intact another month – but Youens, who was intimate with what went on in cabinet, did not think they could leave things that long. Although he felt privately that the matter ought to be thrashed out by a caucus within the MCP, Roberts's official advice was simple: ask the members of parliament whether they supported Banda. The prime minister's resignation, even momentary, would mean the Governor-General straight away having to appoint as prime minister someone who appeared to him to command majority support in the legislature. It was incumbent upon him, therefore, to ascertain the feelings of members of parliament. They could be consulted individually or in groups and not necessarily altogether. Roberts was clear that he need not consult the ministers because they had already told him they wanted Banda as prime minister.[50]

The next evening, 1 September, Jones and Banda discussed the plan to consult members of parliament. When Jones said he would see all members before the end of the week, the doctor retorted that this was too long and he wanted it done immediately. He eventually agreed that the Governor-General had to see all or most of the members before he resigned and was immediately reappointed to form a new cabinet, which was still what he wanted to do. Jones promised to see members in Zomba, Blantyre, Lilongwe and Mzimba, which would involve a good deal of travelling at very short notice.

Early the next morning Banda phoned to say he had changed his mind and wanted to take action immediately. Jones's plan would take too long. He still favoured momentary resignation and instantaneous reappointment, now coupling it with prior soundings of members of the legislature. Two minutes later he phoned once more and said he had again changed his mind and the plan for consultation should stand. Asked to be as quick as he could, Jones promised to proceed with all possible speed. He immediately summoned the commissioner of police, the under-secretary to the prime minister, and his own private secretary to discuss the itinerary for consulting members of parliament.

Banda met his ministers at 10 a.m. He showed no sign whatsoever of meeting their representations, but 'merely lectured them', and the meeting 'ended in chaos'. His mood was one of 'cold resolution and hostility'. At the end he rang a bell, called in Youens, who had heard noisy shouts from the prime minister's adjacent room, and said, 'Mr Youens, I have finished with these people, see them out.' There was 'dead silence' until Chiume interrupted to say, 'But we haven't finished with you.' Banda told them 'You will not make a Nyerere out of me. You can shoot me. I will not be Nyererised.' He then added, 'Well, I am not going to sit here and listen to you any further. If you are not going to leave the room immediately, I am going to leave it.' He rose and walked out 'in anger', leaving the ministers sitting in his office. A little later, Banda not having returned, they left.[51]

As soon as he learned of this, Jones – no doubt realizing that a dangerous impasse had been reached – tried to get Banda to come and see him, but Miss Kadzamira excused him, saying he was not feeling well and would like to see the Governor-General at 5.30 p.m. Again, he was in no immediate hurry to bring Jones up to date.

Jones must nevertheless have felt some very early action was needed. Less than half an hour after the ministers left Banda's office, Jones had a brief discussion with Youens and Roberts. Ten minutes later Roberts called on the doctor, notwithstanding his not feeling well, which may have been an excuse for not visiting Jones. It is most likely that he explained the difficulties and lack of necessity of resigning and being reappointed, and the reasons for advising that all he need do for the present was to have the feelings of members of parliament ascertained. His verbal skill, clear thinking, simplicity and logic of argument and his forthrightness of approach undoubtedly appealed to Banda, and his advice was accepted. It is probable that Roberts, noticing Banda's dithering over what to do, convinced Jones that they should immediately take the initiative and positively advise the doctor on the single course to be taken. Jones, with his reticence to proffer advice which might irritate Banda and bring about an explosion, would have been reluctant himself to undertake this task. Youens, who could and would have been prepared to undertake it, was less familiar with the constitutional intricacies than was Roberts.

Early that afternoon Jones asked Chirwa to see him. Chirwa, who had left his colleagues meeting at his house, described what had taken place that morning. He went on to say that although the ministers still hoped Banda would not resign, there was a growing feeling that it would not be a bad thing if he did; one of the other ministers could easily form a cabinet. Chirwa, surprisingly for the minister of justice, became 'thoughtful' when told that a prime minister was chosen as the person who best commanded majority support in the legislature, not simply in the cabinet. He was despondent and thought stalemate had been reached, especially when Jones told him the ministers had pushed the matter too far and Banda was now unlikely to concede anything. Jones found this meeting 'rather dreary and unproductive'. He was, it seems, losing patience with the ministers, felt they had played their cards badly and had made matters very much worse.

Jones, Youens and Roberts met again in the middle of the afternoon. Chiume's dismissal was being considered, but he had suddenly decided not to go to Addis Ababa as previously arranged. He cancelled his departure within a quarter of an hour of the end of the morning's meeting.[52] Because of Chiume's change of plans, the 'disastrous meeting' and the difficulty of Jones's own position, Roberts advised that the plan for Jones to ascertain parliamentarians' feelings should be abandoned.

> It would be far better to advise the Prime Minister himself to meet his MPs altogether and explain the position fully to them and endeavour to obtain their support to his continuing to be Prime Minister. To sack Chiume at this stage would probably lead to the resignation of the majority of the other ministers and the need to appoint new ministers. This would entail the Prime Minister having to obtain at some time a mandate from the party and the MPs and he would then have his position undermined by the ousted Ministers who would feel free to criticise him forcibly and work against him in all sorts of ways.

Roberts also said that for Jones to canvass the opinions of members of parliament, before he had resigned, on whether they would want the prime minister to be re-appointed would be 'a sterile performance'. Members would feel they were being led into a trap and if later the prime minister fell and some other person succeeded him, the Governor-General's intervention could be viewed with great suspicion and probably hostility. Roberts was pointing out the advisability of keeping all the ministers in office until Banda received a mandate from members of parliament and the party to continue as prime minister.

Later, at 5.30 p.m. Banda, now 'well, confident and cheerful', went to see Jones. The ground having been well prepared by Roberts, the Governor-General followed his advice and suggested that they should not carry out the plan they had worked out earlier: momentary resignation and instantaneous re-appointment following Jones's ascertaining of parliamentary support. He urged the doctor himself to put members 'fully in the picture as to what had been happening' and 'give them his version of the discussions within the cabinet'.

> [Banda] still believed he commanded the support of the great majority of the people and had himself come to the conclusion that it would be wise and advantageous for him to summon MPs to Zomba and have an unofficial meeting. He decided to have the meeting [on] Sunday September 6th. [The] messages [were] not to be sent out until sometime on Friday 4th. He was clearly in [a] fighting mood.

It is likely that Banda's own conclusion that he should summon members was the result of Roberts's visit to him that morning.

Jones did not tell Banda that Chiume had changed his mind about going to Addis Ababa, though he had known for several hours. Banda's decision to delay sending the messages calling members to Zomba was reached in the absence of this knowledge and presumably was designed to exclude Chiume, and to allow only just sufficient time for them to travel to the capital, and too little for any serious attempts to be made to dissuade them from supporting the prime minister. If he had previously shown signs of contemplating making any concessions to the ministers' demands, it is clear from this meeting that he now intended to do nothing of the sort but to dig his toes in still further.

Jones reviewed the position with Youens and Cole that evening and thought there might be 60 per cent support for Banda from the the MPs. Youens estimated it at only 50 per cent, because the ministers were 'sticking' on points commanding fairly wide support, for example dropping the Skinner report, faster Africanization and the hospital fees. Cole thought it would be 'a close thing'.[53] Roberts, it seems, was more sure of Banda's success. As Jones saw it, 'the situation was certainly fluid and ... there now seemed to be no possibility of compromise'.

Up to this point Jones had been in general sympathy with the ministers' objections to the way Banda operated. Furthermore, he could hardly object to the hospital charges and civil service economies – nor to the foreign relations policy which was economic in nature rather than philosophical – since they were part of the financial constraints on which Butler had insisted. Now, however, he felt he and his colleagues should support Banda against his ministers, since they could not sort out their differences themselves. He thought they should do all they could to provide the doctor with arguments for his meeting of members of parliament and remind him that ministers had agreed in cabinet to some of the matters they now strongly criticized.[54] It is clear that for some time Roberts had held the view that they should come down clearly on Banda's side in his conflict with his ministers. Jones was now accepting it.

The next morning, Thursday 3 September, the prime minister called on the Governor-General for ten minutes. Banda was convinced he had taken the right course with his ministers the previous day and 'smacking them down'. He called on Jones again in the evening and when told Chiume had decided not to go to Addis Ababa, he said that while he understood the reasons, it would not deter him from carrying on and summoning the members of parliament to Zomba. 'If I had carried on while he was [out of the country] he might have become a martyr.' Banda said he would like Cameron as minister of justice or, failing him, Sacranie, a lawyer and leader of the Asian community. Jones advised him to await the outcome of the informal meeting with parliamentarians before offering Cameron a post. When Cameron lunched with Jones the next day, he said he 'would seriously consider an offer to be re-appointed as minister, provided the constitution was not altered to provide for detention without trial without the declaration of a state of emergency'. He would also want to have the 'real responsibilities of a minister'.

Banda was surprised the ministers had not resigned and he seemed to hope they would. He was convinced his meeting with them the previous day, when he had walked out on them, was a success for him, and the ministers were cowed by it. He was seeing a good deal of Muwalo, Aleke Banda and Nyasulu, and seemed sure of their support. He had no doubt he would gain overwhelming support at the informal meeting with members of parliament and he intended to hold a formal meeting of parliament the following day or the day after. It was not only the ministers of whom he was now suspicious because, as Jones recorded of their meeting: 'Finally he said ... that [the Governor-General's] servants had been instructed to listen in to [their] conversations and for this reason he had on the last few occasions [he had met with Jones] insisted on all the windows in [the Governor-General's] office being closed.'

The prime minister was up betimes the next day, Friday 4 September, and called on Jones for ten minutes just before 8.30 a.m. He was convinced he had the support of the great majority of the chiefs. It appears that he had his eye on the longer term because, although support in parliament was where he would stand or fall in the immediate term, he was also looking for support in the country as a whole, including the traditional leaders. He now believed he had Mlanje, Port Herald and Zomba districts on his side. He could no doubt rely also on support in his home area of the central region. He had the support of leading non-cabinet members of the party from all three regions of the country. The doctor's parting words were defiant and ominous: 'I'm going to hit them hard.'

The prime minister had another meeting with the Governor-General that evening and, for the first time, showed him a copy of the ministers' written demands. He said Chiume, Chirwa and Rose Chibambo 'must go at once' but he was prepared to keep Chisiza and the other ministers, 'if he came through'. This was the only indication that Banda may have had a doubt about defeating his ministers. It was also the first indication that he intended to dismiss some of them. Up to this point he had been reluctant to do so. Jones advised him to stay his hand until after the meeting with parliamentarians, before sacking anyone. He proposed to move the meeting from Sunday afternoon, 6 September, to Monday morning, 7 September, possibly to ensure that all the members could get to Zomba in time. He still wanted Cameron or Sacranie as attorney-general, and Jones told him Sacranie would cause trouble.

It is likely that Jones's repeated advice to Banda to stay his hand until the meeting of parliamentarians was given in the hope that differences might then be sorted out sufficiently to preserve the existing cabinet, or most of it. It was this preservation which throughout he seemed most concerned to accomplish. It may also indicate that he thought sufficient members – the 40 per cent he believed might not be on his side – might influence Banda in attempting a compromise.

On Sunday morning, 6 September, Banda called at Government House again. He had little to say and seemed 'preoccupied and unwilling to be drawn'. No doubt his mind was still on the list of complaints, the anonymous letters, the advice of the party stalwarts, the rumours of capitulation and particularly the meeting of parliamentarians, upon which so much would depend. It is possible, though, that this unwillingness was part of the general reticence which manifested itself in his not invariably bringing Jones up to date with what was happening and in asking the Governor-General not to intervene but leave him to handle the dispute himself. The doctor said Chiume, Chisiza and Bwanausi had pledged themselves to stick together and 'had got hold of Chirwa and the others. It was a rebellion and [he] would like to have them prosecuted for sedition.' He wondered if he could have their passports seized. When Jones again advised him to await the outcome of the parliamentarians' meeting the next day, he 'quietly agreed'. Banda contemplated the morrow's meeting and was confident of victory.

The following morning, Monday 7 September, Banda, rejecting Jones's recent advice not to take any important action before the meeting of members of parliament, rang the Governor-General and formally advised him that the ministerial offices of Chirwa, Chiume and Bwanausi, together with the parliamentary secretaryship for natural resources, filled by Rose Chibambo, should immediately be declared vacant.[55] The doctor said he would not attend the meeting, adding 'It is not necessary'.

As this telephone call was being made, the informal meeting was taking place. Those present were told by Nyasulu, the Speaker, that a formal meeting of parliament would take place the next day to debate a motion of confidence in the prime minister. They demanded to see the agenda, and when the motion was read out the backbenchers showed 'enthusiastic support' for it, but the ministers 'sat dejected'.

The prime minister rang Jones again soon after the meeting ended and said he would not come to see him that day but he would come the following evening, that is after the day's debate in parliament. Once again he was in no hurry personally to bring Jones up to date, though Nyasulu did. When Jones questioned the wisdom of sacking Bwanausi, Banda became very impatient and said 'I know what I am doing. I want this thing done as quickly as possible – with as little delay as possible.' An hour or so later he rang again, apologized for 'thumping the table' earlier, and asked if Jones was sure he had got correctly the names of those being sacked. Jones repeated them correctly: Chirwa, Chiume, Bwanausi and Rose Chibambo. Immediately after this telephone call, the Governor-General saw the three ministers who were about to be dismissed, at half-hour intervals. Indeed, the first was briefly delayed while the call was being made.

The first to be dealt with was Chirwa, who, Jones recorded, accepted the news 'with calm and dignity'. He considered the prime minister had done the right thing and would win his motion of confidence. 'Most of the MPs do not understand the issues at stake, but they will learn eventually. They do not have the same principles as we have.' Ministers did not wish to criticize Banda publicly and would not do so in tomorrow's debate unless provoked, 'but I suppose we shall be provoked'. He assured Jones he had enjoyed working with him and had nothing whatsoever against the prime minister personally.

The next to come in was Chiume who, also 'calm and dignified', showed no surprise when he received his letter of dismissal. 'I make no apology for what I have done. The Prime Minister has been managing the affairs of four million people without seeking advice from anyone. This is a very undignified form of independence.' Like Chirwa, he had nothing personal against Banda and, according to Jones, said he had enjoyed working with the Governor-General. Chiume's own account is somewhat different: 'I knew that this man had asked for my expulsion from the cabinet in 1963 because he alleged that I had called him an imperialist, and, in 1962 he must have been instrumental in preventing me from becoming the first Minister of the Interior.' When Jones asked him what he was going to do he told him it was none of his business![56] Many years later, Chiume could not recall that he had told Jones he had enjoyed working with him, and thought it unlikely that he and some of his colleagues had said so. He admitted to having called Jones an imperialist.[57]

The third minister to appear was Bwanausi, who also 'received the news in calm and dignified fashion'. He understood Banda's position: 'He does not need men of my calibre. He needs people who will just endorse his policy. I can do more for the country outside politics. I don't like politics and will be glad to get out.' He said ministers had probably only themselves to thank in that they had built up Banda as a Messiah and it was very difficult for him to face opposition now.

These were not the only members of the cabinet to call on the Governor-General that afternoon. When it became clear that only three were being sacked, Chisiza drew Chirwa's typewriter towards him and 'with a confident smile' typed out his own resignation, insisting that they must all 'sink together'. Chokani and then, 'not without some hesitation', Msonthi followed suit.[58] Within half an hour of Bwanausi's departure from Government House, Chisiza, Chokani and Msonthi went to see Jones and handed in their letters of resignation.[59]

> Chisiza was bitter and said he would never withdraw what had been said in their memorandum of complaint ... It would be hypocritical for them to remain after their colleagues had been sacked. There was no difference between them. Chokani was not bitter but said he supported the others

and could not remain a minister after the others had been sacked. He did not agree with the way the country was being run by the Prime Minister. Msonthi said he had been out of all this, since he had only recently been reappointed. 'But how can I stay on by myself?' All said they truly understood [Jones's] position and had enjoyed working with [him] ... They declined to try and see the Prime Minister [as Jones suggested]. They had tried yesterday and he had refused to see them.

Chokani later gave his account of the resignation meeting: 'Sir Glyn ... pleaded with me to reconsider my position and withdraw the resignation. He emphasised Dr Banda had nothing against me. Sir Glyn was definitely unhappy about my resignation.'[60] From this account, though not from Jones's, it is clear that the Governor-General was still desperately trying to retain at least Chokani in the cabinet.

When Jones rang Banda and told him of the resignations 'there was no reaction except that he would see these ministers after the meeting of Parliament tomorrow'. He did not wish the resignations to be given publicity through government channels, only the dismissals.

Early the following morning, 8 September, at 7.20, Msonthi rang Jones from Blantyre to say he wished to see him urgently to withdraw his resignation. He had tried to telephone the doctor the previous evening but had failed. Jones told him to drive over to Zomba straight away. He must have driven very quickly because an hour later he arrived at Government House. He had reconsidered his resignation and wished to withdraw it. He reminded the Governor-General he had said the previous day that he was resigning only because he was 'all alone'. Jones asked him to wait in another room because the prime minister was due to arrive only moments later. Presumably, as soon as he received Msonthi's phone call Jones asked Banda to see him, because he was not scheduled to do so until the evening. When told of Msonthi's change of heart, Banda 'expressed great pleasure' and immediately said the withdrawal should be accepted. Msonthi was then called in and Jones left them alone for about five minutes. After Msonthi left, Jones spent a few more minutes with Banda and advised him to 'let magnanimity and calmness be the motifs of his speech' on the motion of confidence that morning. Banda agreed to heed this advice and thanked Jones for his moral support during the past few days.

During the remainder of that and the following day, parliament debated a motion, drafted for Banda by Roberts,[61] to resolve that the house supported the MCP policy of unity, loyalty, discipline and obedience; supported the policies of the prime minister on domestic and external affairs; and reaffirmed its confidence in him.[62] In this single formula Roberts sought for Banda the necessary mandate of both the party and parliament to which he had referred earlier. Cole described the occasion as 'dramatic and historic':

> The House was packed and several hundred people gathered in the small area outside.
>
> Dr Banda, supported by only Messrs. Tembo and Msonthi, proposed the motion of confidence in a remarkable speech which lasted for an hour and a half. He described in detail the Cabinet proceedings and skilfully built up a picture of a Ministerial conspiracy against him, steering clear of the underlying issue of collective responsibility and claiming that his colleagues had tried to create popular antipathy to his policies ... He said that the Ministers were motivated by ambition and avarice, and by the sinister enticements of Red China ... he deduced a 'Chinese plot' to overthrow him. At one stage he alleged that the Ministers would have murdered him if they thought they could get away with it.
>
> Dr. Banda received an overwhelming ovation from M.P.s, and it was clear from that moment that the vote of confidence would be carried without any difficulty.[63]

Chipembere arrived back from Canada and Chibambo from Britain early in the afternoon of the first day of the debate, 8 September. At 8.20 p.m. Chipembere – with whom a number of his friends on his arrival in Zomba had pleaded that he should attempt a reconciliation[64] – went to see Jones, having been sent there by Banda who had refused to see him. Jones, to Chipembere's surprise, was not expecting him. Chipembere was gravely concerned by the 'tragic situation' which had arisen while he was away, and asked why it had been necessary to sack his colleagues. Jones told him that 'things seemed to be going fairly well' until they put their demands in writing.

> [Chipembere] then said he had not made up his mind what side to take. Before taking a final decision he would like to satisfy his conscience that he had done everything within his power to get a reconciliation between the Prime Minister and the Ministers. Was there still a chance of his doing this in his capacity of a minister who, while being fully implicated in the original approaches to the Prime Minister, had been out of the country when the situation had deteriorated into a cabinet crisis?

Jones thought that if the ministers were 'prepared to make a gesture' there might still be a chance. Chipembere was willing to try and get them to make an approach if the Governor-General would see whether Banda would receive one. Jones then telephoned the prime minister who, although it was not yet 8.30 p.m., had already retired to bed. As Jones recalled:

When I put the proposition to him he at first said he would be prepared to receive an approach only after the debate had been concluded. I said Chipembere very much hoped to have a meeting before the debate was resumed. The Prime Minister said he would consider it but showed very little enthusiasm. I phoned Chipembere and said ... I thought the Prime Minister would not agree to postponing the resumption of the debate to enable the discussion to take place; therefore it would be necessary for the discussion, if agreed to, to take place before 9.30 a.m. ... Later he phoned to say he had contacted all the ex-ministers and they were in agreement. He asked that the meeting should take place in Government House in my presence since I was 'the most neutral of all.'

At a quarter to eight the next morning, 9 September, Jones rang Banda. 'He was not in a happy mood' and was incensed that Chipembere had, even by implication, suggested that resuming the debate should be postponed. He 'absolutely declined' to meet the ministers until after the debate. 'He was angrily emphatic about this.' Jones immediately told Chipembere of Banda's decision and received the response that he and his colleagues felt that no useful purpose would be served by meeting Banda after the debate because strong attitudes would by then have been adopted from which people would find it difficult to retreat.[65] When, half an hour later, Jones told Banda of Chipembere's reply, he simply said, 'That's all right.'

At 9.15 a.m., at Banda's request, Jones swore in Chibambo as regional minister; he had been in Britain when Kumtumanji and Chidzanja were made regional ministers. Five minutes later he received Chipembere's written resignation.[66] Chipembere then drove to parliament and joined his colleagues on the back bench.[67]

At 8.10 in the evening of the second day of the debate, parliament gave Banda a unanimous vote of confidence, having at his insistence sat without break for the whole of the day. Jones with his wife and Youens listened to the whole of the two-day debate, at Goverment House, using equipment installed several years earlier by Armitage. He recorded the proceedings and kept the tape for the rest of his life.[68]

The morning after the debate, Banda called on Jones. He was pleased with the support he had received in the House. He asked Jones to swear in Nyasulu as minister for natural resources, Muwalo as minister of information, Chakuamba as minister for community and social development, Chidzanja as minister of works and transport and Roberts as attorney-general. He himself would take over the portfolios of justice and external affairs. Finance remained with Tembo and communications with Msonthi. He left the ministries of education and local government, of labour and of home affairs vacant, perhaps hoping that Chipembere, Chokani and Chisiza could be tempted back to them.

Banda met Jones on Monday afternoon, 14 September, and spoke of Chipembere, Chokani and Chisiza. Although it was not emphasized, it was their portfolios which had not yet been allocated to other ministers.[69] 'The Prime Minister agreed that he would be in a stronger position if he could get back the ministers who had resigned. He said [Jones] could contact Chokani and Chisiza right away so long as [he] did not let it appear the approach was coming from him. Chipembere should be seen later. [Banda] was still very angry with Chiume, Chirwa and Bwanausi – latter almost most of all.'

Banda rang the Governor-General the next evening, 15 September, to say he 'had it on good authority' that Chisiza, Chokani and Bwanausi would be prepared to rejoin him. He asked Jones to approach them 'behind the scenes' and 'see what he could do'. During the following week Jones had a number of meetings to try and repair some of the deep damage caused over the past week or so.

On 16 September, the day after Banda asked him to see what he could do behind the scenes, the Governor-General spoke with Chokani who hoped very much that Jones would 'promote a reconciliation ... this week before the attitudes had hardened beyond recall'. Jones was not confident he could get Banda to accept Chiume and Chirwa and asked how important Chipembere was. The tactic of dividing the ex-ministers, originally attempted by Banda to get rid of some of them, was now used by Jones in an effort to get some of them back. Jones recorded:

> [Chokani] said no reconciliation could take place without Chipembere. The [ex-]ministers would press for all to be taken back. I said that if they adopted an 'all or nothing' attitude the prospects of getting things back to normal were very slight indeed, [though] there might be a possibility that the thing could be solved if all except Chiume came back. Chiume might be given a job outside the Government. Chokani said, 'If Chiume as Minister of External Affairs is unacceptable why could he not go back to Education or Information?'

Under no existing, and probably no future, circumstances would the prime minister have Chiume back in his government, but Chokani does not seem to have grasped this point.

The Governor-General carefully explained that his line of approach was without Banda's prior agreement, that he had no authority to make any concessions and that any argument and bargaining would have to take place directly with Banda; he could take no part in it himself. He then spoke in very pointed terms, which reveal how deeply disturbing he believed the position to be and which explain why he had gone, and was continuing to go, to such lengths to heal the rifts and bring about a return to stable government. He almost certainly intended his words, their tone and his view of the profound seriousness of the situation to be conveyed to the other ex-ministers:

> Malawi was now disunited and the laughing stock of the world. If I could not promote a reconciliation I would have to go. The situation could go from bad to worse and civil war on a Congo scale could happen. The ex-Ministers must recognize that they had over the past three years conceded full power to the Prime Minister; he had got them what they wanted; they could not, having regard to his very authoritative methods, get him in one fell swoop to reverse all his policies and decisions. They must be prepared to meet him half way. All was going well in their negotiations until the memorandum of demands was drawn up. That document was in my view disastrous.

Jones's statement that he would have to go if he could not secure a reconciliation is puzzling and it is not clear how extensive that reconciliation would have to be for him to stay. It is extremely unlikely that he would have wished to avoid the challenge of being Governor-General in the event, appalling as it would be, of a Congo-like civil war. Rather, it may be that having learned from Banda the efficacy of threatened resignation, he was applying the same tactic. Perhaps he hoped Chokani and at least some his colleagues believed they needed him as Governor-General. Perhaps a threat to go might pull them round? On the other hand, Chiume disliked him and Chipembere believed Jones had become ineffectual and Banda treated him as a junior officer.[70] Perhaps, too, the prospect of remaining in Banda's ill-favour without having Jones to turn to for advice and support, which would leave them marooned and entirely at Banda's mercy, would induce a greater willingness to attempt a reconciliation. In the absence of an immediate conversion to republican status, Malawi would have to have a new Governor-General if Jones resigned, and the prospect of having either an unknown replacement – and one less trusted by Banda – or an executive president, would not have appealed to them. It is possible, too, that Jones feared that if he could not effect a reconciliation, if necessary by threatening to resign, and sucessfully resolve such a devastating and revealing crisis so soon after independence, the sacrifices he had made and the trials he had endured over the past four years would be to no avail. The defects of the past few years – politically motivated violence, murder, arson, intimidation, intolerance, victimization and the rapid drift to one-party dictatorship – would be exposed and grave doubts cast on the validity of the outstanding public reputation which he enjoyed, especially for influencing Banda and guiding and restraining his lieutenants. This would be a profoundly unhappy, humiliating way to end his career. Be these as they may, in the event he neither promoted a reconciliation nor did he resign.

Chokani agreed that Jones should try to get Chisiza and Bwanausi together with himself and Chipembere, for a meeting on Friday 18 September, two days hence. When, on 17 September, Jones asked Chipembere to see him he replied, 'At the present stage I cannot see [the Governor-General] by myself alone. I can only see him together with ... the former ministers who are likely to be in Zomba and Blantyre at the end of this month', which was two weeks away.

The next day, 18 September, Jones saw Chokani, Chisiza and Bwanausi. Chokani phoned him in the morning and was strangely guarded in his phraseology, asking, 'Is the gentleman from the north coming down?' to which Jones, taking this to refer to Chisiza, answered that he had not received a reply but he might be on his way. Chokani then said, 'Augustine [Bwanausi] and I have spoken to the one who refused your invitation for yesterday [Chipembere]. He says he will join us if the man from the north comes down. Then there will be four of us.'

Chisiza arrived at Government House early that afternoon to see Jones in his personal capacity and not as Governor-General. He agreed to come again in the evening with Chipembere, Chokani and Bwanausi and 'promised to do all in his power to remedy the very difficult situation that had arisen by all means short of abandoning his principles'. He said the situation was not beyond repair. Jones explained his position as honest broker and said he would tell Banda of the proposed meeting with them. He added that he thought the memorandum deplorable: 'it had a disastrous effect on the Prime Minister.'

At seven o'clock that evening Chisiza – 'slightly tight' in Jones's opinion – Chokani and Bwanausi, saw the Governor-General but Chipembere did not join them. His colleagues excused him on the ground that 'he did not know there was to be a meeting.' Jones recorded: '[They] all spoke saying they were willing to do what was possible to heal the breach. There could be compromise but [they] strongly felt the doctor should see all the ex-ministers. I said I doubted if the Prime Minister could agree to that. Why could not those whom he would agree to, go and see him in the first place?' He made it clear that though he had no mandate from Banda and no proposals, he sensed that at present Chiume and Chirwa were unlikely to be received by the prime minister. Chisiza responded that Banda wanted to divide them, 'But we shall stick together and must be loyal to our friends.' Jones pointed to possibly an even greater loyalty: to the country and the people. 'The Prime Minister [was] a man of strong heart and spirit. They could not expect him to reverse his policies. Their document had been an arrogantly worded ultimatum probably unique in history.'

Jones repeatedly, almost obsessively, told the ministers about the damaging effect of the Kuchawe manifesto, but he does not seem at any stage to have suggested they withdraw it. He may have been miffed by Chirwa and his colleagues not speaking with him about compiling and submitting it and by Banda's delay in mentioning it to him. Alternatively, he possibly felt the damage done was irreparable and withdrawal would not help. More likely, he felt it would have been too much to ask of the ministers, especially since they knew he agreed with the substance of much of it.

The Governor-General continued that if they got four cardinal principles of cabinet government they should be satisfied: the prime minister should back them up particularly in public; delegate functions; take his ministers into his confidence; and accept collective responsibility to parliament, as laid down in the constitution. All these points were directed at Banda reforming his method of governing, and none of the substantive policy issues was mentioned. While they were capable of meeting all the ex-minister's demands, Jones must have known that there was no chance of them being accepted by Banda. Quite obviously, he still agreed with their demands. The three ex-ministers promised to reconsider their decision not to meet Banda unless all ex-ministers were present, and agreed to meet again the following evening.

They – Chisiza, Chokani and Bwanausi – met Jones, as agreed, at 6.30 the following evening, 19 September. Again Chipembere was absent and his colleagues excused him by saying he was 'on his way but had probably had a puncture or something'. They would see him later in the evening. This time Bwanausi was the spokesman. They had decided, in the interests of the country, to try and see Banda without insisting on all the ex-ministers being present. They seemed 'more cheerful' than the previous evening. It was left that Jones would suggest to the prime minister that he should meet them and Chipembere the following Monday. In the meantime he would 'try and create as friendly an atmosphere as possible for the meeting'.

Just after they left Jones, Banda, as arranged, arrived. He was in a 'very confident and, from the point of view of the purpose in hand, very difficult mood': 'He was going to teach the ex-ministers a lesson they would never forget. They had picked on the wrong man to try and "Nyererise". But for the fact that [he was] telling the people to exercise restraint some of them would be dead and under the ground by now. All the people were solidly behind him even in the north.' The doctor's mood made it extremely difficult for Jones to create a friendly atmosphere in which the former ministers could meet the prime minister. He told Banda that those he had met at his request wished to see him without asking for Chirwa and Chiume to be present. As Jones recalled:

He was very lukewarm about it, saying, 'I cannot see them until I have finished all my meetings throughout the country' ... I protested that such a decision left me in a most awkward situation. He then agreed to meet the four sometime on Monday 'but only to shake hands with them, not to talk business. We will talk after I have had my meetings' ... I could get no further with him and agreed to inform the ministers. He was very cordial to me and thanked me very much for all the trouble I had taken. But he was in a mood of rather devastating confidence and quite unshakable.

The likelihood of a meeting between the prime minister and any of the ex-ministers, limited as it already was, faded significantly that weekend when Chipembere, Chokani, Chisiza and Bwanausi held what they claimed was a cocktail party in Blantyre to which the press were invited. They criticized Banda's policies, particularly on external affairs, and vowed they would return to the government only if he changed that policy. The 200 or so people present gave them a standing ovation.

Jones believed the doctor knew this party had been arranged when he spoke with him on Saturday evening and was 'so difficult'. He also believed that when Chipembere 'probably had a puncture or something' he was in fact arranging the function. What was said at the cocktail party and the dismissive tones of a speech made by the prime minister at Ngabu the following day, persuaded him to reconsider the appropriateness of a meeting between the ex-ministers and Banda. Consequently, well before eight o'clock on Monday morning, 21 September, he met with Youens and Roberts and they quickly decided to ask Banda if he now felt any helpful purpose would be served by a meeting simply to shake hands. Youens rang later in the morning to say that, when asked, Banda said there would be no useful point in a meeting at the present time. Having received Banda's response, Jones rang Chokani and asked him to tell his colleagues that Banda, having reluctantly agreed to meet them, now felt that it would serve no useful purpose. He added that he was sorry his efforts had failed, but he did not say that he also thought there was no point in a meeting. Chokani was sympathetic but sounded relieved by Banda's decision. It may be that Jones wondered if either side was being open and honest with him and was not simply using or toying with him, playing for time and not being seriously intent on reconciliation. The three ex-ministers had given implausible excuses for Chipembere not joining their meetings with him, and he believed Banda knew in advance of, but did not mention, the 'cocktail party' meeting.

On Friday morning, 25 September, Banda visited Jones just before departing on a tour of the central and northern regions. He seemed very fit and was confident his tour would go well. He was still quite adamant that he would accept no ministers back on the 'all or nothing basis'.

If that was their stand then he would chose nothing. Nevertheless he was willing to have some back on his own terms – Chokani, Bwanausi and even Chirwa. I told him Chirwa had asked to see me and he said he hoped I would agree. I received the impression that the Prime Minister would be very glad indeed to have the three of them back. But 'never Chiume and probably never Chipembere [who was 'mentally deranged – there is insanity in the family']: possibly never Chisiza [who] is a much more treacherous man than you think.'

Chirwa went to see the Governor-General on Saturday 26 September. He would like to do something to reduce the tension before it was too late. Jones told him that Chokani, Bwanausi and probably he himself could get back their ministerial jobs but certainly not Chiume and Chipembere and possibly not Chisiza. Banda had said 'probably never Chipembere' but Jones now said 'certainly not Chipembere'. Whether this was deliberate or a slip of the tongue or memory is unclear. Chirwa doubted if he personally could get a polite word out of the doctor. The last time he had tried Banda had 'blown him off the phone'. He thought perhaps he should write to Banda, and Jones encouraged him to do so and continue to think in terms of 'more friendly overtures'. Jones, repeating the point he made so very often, told him 'what he thought of the document: arrogant and peremptory in tone, smacking of an ultimatum'.

That same morning, Banda rang Jones. He had banned public meetings without police permission and he understood 'Chipembere's gang' was going to Blantyre to organize a meeting the next day. He was adamant the meeting should not take place because it would lead to violence. 'If necessary, force must be used to stop it taking place. If necessary people must be shot and I mean that the Police must shoot to kill. You are in charge of public order, Your Excellency, while I am away in the North. The maintenance of public order and security is paramount at this time. One person cannot be allowed to endanger the security of the whole state.'[71] Banda remained fairly calm during this telephone conversation but Jones believed this was only because he had kept him so. 'He could have become excited fairly easily.' This may explain why Jones made no attempt to question him on the wisdom and propriety of instructing him that the police should, even 'if necessary', shoot to kill.

Later that day 200 youth leaguers arrived in Blantyre, probably to stop people attending Chipembere's meeting the next day. Fighting broke out and twenty people were injured. The following afternoon Chipembere's meeting was banned on the grounds that police permission had not been obtained. Nevertheless, 'gangs of pro-Banda Malawi Youth arrived in Government lorries, heavily armed with clubs and iron bars, and attacked the audience. The riot act was read and the crowd dispersed.'[72]

Meanwhile, ten miles from Zomba, the youth league set up a road block to prevent Chipembere's supporters reaching Blantyre for the banned meeting. In the evening there were violent incidents in which two cars were burned, one of them belonging to Chirwa, who was 'chased in the darkness into the bush where he was fortunate to escape with his life'.[73] He then made his way on foot in the darkness to Zomba – a distance of ten miles – and to Government House. He arrived, 'very shaken, with a cut face and torn clothing. He said Government House was the only safe haven in Zomba.'[74]

The following week was very troubled. It opened on the Monday, 28 September, with rioting between youth leaguers and civil servants in Zomba.[75] On Tuesday afternoon Jones received a calm but verbose telephone call from Chipembere in Fort Johnston. He said the people were expecting the Governor-General to take action to 'remedy the present unfortunate situation'. Jones replied that he had made several attempts at reconciliation but all had failed. He was willing to try again if the ex-ministers gave him a lead. Chipembere was prepared to help but could not do so as long as the prime minister made public allegations against him and his colleagues which made rebuttals imperative. Jones said he would convey this to Banda. Chipembere said he would ring Jones in two days' time 'if he was still alive'. He then protested about Banda's violent use of the young pioneers, and Jones agreed to pass on the complaint to the prime minister's office. He did not, it seems, intend to pass it on to the prime minister himself. This is odd, since the youth league were part of the MCP controlled by Banda, over which Youens, head of the prime minister's office, had no authority.[76]

The following day saw all government employees on strike in Zomba. Most shops in the urban areas of the south were closed. Government offices in Zomba closed early and civil servants stayed at home to protect their families. Large crowds assembled to ward off pro-Banda gangs which were thought to be on their way into the town.

> The situation was tense and explosive, and the Army stood by in support of the Police, one company of troops being on immediate notice. During this difficult situation, not a single African Minister was in Zomba ... The Governor-General, the Army Commander and the Police Commissioner and senior officials, all expatriates, were left in charge ... During the late afternoon the leaders of the civil servants in Zomba demanded to see a Minister. The only one who could be contacted in Blantyre refused, on a flimsy excuse, to show himself in the capital. Mr. Youens [was sent] to

try and reassure the people that all would be well if they returned to work.[77]

Later that day Jones and Youens met the British high commissioner. Cole was worried about the prominent executive role being played by British civil servants and spoke 'about the need for British involvement to be as unobtrusive as possible and for Africans to be openly associated with any major decisions or politics'.[78] He did not say what he would have done had he been in Jones's or Youens's shoes that afternoon. Nor did he explain his authority, as a diplomat, for addressing a Governor-General and head of the civil service of an independent state on this matter. There had been previous occasions when senior government officers had addressed disturbed crowds of civil servants at times of strikes and violence, so it is unlikely that many Malawians would have thought it improper. It would have been irresponsible of Youens to stand aside and risk the army and police having to take forceful action. No ministers were available and no doubt they were very grateful to him for acting on their behalf. He was head of the civil service and was addressing civil servants. Banda had told Jones he was in charge of law and order and that if necessary the police should open fire and shoot to kill. His and Youens's response to the deeply difficult events fell a good deal short of what, on behalf of the prime minister, they were authorized to do.

The following morning, 1 October, the police and a company of the Malawi Rifles moved into the African residential area. They were welcomed by the civil servants who, being thus reassured, promptly returned to work.[79] Thereafter things quietened down for a while.

On the last day of September, regulations were introduced, empowering Banda to restrict people to specified areas.[80] Immediately, he signed an order confining Chipembere within a four-mile radius of his home at Malindi. Chipembere wrote to the British prime minister appealing to him to advise Jones to resign as Governor-General.[81] Jones then lost touch with him for more than five months.

The situation remained tense. There was a persistent rumour in Zomba that civil servants were to be attacked again, their families molested, and on Banda's return to Zomba he would be accompanied by 'a massive force of League of Malawi Youth' who would beat them up. Jones was concerned about these rumours and asked Kumtumanji, Muwalo, Chakuamba and Aleke Banda to meet him on 9 October. They reassured him and he wrote to the prime minister the next day, still, apparently, sure that the party leadership was not behind the outbreaks of violence, and confident of the efficacy of Banda's appeals:

> I know from the Ministers I met yesterday that there is not the slightest vestige of truth in these rumours but it is very difficult, as you know, to

scotch them. The people who spread them are insidious people who work in secret. I wonder if it would be possible for you to say, when you make your speech in Kota Kota, that your policy is still peace and calm ... Your statements about peace and calm in the past have always had very good effects, and I would expect that a similar statement on Sunday would also have a good effect.

Jones told Banda he was sure the great bulk of African civil servants in Zomba were loyal to Banda. Youens had quite the opposite impression.[82] The issue now, Jones continued, was not their terms of service, following the Skinner report, but the rumours of intended violence. He was convinced that the best prospect of retaining a devoted and loyal service was to show them that he, Banda, had confidence in them and would protect them from violence.[83]

When Banda returned to the south on 14 October, he was confident of his position everywhere in the country except Zomba, notwithstanding Jones having said he was sure the great bulk there were loyal to him. He called on Jones three days later and asked if he would 'do him a favour' and go to London to help Tembo in the financial talks with the British government. He would find it difficult and, although he did not say so, politically dangerous to be away and, since there was a new government in Britain – Labour having assumed power the previous day – it might be more appropriate for Jones to go. Jones promised to give the request some thought and in any case he proposed to take leave about that time.[84] A week or so later, he told Banda he thought it unlikely the British government would agree to him being present at the financial negotiations in London and he explained the reasons as he saw them. Banda did not accept them and said he would write to James Callaghan about it. At the very least he wanted Jones to be in London and available to advise Tembo. He argued that although appointed by the queen this was in her capacity as queen of Malawi, Jones represented her in that capacity and Malawi employed him. Consequently there should be no objection to him taking part in discussions vitally affecting the country.[85]

Banda went on, at their meeting on 17 October, to say he did not propose to make an announcement, as he had intended at the next meeting of parliament, about Malawi becoming a republic on 1 April 1965. He had changed his mind and the country would not become a republic 'for at least six months after that [and] possibly a year'. The Governor-General then asked about the ex-ministers. Though he did not say so, Jones was very keen that Malawi should not completely lose the services of the former ministers – some of the best educated and most able people in the country – and he may have hoped that by retaining them in some way they would continue to be of use to their country and be available to rejoin the government if ever this became a possibility. He recalled:

> I suggested that it might be a good thing for the ex-Ministers to be given some employment if they would accept it ... I told him that when I had last seen Orton Chirwa some weeks ago he had himself said that while acknowledging that it would be impossible for him to re-enter the Government [he] would like to perform some useful service. He seemed definitely to be hinting that he would like a job. The Prime Minister's reaction to my suggestion was not unfavourable and he agreed that I should summon Orton Chirwa to come and see me in Zomba to see if his views were still the same.[86]

He lost no time in contacting Chirwa who arrived in Zomba by plane in the afternoon of Monday 19 October. Jones thought it no longer possible for any ex-minister to return to the government.

> He would therefore be well advised to think in terms of serving Malawi in some non-political capacity, for example on the Bench. Clearly Orton had already given this some thought and said that he thought that not only he but Chisiza and Chipembere also might agree to retire from politics and serve Malawi in some other way ... I then gave Orton a lecture on the position of a Prime Minister who was not bound to accept the advice tendered to him and certainly was not a person who could be dictated to.

Jones's 'lecture' reinforced the conclusion at which Chirwa must already have arrived: there was no way in which Banda would agree to the partially collective approach he was proposing – solidarity between Chirwa, Chipembere and Chisiza, but excluding the others. He said he would nevertheless like to call on Banda, 'merely to pay his respects'. Seizing this late chance of re-establishing contact between the prime minister and one of his former ministers, contact he desperately desired, Jones immediately spoke to Youens, who recalled:

> I was called up by Sir Glyn Jones and told what the situation was and asked to go and see the Prime Minister, and ask whether, in fact, he was prepared to talk to Orton Chirwa. I remember going to his house, it was fairly late at night, very dark, and explained the situation to him and he grinned at me, I remember, and said, 'Oh, yes, well, alright, bring Chirwa here and I will talk to him.' And he then rang his bell for his chief of bodyguard who appeared, and he said to him, 'Orton Chirwa is at Government House, Mr. Youens is going to fetch him and bring him here. See that the gate is open for them when they come through'.[87]

When shortly Youens drove Chirwa to Banda's house, the guards tried to force open the doors and get Chirwa out. When this failed they started beating the car and especially its windows. They tried to overturn the car and Youens feared they might set it on fire. He decided he must try to escape as quickly as possible. He put the car in gear and accelerated away quickly.

When he got back to Government House and said what had happened, Jones was very angry because Banda had, he felt, taken advantage of him in that he 'had been responsible for encouraging Chirwa to go and make his peace and he had seemed to acquiesce'. When Jones rang the doctor to remonstrate, as Youens recalled, Banda roared with laughter and said,'Oh, well, it just shows the strength of opposition to these people and the dedication of my own following.'[88]

Jones decided to increase the guard at Government House. Chirwa was to spend the night there and Jones must seriously have thought an attack might be made on him. He also decided that early the next morning Youens should arrange another meeting and say the Governor-General was anxious about Chirwa's safety and hoped Banda would agree to his being escorted by an adequate guard.

Early the next morning, 20 October, Youens saw Banda, delivered Jones's message and was assured that a police escort was unnecessary since the doctor had warned everyone that Chirwa was not to be molested. Youens reported this assurance to Jones.

> At 9.0 a.m. Youens and Orton left in a Government House car with chauffeur Wilfred, without escort, Orton saying he felt most uneasy and apprehensive. Miss Kadzamira was at the gate to meet them. The leader of the body guard was on the verandah and was extremely polite ... They had a good meeting with the Prime Minister who, while being very frank, was cordial and said he would be very pleased to give Orton a non-political job.

Youens and Chirwa took their leave. As they walked along the verandah of Banda's house the head guard and a number of his colleagues brutally attacked Chirwa, beat him severely, and, as Youens, an Oxford boxing blue not given to over-statement, said 'really made a rather unpleasant mess of the poor chap'.[89] When Chirwa arrived back at Government House he 'showed no bitterness at all about his unfortunate experience' and hoped Jones would be able to prevail upon the prime minister to give him a job as a judge.

Jones knew that all the former ministers, except Chipembere, had considered it prudent to leave the country and that a few weeks earlier Chirwa 'had narrowly escaped with his life from a hostile mob when his Mercedes Benz motor car was burnt out'.[90] He knew, too, that Chirwa only just escaped being badly beaten with heavy sticks and knives the evening previously when he had gone to Banda's house. He had himself taken precautions to strengthen the guard at Government House overnight. He was aware of Chirwa's unease and apprehension just before the morning visit. He must have been most desperately anxious to re-establish some contact between Banda and at least one of his former ministers, otherwise it is unlikely that he would have run the grave, obvious and some might think utterly irresponsible risks involved in twice encouraging and helping Chirwa to see Banda. He must have been relieved that Chipembere, Chisiza, Chokani and Bwanausi had been sufficiently wise not to see Banda a month earlier so that he could 'only shake hands with them'.

The following evening, 21 October, Jones told Banda how shocked he was by the attack on Chirwa. He protested at the reports on the radio and in the press that Chirwa had 'come crawling back for forgiveness'. The grounds for this protest are unclear. It was typical of Banda to describe what happened as 'crawling back' and it was not stretching the words excessively to describe Chirwa's return to Banda's house after all he had been through, as 'crawling back'. Youens's account of the interview makes it clear that forgiveness was in fact discussed, so it may have been Banda's publishing the fact of holding the interview or, less likely, the use of the belittling word 'crawling' which brought about Jones's protest. Banda said the assault showed the depth of feeling which people had against Chirwa, and Jones retorted that it also showed a lack of discipline in his guards, which gave little confidence in their competence to protect the prime minister if things got tough. On no previous occasion had Jones spoken with anything like this, albeit very limited, degree of firmness to Banda, but the doctor was unaffected by it. Unlike Youens, Jones believed the guards had acted independently of the doctor. By this time, however, Chirwa had 'got the message and he left [Malawi] pretty quickly'.[91]

On 22 October Jones flew to Lusaka for Zambia's independence celebrations. Among the representatives from the Commonwealth Relations Office was Duncan Watson, assistant under-secretary of state, who spoke with Jones about 'the possibility of [his] becoming too much involved in the business of government' in Malawi. Watson instanced the request that he be present at the financial negotiations in London, which for the queen's representative was 'no go'. He advised Jones to 'be careful'. In the case of assenting to Bills he 'could threaten to resign if it gets too draconian'. The CRO, then, was prepared for him to make this threat – one which he had never made to Banda although, very late in the day, he had to Chokani. This conversation perturbed Jones who, having discussed it with Roberts on his return to Zomba, wrote to Watson and said that he believed he had 'a true understanding of the limitations that lie upon a constitutional Governor-General in an independent Commonwealth country, particularly with regard to participation in the conduct of the political Government of the country's affairs'.

> I have scrupulously avoided any attempt to exercise any authority in these fields, but, as Governor-General enjoying a degree of mutual confidence and respect with the Prime Minister, Dr. Banda, I have always been prepared, at his invitation, to give him and his Government independent counsel, on a confidential basis, when he has asked for it. When the Prime Minister has sought advice on security and constitutional matters this has extended, with his knowledge and support, to permitting the senior officials of the Government ... to meet in the neutral forum of the Conference Room at Government House, to discuss day-to-day security problems, and to keep me informed of the factual situation. I have, from time to time, offered advice when it was sought but decisions taken have always been made by the proper constitutional authorities, either at the level of the Prime Minister and his Ministers or by the individual officials concerned.

He concluded that in all cases it had been Banda or members and officers of his government who had taken the initiative in seeking his counsel. They had, he believed, felt there was 'some advantage in a newly independent state in informally inviting the advice of a Governor-General with considerable experience of the administration of governmental affairs in African countries'.[92]

This was not an entirely accurate portrayal of the extent to which he had involved himself in Malawi governmental and political affairs after independence. He had discussions with Chisiza and Chirwa about the imminent crisis without the prime minister's knowledge. At his own behest he invited ex-ministers to see him without Banda knowing in advance. He gave advice to the ex-ministers without Banda always asking for it to be given. He held 'vespers' (evening security committee meetings) on his own initiative without Banda always knowing of them and he involved Youens, Roberts, Lomax, Long and Lewis in them.[93] Roberts had to dissuade him from implementing his proposal to travel the country to ascertain the support which parliamentarians had for Banda. He decided that he, Youens and Roberts should support Banda in his opposition to the ministers at the informal meeting of parliamentarians. He had discussions with dissidents who had fled the country for Zambia. He was regularly briefed and kept up to date by the secretary to the prime minister and head of Special Branch to a degree which, it could be argued, went beyond the constitutional requirement that the Governor-General should be kept 'fully informed [by the prime minister] concerning the general conduct of the government of Malawi'.[94] Throughout the ministerial revolt – arguably exclusively a political matter in which he should have been cautious of intervening – he had involved himself in many ways more intimately than at any previous time. These were precisely the reservations the Colonial Office had when agreeing to a Governor becoming Governor-General, and of which Cole had warned him.

Watson had not simply by chance mentioned the matter in Lusaka, nor was he to be diverted by the high tone of Jones's written response, which has more echoes of Roberts's drafting style, tone and phraseology than of his own. Shortly, when Jones was in London in November, Snelling, under-secretary of state at the Commonwealth Relations Office, brought it up again and made British doubts about his close involvement with Banda in the politics of Malawi even more clear: 'Is Britain courting trouble appearing to support Banda who might fall at any time? Would it not be worthwhile to continue to keep in with [the] ex-Ministers? Will they not take it much amiss if they see Britain giving financial support to a dictator? [Jones's] position and embroilment in [the] financial talks caused much raising of eyebrows.' Jones did not point out that it would be surprising if a Governor-General did not attempt to support his prime minister, nor that he was in fact trying to keep in with the ex-ministers. He did, however, point out that even if he confined himself to his legitimate constitutional functions he 'would be showing support for the Banda regime', for example by his assent to the Preventive Detention Bill which he could not withhold.[95] The constitution did provide for the Governor-General to withold assent. Indeed, a year later he made representations offering to withhhold assent from a Bill, notwithstanding what he now said about the Preventive Detention Bill.[96]

While he was in Zambia, Jones met Chokani:

> We had a long discussion about affairs in Malawi. He would like to come back in a non-political capacity – e.g. as teacher. He asked me to see P[rime] M[inister] about this and then write to him ... I later wrote to Chokani and told him that while the P[rime] M[inister] seemed agreeable to his returning to Malawi to work in some non-political capacity, I did not think the present time was suitable. I advised him to keep in touch with me and I would let him know when it would be wise for him to return.

Chokani recalled this meeting, but his account has different emphases:

> It was at his request through the Zambia Government. Sir Glyn felt that I should return to Malawi. I politely declined the offer. There was no question of going to Malawi, as both Orton Chirwa and Kanyama Chiume who 'delayed' coming out, were manhandled and had motor car incidents.

My own personal body-guard in Malawi was chased like deer in the blue gums at Limbe and murdered in broad daylight.[97]

Jones was still very keen that at least some of the ex-ministers should return to Malawi at some stage in a non-political capacity, notwithstanding the way Chirwa had been attacked when he took steps to remain in the country. In Chokani's case he seems to have recognized that his attempts would not persuade him to take the risks involved, which were graphically clear to Chokani if not to the Governor-General.

While Jones was in Lusaka, from 22 to 27 October, the Zambian Special Branch received reports that an attempt was to be made on Banda's life and a coup brought about. This information was given to Jones and he immediately sought the advice of Leonard Bean, a former colleague in the secretariat. He also asked for a plane to stand by to return him to Malawi. Bean's advice was that he should stay until the main celebrations were over. Jones accepted this advice, attended the main celebrations and returned to Malawi the next day.[98]

On his return to Zomba he saw Banda, safe and well, to tell him about the Zambia independence celebrations and convey to him the good wishes of many people he met there.

> At the end of the meeting I told him that the delegates to Lusaka from all over the world had approached me to express their deep concern at what was happening in Malawi. Malawi had been held up as a model of peace and calm during the past three years and now she seemed to be drifting into a state of violence in which people were taking the law into their own hands. He agreed that the present pattern of violence was not good for Malawi but said that he must teach the rebels a lesson which they would never forget. He was going to make an example of the ring leaders. I pressed him ... to make a statement urging his people to observe peace and calm and he finally said he would consider it.[99]

Violence in the country and the people taking the law into their own hands were nothing new. It is odd that he should represent Malawi as a model of peace and calm over the past three years since this was precisely his period of governorship and he knew well that there had been countless politically motivated cases of lawlessness, violence, assault, arson, intimidation and several of murder. The country could scarcely be said to be a model of peace and calm. In the past Jones had always said he was convinced the doctor and his senior party colleagues had not authorized the outbreaks of violence and he had given the impression that it was inconceivable that they should have. This, he must have judged, was the best way of inducing Banda to appeal publicly for peace and calm. On this occasion he must have thought it advisable in his approach to

Banda to make it sound as if it were something new – formerly a model of peace and calm but now drifting into violence and lawlessness – even though he, Banda and everyone else knew it not to be the case. In the past Banda had from time to time made appeals to his people to be peaceful and law-abiding, never of his own initiative and always at Jones's imploring; they were usually delayed, often until additional damage had been done; they, from the time of his return to Nyasaland in 1958, were thought by many not to be genuine; and they were never effective for longer than a very short time – as the periodic need to repeat them shows – despite Jones's frequently expressed confidence in their efficacy. Now, Banda was prepared, and reluctantly so, only to 'consider' making an appeal to his people. Furthermore, the clear implication of what Banda said was that the present violence was designed to teach the ex-ministers a lesson they would never forget and make an example of the ringleaders, whatever Jones's previous views were of Banda's innocence in the outbreaks of violence.

The day after Jones returned from Zambia, Banda introduced into parliament a Bill to amend the constitution so as to restore preventive detention without trial 'so that men like Chiume, Chipembere, Chisiza, and those of their dupes can be dealt with swiftly and without mercy'.[100] The Bill was agreed to.

At the very beginning of November, a number of politically prominent Europeans and their families left Malawi permanently and at short notice as a result of what the press dubbed 'deportation by intimidation'. They were, in fact, placed in fear of their lives. Banda was unable to give them an assurance that they would be safe and the British high commissioner advised them to leave. Jones yet again asked Banda 'to do everything in his power to ensure that peace and calm returned to Malawi'. Again, Banda replied only that he would 'consider' doing so.[101]

Meanwhile Chipembere had been served with a restriction order. This was his third period of confinement and he had been free for less than two of the previous five and a half years. The area to which he was restricted has mountains to the east and the lake to the west, and he not unnaturally felt imprisoned in the narrow strip north and south of Malindi village. Shortly before parliament passed the constitutional amendment permitting detention without trial – a little under a month after he was restricted – he decided to break the order and go into hiding with his followers. He knew that, just as he had been the first to be restricted, he would be the first to be detained.[102]

On the night of Friday 12 February 1965 a unit of about 200 of Chipembere's forces moved into the Fort Johnston area, attacked the police station, killed the wife and child of a policeman, destoyed all telephone installations at both the police station and the post office and stole guns and ammunition from the police station armoury.[103] They then started towards Zomba in four lorries. Shortly after they left, the officer in charge of police at Fort Johnston, who had been away from the township when the attack took place, was able to get to a telephone and give news of the attack to his commissioner in Zomba.

Chipembere and his men arrived at Liwonde ferry, midway between Fort Johnston and Zomba, between 2 and 3 a.m. on Saturday. Quite by chance, the ferry had been secured on the Zomba side of the Shire river. Discovering this, Chipembere returned to Fort Johnston. At about the same time that they arrived at Liwonde, a company of the Malawi army left Zomba to pursue them. Their progress was slow because they took precautions against possible ambushes and road blocks. By noon, however, they were in hot pursuit and caught up with one of the lorries. They opened fire and all save one of the occupants, who was captured, ran into the bush and escaped.[104]

Jones had been away since 21 November, first for the finance talks and then on leave. Late in January, about two weeks before the attack on Fort Johnston, Banda wrote to say it would be 'quite alright' if he returned in mid-February, adding, 'There is no need for you to hurry back. Things are quiet and peaceful here.' Clearly, the prime minister was not expecting an attack. Jones arrived back in Malawi on 16 February, four days after Chipembere's attempted coup.[105]

Three weeks after he returned from leave, on 9 March, Jones received a letter from Chipembere.[106] They had not been in touch since their telephone conversation on 29 September. The first purpose of the letter was to give Chipembere's side of the story in the hope that Jones would see he was 'not quite the villain' he had been called. He then came to the main point of his letter: an offer to call off his fight if Banda would agree to 'some sort of amnesty'. If this were to happen he would tell his supporters to cooperate with the government and he would do his best to persuade his colleagues in Tanzania to abandon 'whatever military preparations they may be making', if indeed they were making any, and return to live in Malawi peacefully. He himself would then be willing either to leave Malawi and work abroad or to live on Likoma Island with his wife's family and 'keep away from pressmen'. The only choice was between war and an amnesty. He asked Jones to mediate and seek an amnesty and hoped he would be able to act quickly.

As soon as Jones read the letter he sought the advice of Youens, Roberts, Long (commissioner of police), Lomax and Major Matthews, second in command of the Malawi Rifles, and they met in the early afternoon. He decided Youens should take a copy of the letter to Banda and ask him not to make any public reference to it until he had discussed it with him early the next day. When Youens delivered a typed copy at about 5 p.m. that day, the prime minister immediately said he was not interested in an amnesty and would rather not see Jones on the subject. Early the following morning he telephoned Jones, thanked him and repeated, 'I am not interested in the letter. I am not at all interested.'[107]

Jones wrote briefly and formally to Chipembere on 17 March, acknowledging receipt of his letter and saying he had passed a typed copy to the prime minister, as he had suggested.[108] He did not say what Banda's reaction was: to have done so would have closed off the only alternative, as seen by Chipembere, to war.

At this time Banda published a Bill to define the law of treason more stringently and give it retrospective effect from 1 January 1965.[109] Jones was 'seriously disturbed' by this and drafted – or more likely, from the wording and tone of the letter, got Roberts to draft – a letter to the prime minister to tell him so and to ask if they could discuss the matter before the cabinet met. He was gravely concerned about the principle of retrospectivity and the proposed 'violation of certain fundamental principles'.[110]

Whether Banda and Jones did discuss it is unclear but, as Jones no doubt expected, Banda did not change his mind. Some three weeks later he introduced the Bill in parliament. He argued that the changes were not making unlawful an act which when committed was not forbidden by law. The law of treason already existed and he was simply clarifying it. He made it clear that he had the activities of Chipembere in mind: 'In the light of what has happened at Fort Johnston we can't have a vague law in this country.' The motion to enact the alteration to the law was carried.[111]

On Saturday 27 March Jones left for a three-day tour of the Fort Johnston district. He inspected army units stationed in various villages and had three meetings with the district operations committee. He also held a number of meetings in villages where he found the people 'sullen and unresponsive but not rude'. He told them the 'soldiers and police were doing their duty, [he] hoped they would have good crops and that there would be peace'. 'One man, ex-KAR, said they were not happy. Soldiers were beating them, looting, burning houses. [Jones] said if he had evidence he should produce it to the officers who would take action.' Others told him of houses and cars being damaged, and a European missionary said that 95 per cent of the people in the district were for Chipembere. It is unlikely that either the villagers or the Governor-General found his visit reassuring.[112]

At about this time Chipembere wrote to the US ambassador, Sam Gilstrap, who received it probably on 4 April.[113] Late in the morning of 5 April Gilstrap saw Jones 'on a matter of urgency' and showed him the letter. Its gist was that Chipembere was confidently expecting an amnesty to be declared for himself, the former ministers and those who had taken part in the raid on Fort Johnston. In this event he wished to leave Malawi and go to America to study for an MA degree in history. He would also like his wife and two of his children to follow him, and his wife to be given a teaching post in a secondary school there.

Gilstrap told Jones 'there would be no difficulty whatsoever in finding Chipembere a place in a university and his wife and family could be looked after'. He thought the best solution from all points of view would be for Chipembere to leave Malawi and go to a place like America for some years. Jones replied that he would give the matter some thought and, the ambassador having left him temporarily, he asked Youens and Roberts to see him immediately. They agreed there could be no harm in Jones mentioning the letter to Banda when he saw him, as previously arranged, later that day. He could then note Banda's reactions and have further discussions with Gilstrap in the light of those reactions. Gilstrap agreed with this.

Later that day, when Jones mentioned the letter from Chipembere, Banda's reaction was immediate. He required no advice or persuasion: 'He would not wish to block Chipembere's leaving the country for the purpose of acquiring further education, provided it was clearly understood that he should not use his time in America to plot against this Government and to make speeches of criticism against the Prime Minister personally.' Banda saw political advantages in Chipembere's removal from the country. He would no longer be viewed as a martyr and everyone would see that the former ministers' solidarity was crumbling. Jones reported this meeting to Youens and Roberts and they decided that Lewis, Long and Lomax should be told about it later that evening.

Within a few days a letter was sent to Chipembere telling him that Banda had agreed to his departure and the conditions he attached to his permission, that Gilstrap had agreed to find him a place at an American university and that arrangements would be made for his wife to join him. It also asked him to select a date and an alternative date for him to leave Malawi. The letter was sent by Gideon Banda, a pseudonym.

Chipembere replied on 16 April, accepted Gideon Banda's proposals and selected a date, and an alternative, for him to leave.[114] The operation was masterminded by Lomax. The person executing the actual operation was an expatriate police officer, who was told to be at Government House one day the following week, 19–24 April, for a meeting. The meeting was chaired by Jones and attended by the police officer; a senior officer of the Malawi Rifles; Lomax; Youens; and Roberts. Lomax outlined the arrangements made with Gilstrap for a university place for Chipembere to which the US government had agreed. He also said contact had been established with Chipembere who was prepared to accept the offer. Roberts produced a letter for Chipembere, outlining the proposals, saying he would be picked up at a certain time and place the following Monday. Jones was much concerned about the police officer's safety. While he was prepared to go along with the evacuation he was conscious of the danger involved and worried about the possibility of the officer being harmed. As he left Government House at the end of the meeting, Jones called him aside and said, 'If things go wrong shoot your way out, and for God's sake be careful.' Such was his concern.

The following Monday, 26 April, the first of the two dates Chipembere had mentioned, the police officer set off for Fort Johnston in a police Land Rover. All army and police patrols in the Fort Johnston area were withdrawn. The police officer left Fort Johnston police station, alone, just after six o'clock and made his way to the pick-up point outside a maize mill in a village of a few scattered huts some four miles east of Fort Johnston. Almost immediately two young Africans came up to him and asked why he was there. He replied that he was from Zomba and was waiting for a friend. They then disappeared back into the bush and a few minutes later some two dozen men appeared from the bush, armed with shotguns, pangas and other weapons. The officer recognized one of them as Chipembere, who introduced himself, hesitated momentarily and then said, 'I will come with you.'

Chipembere went to get his belongings and was away only a few minutes before returning with a battered suitcase. He climbed into the Land Rover's back seat which had a blanket on it and the police officer told him to get down and cover himself with the blanket whenever he told him to. The pick-up had lasted less than half an hour.

The youth league had set up a number of road blocks on the roads out of Fort Johnston. Had they intercepted a vehicle carrying Chipembere, the consequences for him and the police oficer would have been disastrous. In order to avoid such a catastrophe, another police officer, who had been waiting nearer to Fort Johnston, led them in his Land Rover through the road blocks, explaining to the youth leaguers – to whom he was well known – that the vehicle immediately behind him was accompanying him and was to be let through. This worked well and they drove through each road block without incident, with Chipembere on the floor covered by the blanket. They arrived safely back in Zomba during the night and went straight to the airstrip where Lomax was waiting for them and immediately told Jones that everything was going to plan, 'apparently much to the Governor-General's relief'.

The civilian air wing of the British South Africa police had provided a light aircraft that had arrived the previous day, and at first light it left Zomba and flew Chipembere and the police officer who had picked him up to Salisbury.

That night, Tuesday 27 April, the police officer and Chipembere left Salisbury airport for London aboard a South African Airways plane. They arrived in London about noon the next day and were then joined by a CIA officer and a senior immigration officer who took them directly to a TWA flight for New York that had been held up for Chipembere to join it. Chipembere flew on to New York and the police officer flew back to Blantyre. There was a final debriefing with Jones in the chair, together with the individuals who had been present at the meeting prior to the operation taking place.

Jones was much relieved the operation had been a success, mainly, the police officer thought, because he was still alive to tell the tale! Years later, from time to time, Jones 'still woke up with the hairs standing up on the back of his neck' thinking what might have happened to the officer. Ten days later Jones told Banda that the operation had been successful and Chipembere had arrived as planned in California. The doctor was 'very pleased' and said he would announce it the next evening on the radio and at a meeting at Fort Johnston itself.[115]

The number of people, other than those at the Governor-General's meeting, who knew anything about the evacuation via Rhodesia and Britain was very limited. Those who knew the details were even fewer; those who did not need to know were not told, and this applied even to those who were closely involved. It would not have been necessary for Gilstrap, having got his government's agreement to Chipembere entering the USA and being given a university place there, to know any of the details of the evacuation operation. US intelligence officers would need to know about only the London–USA part of the exercise. Cole would have needed to know even less, if anything, since the passport and transit arrangements in London were handled by the British Special Branch. Chipembere knew nothing in advance about how he was to be evacuated except the place, date and time of his being picked up. He later referred to the 'vagueness' of the safe conduct plan.[116]

Despite Chipembere's evacuation, the security forces did not lessen their attempts to arrest his followers who had joined him in the bush. Towards the end of October 1965, Medson Silombela, one of 'the so-called generals of the so-called Chipembere's army', as Banda expressed it,[117] was caught by the police, army and young pioneers near his home just south of Zomba.[118]

On 10 November Banda introduced into parliament a short Bill to permit judicial execution to be carried out in public. He was explicit that he wanted this provision so as to hang Chipembere's terrorists in public. Silombela was tried, convicted and sentenced to death. Banda had already announced that the execution would be in public. This, as he expected, caused an international outcry and allegations of barbarism, but he pointed to precedents in many other countries at different times, including Britain. Many pleas were made to Banda to change his mind.[119]

Such was the outcry against the proposal to hang Silombela in public and such was Banda's determination to do so, notwithstanding its effect on his reputation, that his official advisers sought ways of satisfying, or at least securing the acquiescence of, both Banda and those wishing to persuade him to reverse his decision. In the event, Roberts suggested that Silombela should be hanged within the prison walls and before an invited audience of villagers and those whose relatives had been murdered. This was done.[120]

Jones told friends 'with great emphasis' of the way in which he had 'used all his powers of persuasion to talk Dr Banda out of it' and repeatedly pleaded with him not to hang Silombela in public, but the doctor was emphatic that the majority of the people of Malawi were demanding that the 'invulnerable' Silombela should be seen to be hanged.[121] On the other hand, Jones wrote of his private attitude towards the public execution of 'this rebellious ruffian ... who claimed a supernatural power of invulnerability':

> Privately I ... considered that the public good would be served if witchcraft murderers could be executed in public, but the bill was presented to me for assent 'on behalf of Her Majesty.' I conveyed a message to the proper quarter offering to withhold assent and to resign. I was told not to resign ... Silombela was hanged within the precincts of Zomba gaol before invited guests – Chiefs, headmen and relatives of the victims. In the circumstances this procedure was entirely in accordance with my private wishes.[122]

Chipembere's worries at this time about what was happening in Malawi were profound. As his anxiety approached desperation, mingled with remorse for his responsibility, as he saw it, for the plight of his relations and followers, he wrote to Jones. He hoped the contents of the letter would be communicated to Banda.[123]

His letter was more formal than his earlier letters and its purpose was 'to find out what ha[d] in fact been done about [his] supporters in restriction, detention and prison'. He reminded Jones that it was on the basis of the promise that something would be done about an amnesty that he decided to stop fighting and to leave Malawi. If the amnesty suggestion had been rejected out of hand he would never have left the country but would have intensified his guerrilla activities. He had placed faith in both Banda as 'a man who would honour his word' and in Jones as 'a man of great humanity and one who commanded great respect in the heart of the Prime Minister'. It is unlikely that Jones mentioned this letter to Banda.

Jones did not tell Chipembere, either at the time or later, that Banda had indeed rejected out of hand his amnesty approach and had treated the request to be allowed to leave for America as an entirely separate matter to which he readily agreed. Jones had taken a week to reply to Chipembere's original amnesty letter. Maybe he hoped that in the interim Banda might change his mind and accept the offer. The failure to communicate the rejection to Chipembere caused him to believe he had been double-crossed, but also had the important effect of keeping him in play and not intensifying his guerrilla activities.

During November Jones learned that Chipembere had addressed audiences in the USA. He was concerned, not so much about the speeches in themselves but about the danger that they might bring about disclosures of his evacuation and those involved in it. Malawi's ambassador to the USA, Vincent Gondwe, did not know how Chipembere had got to America but he became suspicious of US government involvement.[124] It is likely either that Banda indicated he would demand Chipembere's return to Malawi, or the Americans feared he would, on the grounds that the undertaking, which the US government had agreed to assure, not to criticize Banda or engage in activity hostile to Malawi had been broken. Since the Americans would not be prepared to return Chipembere, and in order to counter a possible demand for this and to shut Gondwe up, they threatened to publish confidential information and to reveal Banda's and Jones's involvement in the evacuation.

Banda told Jones he had nothing to hide and the Americans could publish what they liked. Jones none the less 'went through everything with him', whether to ensure that he, Jones, recalled the circumstances correctly, or whether to refresh the prime minister's memory, or whether otherwise to rehearse a joint account of what happened, is unclear. They agreed that the approach had been from Chipembere to Gilstrap to Jones to Banda. In view of Chipembere's illness, his desire to study and his determination to get out of politics, Banda had decided that he would not block his way to America, provided the Americans agreed to two conditions: they would ensure that Chipembere engaged in no hostile activity against Malawi and made no criticism of Banda. 'That's all he knows and is not afraid of that coming out.'[125]

The Americans did not publish any of the details of the arrangements for Chipembere's departure to the USA, but there was a further worry some six months later when Jones learned that he might move from America to London. When the Governor-General spoke with Banda about this early in June 1966, the doctor said that if Chipembere did go to London he might ask for his extradition on the grounds that he led an armed rebellion in February 1965. Jones asked the British high commissioner to request the British government to put pressure on the

Americans to ensure that Chipembere stayed in America, and Banda was content to leave the matter there.[126]

On 13 July 1965, Banda announced that Malawi would become a republic on 6 July the following year. In April 1966 a Bill to introduce the republican constitution was published, a month later it was passed by parliament and Jones assented to it on 14 June.[127]

Virtually the whole of Jones's time as Governor-General had been taken up with the cabinet crisis and its aftermath. In his final three months in Malawi he paid farewell visits to each of the three regions, meeting chiefs, headmen, and missionaries; visiting hospitals, schools, colleges and community centres; making speeches, receiving gifts and attending receptions and private parties.[128] He was given a farewell dinner by Banda who made it clear how greatly he had valued Jones's contribution to Malawi and the support which he had given him as prime minister personally. The highlight of Jones's reply was his remark: 'You will have at least one reason to regret my leaving: you will no longer be able to come to me when you have a problem with the British Government and say "Send me back to Gwelo!"' Guests present had never seen Banda look more amused.[129] The Gwelo card was one on which the doctor had relied with great efficacy to get his way since Jones took office in 1960. It must have brought happiness as well as amusement to both of them that, at the very end, they could acknowledge that each knew what had gone on and was able to do so with such good humour.

In his public farewell message to the people of Malawi, delivered at the beginning of July,[130] Jones briefly reviewed the country's progress during the previous six years and said these were years which represented for him the culmination of his career in the colonial service, and added:

> When I was a probationer in the Colonial Service ... I was told that the role of the Colonial Service in Africa was to prepare the local people for self-government since it was British policy to grant freedom as soon as conveniently possible to the Colonies and Dependencies in Africa. Thus, though some may complain that the process has been unduly slow and others that it has been unwisely rapid, and though the process towards Self-Government has been attended by frustrations and some bitterness, Britain in the end has discharged her trust in Malawi and in other parts of Africa. I am proud to have played a small part in the discharge of this trust, both here and in Zambia where I served for twenty-nine years.

Although the last six years had not been easy for him, they had been rewarding and he would treasure them for a number of reasons. First, because they brought him into close contact with Banda, who 'throughout all the anxieties and tensions of the past few years ... pursued his aims with tenacity and fidelity and always ... insisted that his followers should maintain peace and calm'. Second, because he, his wife and children had enjoyed the friendship of many people of all races, for whose kindness and friendship they were most grateful. Third, because of the loyal assistance given to him by 'members of the Armed Forces, the Police and the Civil Service'. He concluded: 'Shortly we shall be leaving this lovely country. We shall never forget its beauties and its hospitable people. We shall ever pray for its happiness and prosperity ... May God Bless you all.'

In the afternoon of 5 July, a crowd of thousands gathered at Chileka airport.[131] A 'resplendent guard of honour' of the first battalion of the Malawi Rifles marched on to the tarmac, headed by the regimental band, and completed a square, the other three sides of which were formed by the crowd and a 'Viscount aircraft gleaming in the smart livery of Air Malawi'. A white uniformed motorcycle escort led Banda in his bright red open-topped Rolls-Royce – the financing of which had caused consternation in Whitehall for a while a few years earlier – into the square where he took the salute as the Malawi national anthem was played. A few minutes later another motorcycle escort led the Governor-General's 'elderly black Rolls' with pennon flying, into the square, carrying Jones, dressed in full ceremonial uniform, and his wife. Again there was a military salute and the Malawi national anthem. Banda then made a speech, using his fly whisk to give 'dramatic force' to his points:

> He was plainly moved. He told the crowd much of the history of the past six years, and of how Sir Glyn had helped him again and again in his battles with [the federal government]. He emphasised his sorrow that 'what some people call protocol' meant that with the constitutional changes Sir Glyn must leave. He plainly intimated that he would have liked him to stay as an adviser ... He ended with an emotional tribute that brought a roar from the crowd.

Jones then rose to make his final speech as Governor-General, standing with 'the feathers of his great cocked hat fluttering in the breeze'. He was much briefer than Banda. He expressed his affection for the people of Malawi and their prime minister, 'and ended with a "God Bless you" which sent a tremor through the crowd'. He inspected the guard of honour as the band played 'Men of Harlech', and took his last salute as the Malawi national anthem was played. With Banda and Lady Jones he walked along the red carpet, shaking hands with those who lined the route to the waiting aircraft. At the aircraft he had a final few words with Banda and then climbed the steps, waved goodbye from the open door, as the band – strangely but movingly – played 'God Save the Queen' and the crowd 'rose stiffly to attention and dead silence'.

A moment later the aircraft door closed, and the Viscount, a governor-general's pennon trailing above the flight-deck, taxied away to the main runway for take-off. In a very short time it came thundering back, climbing quickly into the setting sun. As it came past, the Governor-General could be seen waving through the oval window – and the crowd, headed by Dr. Banda, waved back.

All was not over. The aircraft climbed, made a sweep over Blantyre and then turned back, now at speed, and ... came past some fifty feet above the runway. More waving, and then it climbed away towards the mountains. As [the crowd] turned to go, the last light fell on the lonely figure of Dr. Banda, still waving his fly-whisk at the darkening sky.

CHAPTER 8

Retirement

THE Joneses arrived in Beira in the evening of 5 July. They were guests of Jardim, Malawi's Portuguese consul, to whom the rebel ministers had taken such grave exception two years previously. They stayed there six days and then flew, in Jardim's Aztec, to watch game in the Gorongoza reserve and on to Nyamakala where Jones – reliving his early district officer days – shot three hartebeest bulls, a sable bull, a buffalo bull, a nyala bull, a reedbuck ram and a zebra. They returned to Beira on 17 July and flew with the Jardims in their aircraft to Paradise Island for four restful days, mainly fishing. After a few more days in Beira they boarded the *Africa* and began their voyage back to Britain, arriving in Trieste on 15 August. Over the course of the next three weeks they motored by easy stages to Holland and then by air to Lydd and car to London, arriving on 10 September.[1]

They took a flat in London and suffered the inconveniences of many returning from a lifetime in the colonies: installing a television set which failed to work and putting money in the meter before being able to use lighting, heating and cooking facilities. Jones spent several days shooting hares, pheasants and pigeons, and they went to the opera at Covent Garden, attended an evening reception at Buckingham Palace and went there again to lunch with the Queen. He also saw at least two doctors for consultations. They spent two weeks, including Christmas, in Switzerland, skiing.

Over the next several years Jones continued to take an active interest in African and particularly Malawian affairs. The principal aspects of this were his continued interest in the fate of the former ministers from Malawi, working with the newly created Malawi Buying and Trade Agency, advising the Lesotho government, being deputy chairman of the Pearce commission in Rhodesia, officially observing the 1980 Rhodesia–Zimbabwe elections, representing Banda in a dispute over a proposed biography of the doctor and advising Granada Television on the *End of Empire* series.

When Jones left Malawi the former ministers were all in exile: Chirwa, Chiume, Bwanausi and Chisiza in Tanzania, Chokani in Zambia, and Chipembere in the USA. Although Chokani seemed content to continue to live in Zambia, and Chiume and Bwanausi in Tanzania, the other three wished, for differing reasons, to return to Malawi.

About the middle of June 1967 Chirwa – now assistant registrar of lands in Tanzania – travelled to England to see his wife, Vera, who was studying law. His return air fare was paid by Lomax, who was in London at the same time. Lomax also gave Jones money to help Vera with her rent.[2] Jones saw both Chirwas, and then, still trying to effect a reconciliation and their return to Malawi, wrote to Banda: 'I found [Vera's] demeanour was calm and peaceful and she assured me that she is having no communications with the rebels ... She told me that she considered that you are doing fine work for Malawi and that no other person could lead the nation at the present time.'[3] Chirwa, too, 'appeared to be of a peaceful disposition and expressed his admiration for [Banda] and his desire to help Malawi under [his] leadership as soon as an opportunity occurred'. He would like to leave Tanzania if a suitable job could be found for him elsewhere. He realized it would not yet be possible to return to Malawi but hoped he and his family could return in the not too distant future. Jones's view was that 'if some post could be found for him in an organisation such as the UN ... this would be ideal for him in the transition period.' He told Banda: 'I believe that if one or two of the rebel ministers could be seen to accept your authority once more and to be working under you for the good of Malawi, the effect on the people of Malawi and the outside world would be most favourable. Conversely it would tend to dissuade the other ex-ministers that their cause is hopeless.' He seemed to be overlooking the fact that Chirwa was one of those Banda had sacked, with Chiume and Bwanausi, and it was virtually inconceivable that that the doctor would ever have those former ministers back.

Jones continued that he had learned from Chirwa that Chisiza was 'unemployed and rapidly degenerating'. He had no communication with the other rebels and 'seems now to accept that you are the only possible leader for Malawi'. This last impression was a grave miscalculation. Very soon, early in August, Chisiza went to a training camp in Western Tanzania and then sent 'a number of disciplined rebels' in small groups to a camp near Broken Hill in Zambia for further training, so that they could infiltrate Malawi and assassinate Banda and his ministers. By early October, a unit of twenty-six was already in the Mwanza-Neno area north-west of Blantyre. On Saturday 7 October the security forces captured three of the insurgents, from whom they learned that the unit was led by Chisiza himself. Four days later the security forces tracked him to his 'lair'. After a two-hour gun battle he was shot dead and the rest of the gang escaped under cover of darkness. Most were shortly arrested, 'tried, publicly, for treason ... and were hanged'.[4]

About three months after Chisiza's death Chipembere, who had left the USA in August 1966 and was living in Tanzania, asked Judith, Lady Listowel, then visiting Dar es Salaam, to see him urgently.[5] This she did, and Chipembere told her: 'I am finished and useless. I can accomplish nothing, am unemployed, receiving a small pittance from the Tanzanian Government ... There is only one man I can trust to help me and that is Sir Glyn Jones. Please tell him to help me. I do not wish to crawl back to Dr. Banda but I am desperate.'

On 18 February 1968 Jones arrived in Malawi on his way to Lesotho and was told by Lomax that Lady Listowel was acting as a go-between and was anxious to meet him urgently. The following day, when Jones met Banda, the doctor said he was aware that she wanted to see him and convey a message from Chipembere. Jones thought he should meet her and find out what she had to say. Banda agreed. The next day Jones had lunch with Roberts who was also entertaining Lady Listowel. After lunch she and Jones had a private meeting in which she told him of Chipembere's request. She had advised him to try and get a job with the United Nations somewhere

After this meeting Jones went to see Banda. The doctor said he would be glad if Jones would try and meet Chipembere and probably the best place would be Nairobi. He 'would be prepared to consider forgiving Chipembere' if he wrote a statement showing that 'he is finished as a political opponent of Malawi', regretted his 'former rebellious activities' and recanted, supported Banda and the policy of the MCP and would 'never again intrigue against the President and Government of Malawi'.

Later Jones agreed with Roberts and Lomax to visit Nairobi after his business in Lesotho. Lomax would make the arrangements to get Chipembere there. After the meeting Jones would return to Malawi to report to Banda what had transpired. He then went off to Lesotho. While he was staying in Johannesburg overnight on his return journey, however, Roberts rang to say they had been unable to contact Chipembere and he consequently asked Jones to go to Zomba instead of Kenya.

Jones arrived in Zomba on 10 March and the following day Lomax received a message from Chipembere saying he did not wish to meet anyone from Malawi. Banda was disappointed and felt they had made a tactical error in sending a message through Lomax because this would make him unduly suspicious. Privately Jones disagreed with this view because he had had other dealings with Chipembere through 'the Lomax channel'. They decided not to make a further approach to Chipembere but wait and see if he sent further messages. Jones made it clear that he would be willing to meet him at any time and in any place, if it would help Malawi.

Chipembere returned to the USA in 1969 and died there in 1975.[6]

At about the same time as Chipembere returned to the USA, Chirwa also left Tanzania, where he had set up the Malawi Freedom Movement dedicated to restoring 'democracy, justice and liberty', and went to live in Zambia. From there he and his wife were abducted in 1982. They were taken to Malawi, tried for treason and sentenced to death. This occasioned a great international outcry with many pleas for clemency. The British government was embarrassed because Banda was due to make a state visit to Britain in June 1984. To go ahead would risk either a last-minute cancellation if the executions were confirmed or, alternatively, the visit being marred by criticism and demonstrations if no decision had been taken by then. The British government, as fearful of upsetting him as their predecessors had been nearly a quarter of a century earlier, did not want to discuss the matter directly with him because of the grave offence they were sure it would cause him.

> In the circumstances [they] wondered whether Sir Glyn Jones would be prepared to help ... Without suggesting any conditional link between the two, would he perhaps consider offering the President ... the advice that it would be in his best interests to get the Chirwas' case settled favourably before the State Visit ... anything he could do to obtain an insight into Banda's thinking and nudge him in the right direction would be much appreciated.[7]

Jones did in fact write to Banda, a fortnight later, but confined himself to saying 'a few words on their behalf in mitigation of the sentence' passed on the Chirwas. He did not mention, even indirectly or by inference, the state visit. He had, he told the president, until now refrained from approaching him, despite numerous requests to do so, because he did not want the doctor to think that he, Jones, considered himself as retaining any of the powers or influence which he had when he was Governor-General. Nor did he want Banda to think that he regarded the traditional judicial system as inappropriate to the needs, circumstances or welfare of Malawi. He had not forgotten that the system had been 'subscribed and sponsored' by Chirwa himself and had not been disallowed by the British government despite the death sentence having been abolished in Britain. Having himself had to 'choose between the life and death of a convicted person' he had no wish to add to the doctor's burden. Nevertheless, he pleaded for clemency:

> I believe that your successes in 1963 and 1964 went to Chirwa's head and his growing insobriety led to his becoming an easy prey to men of

stronger and more seditious character. His final rejection by the people in 1964 after you had graciously consented to offer him a higher post in the judiciary, and his self-sought exile, caused a total lowering of his morale ... My recent visit to Malawi confirms my view that you and your policies command universal respect and support throughout the country.

My plea to you therefore is that you exercise clemency towards Orton and Vera Chirwa on the grounds that they command so little support that they cannot constitute a serious threat to the stability of Malawi, and also that my wife and I personally believe that prior to the cabinet revolt in August 1964, inspired and led by Mr. Chiume, they were loyal servants of yourself and the Government of Malawi.[8]

He must have thought it prudent to exclude from his reference to Banda graciously consenting to offer a judicial post and to self-imposed exile, the grievous assault which immediately followed the offer and which, rather than 'rejection by the people', induced the exile.

There were many other pleas, made by distinguished people to whose views Banda might have been expected to listen. One such was Andrew Doig, former missionary in Malawi and recently retired Moderator of the Church of Scotland, of which Banda had been an elder. Doig had worked in Malawi for a quarter of a century, had been instumental in persuading Banda to return to Nyasaland in 1958, and his church had staunchly supported him.[9]

Banda was not the sort of man to pay a great deal of heed to pleas such as those made by Jones and Doig. Indeed, he declined even to see Doig and he seems not to have replied to Jones's letter. Ironically, neither of them knew that Banda had decided several months earlier not to hang the Chirwas.[10] The state visit took place in April 1985. Chirwa died in prison in 1992 and his wife was released from gaol in 1993.

Towards the end of September 1966, very soon after Jones arrived in Britain on retirement, Roberts, now secretary to the president and cabinet, wrote that Banda had asked the new British prime minister, Harold Wilson, to appoint him, Jones, as British high commissioner to Malawi in succession to David Cole the following year. In the meantime Banda was thinking of setting up his own Malawi agency in London because he was dissatisfied with the service he was getting from the Crown Agents. He asked if Jones would be interested in working with the agency.[11] On 24 October Banda also wrote to him:

I am glad to hear from Mr Roberts that you will be glad to continue your association with this country by undertaking the work I have in mind for you in London. About a month or so before you and Lady Jones left, [Cecilia Kadzamira] told me what Lady Jones had told her, as I was at that time thinking of establishing our own buying office or Agency in

London. I told her to tell Lady Jones that I had this office in mind and if you were prepared to take this job on, I would be glad.[12]

When Roberts wrote to Jones, on 25 November, he said that Banda had in mind 'a large agency which would completely take over the whole of the functions at present performed by the Crown Agents and formerly by Lonrho in the railways field and similar organisations'. It seemed to Roberts that it would be 'an extremely difficult and expensive project'. On the other hand, he could see it would be very helpful to Malawi if there were in London an organization representing its special interests in dealings with those from whom direct purchases were made, especially if the organization included a Malawi trade office. He was aware that this was 'not altogether in accordance with the way [Banda was] at present thinking',[13] but his concept was clearly more realistic than was Banda's. He was, in effect, trying to secure Jones's assistance in reducing the project to a more realistic level.

Shortly, Jones accepted the offer of full-time chief agent of the newly created Malawi Buying and Trade Agency (MBTA). He accepted a four-year contract from 1 June 1967 and this was renewed for a further three years in June 1971. The post was offered to him personally by Banda under somewhat mysterious circumstances. In his letter of 24 October 1966 Banda referred to a conversation which Lady Jones had with Cecilia Kadzamira in May or June 1966. Almost eight years later the doctor, in different circumstances, wrote: 'It is true that I asked you to join the agency myself, personally. And when I did this I did not think it necessary or in good taste for me to tell you why I was doing that ... Even now, at this late stage, I do not think it would be in good taste to tell you. Because it involves Lady Jones.'[14] It was the case that Lady Jones had been worried that her husband would be 'lost' in retirement without a job, after a very busy life.[15] It appears that, with this anxiety in mind, she asked Cecilia Kadzamira if she would ask Banda to find a job for her husband when he retired. Banda did not take this request amiss and, as a kindness to Jones and in response to Lady Jones's request, since he was contemplating setting up a buying agency in London, thought heading it might be the sort of job Jones would like. Either Cecilia Kadzamira failed to tell Lady Jones that the doctor had the post in mind for Jones, or Lady Jones failed to tell her husband.

A few months after the MBTA was opened, Banda appointed W. J. R. Pincott as the deputy chief agent. Pincott, formerly deputy secretary in the Nyasaland ministry of finance, had taken his gratuity and pension and left the service at independence. Banda very rarely re-engaged officers who had left the service in this way and did so in Pincott's case only because Jones pleaded with him to do so. In 1970 Pincott took over as chief agent and Jones became adviser to the agency. Their contracts were due for renewal at the end of May 1974 and in anticipation of this Pincott asked the agency's auditors to review the work and responsibility levels of Jones and himself. The auditors assessed the commercial rate value of the posts and recommended that Jones and Pincott should receive very substantially increased salaries. Pincott forwarded these recommendations to George Jafu, Roberts's successor as secretary to the president and cabinet in Malawi. One way or another, Jafu understood that Jones and Pincott were saying they would leave the agency unless their salaries were increased.[16]

During January 1974 Jafu asked Vincent, a member of the MBTA staff, to visit Malawi immediately, ostensibly, Jones claimed, to discuss military equipment procurement but in reality to discuss the agency's future after Jones and Pincott left. Vincent reported these discussions to Jones. This was the first indication he and Pincott had that their contracts were not to be renewed. Shortly, Jones received 'a courteous letter' from Jafu saying the president had decided not to renew their contracts when they expired. Jones apparently doubted whether Jafu was acting with Banda's authority, because, in addition to thanking Jafu for his letter, he wrote to ask Banda to confirm that the contracts were not to be renewed.[17]

Jones was much concerned about this turn of events. Having received no replies to the three letters he had written to Banda over the past six months, he wrote again on 11 April and sent it personally by hand of the president's private secretary. What concerned him, he said, was not that his and Pincott's services were to be dispensed with, but the way in which Jafu had handled the matter by discussing it with a junior member of the agency's staff before discussing it with Jones or Pincott. In truth, however, despite his repeated protestations that he was not complaining about his services being terminated, he was at least mildly miffed: 'I do feel that the manner of terminating my seven years faithful service for you and your country in this Agency is disgraceful.' Jafu had given more than the contractual period of notice so there was nothing disgraceful about that aspect of terminating the contract. Rather it must have been the involvement of Vincent that he saw as disgraceful. He went on to assure Banda that he remained his loyal supporter and would always be ready to help the government and people of Malawi.[18]

Banda's response was a masterpiece, combining courtesy with forthrightness.[19] At the outset he reassured Jones he had not offended him, either personally or as head of state and government. He was very happy to hear Jones say he remained a loyal supporter and would be ready to help the country's government and her people: 'I know you are absolutely honest, sincere and genuine when you say this. On my part, I accept this assurance without any reservations.' Avowals of loyalty, as Jones knew from experience, always pleased the doctor. If any of Jones's letters had gone unanswered it was not, he continued, because he was offended but because in the case of one he could not remember having received it ('It is possible that my memory is letting me down') in the case of another he had not felt it required an answer because Jones had written it after Banda had written to him, and in the third case it was because of pressure of work. He confirmed that he had decided against renewing the contracts and reassuringly added that this was not a sign on his part that Jones had offended him: 'Not at all.' With this 'preliminary statement', he continued:

> I was shocked, literally shocked, when Jafu told me that you and Pincott were demanding increases in your salaries, as conditions of renewal of your contracts in June ... Whether Pincott ever discussed them with you before sending these demands to Jafu, I am not sure. But since Pincott spoke not only for himself, but for you, I took it for granted that you had discussed the demands and had agreed to them between you.

He considered the demands most unreasonable on a number of grounds. First, both Jones and Pincott were receiving a pension from Malawi. Second, what Jafu had been told Jones wanted as a condition for renewing the contracts was the same salary as he had received as Governor-General, a figure which Banda had inherited for himself when Jones left in 1966 and which he had not increased since then. For Pincott, the salary demanded was 'much higher than that'. In his view the demands were 'something bordering on the grasping'. This was the more so, he added, in Jones's case because for all practical purposes he ceased to work for the agency when he handed over to Pincott as chief agent. It was only because of their past relationship that he did not mind keeping Jones on as an adviser, and he considered the salary which they then agreed to be 'quite enough'. The only way he could explain the demands was to assume that this was their way of saying they wanted to leave the agency. He was not prepared to accept the conditions. In any case, he wanted changes in the agency to put it 'more under our control than it has been for the past eight years'. He wanted it to be run exactly as the statutory bodies were run in Malawi, 'not kingdoms on their own, not even kingdoms within a kingdom'. This implied dissatisfaction with Jones's 'empire building' and lack of accountability to the Malawi government.

After all the pleas by Jones, Butler and the British treasury to economize, and after the catastrophe and near toppling of Banda which African civil service salary economies and accusations of paying expatriates high salaries had, as Jones knew only too well, brought about in 1964, it is little wonder Banda was sensitive on the salaries issue.

Jones said he was 'very pleased indeed' to receive Banda's letter, and he wrote straight away to tell him so and how much he looked forward to their 'continued correspondence'.[20] There can be no doubt that he was hurt by the differences between them: 'I am very sorry to have to cross swords with you at this stage of our long and, for me, very pleasant association.' Nevertheless, rather than let matters rest, which in the past he would have considered the manifestly prudent course, he felt obliged to 'put the record straight by answering allegations with the true facts', but with no intention of trying to get Banda to alter his decision. Indeed, with his knowledge of the doctor gained over the years he knew of his great aversion to altering his mind and certainly to others seeing that he was altering it.

He had always told Banda that he considered he was well treated as Governor-General with a salary which Banda put up, without being asked, from £5000 to £6000 a year tax-free, an entertainment allowance of £2000 a year which he consistently over-spent on hospitality, with three houses, servants, water, light and cars provided free. To earn in Britain what he earned as Governor-General with all the benefits and privileges of head of state he would have to receive a salary of about £60,000 a year[21] of which two-thirds would go in taxes. He knew of three other former Governors-General whose responsibilities were no more onerous than his who were earning salaries of £10,000 and in one case £15,000 a year: 'The fact that I choose to work full time for Malawi for less than half what they are drawing is my business and I care not whether people think I have been a fool to do so.' He had been working full-time at the agency, not part-time as Banda supposed, and had taken no leave for the past two years. 'You will have gathered by now that I resent your use of the epithet "grasping": it is quite unjustified by the facts. I would not have mentioned this sordid subject of salaries if you had not brought it on yourself, stating in fact your own salary of £6000 as Head of State.' Not to be outdone, Banda replied immediately, before, as he said, he got too busy again, which suggests that he hoped the correspondence could be at an end.

> I can understand you resenting the use of the epithet 'grasping'. But I would be dishonest if I denied that that is my view of the whole thing. And I do not want to be dishonest.
>
> In doing so I am not unaware of what is going on in the City of London and other centres of commerce and industry in Britain. I know that people [there] have an exaggerated opinion ... of former Governors-General and Governors ... They offer them inflated salaries when they are back home from any overseas territory. This is because, in my view, the people in the City ... have an exaggerated opinion of themselves,

their importance, their expertise and their worth. They offer and vote themselves highly inflated salaries ... out of proportion to their worth.[22]

Save for an outspoken and in parts grossly insulting letter from Pincott to Jafu on his last day in the agency in which, as he saw it, he 'put the record straight',[23] this, at least superficially, was the end of the affair, though Jones was undoubtedly gravely and irreparably hurt by it. It was a sad turn of events towards the close of a long relationship in which, save for a single very early exception on Banda's part, they had always addressed each other in courteous, respectful and often flattering, terms. It was a turn that would not have taken place had Jones realized earlier that Banda had given him the job at his wife's instigation via Cecilia Kadzamira, and as a kindness to him.

During his seven years at the MBTA, Jones undertook a number of other assignments including one in Lesotho and another in Rhodesia. About the middle of 1967 he was told the prime minister of Lesotho, Chief Jonathan, wanted the services of 'a political adviser particularly in the field of foreign affairs'.[24] The country was experiencing 'serious administrative weaknesses' on which a report had recently made recommendations. Jones offered to go for a short visit at the end of 1967 and thereafter periodically to advise 'both on how they should bring [the] recommendations into effect and also generally on any matters the Government cared to consult [him] about'. The Lesotho and British governments accepted this offer and in August he was appointed 'Adviser on Governmental matters to the Prime Minister of Lesotho'. Over the course of the next two years he paid five visits to Lesotho, averaging three weeks each.

There were a number of disappointments in this assignment. Regarding foreign affairs, the premier 'used [Jones] very little in this capacity and [he] suspected that he was in much closer contact with South Africa than with [Jones himself] or with Britain in these matters'. Most of the work he in practice undertook was of an elementary organization and methods nature and Jones 'could not truthfully say [he] achieved much more than marginal economies'.

Jones's thoughts at the end of his Lesotho assignment were revealing:

> The territory has been given its independence before it was ready for it ... It was politically unstable because the election could not produce a party sufficiently strong to govern with determination ... What Lesotho seems to lack is a strong, well organised nationalist party capable of commanding the emotive support of the bulk of the population and of introducing tough measures to meet the economic needs of the country. In my view this is an indispensable desideratum for self-government in Africa and while it may in unscrupulous hands lead to intimidation and

the one-party state and the regimentation of the youth, these are, I believe, avoidable features of a strong party system which seems to be the only means of instilling a sense of urgency into the Government and a sense of duty, loyalty and discipline into the people.

In this statement, Jones seems to be setting out his political beliefs. It gets close to rejecting for Africa the Westminster model with its effective opposition acting as a check on the government and as the government-in-waiting. He advocates government by a strong, tough, determined, well-organized nationalist party commanding mass support and instilling a sense of urgency, duty, loyalty and discipline. In Malawi, intimidation, youth regimentation and the *de facto* one-party state, which he believed could be avoided in scrupulous hands, were precisely the means of securing the strong party which he saw as the indispensable desideratum for stable government. Their dangers, even if avoidable, were not avoided, and were obvious long before the country became a *de jure* one-party state. It is unclear whether he believed that they had been avoided, which is scarcely possible, or that Banda was unscrupulous, which he would scarcely admit. These beliefs almost certainly guided him during his time in Malawi and help to explain his unwavering support for Banda whom he correctly saw as the only person able to bring about the strong party and its indispensable stabilizing role. That the dangers might not be avoided was a risk which he could not escape.

In the case of Rhodesia, the country had unilaterally declared itself independent in 1965 and, after a number of attempts to resolve their differences, the British and Rhodesian governments agreed a set of proposals on 21 November 1971.[25] These proposals were conditional upon their acceptability to the people of Rhodesia as a whole, which would be tested by a commission appointed by the British government. Four days later, on 25 November, the foreign secretary announced that Lord Pearce would be the chairman of the commission and that Lord Harlech and Sir Maurice Dorman would be deputy chairmen. Three weeks later it was announced that Jones also would be a deputy chairman. The delay in announcing Jones's appointment was so that, at his request, the foreign secretary could ascertain that Banda had no objection to his doing this work.

Immediately on being appointed, Pearce, Harlech and Dorman decided that they would need as commissioners people 'who had experience of rural and urban Africans, who had shown their capacity for handling people and crowds, who would be able to operate independently and who were capable of forming a balanced and impartial assessment of what they heard and saw'. The task of interviewing and selecting originally sixteen and later four more of these commissioners fell to Jones and Dorman. Dorman had been Governor and, after independence, Governor-

General of Sierra Leone. Seven of those selected, and the statistician who joined them, had served in Northern Rhodesia and five others in Sierra Leone. One had served in both. Almost without exception the commissioners had been members of the provincial and district administration. A small advance party left for Rhodesia on 4 January 1972 and the others, including Jones, arrived in Salisbury by air a week later.

The commission spent two months in Rhodesia and heard evidence in London before submitting the report. It was the chairman and his deputies' task to submit the report, and the commissioners' task to provide the material on which it was based. They concluded that while the proposals were acceptable to the great majority of Europeans, the majority of Africans rejected them, and consequently they were not acceptable to the people of Rhodesia as a whole. Pearce divided the job of drafting between members of his team. Jones wrote the section on chiefs 'for which his experience made him particularly well qualified'. His role in writing this section was 'vitally important because it was a refutation of the Smith regime's claim that the chiefs had lost their political significance and could not be held to speak for their people'.[26] The question of chiefs losing their political significance was one with which he had been familiar in Malawi.

Members of the commission recalled many years later that most of their discussion was over a drink in Pearce's suite in the evenings. Jones spoke less than the others, though when he spoke he was always listened to. He clearly enjoyed visits which took him into the rural areas. He and the commissioners were delighted to be back in the environment in which they had spent most of their lives.[27]

> The Commissioners tended to resolve themselves in 'cliques' according to the age and colonial background. The FCO clique used to joke about Sir Glyn's obvious delight in mixing with his 'boys'. He seemed rather to ignore the rest of us ... My impression is that he enjoyed relaxing with his former senior officers of Northern Rhodesia more than with his fellow chairmen ... Sir Grin, as the back-up staff called him, perhaps unjustly, was something of a joker ... Everyone sensed that [he] relished his return to 'active service'; the chance to renew former contacts; and to relax with his 'boys'.[28]

Jones played his part with energy and enthusiasm, and it was obvious that he thoroughly enjoyed being back in the field and exercising control over things.

In referring to Jones's work with the Pearce commission, it was later, with some authority, said that 'Those who knew reported that he exerted vital pressure behind the scenes to enable an appropriate solution to be reached.'[29]

One of the other tasks Jones undertook while employed at the Malawi Buying and Trade Agency, but this time personally for Banda, was to try and prevent the publication of a biography of the doctor, written by Philip Short, a journalist who had spent some time in Malawi. The book was to be published by Longman and 3000 printed and bound copies were ready to be sold.[30] Banda took grave exception to the publication partly, although this was never said, because he wished to be the sole authority on his life story, aspects of which (his age, for example) he had kept secret. There were, in addition to a number of general and not particularly convincing grounds of objection, three specific references which disturbed Banda deeply: his being a white 'stooge', his having suffered from schizophrenia and his association with Mrs French.

Jones was accompanied in his dealings with Longman by Malawi's attorney-general, Richard Banda; the doctor's personal legal adviser, Sattar Sacranie; and lawyers whom they briefed in London. A number of meetings were held in the latter part of 1972. While in no way accepting that the passages to which exception was taken were untrue, Longman eventually decided not to publish the book. Their stated reasons were that they recognized it ought not to be published in Malawi for the general reasons given by Banda and that publication in Britain would 'severely jeopardise the good relations which Longman enjoy in Malawi'. Publication would put at risk their extensive market for educational books in Malawi and elsewhere in Central Africa. It was not explained how this market would be affected unless Banda intervened to damage it. There was, however, a very different interpretation placed on the withdrawal by the press in Britain:

> Curiously, it appears that the method of persuasion employed by Dr. Banda was not the obvious one of a threat of legal action. Instead a more subtle and personal technique was adopted by the Malawi Life President. His representatives pointed out that resident in the country as chief representative of Longmans was a Malawian citizen, Mr. Alex Malinki and three assistants operating the office in Blantyre ... it was made clear that Mr. Malinki and his colleagues would be clapped in prison if the book went on sale in Britain or anywhere else.[31]

The Malawi high commissioner in Britain denied this was the reason for withdrawal. There was a possibility Banda might sue the *Guardian*, but when counsel asked if it was 'at all conceivable that any warnings, however veiled or muted, were made ... to Longmans' representatives that they might risk imprisonment if publication went ahead', the suit was dropped.[32]

Jones asked Banda's solicitors and Longman to 'exercise the greatest vigilance' to make sure that the doctor got early warning of any further proposal to publish the book, which was Short's intention. 'They say they would be very surprised if any reputable publishing firm would now agree to publish it but there are a large number of smaller publishing firms who are less reputable.'

In any event, Longman pulped the printed copies – save for perhaps half a dozen copies. They did, however, sell the type to an outstandingly reputable and by no means small publishing firm, Routledge and Kegan Paul, who intended to publish 3000 copies themselves.

Banda now asked Jones to represent him in attempting to secure a similar withdrawal from Routledge.[33] Routledge were a much tougher opponent for Banda and Jones to tackle. Having no representatives resident in Malawi and no equivalent to Longman's educational book market in Central Africa, they were from the outset significantly less open to, or inclined to tolerate, extra-legal pressure.

Jones, accompanied by two of Banda's London lawyers, met with Routledge's representative, accompanied by two of their lawyers, in London on 13 February 1973. Banda's lawyers were instructed to 'endeavour to dissuade Routledge and Kegan Paul Limited from publishing the book' and they asked Jones to present their case. He repeated the general objections which Banda held and the steps taken by Longman.

> [Routledge's representative] duly noted what Sir Glyn Jones had to say but stated that his company were determined to publish the book. He believed that it was a fact of life which politicians had to accept that biographies would be written of them which were both critical of them and contained material which the subject would prefer to remain private. However, he was anxious to ensure as far as possible that there were no factual inaccuracies in the book (which he believed on the whole to be a sympathetic portrait) and with that in mind he was certainly prepared to consider amendments and deletions where there were good grounds for complaint.

They then considered each of the passages in the book to which Banda took exception.

In the closing paragraph of Short's introduction he asked, 'Which is Banda – black saint or white stooge?' Was he as Godfrey Nicholson claimed, 'possibly the most remarkable living African' or was he as a Ghanaian medical colleague suggested, 'the greatest rogue that ever went unhung'? 'The real Banda', Short went on, 'is both saint and stooge.' Jones explained that the word 'stooge' had a more serious and precise meaning in Malawi than in Britain. Routledge were reluctant to remove the word because they were concerned with the British market where it was much less objectionable, but they were prepared to mark it with an asterisk to indicate that the word was being used in its usual English connotation. In the event, this they did and many readers must have wondered why the asterisk was necessary.

Jones went on to express Banda's objection to passages in the book which suggested that he, when living in Ghana, was suffering from schizophrenia, was unstable, chronically depressed, suffered from a protracted breakdown and was mentally deranged. Routledge accepted that Banda had never suffered from schizophrenia but they were nevertheless satisfied that he 'had been under severe mental stress during the material times'. In the event they made amendments such as to replace 'instability' by 'conflict', 'chronic' by 'acute', 'protracted breakdown' by 'difficulties in Ghana' and 'mental derangement' by 'pathological hatred'. They also deleted two short passages.

Perhaps the matter to which Banda took the gravest exception was the references to his relationship with Mrs French in whose divorce case he had been cited as co-respondent and with whom he lived in Ghana. This part of Banda's background was not well known and was not publicly discussed in Malawi even by those who knew of it, though, when Banda first returned to Nyasaland, the government had information that he might bring Mrs French with him; he did not. In fact, there were only two brief – and many would think sensitive and discreet – passsages dealing with it in Short's book. Routledge had looked very closely into Short's allegations and were 'entirely satisfied that what appears in the book is quite true'.

Banda had instructed his lawyers that he had never been officially notified of the divorce proceedings nor served with any of the documents in the proceedings, but Routledge's lawyers showed that the doctor's memory 'must be at fault' by producing a copy of the acknowledgement of service of the relevant documents signed by Banda on 21 December 1954. Routledge's lawyers knew – and they told Jones – that the 22 December 1934 marriage of William Henry French to Mirene Margaret Ellen Robbins had ended, undefended, in a decree nisi, granted by Judge Elder Jones, on 25 April 1955, in which Banda had been cited as co-respondent, on grounds of adultery and three years' desertion.[34] Consequently Routledge made no changes to the wording of these parts of the book.

Jones's efforts on behalf of Banda failed, and Routledge published the book in 1974, save for a few minor adjustments, precisely as Short had written it. When the book was first withdrawn by Longman, Banda decided to write his autobiography and he asked Longman to consider publishing it.[35] The idea of an autobiography by Banda persisted vaguely on and off for a number of years and became intertwined with the notion of a free-standing biography of Banda by Jones.[36] It is likely that after the publication of Short's biography Banda was keen that a work more acceptable to him, more completely favourable to him and excluding parts he wished to supress should be published, and Jones indicated his willingness to help achieve this.[37] In the event, regrettably, these ideas made next to no progress and eventually came to naught. Both Jones and Banda became involved, however, in the preparation of another book and a television series.

In the early 1980s Brian Lapping made a series of television programmes and wrote a book, both entitled *End of Empire*. One of the programmes in the television series, and one of the chapters in the book, was devoted to Rhodesia but included a good deal about Nyasaland because of its role in the Federation. Lapping was keen to interview both Jones and Banda. Having first consulted Armitage and Blackwood, he asked Jones to make the initial approach to Banda and this was done in October 1982. Jones made it clear that he would advise the doctor on 'no other basis than [his, Jones's] genuine view of his [Banda's] best interest'. The doctor agreed in principle but would need to approve the detailed arrangements. When Jones told Lapping this, they thought the interviewing should be by someone in whom Banda had confidence and who knew him well: Professor George Shepperson, a distinguished historian, Donald Trelford, formerly editor of the *Nyasaland Times*, or Sir Bryan Roberts. After thinking about it, Lapping wrote to Jones and said that on reflection he believed the best chance of Banda agreeing to be filmed lay through Jones himself. Jones was very unsure about undertaking this task himself, possibly because he was still feeling the effects of the MBTA rift between them, or because he recognized his limitations as an interviewer especially on film, or because of his awareness of advancing age. Eventually he agreed, as a 'last ditch' option, to doing it himself.[38]

On the last day of May 1983, Lapping, with his colleague Sarah Curtis, interviewed Jones at his home at Goudhurst. Maxine Baker, the producer, also interviewed him there, and as Peter Connors, who accompanied her, recalled:

> He then struck me as entirely typical of the long-serving former members of the Colonial Service that I had met on other research trips. It was clear from what he said that our access to Banda could only come about via him; this was not unexpected and I read no great significance into it … He was certainly part of the group of ex-Colonials who thought that Banda had received a bad press.[39]

The Granada team interviewed Banda on film on 9 February 1985 at his house at Kasungu. He was interviewed by Jones whose expenses and those of his wife were paid for by Granada. When they arrived, Cecilia Kadzamira told Lady Jones she did not know how successful the interviews would be because 'My old man is almost stone deaf.' 'Don't worry', replied Lady Jones, 'so is my old man.'[40] The programme was directed by John Shepperd, who recalled that 'Sir Glyn was very old and very much "Malawi Jones". I had the impression that even the mildest of devil's advocacy would not have been well received.' Shepperd also interviewed Jones just before the visit to Malawi but Granada decided not to use the interview 'because of his phenomenally slow rate of talking'.[41]

Connors, who travelled to Malawi with Jones and his wife, recalled:

> Prior to travelling to the Life President's summer residence we spent a little time in Lilongwe, during which time the former Governor General announced that he was going to the bank. We were intrigued by the officials' response to this: there appeared to be some consternation that he had announced this in our presence. One could read a number of interpretations into this; perhaps they were concerned that this would upset some closely woven timetable.[42]

Connors recalled, too, how Jones insisted that all members of the filming and interview team should dress 'in a manner appropriate to a Buckingham Palace garden party'. He thought Jones's insistence might be because of his conception of how film crews dressed and conducted themselves, rather than an exaggerated respect for Banda. He believed that Maxine Baker had never before, or since, 'had occasion to wear long gloves, hat and matching handbag.'

At the interview with Banda, 'Jones put the questions on [their] behalf in a respectful manner' and this, unfortunately, did not allow the team to ask the supplementary questions that 'are customary to fully illuminate the topic'. For the interviewing team, the answers held no great surprises and appeared to add nothing to existing histories of the Federal era. They got the clear impression that Jones had prepared Banda and that each was rehearsed. They had expected Banda to be a little more 'away with the fairies' than was the case and thought maybe they had 'arrived during a good patch'. They found the formality requested of them 'somewhat overdone'.

One other 'interesting event' long stayed in Connors's memory. When the interview and filming were complete, Jones was expected to be guest of honour 'at a gathering at a local community', but instead he announced his intention 'to go to the lake and do some fishing'. This surprised everyone else, and the ministry of information officials, rather than disappoint the local community, prevailed upon the Granada team to go to the gathering:

> We found that the population of a village, the pupils of a school and local dignatories were arrayed waiting to present a full programme of

events to Jones. The choir of blind children was followed by speeches from local worthies and an imprompu speech from Maxine. An individual then shuffled forward on his knees with a gift for Maxine [intended for] Jones [in] a plain brown envelope ... We did not see Jones again.

The *End of Empire* television series was ready for broadcasting soon after this filming was completed, and Lapping's book was published the same year, 1985. Lapping wrote to Jones and offered to include his name as a consultant but he declined because, in his view, it would be dishonest to accept:

> While there is much in the film with which I agree, there is almost more with which I disagree – e.g. the inadequate space given to Dr. Banda as opposed to Sir Robert Armitage: the almost total elimination of the history of Nyasaland between 1960 and the secession from the federation: the exclusion of my meeting with Dr. Banda in Gwelo prison: and of my meeting with Mr. Macleod at the end of 1959: and, possibly most important, the failure to make adequate mention of the part played by Rab Butler in relation to Nyasaland's independence ... I note that the only mention of myself in the programme is at page 10 of your book. You drew my attention to this *after* the book was published and I told you that the record was inaccurate. I find it difficult to understand why you failed to do me the courtesy of verifying the report before publishing it.[43]

In the foreword to the Paladin edition of 1988 Lapping said it was little changed from the original but he had made some corrections on the Rhodesia chapter at the suggestion of Jones. There was, however, an interesting – and extremely rare – misunderstanding retained from the first edition. Lapping said Chipembere was arrested for sedition in 1962 (it was in fact 1960) and that Jones, as Governor, could have persuaded his attorney-general that a prosecution was against the public interest but that he was assured by Banda that he approved of Chipembere's imprisonment. Jones was in fact not in the country at the time; still less was he Governor, not even acting Governor, and it was Armitage who was in a position to prevent a prosecution but did not do so. What is interesting is that Lapping checked this statement carefully for the second edition and Jones did not deny the substance of the story nor tell them anything about it. Lapping's explanation was that perhaps 'he felt my telling a story about him on which he had declined to comment was at the least discourteous'.[44]

Jones was clearly much put out by the shortcomings, as he saw them, of Lapping's work and failure to portray Banda in an adequate light – both from the point of view of space and role – especially as compared to Armitage. He believed, too, that Lapping was gravely remiss in giving insufficient coverage to himself in relation to Banda and to Macleod, and to Butler's contribution. Lapping concluded that 'in the end he was disappointed, both that we did not include him in the programme and that we did not, as he had come to expect, follow his line on the Northern Rhodesian and Nyasaland stories'.[45]

> [Jones] was not entirely happy with our programme. I think the reason was that we cut out almost all the stories he told us. This wasn't because we thought there was anything wrong with [him] or his story-telling; merely that he took over after Armitage when the exciting conflict was over and a smooth transition was assured. Similarly his stories about Northern Rhodesia, though many of them were interesting, failed to make a big impact in the television series.[46]

Granada paid Jones £1000 for his services, but since he had told Banda at an early stage that he 'would be performing this service of obtaining his cooperation with the *End of Empire* series without receiving payment', he came to believe it was wrong to have accepted it. Consequently, in the letter in which he told Lapping how much he disagreed with the programme, he sent a cheque for £1000 as a repayment to Granada and added, in tones reminiscent of his correspondence about the MBTA salary: 'At the same time I consider that a thousand pounds is by no means too much for a company like Granada to pay someone of my qualifications for a service which no one else seemed able to perform.' He therefore asked Granada to arrange 'to pay out at least a thousand pounds in four equal portions' to each of four named charities.[47]

It is likely that he anticipated Banda's displeasure when he learned that Granada had taken a different view of the part he had played in Central Africa. He believed Granada was being grossly unjust to the doctor and especially in giving a great deal more prominence to Armitage than to Banda or to himself. Consequently, he was distancing himself from the television series and the book, not as a public gesture – for the repayment of the fee and its allocation to charities was entirely private – but as a gesture to the doctor, should it be needed. He may still have been smarting from Banda's 'grasping' allegation at the close of his service with the MBTA, and would not have wished to re-open that painful wound.

The Granada team had the feeling that, having remained in the paid service of Malawi for several years after retirement – 'on Banda's payroll' as they put it – he was more propagandist than historical witness, and wished to counter that feeling.[48]

Lapping was engaged on the 'task of historical evidence gathering',[49] and his explanation of Jones's objections was:

I was at the time convinced that what annoyed Glyn Jones was my having hit the nail exactly on the head. He wanted himself to be regarded, and he thought it his duty to ensure that the departing British were regarded, as adherents to the rule of law. And my clear statement that he conspired with Banda to get Chipembere locked up reduced him from a neutral instrument of fair-minded government to a political partisan. He didn't like that at all.[50]

While Lapping was mistaken over the part played by Jones specifically in relation to Chipembere's arrest, he may well have hit the nail on the head and been correct in thinking that Jones would not wish to re-expose the extent to which the rule of law had been so gravely eroded under his governorship and to which he had been so strongly politically partisan.

Though Banda enjoyed the experience, the Granada episode was an unhappy affair for Jones and he long remained bitter about his treatment at their hands.

In his retirement, Jones had time to reflect on his early education. It seems he wished to make an attempt, however small as he might have seen it, to repay some of the debt to his school and college for the contribution they had made to his education, and thereby to his life and career.

In the case of the King's School, Chester, he wrote confidentially to the headmaster in 1972. For the first time in his life, he said, he had 'a little more money than [he] need[ed] to live on':

> I wonder if there is any way in which I can provide some unobtrusive help occasionally for a needy boy at the King's School. Perhaps you do not have that type of boy at the school, these days. But if there were anyone finding it difficult to get books or sporting equipment or anything else required, that would be the kind of boy I would like to help.[51]

It may be that he was reflecting on his own school career, half a century earlier, when he found 'it difficult to get books or sporting equipment', and now that he was able to afford it he wished to help someone similarly placed.

The case of Oxford was rather different, although in his later years he donated generously to his college.[52] When he went up in 1927 he was admitted as a non-collegiate student to St Catherine's Society. A few years before he retired from Malawi, St Catherine's College was founded and the society ceased to exist. What did not cease to exist, however, was the St Catherine's association of alumni which Jones had joined on going down in 1931.

In 1970 he took his MA *in absentia* and in the same year he was invited to join the committee of the association. Two years later he became its chairman. He retained this post for a decade. He was made an honorary fellow of St Catherine's College in 1977 partly, it was thought, because he was a distinguished alumnus and partly because the governing body considered him a suitable person to help forge closer links between the College and its alumni.[53] He prized the honorary fellowship highly and was as proud of it as any of his other awards and honours.[54]

In 1982 he was asked to become the chairman of a transitional body for alumni affairs created after the winding up of the college association. Jones's 'standing with the older alumni meant that they had complete confidence in him'. Furthermore, 'his ideas, his prestige in Africa and his total lack of stuffiness made him acceptable to the younger generation'.[55] He had a 'natural rapport' with Sir Patrick Nairne, the master of St Catherine's, and there was 'a natural understanding and respect' between Jones and Lord Bullock, the founding master. Their work culminated in 1988 with Jones's acceptance of the unique title of President of Alumni for life, a step proposed by Nairne.

In April 1992 the Joneses flew to Turkey for a holiday with their daughter, Elisabeth, and son-in-law, Colin Perchard, the British Council representative there. Before they left Goudhurst, where they were now living, he was examined by his doctor and pronounced fit to travel. However, while in Turkey he became very ill and a consultant diagnosed liver failure. He had suffered from a good deal of malaria as a young man in Northern Rhodesia and this had damaged his liver. He had also, as was not unusual in his colonial generation, drunk rather more alcohol than perhaps became the custom in a later generation. It is the case, however, that those who knew him well never saw him adversely influenced by this, and indeed his local doctor at Goudhurst, bearing in mind his age, advised that drink would not harm him. The consultant's diagnosis in Turkey was serious and Jones was flown back to Britain for treatment, accompanied by his wife and daughter. After a fortnight back in Britain, Elisabeth – desperately and increasingly worried about her father's condition – had him admitted to hospital. He continued to decline, and two weeks after being admitted to hospital, he died.[56]

Nine months later, on 13 March 1993, a memorial service was held by St Catherine's College at St Cross Church, Holywell, Oxford. There was a massive congregation of friends, former colleagues and representatives of numerous bodies. The haunting lilts of Elgar's ninth Enigma Variation, Nimrod the great hunter, a favourite of Glyn's, opened the service, and his favourite hymns were included: 'For all the Saints who from their labours rest'; 'Guide me O thou great Redeemer' to the tune 'Cwm Rhondda' in which he must have joined so many times when watching

Wales play international rugger matches; and 'Jerusalem: And did those feet in ancient times walk upon England's mountains green?', a hymn chosen as if to balance the English side of his make-up.[57]

Many of those who attended the reception after the memorial service saw it, despite the sadness of Glyn's passing, as a joyous occasion, in many ways resembling the parties he himself had given over the years. It was, in their eyes, a reception he would himself have enjoyed immensely.

At the bottom of the grounds of their home at Goudhurst in the Kent countryside, Nancy and Elisabeth had a local carpenter make and erect a small pillar fashioned from darkened Mlanje cedar wood – indigenous to the upper levels of Mlanje mountain in southern Malawi, a mountain which he frequently climbed at remarkable speed and on whose plateau he enjoyed the peace and solitude of fishing. This pillar was intended to mark the final resting place of his ashes. A little later, however, Nancy decided that an earlier idea which she and Glyn had discussed should be adherred to: his ashes should be taken back to Malawi and laid to rest beside their son, Timothy, in Zomba cemetery, gently cared for over the years by Wilfred, the former Government House chaffeur. In 1993, Elisabeth flew to Malawi and, at a dignified ceremony, arranged by Cecilia Kadzamira and the Anglican priest, John Parslow, with many chiefs present, she laid her father's ashes to rest, beside her brother. Later, in 1999, she travelled again to Malawi and laid her mother's ashes at the same spot. Among many others, Cecilia Kadzamira, John Parslow and Wilfred were again present.[58]

The cemetery in Zomba is a quiet, peaceful, well cared-for, almost private place, only a short distance downhill from Government House and across the road from the *boma*. For Africa it has a silent air of eternity about it. It is the last resting place of another Governor, another Governor's widow and another loved son. They and others are at peace there.

CHAPTER 9

Proconsul of the Wind of Change

GLYN Jones's family background and upbringing were modest. His parents lived in one of the less fashionable parts of Chester. His father was a grocer's assistant and had been described as somewhat footloose. Although only twenty-one and not long married when her son was born, his mother, a milliner, was the dominant influence in the family. Glyn had no brothers and for the first seven years of his life, until his sister was born, he was an only child. He was much closer to his mother than to his father, who, for example, he would not allow to watch the football games in which he played. Glyn's primary education was at an elementary council school. His mother was ambitious for him and sent him to an English-language church – the only member of the family to do so – for proficiency in English which was seen as the key to a good education and subsequent entry to a worthwhile career.

The environment in which he was brought up was relatively narrow. The Love Street primary school was but two minutes' walk from his parents' house and his secondary school, the King's School, was within ten to fifteen minutes' moderate walking distance and he easily returned home for lunch each day. The churches which he and his parents attended, on opposite sides of the same road, were only a street away from where they lived.

The King's School was a day school and consequently those who attended it lacked the particular character-building aspects, for good or ill, of the major public schools where boarding was the norm. These aspects are often believed to include heirarchy, fagging, beating, cold showers and instilling such concepts as right and duty, leadership and public service. A day school necessarily lacked the broadening influences of mixing with boys from other parts of Britain and from other countries, several of whom, in boarding schools, were the offspring of fathers in crown service overseas. Compared to the major public schools, too, the King's School was quite small – less than half the size of most.

It was at King's – where there was great competition to be admitted, for there were twice as many applicants as there were places available – that the first sign of Glyn's strong competitiveness, which was to remain throughout his life, emerged. This competitiveness displayed itself in his keenness to undertake any task asked of him. More importantly and clearly, it manifested itself in a determination in everything he tackled to do better than anyone else and better than he himself had previously done. It was clear in his outstanding record of successes in football, rowing, athletics and swimming. It was clear, too, in his successive – and not strictly necessary – sittings of the higher school certificate examinations. Whereas leadership was assumed as a right and duty in the major public schools, it was more a matter of individual choice at King's and was often pursued through sports and athletics. In these fields Glyn not only excelled personally but also developed his leadership qualities as captain of soccer, swimming and boats. Sports helped to cultivate a pragmatic flexibility, which was to become a useful attribute in later life. In school soccer he played successively at outside-left, centre-forward and centre-half, and at Oxford outside-right, inside-right and centre-forward. The common position at both, to which he successfully aspired, was centre-forward – the middle of the front, attacking, line. At school he rowed first at number three and then as stroke, from where the pace for the whole crew is set. His leadership qualities also developed as senior prefect, headboy, captain of the school, house captain and vice-president of the literary society. He accepted 'his very considerable responsibilities ... without hesitation and exercised [them] with discretion, combining with a natural gift of leadership a social conscience'.[1] In virtually all of the very many activities in which he engaged at school, he excelled. He gives the impression of entering into every possible activity, putting his all into them with great determination, doing well and usually coming out on top. He showed no sign of the narrowness which his family background may have implied.

It may be that this competitiveness, this entering into every activity and working hard at them, affected his academic accomplishments at Oxford – though not necessarily at King's – which fell below the level of which he was intellectually capable. He undoubtedly devoted a great deal of his undergraduate time to soccer, rowing and debating, and did not neglect the social side of life, and these may have had an influence on his academic work: he was awarded a third-class degree. Yet, his Oxford career, like his school career, was both full and fulfilling, and his lack of scholastic distinction may well have been a disguised blessing. Had he done better academically – and his tutors certainly thought him capable of it – he might have been offered, and accepted, one of the teaching appointments for which he applied. If this had happened he would not have sought a post in the colonial service where his all-roundedness, leadership qualities, love of outdoor pursuits and physical activity, and his team spirit were precisely the qualities for which the selectors were looking.

The selectors were also looking for self-sufficiency and the ability in a man to tolerate, indeed enjoy, long periods with no company other than his own. Finding men with this ability was not easy, yet they existed and Jones was, or became, one of them. It may be that the quality was developed through his living in a part of Chester where few of his fellow secondary schoolboys lived, and through going from school each evening to a home in which his father played a negligible part, in which his mother was the stronger personality, in which he had no brothers and only one, significantly younger, sister. King's was an all-boys school and tended to accustom, but not always to reconcile, the pupils to the absence of female company. His homework, in the sort of family in which he was brought up, was a lonely occupation, and some others of his activities – singing and playing the piano – were also largely individual pastimes.

There was another influential element in his upbringing. His family background freed him of the inbuilt non-egalitarian aspects of the families from which colonial service officers were typically drawn: middle-class, professional, crown service, major public school families. The King's School education contained a number of egalitarian elements. Save for the prefects' caps and sporting colours, there was relatively little differentiation in the uniform worn by the boys – unlike the numerous, subtle but important hierarchical sartorial differences common in some public schools. The complex marking system for the efficiency competition was designed to 'make it possible for every boy to feel that by his success or failures ... he was contributing something'. The competition was designed also to encourage 'the average, rather than the exceptional, member'. It may have been the egalitarian element that made Glyn reluctant at school to have resort to corporal punishment by prefects. Much later in life he privately expressed the view that African women should not be exempt from corporal punishment on grounds simply of their sex.[2] The Duke of York camps, which left a deep impression on those who attended, were egalitarian in mixing boys from public schools and from industrial backgrounds. There may have been significance, too, in the cadet corps, with its inbuilt heirarchical rankings, being abandoned mid-way through Jones's time at the school. In any case, the corps was designed to train officers *and* men for military service. Again, there may have been something in his being a non-collegiate student at Oxford which reinforced the egalitarian influences of his school.

The first part of his service in Northern Rhodesia, from 1931 to 1951, was spent in the rural areas of the country, some of them very isolated and remote from centres where more than a very few Europeans lived. Although, like most young men, he enjoyed the bonhomie and lack of inhibition of his occasional visits to larger centres, in his everyday life he was dependent, though usually without regret, on his self-sufficiency. His personal and professional lives were not separate but rather were intertwined to become one and the same thing. It was a life in which he did a great deal of walking, game and bird shooting, and fishing. As district commissioner, he was the senior government officer, representing the government and responsible for the African population of his district. District commissioners looked upon the area to which they were posted as *their* district, and the people in it as *their* people.

It is not surprising that these proprietary elements of district administration, when coupled with the 'huntin, shootin and fishin' which he so much enjoyed, tended to develop a 'squirearchical' feel to Jones's life. He came to enjoy an existence in some respects not unlike that of the English country squire, notwithstanding that his parents were Welsh and notwithstanding the egalitarian elements of his upbringing. The sort of life he led and enjoyed also developed a close affinity with the rural African people and a belief in the values associated with tradition and the role of the chiefs in society and the government of the country. The importance of these values particularly impressed itself on him in Barotseland. Here, where he was resident commissioner, albeit for a relatively short time, in charge of a whole province, the opportunities to enjoy the squirearchical aspects of administrative life, originating and developed in the more isolated areas, were at their greatest. The travelling to visit *his* chiefs, *his* district commissioners and the mission stations in *his* province, the barge trips, the river picnics, the fishing and the shooting, the entertaining at the residency were all part of this quiet fondness for the life of a squire.

It was a fondness many elements of which he shared with Governor Benson. The memorable Barotseland tour he arranged for the Governor, whom he accompanied, was a fine example of this: being welcomed by deferential traditional chiefs and headmen, travelling by barge, carefully arranged fishing, hunting, well constructed and splendidly located camps, quiet sociable evenings, congenial companions, under the African skies, with the bush and its peculiarly African night noises close to them, all far from Lusaka's madding crowd. Benson was reliving his earlier life as a district officer and doing so in gubernatorial comfort – the squire *par excellence*. His recreations, as recorded in Who's Who were fishing and shooting, as were Jones's. Benson knew that Jones shared his strong belief in the values of traditional, chiefly, African leadership, and in 'his pet theories about indirect rule and the vital importance of the chiefs in British colonial rule'.

In writing Jones's biography one has the disconcerting sensation at times that one is writing the life story of two different men: the Northern Rhodesia Jones and the Nyasaland–Malawi Jones. A difference was to be expected when he moved to Nyasaland, since the assumption of high office, particularly as Governor, brought with it an inevitable degree of isolation from other members of the community, including colleagues and even many friends. He was now removed from direct contact with the numerous friends with whom he had associated over many years in Northern Rhodesia, and it would take time for similar friendships to develop, if ever they did, in Nyasaland. He was removed, too – certainly as Governor and largely as chief secretary – from direct contact with chiefs, headmen and village people, indeed from most Africans save quite a small number of leading politicians. The death of his mother soon after he became chief secretary and especially the tragic death of his son soon after he became Governor, tended to make him more withdrawn, more taciturn,[3] more introspective, less gregarious, less fun-loving than he had been in Northern Rhodesia. These factors undoubtedly contribute to the impression that Jones in Nyasaland was a very different sort of man from Jones in Northern Rhodesia, but they do not provide a full explanation.

The important professional difference was in his dealings with African leaders. In Northern Rhodesia he was a profoundly convinced supporter of the traditional chiefs and of their continued leadership role; this was why Benson promoted him and made him secretary for native affairs.[4] Together, as he himself recalled, they 'fought a long, losing battle over the chiefs, who, [they] thought would overcome the modern politicians'.[5] In Nyasaland, despite early visits to meet as many of them as he could and later attempts to get Banda to stop criticizing them, he did little, and in most cases nothing, to support them in their traditional role. Indeed, at Banda's behest, he soon removed from some of them, including some of the most senior and most loyal, their status as chief, and assented to the removal of their judicial functions from all of them, though he was able to secure pensions, which Banda insisted should be small, for some of those whom he removed from office. He told them to toe the line in their relations with the MCP, and he paid overwhelming regard to, and gave almost total support to, the new elite of professional African politicians. This was not, in broad terms, exceptional. In Jones's case, however, there was an intriguing and massive change of attitude, from being a great supporter of, and believer in, the role of traditional leaders and its continuation, to being an even stronger supporter of, and believer in, the new politicians, who secured a following often only by demagogy, intimidation, violence and lawlessness. He gave them this support and condoned much of their law breaking long before their popular following was tested in any election. The shift from supporting one to jettisoning them and supporting the other was not marginal: it was chasmic. Its being accomplished in a very short period of time – overnight as some saw it – emphasized the magnitude. Understanding this change depends upon seeing that Jones, devoted to the best interests of the African people and pursuing those interests through supporting the leaders most likely to bring them about, was quick to recognize the altered circumstances: that the leadership was changing, was being wrested from one set of hands and seized by another. No longer was constitutional progress to be achieved, and the will of the people expressed, through traditional authorities, but henceforth through professional politicians.

Furthermore, by 1960 Jones had spent virtually the whole of his career in close touch with rural Africans and their way of life, which he admired and respected. He was very much a field man. Even his years in the Lusaka secretariat were intimately concerned with the rural African population as commissioner for native development and then secretary for native affairs. He never lost touch, in Northern Rhodesia, with the chiefs and the rural Africans, and rarely missed an opportunity to visit them. At the age of fifty-two, and with his experience and views, the leap which he took in shifting his support from chiefs to politicians was a good deal larger, quicker and more complete than many would have been able to take. If it was a leap which had to be taken and someone had to take it, one might expect it to be more easily taken by a younger person, and one less rurally inclined and less firmly supportive of the traditional chiefs. Whether Benson, whose views he shared, could have taken the same sort of leap is debatable, but the point never arose, because Benson retired shortly before Macmillan undertook his African 'wind of change' tour. Jones's appointment to Nyasaland coincided with it.

There are a number of explanations for the change. First, in an interview in May 1983 he said that generally speaking the colonial service believed the 'liberation' of Africa would happen through the chiefs and their councils. He and his colleagues in Northern Rhodesia tended to deprecate the leading African politicians. Indeed, he took pride in personally signing restriction orders and having them served on a number of leading African politicians. However, when he moved from Barotseland to become secretary for native affairs, he began to move 'from being a dyed-in-the-wool conservative to recognising the importance of urban politicians'. Service in Lusaka, as secretary for native affairs, contributed to his 'evolving view that [they] were the men who had to be dealt with'. Presumably, he was beginning to recognize that his and Benson's belief that the chiefs would prevail over the politicians was profoundly mistaken, and the time to swap horses was fast approaching. He also recalled that during the tour of the country that he undertook as soon as he arrived in Nyasaland he was impressed by the existence of an MCP office and flag in every village. This very short tour, in which in fact he saw very few villages, 'completed [his] change of mind about the influence of African political leaders'. Understanding this change of mind depends upon seeing that he was using the words 'had to' and 'influence' descriptively rather than prescriptively. The politicians' influence was a fact, which could not be ignored, and, similarly, the inevitability of having to deal with them was a fact. This had occurred to Macmillan almost a year earlier. It was a pragmatic perception which he and Devlin impressed upon Macleod and which no doubt the secretary of state impressed upon Jones.

A second explanation of the difference between the Northern Rhodesia Jones and the Nyasaland Jones lies in his competitiveness. It would have been against his nature to decline the challenge which high office in Nyasaland presented, particularly at such a troubled time. He understood Macleod to have told him the Nyasaland post was 'the most difficult job in the colonial service'. If anything was calculated to get a positive, almost Pavlovian, response from Jones, it was precisely this sort of challenge. He believed, as did Benson, that the Nyasaland administration had over-reacted in declaring a state of emergency in 1959 and had consequently embittered the African population. He believed, too, that the government had lost touch with the African people. He would have reacted positively to the challenge of transfer to Nyasaland, determined to do his best to put matters right and do better than his predecessors had done. In this determination, he would have realized that his approach to the question of to whom to give prime support – traditional rural leaders or urban professional politicians – would need radical readjustment, for without it he could not put matters right and do better than his predecessors. In any case, Macleod made it clear that Banda was the man to support, exclusively if necessary. Competitiveness, and pragmatism, gave speedy impetus to his evolving view and turned it into a conversion. If his conversion was not completed before he left Northern Rhodesia, it was given an irreversible push by Macleod and was completed once he arrived in Nyasaland and faced Banda.

A third explanation lies in the reception he received when he arrived in Nyasaland. His appointment was at first welcomed by expatriate civil servants, especially those in the administration who looked forward to working with a man who was 'one of them', a district officer who had long and recent experience of field administration in a neighbouring and in some respects similar country, spoke local languages and had a reputation both for toughness and for being closely in tune with rural African needs. They looked forward to having a head of the civil service who was prepared, unlike his predecessor who, they humorously and with mild exaggeration said, had never ventured north of Liwonde.

Jones's arrival in Nyasaland was none the less unexpected, sudden and widely seen as designed to replace a gentle man who had ruthlessly been made a scapegoat by the British government. Moreover, it coincided with a time when the vast, recently decided but largely unannounced changes on which Macmillan and Macleod were determined were dimly beginning to dawn on expatriate minds, and this roused suspicions, which Macleod did nothing to allay, in those minds. Jones's explanation for his belief that the Nyasaland administration had over-reacted and panicked in declaring a state of emergency, was that there had been no need to bring in federal troops 'because Nyasaland had a stronger army than Northern Rhodesia had: two battalions compared to only one'.[6] This was a baffling statement, because neither Nyasaland nor Northern Rhodesia at the time had an army. Of the two battalions of the King's African Rifles in the federal army, one each was posted to Zomba and Lusaka. Northern Rhodesia additionally had a strong territorial army battalion, whereas Nyasaland had none. Even so, Jones's – and his wife's[7] – feelings about the Nyasaland administration's actions in having, unnecessarily as they saw it, declared a state of emergency, especially their implied comparisons with Northern Rhodesia, seem to have communicated themselves to the Nyasaland civil servants. What was seen by some as his precipitate and unkind insistence on taking over Footman's house, leaving him and his family to live in a small hotel, was commented on with sorrow by civil servants. His invitation, even though it may have originated with Macleod, to the southern provincial commissioner and officer in charge of police to dine with the secretary of state rather than stay in attendance on Armitage, the Governor, caused lasting resentment. Within the secretariat, too, the fact that Macleod, who was not invariably admired by members of the colonial service, took the unprecedented step of openly writing to thank Jones, and not Armitage, for the arrangements for his visit when Banda was released, did little to reduce any suspicions which officials may have been harbouring.[8] What was fairly soon seen as his lack of understanding of, and sympathy with, the district administration in Nyasaland brought forth charges of lack of contact, trust, candour and support.

The antagonism, whatever its nature, its extent, its causes and the degree of accuracy with which it was perceived, which faced him in his early days in Nyasaland, especially after many years of bonhomous relationships with colleagues, especially those in the administration, and non-officials in Northern Rhodesia, must have been a sad blow which hurt him deeply. In contrast to this, Banda, whom he found charming and a person with whom he could work, welcomed his appointment. It may not have been from traditional chiefs alone that his conversion was completed. Jones later recorded: 'When I arrived as Chief Secretary in Nyasaland, the settlers were against me and took it out on my wife.'

What he saw as the antagonism of the settlers and soon many of his civil servant colleagues made this period 'the most unhappy part of [his] colonial service'.[9]

The most fundamental explanation of the difference between the Northern Rhodesia Jones and the Nyasaland Jones, however, lies in the abrupt change in the application of British policy in Africa. When Jones went on leave from Northern Rhodesia in August 1959, Britain's Africa policy under Macmillan and Lennox-Boyd showed no public signs of early change. Indeed, they had recently in parliament stoutly defended the actions taken by Armitage in declaring and maintaining a state of emergency in Nyasaland. Soon after Jones arrived in England on leave, the October 1959 general election was held and Macleod succeeded Lennox-Boyd, with a remit to get a move on in Africa. Early in January 1960 Macmillan set out for a major tour of Africa. Jones, in blissful ignorance, was relaxing on a skiing holiday. When he returned he found waiting for him the offer of the chief secretaryship of Nyasaland. Two weeks later, Macmillan having visited Nyasaland, he was asked to take up the appointment immediately. On 3 February Macmillan delivered his 'wind of change' speech in Cape Town – the very day Jones and his wife were due to sail back to Africa. By the time Jones reached Nyasaland, Footman had already been relieved of his office. Nowhere did the wind of change blow more speedily than in Nyasaland, and no one was swept up by it more quickly and fully than was Jones.

Jones first met Banda in March 1960 in Gwelo gaol. The doctor had been in detention for a year and was confident that in time he would be released and the government would be obliged to deal with him as the political leader of Nyasaland's African people. Jones's visit followed very soon after a similar visit by Footman, and in the meantime Macmillan had visited Nyasaland. Given this prime ministerial visit, and with Jones's Gwelo visit following so soon after his appointment as chief secretary and so soon after Footman's visit, Banda must have realized that important early changes were afoot. He probably assumed that Jones had been brought in at short notice to help do something about solving the problems in Nyasaland, including his own release and constitutional advance. Their meeting was amicable and they immediately struck up a friendly rapport. It was a good start.

Thereafter, in the six months following that meeting, Jones did not see a great deal of Banda. It was Armitage, with Macleod, who played the leading part in Banda's reception at Government House on release from detention. Jones's part was minor and he was not even present when Banda arrived and met the Governor and the colonial secretary. Armitage had ensured that the meeting should be on his own ground, at Government House, rather than, as Macleod had proposed, in the chief secretary's office. It was Youens and not Jones who had flown to Southern Rhodesia, released the doctor and accompanied him back to Nyasaland.[10] It was Armitage, not Jones, who, having revoked the state of emergency in June, released all but a handful of the remaining detainees. Banda was away in Britain and America for several weeks after his release. He then attended, with Armitage who went out of his way to wish him well before he left, the Lancaster House conference in July and early August 1960. So, the doctor was not in Nyasaland a great deal during the first few months of his freedom and of Jones's service in Nyasaland. Jones's opportunities for developing a close relationship with him during this period were limited and much of the opinion which each had of the other was based on their Gwelo meeting.

So far as British policy in Central Africa was concerned after the October 1959 general election, Macmillan and Macleod saw that they must deal with Banda as the leader of the Nyasaland people. Not surprisingly, dealing with the chiefs as leaders of the people did not enter their minds. They also saw that the protectorate's constitution must be altered so that the country could move towards self-government, and then independence, but within the Federation, albeit with a changed federal constitution.

Over-arching all other elements in Britain's policy regarding Nyasaland, however, was the determination that they should never again be placed in a position where they had to declare a state of emergency and bring in military forces to make the country governable. Only by ending the 1959 state of emergency, releasing Banda and dealing with him could the political impasse, which declaring it had created, be broken. Only then could the country become peaceful and advance constitutionally, rather than continue to be ruled by force in a repressive and costly manner. The cost would be in terms of political standing for the government in Britain and internationally, and also in terms of bloodshed, finance and economic development in Nyasaland. The determination to avoid a state of emergency was as near absolute as the British government's, and therefore the Governor's, actions could make it. That is to say, they would adjust their actions and would move towards the pragmatics extreme of the principles–pragmatics spectrum to avoid another state of emergency in which they ruled by force of arms.

Given this over-arching determination, Jones, as Governor, knew that in order to accomplish anything worthwhile in the three years for which he was appointed, his relationship with Banda would be crucial. Above everything else, the relationship had to be such that the need to declare a state of emergency and return to an impasse would be avoided. Achieving this necessitated preventing Banda breaking off his cooperation with the British government and making Nyasaland ungovernable as he had in 1959, no matter what unpalatable steps had to be taken to achieve that end. If at the same time Jones could get on sufficiently good terms with the doctor as to influence him, guide him and persuade him to whatever steps the British government wished to take, so much the better, but they would be bonuses.

There was a further consideration of profound importance, held personally by Jones: in all matters that faced him and in all decisions that he made, the best interests of Nyasaland–Malawi and its people were paramount, and all other considerations – personal, professional and political – were subordinated to these. Furthermore, he was genuinely and utterly convinced that Banda was far and away the person most able – indeed, the only person able – to bring about those best interests. But Banda could do this only if his hegemony were maintained. Consequently, he had to be protected from anything which might dislodge him (for example, opposition parties and his own lieutenants) or which might weaken him (for example, his own actions and serious doubts in British government minds whether he was, after all, acting in the country's best interests).

The protection against being dislodged required Jones to advocate concessions in order that the lieutenants should not resort to rousing the masses on the grounds that Banda was not securing the advances they were pressing him to obtain. In a sense, it was the lieutenants as much as, and on occasion possibly more than, Banda whom Jones had to keep in play or at bay. For example, when Jones and Foster noticed that Banda had 'less assurance in his demeanour' a few months after the 1961 elections, he said:

> We have a feeling that [Banda's] policy of peace and calm, cooperation with the Government and determination at present not to embarrass the Secretary of State or myself, is coming in for increasing criticism. This can obviously lead to a hardening of his heart for purely defensive purposes, and in such a case I must obviously be sympathetic and go a long way to meet the demands which he makes.[11]

Protection against being dislodged also involved the Governor in standing aside while African opposition parties and others were bludgeoned into oblivion.

The protection against the doctor being weakened required Jones, in reporting to the secretary of state, to defend Banda by, for example, claiming that he did not authorize or approve of any of the frequent outbreaks of violence, that he genuinely appealed to his people to be peaceful, that reports of lawlessness were inaccurate, exaggerated or fabricated, that the press and opponents were simply stirring up trouble and that the situation was improving. Protection against Banda being weakened was also accomplished by Jones sedulously advising him in his best interests even when the advice was not in accordance with his own private views on a particular matter. For example, in order to protect Banda's reputation, he advised against the public execution of Silombela and against hanging women even though he privately agreed with both. Even two decades after he left Malawi, he agreed to participate in the Granada *End of Empire* series only on the basis of acting exclusively in Banda's best interests, and not, by implication, necessarily on the basis of accurate historical evidence-gathering.

The combination of these dominant factors – Britain's determination to avoid declaring another state of emergency and Jones's profound commitment to the best interests of Malawi and its people, as he saw them, coupled with his equally profound conviction that Banda was the only person able to bring these about and consequently needed protection – was fundamentally important in determining Jones's actions at the time, and is crucial to understanding them subsequently.

We do not know when Banda first realized the British government, come what may, was determined never to declare another state of emergency. Once he did realize it he knew that to get his own way, to continue to be in a position to bring about the country's best interests as he saw them, to remain in power and retain the support of his lieutenants and followers, if all other methods failed or if he chose not to attempt them, he had simply to warn or threaten – the difference was rarely clear and seldom mattered – that he could no longer guarantee to restrain his followers, or that he would resign and have to be sent back to Gwelo gaol. Everyone recognized there was no acceptable alternative leader. Consequently, his resignation, inability to guarantee to restrain his followers, or even lack of cooperation, would inevitably lead to serious widespread violence, the declaration of another state of emergency, mass detentions and a fresh impasse. No alternative leaders had emerged during the 1959–60 state of emergency, still less subsequently, and Banda's hold on the African population – deliberatately built up by his party lieutenants and reinforced by Britain's exclusive support of him – was virtually complete. Provided the Governor believed that Banda's threat to resign and go back to Gwelo, or his warning that he would be unable to control his followers, was serious, or even might be serious, he would be bound to accede to the doctor's demands or wishes – again the difference was rarely clear and seldom mattered. To do otherwise would risk a state of emergency – a contingency the British government was determined to avoid, virtually at any cost.

Taking risks is a matter of considering both the likelihood of the thing risked occurring and also the magnitude of the damage which would be occasioned by its occurrence. The greater the latter, the less the importance placed on the former. In Nyasaland, the potential magnitude of damage – the consequences of another state of emergency – was so great, that Banda had only to place in Jones's mind the possibility – not probability, still less certainty – of a security breakdown, in order to induce him to act as he, the doctor, whether of his own volition or under pressure from his lieutenants, wished.

Banda took an early opportunity to test the efficacy of using the overarching policy of emergency avoidance as a sword in his own hands while the British government was using it as a shield for its own protection. From August to November 1960, while Armitage was on leave, Jones was Acting Governor, and this presented the opportunity. There were still a dozen or so of Banda's followers in detention, all of them considered to be hard core and two of whom later led armed *coup d'état* attempts. The law provided for them to be kept locked up indefinitely, although the state of emergency itself had been revoked. Banda made no attempt to get Armitage to release these men before he went on leave, possibly because he recalled how the Governor had talked him out of boycotting the Lancaster House conference unless they were released. Nor did he make any representations to Macleod about it, as might have been expected, for example during the conference. Indeed, Macleod was not expecting any approach to be made. Yet, almost immediately Jones became Acting Governor, Banda – himself pushed by Chiume who no doubt also recognized the opportunity – exerted pressure on him to release the remaining detainees. The doctor was no doubt relying on the impression of Jones's keenness to help which he had formed at their first meeting. He threatened that if Jones would not agree to the releases he would 'go back to Gwelo', and as a result of this threat Jones quite quickly revoked all outstanding detention and control orders and released the remaining hard core detainees, including Chipembere and the Chisiza brothers. Banda first raised the question with Jones on 5 September. Although Jones later said he 'resisted strongly at first', within two and a half weeks he had discussed the matter with Banda himself, Colonial Office officials – who were doubtful about such early releases[12] – Macleod, the provincial commissioners, Blackwood, Dixon, Welensky and his own official advisers, and then on 22 September he told Banda he agreed to the releases. Banda's threat was not only effective but it produced extraordinarily swift results. Jones said he released the detainees in the hope that it would remove any remaining bitterness and lead to peace, cooperation and a reasonable approach to federation, but in reality, although the hopes were undoubtedly sincere, he had little choice in the matter: he was committed to achieving Nyasaland's best interests by keeping Banda in power and out of gaol, and the country out of a state of emergency. This, not cooperation which was simply a hope, was the motive for his action. It was the first, but by no means the last, time Banda played the Gwelo card. He was interested in the outcome – release of his hard-core colleagues and satisfying his other lieutenants – not in Jones's hopes, which in the event were soon frustrated.

Britain's over-arching policy could indeed, Banda had now proved to himself – and others, including Jones – be used as a conquering sword to achieve his aims and fulfil his political ambitions. Indeed, provided the clear possibility of his actually drawing the sword existed, he might never need to do more than merely rattle it in its scabbard or simply move his hand towards its hilt. Although Armitage came back from leave a few weeks later and the question of the releases could have been delayed until he, as substantive Governor, returned, there would have been no point in Banda deploying the sword against Armitage, for two related reasons. First, it was at the time an untried weapon. If he had tested it when Armitage was in the gubernatorial seat and had failed, Jones, the Governor's closest official associate, would immediately have seen that the sword, at the first attempt to use it, was indeed capable of being parried and the wielder certainly delayed in, and maybe even diverted from, his purpose. There was no point in risking wasting the Gwelo card on Armitage when he was going to leave shortly, and in any case Banda may have felt that he was a particularly tough nut to crack not only because Armitage had little to lose at this late stage of his career but also because when he was Governor of Cyprus he had been unaffected by dangerous threats including actual bomb attacks on his life. In any case, success would almost certainly have been delayed. Second, by this time it was publicly known that Armitage was to leave the country on retirement in April 1961 and be succeeded by Jones. It was the longer term strategy of using the sword over the coming years when Jones was the Governor that was important to Banda: immediately releasing the detainees was not nearly as important as securing secession and independence in the future. In the whole three and a quarter years of Jones's governorship there was no case in which he attempted to call Banda's bluff over his threats to go back to Gwelo or his warnings that he might not be able to hold back his followers. The consequences of an unsuccessful attempt during that period could have been catastrophic. Alienating Banda by the attempt would remove the one man capable of leading Nyasaland in an orderly, peaceful fashion to independence, and either his replacement by a less able, less pro-British, more violent, lieutenant, or, more likely, mass uprisings necessitating the declaration of a state of emergency, the bringing in of military forces and a return to the political impasse.

Nevertheless, Banda realized that he should not over-use this overwhelmingly superior weapon which he had. To threaten too often to resign, or to warn too frequently that he might be unable to restrain his followers, would run the risk that he would be thought, by the Colonial Office if not by the Governor, to be crying 'wolf, wolf' and might not immediately be taken seriously. Indeed, there was usually little reason to deploy the weapon, because he must soon have realized that Jones saw him as the only person who could bring about Nyasaland's best interests and was genuinely committed to do all he could to help him achieve them. Instead, he set about getting on good terms with the new Governor, praising him in public and helping to build up for him a deeply pro-Malawi image and reputation for getting on well with the Africans and in particular with himself. The image and reputation were deserved – they were not in any way fabricated or invalid – and they were enhanced by Banda consistently doing nothing publicly to hint at criticism, even when privately they had not reached agreement on an issue. For most of the time this stood the doctor in good stead with the British government, as well as with his own party.

Through his good working relations with Jones, Banda was able on most issues to secure the Governor's support and advocacy with the British government. This usually ensured his success without having to risk overplaying his hand by too often threatening to resign or claiming he could no longer guarantee to restrain his followers. Banda's violent outbursts, whether thespian or pathological (few could decide which) were well known, though none the less alarming and, for some, terrifying. Thus, chary of the consequences of alienating, or even upsetting, him and thereby risking widespread disturbances which would necessitate declaring the state of emergency they wished so determinedly to avoid, and still generally reposing their traditional confidence in 'the man on the spot', the British government normally accepted what Jones and the doctor jointly recommended, though the actual recommendation generally came from the Governor alone, even when they had clear doubts about what was being proposed. In his turn, Jones was able vicariously, and entirely genuinely, to deploy Banda's trump card and in effect say: Much as we may prefer a different outcome, if we don't go along with Banda, who is in an angry mood and is being pressed by his lieutenants, I have the very real fear that he will withdraw his cooperation, I shall lose contact with him, we shall have lost everything we have so far gained and into the bargain we shall have a state of emergency on our hands and the need to bring in outside military forces with predictably dire consequences. If these forces come from the federal army there will be an unprecedented blood bath.

A frequent expression used by Jones and the secretaries of state was that they must 'keep Banda in play and not lose touch with him'. Banda used Jones to get his way with the British government, consciously or sub-consciously recognizing that Britain was anxious not to alienate him, that they were determinedly opposed to risking another state of emergency and that Jones had a profound commitment to the country's greater good, a deep conviction that only the doctor could bring that good about and a determination to keep him in a position to do so. This recognition was an immensely valuable asset and one which, quite apart from any personal feelings he may have had towards Jones, made it prudent for Banda to establish and then be seen to retain good relations with him. Jones was valuable to him as a go-between, ardent supporter, personal admirer and advocate, not only while he was Governor but also when he was Governor-General and long into his retirement.

Since Banda knew precisely and very clearly what he wanted to achieve and how he wished to achieve it, he neither needed nor sought Jones's or anyone else's advice on how to secure constitutional advance and how to handle the business of government. He was a master of both. But he did need someone to deal with the British government and help him keep up the pressure on them, and it was in this that Jones's value lay, both before independence in securing constitutional advances and in maintaining the British government's confidence in him, and after independence in securing Britain's continued support, especially financial. It was a role which Jones played spendidly and to the full, even though it caused Whitehall occasionally to wonder on whose side he was working. It was a role he was able to play because of his reputation for integrity and because of the relationship of trust which developed between the two of them.

Banda's strategy of using the Gwelo card was, deliberately or otherwise, backed up by his followers breaking the law, intimidating and assaulting opponents, committing arson and murder, and generally causing disturbances in various parts of the country. These disturbances flared up in different areas at different times. No district was immune and consequently their effect was considerable and a continuous worry to the government. Yet they never occurred over sufficient districts at any one time to give cause to allege that there was a general breakdown of law and order. A number of administrative and police officers believed that Banda's public appeals for good order were deliberately phrased or interpreted in a way that made their disingenuity and contrary intent obvious to his African audiences. Jones's most senior official advisers believed that the doctor deliberately stirred up, or allowed to be stirred up, violent disturbances as a means of manipulating the general situation in the country and exerting pressure on the Governor and secretary of state, in order to stay in control of events.[13] Jones himself must have been struck by the way in which from time to time, Banda, having said he would not be able to control his followers, none the less, once he had been told he could have his way, even though he could not yet tell his followers, undertook categorically and successfully to control them. The existence of this grave and widespread lawlessness lent credence to any warnings from the doctor that he might not be able to restrain his followers as they became increasingly impatient with the government's tardiness in doing whatever it was he was demanding. He shared, in still greater measure, Jones's profound conviction that he, Banda, was the only person capable of securing the country's best interests and of bringing it to independence with further economic and social progress. Presumably, he would have justified his actions, or inactions, on these grounds, had anyone had the effrontery or temerity to inquire.

Jones's strategy, in attempting always to secure the best long-term interests of the country and its people, and convinced that Banda was the only person who could secure those interests, was to get on such good and preferably exclusive terms with the doctor that he would stand a chance of influencing him, basically to avoid a security breakdown but, he hoped, also in more constructive ways. He backed up this strategy by frequently telling the Colonial Office how well he was getting on with Banda, how even their more stormy meetings ended cordially and how in troubled times things were getting better. He told them, too – as a protective means of securing and maintaining their confidence in the doctor – how Banda knew nothing in advance of, and certainly did not authorize or approve of, any of the law breaking of his followers, and how he had, at the Governor's request (and, though he did not say so, usually after a further damaging, and almost certainly deliberate, delay) publicly called for peace and calm and an end to violence. That Banda made these calls not infrequently must cast the gravest doubt on their sincerity or efficacy. From time to time he resorted to explaining violence by saying that it simply showed how strongly his followers felt about an issue. When given to Youens, though not to Jones, these explanations were usually accompanied by a knowing and revealing grin. Also, on occasions Jones tried to justify or minimize the significance of matters which *were* within Banda's knowledge and control. Reassuring the British government in this way was important in order to avoid them saying, 'Well, if things are that bad, you'd better start getting tough.' This would have run counter to Jones's basic strategy, probably would not have been effective and could well have resulted in precisely the conditions of unrest which they and he wished to avoid.

On the other hand, from time to time Jones also told the Colonial Office that things were particularly dangerous and worrying, that Banda was in an excitable and angry mood, that only with great difficulty had he persuaded him to 'stay in play', that the doctor had remained calm only because he had kept him so, that he was not sure if he could continue to restrain him and that he did not know how long any peaceful conditions would last. Just as Banda kept Jones on the edge of his seat by allowing or stimulating sporadic but none the less widespread law breaking, so did Jones keep Colonial Office officials on the edge of their seats by telling them how delicate, precarious and ominous the situation was in Nyasaland and how it demanded great care, patience and skill – and concessions – if it were not to get out of hand. He gradually allowed to be built up an image of himself as *the*, and certainly the only credible, authority on Banda, his moods, his deeper feelings and likely responses and on how he should best be handled. Allowing this reputation as the sole authority on Banda and sole satisfactory channel of communication with him to be cultivated or fostered, would have ensured, as far as he could, that no one – except possibly the secretary of state – should get close enough to the doctor as to pry into the genuineness of his threats and warnings, or otherwise bring about an explosion from him. He was quick, for example, to tell Alport that he had seen him on a good day and had raised no contentious issues with him, so he should be careful of basing his assessment on the one meeting and assuming that the situation was not explosive. It was hard enough for him to succeed without having anyone else step into the boat and risk rocking it. He would have gone to considerable lengths to keep at bay anyone, and there were many, who did not share, or might begin to doubt the validity of, his conviction and his admiration of Banda, and thereby lessen the British confidence in both Banda and himself, and his own ability to work with the doctor and maintain his hegemony.

The relationship between Jones and Banda was an important ingredient in Nyasaland's advance to independence and its progress thereafter. Ensuring that it was close and amicable was a task which fell to Jones rather than to Banda. It was not a simple matter, because neither man was easy to get close to.

Banda made occasional generous public displays of great friendship towards those who had, as he saw it, helped him in achieving his political objectives. For example, he invited expatriates to share the platform with him on state celebratory occasions and made flatteringly complimentary remarks about their contribution; not only Jones but also Armitage, Roberts, Neale and even his gaoler from Gwelo.[14] A British high commissioner said that Jones was 'a great favourite of Banda's, who was always quoting him in speeches, although [he] sometimes thought the quotations were of what Banda had told Jones'.[15] Nevertheless, Banda saw it necessary generally to isolate himself from people, believing that a leader must set himself apart, and in the early stages of the cabinet crisis he warned his cabinet colleagues against being too familiar with junior officers. It is likely that he confided only in Cecilia Kadzamira, though to what extent cannot sensibly even be guessed. It is clear that he trusted none of his African ministers and he would not have confided in them. He kept much of his past a secret from everyone. Though he normally made his views well known there was a great deal that he kept intimately to himself. At the time of the February 1966 coup d'état in Ghana, for example, when Banda's close friend, Nkrumah, was ousted, Cole reported: 'We may never know Dr Banda's innermost personal reaction to the coup. This may remain a secret, like so many others, he locks in his own heart.'[16] He was unmarried and had little if anything to do with the relatives he had left in Nyasaland four to five decades previously. His principal lieutenants saw him as more of a European than an African and rarely felt comfortable in his presence. The same British high commissioner's view was that 'all Malawians who came in regular contact with him were terrified of him'.[17] He retired early each evening, spent much of his time reading – his private library was enormous and the breadth of his reading quite extraordinary – and he had no other leisure pursuits. Although he made long public speeches with ease, he rarely engaged in social conversation. He was a very private man. The Commonwealth Office assessment summed him up well:

> Though he does his duty he does not enjoy organised social life. He does not smoke or drink, and prefers to work or read at night or simply go to bed early. He cannot walk far, having many years ago had a thrombophlebitis in his left leg. He has a weakness of the eyes (sensitivity to bright light) which causes him to wear dark glasses much of the time. He also has a nervous twitch of the mouth ... for female company he relies entirely on Miss Kadzamira, a young trained nurse, elegant, charming and pleasant who works for him as private secretary as well as nurse and housekeeper but who often arrives in his company on public occasions with the presence and panoply of consort.[18]

Jones, too, in many ways was not easy to get close to. In Northern Rhodesia he was known as a very sociable person, enjoying the company of others and entering into all sorts of social activities – the life and soul of a party. Even in that country, however, few knew anything about his family background and hardly anyone knew of his first marriage. A close colleague and admirer commented: 'He was quiet and modest to a fault. Even his closest relations and friends often knew little of his doings, which he kept under wraps.'[19] His private secretary commented on how 'he was the last person to bang on about his personal affairs'.[20] A leading businessman friend in Malawi asked, 'Is there anyone who really knew him? He was a very private person and kept things very close to his chest.'[21] He had, too, the solitariness characteristic of the angler; fishing is a quiet, indeed silent, private, pastime. We have already commented on the differences between the Northern Rhodesia Jones and the Nyasaland–Malawi Jones. Many circumstances contributed to this difference. Of all those bearing on his becoming a more withdrawn person, the death of his son, in whom he took such pride and in whom he saw so much promise, was the greatest. He bottled up his anguish and never really recovered from the tragedy. Jones, too – though a devoted family man and, at least in Northern Rhodesia, a very sociable person – was a very private person.

Given these factors in the make-up of the two men, it is not surprising that they did not become really intimate. Save for one slip, which was probably deliberate, on Banda's part in September 1960 when he accused Jones of being like all other civil servants, they invariably treated each other with the utmost respect. There was, however, an inevitable tension. Banda always made his wishes clearly known and spoke frankly to Jones, as he did to most others. Indeed, this was part of his strategy: to state his wishes and accompany them with warnings of what would happen if he were delayed or thwarted. Subtlety of expression and indirectness of approach were not compatible with this technique; a favourite expression of his was that he did not believe in 'beating about the bush'. Jones, however, was faced with the need studiously to avoid alienating the doctor in any way. This inevitably severely restricted, and very often removed entirely, the frankness with which he could discuss with Banda disconcerting and controversial issues. It could extend even to vitally important matters. For example, and surprisingly, he never asked Banda precisely what it was that Sandys had said in Dar es Salaam about secession. Though frequently relaxed, their meetings always had a formality about them. 'Dr. Banda was [always] received formally at the main entrance [of Government House] by the aide-de-camp, whereas the routine official visitors were received in the Private Secretary's office.'[22] The doctor never dressed informally even on the least formal of occasions. Even their closest conversations were on a largely formal basis. Banda was punctillious in addressing Jones as 'Your Excellency' – even long after he ceased to be Governor-General[23] – or 'Sir Glyn', even in private. Jones, on his side, addressed Banda as 'Prime Minister' or 'Doctor Banda' and, later, 'Your Excellency', though in private with others he would occasionally refer to him as 'the doc'. It was inconceivable that Banda should address Jones or refer to him by his familiar name, 'Jonas', even though virtually all his friends and expatriate colleagues regularly did so. Curiously, the doctor did address the expatriate commander of his army by his Christian name on private social occasions. Youens got closer to Banda, in the sense that their frequent meetings were less formal and the doctor would from time to time grin at him and indicate clearly that what he was saying was said with his tongue in his cheek. Roberts, too, got closer, in the sense that, while couching what he had to say elegantly and in respectful, diplomatic language, he made it quite clear to Banda when he disagreed with him or thought he was not acting in the most appropriate manner, and he invariably frankly gave him the advice he felt necessary or desirable. Banda, in fact, much appreciated frankness from those who advised him, as is demonstrated by his appointing first Youens and then Roberts as his secretary to the cabinet and head of the civil service.

It was important to Jones, if he was to help Banda in his pursuit of the country's best interests, that the doctor should be seen as a reasonable, non-violent, law abiding, gifted and altruistic leader, devoted to his country and people's progress and welfare: a great man. Otherwise, how could his unwavering support of him be justified and how would others – the British government, foreign aid donors and expatriate civil servants – be prepared to help the country? It was important to Banda, if he was to retain the support and acquiescence of his lieutenants and followers, that Jones should be seen as a person devoted to their cause, a man working selflessly, skilfully and wisely on their behalf: a great man. Otherwise, how could they be expected to share Banda's trust and confidence in him and exercise patience when the doctor was unable to get him to move things as fast as they wished or he promised. It was in the interests of each to add colour and conviction to the picture which was being painted of the other. Jones could say, in effect, to the British government, 'I get on well with Banda, he's a great man, he's devoted to the county's best interests and he trusts me, so you can safely leave it to me to handle him.' Banda could say to his people, in effect, 'I get on well with the Governor, he's a great man, he's devoted to our cause and he trusts me, so leave things to me, and all will be well.' Theirs, whatever their private feelings, was publicly a relationship of mutual respect and admiration, designed to support their individual efforts to bring about the country's best interests.

When eventually the Colonial Office got fed up with the appalling reputation Nyasaland was gaining – and fearful both of the security of the investment Britain was making in the country by annual budgetary grants, and of the possibility that after all they might have to step in with military action to restore order and reputations – Jones's ultimate, if reluctant and unhappy, response was to say, 'What else do you expect in Africa?' Being driven to respond in such a way, which he must have felt was disloyal to the continent and the people whom he had served for so many years, no doubt saddened him deeply. When, too, after independence, British officials were critical of what they saw as his too close support of Banda's government, he asked what else he could do: it was not, for example, constitutionally open to him to refuse assent to legislation even if it were tyrannical and thoroughly objectionable. He made this statement notwithstanding that provision to withhold assent clearly existed, though of course it might not have been prudent or helpful to take advantage of it.[24]

Gradually, Jones became increasingly pro-Banda. This may have been inevitable, given his and Banda's strategies within Britain's determination to avoid a state of emergency and their joint conviction that only the doctor could secure the country's best interests and take it peacefully to independence and further economic and social development. He defended Banda against criticisms by the press and the Colonial and Commonwealth Relations Offices. He praised him both publicly and, usually, privately – certainly in private correspondence with him – though on occasion this was undoubtedly a question of using flattery to influence him. To the British government he played down the importance and significance of many excesses by Banda's followers, saying they were misreported, exaggerated, fabricated, the work of those trying to undermine the doctor and the Nyasaland government and were now getting better. It went far beyond the public servant's traditional sang-froid and tendency to turn mountains into molehills. Jones's most senior officials believed there was nothing he or anyone else could do to influence Banda to be moderate or accept advice and guidance, so he had no choice but to go along with him, back him up in what he was doing and occasionally anticipate, though not always correctly, his wishes in the hope, invariably forlorn, that it would buy goodwill for the future.

One could attribute this increasingly pro-Banda stance to his competitiveness. The challenge which the offer of appointment to Nyasaland presented was one which it was not in his nature to forgo. Having taken on the job, his competitiveness and determination to succeed would have persuaded him to persist beyond the point where it became clear that Banda was not the sort of man he originally thought he was. Indeed, he himself referred privately to his 'determination to survive while walking ... along the perilous path towards self-government, endeavouring to avoid the snags and pitfalls and slippery slopes leading to disaster'.[25] To attribute his perseverance to his competitiveness and determination would, however, be insufficient an explanation, for there was a good deal more to his opinion of Banda than that. As the years passed he adopted an extraordinary deference towards the person he saw as 'Kamuzu, the man of destiny'.[26] This deference was based on genuine admiration of a truly remarkable man, notwithstanding the rift over the Malawi Buying and Trade Agency and particularly his long awareness of the doctor's gravely disturbing defects, his ruthlessness, his dictatorial behaviour and his manifest and continuing failure to curb the atrocities of his followers and eventually the outrages of his own regime.

It required an acute perception of the longer-term public interest to act always in a realistic and pragmatic way in what he genuinely believed to be best for the country and its people. He consistently believed, as for many years did the British government, that Banda was the only person who could develop the country into a viable and civilized state. He did not see him as an ideal ruler but as far and away the best available or likely to be available for a long time to come. Save for some of his principal lieutenants and their relatively limited following, few, either in Nyasaland or the British government, would dispute Jones's view that the possible alternative leaders would not match Banda's ability and potential for securing the country's best interests and that some of them would act markedly contrary to those, and Britain's, interests. The Commonwealth Office shared Jones's view and was convinced that the doctor 'puts the interests of Malawi above all else, and everything he does inside the country or beyond is governed by this consideration'.[27]

Assiduously following these beliefs must frequently have been profoundly painful and distressing to Jones. He risked sacrificing, and indeed did sacrifice, the loyalty and respect of many of his officers, perhaps especially administrative and police officers, for failing to prevent increasing lawlessness and, in many politically motivated cases, failing to prosecute the offenders; for instructing them to turn a blind eye to certain politically motivated offences; for abandoning the support and safeguarding of loyal traditional chiefs whose only offence had been to carry out government policy; for not preventing the drawing up and implementing of a list of 'unacceptable' expatriate officers whose services were to be compulsorily and prematurely terminated, while denying that there was a 'blacklist' of such officers; for encouraging the early departure of all his provincial commissioners and their deputies and a number of senior district commissioners – men much admired in the service. At least two district commissioners were 'summarily dismissed' at Banda's behest, and one of the provincial commissioners 'was summoned to Government House and told by Sir Glyn that he had to leave'.[28] Another provincial commissioner was so disillusioned that he neglected to call on the Governor to say farewell.[29] Jones incurred much public criticism for failing to stop the repeated waves of violence and drift to despotism, and generally for what was seen as his overly enthusiastic support, indeed encouragement, of Banda and his manifestly and increasingly tyrannical regime. He did nothing to prevent a number of men who occupied vital statutory safeguarding positions under the constitution from leaving or having their services disposed of: the chairman of the public service commission, the chief justice and the director of public prosecutions. There were to his knowledge many political murders committed, often in a savage and most brutal fashion, during his term of office both as Governor and as Governor-General. His response to the beatings of innocent members of the public by Banda's personal bodyguard – which he unconvincingly likened to the entourage of traditional African chiefs and whose uniform, with even less conviction, he likened to that of the boy scouts – was that perhaps the bodyguard should be absorbed into the regular police force, for the future commissionership of which he recommended that Yatuta Chisiza, long well-known for his violent tendencies and who was later shot while leading an armed rebellion against Banda's government, should be acceleratedly groomed. None of this means that he did nothing behind the scenes to attempt to get Banda to put things right or to lessen the impact on individuals involved,[30] but in many cases, perhaps in most cases, he believed he stood no chance of getting him to insist upon more democratic, civilized, law abiding and acceptable behaviour in his government of the country.

Virtually from the outset, and throughout, he failed to get Banda to ensure, as opposed to promise, general peace, orderliness, an end to violence and political intimidation, and the good behaviour of the released hard-core detainees, principally Chipembere. This was notwithstanding his clear perception at the time, as he told the doctor, that if their release was not matched by peace and good order he would come in for strong criticism, would be discredited and his belief in Banda's good faith would be shaken. Curiously, he did not show any sign of his belief in Banda's good faith being shaken when peace and good order did not follow their release. He was unable to secure a number of deeply important matters which the British government aimed at and hoped he would achieve: to persuade Banda to give reasonable consideration to the Monckton report and adopt a reasonable approach to the federal review conference; to induce the doctor, through experience of ministerial office and with Jones's guidance, to come to appreciate the benefits of federation; and to get him to consider future forms of association between the states of Central Africa. His efforts to get him to take a seat on the executive council in 1960 came to naught. Intimidation before the 1961 elections became prevalent despite his attempts to stop it. He was unable to secure for the UFP a seat on council in 1960, and to resist the surprisingly early replacement of the nominated official members in 1962, even though these undermined the basic intention of the Lancaster House agreement that executive power should remain effectively in official hands and even though the latter meant that Banda and not Jones was governing the country from that point onwards. His efforts failed to get Banda to prevent Kettlewell's and Ingham's retirement being publicly referred to by the MCP as their being 'sacked' and 'kicked out'.[31] He was not able to get Banda to stop criticizing the civil service even though he agreed to do this when the official nominees left council. He failed to protect and support the chiefs in their traditional role in Nyasaland despite his deep commitment, with Benson, to them and their role in Northern Rhodesia.

He failed consistently to restrict the wide range of Banda's portfolio responsibilities. Nor could he secure a *modus vivendi* from him in relation to the operation of federal functions, notably the Nkula Falls scheme, despite the desperate need for it in the implementation of the country's development plan. Banda rejected his 1962 suggestions that one of the ministers replacing the nominated officials should become a minister without portfolio, that Dunduzu Chisiza should become a full minister and that a new parliamentary secretary should be appointed to Banda's ministry. Despite his efforts, the victimization of political opponents and Jehovah's Witnesses, the murders, other atrocities, violence and intimidation accompanying the electoral process in 1961 and 1964 long continued unabated. He was unable to get Banda to meet Welensky, notwithstanding repeated attempts and the great store which Sandys placed on it. Later he failed to dissuade Banda from allowing his ministers to meet with federal ministers to discuss handing over federal responsibilities prematurely in July 1963 – which the British government strongly resisted – though the need for such meetings subsequently disappeared. He was unable to convince Banda's ministers of the financial realities of independence, though Banda accepted the same points when Jones passed them on to him from Butler. There is no evidence in his papers that he attempted to convince the ministers individually or directly. He failed to secure Banda's cooperation in prosecuting members of his bodyguard when they assaulted European teenagers and other members of the public. His recommendations on the allocation of specific ministerial responsibilities to Bwanausi, Tembo and Cameron in the independence cabinet were ignored or rejected. Banda did not accept his view of the desirability of Malawians joining 'European' clubs. During the cabinet crisis he failed to get Banda to alter his methods of working and his policies, despite agreeing with the objections of the dissident ministers. Banda rejected his advice both to 'play it cool' and then not to sack any ministers before the formal meeting of parliament on 8–9 September 1964. He failed to persuade Chipembere to see Banda by himself, and other ministers to see him without all of them being present. He did not ensure Chirwa's safety when he went to see the prime minister in October 1964. He did not succeed in his efforts at that time to hold the cabinet together and to effect a reconciliation. He failed to persuade Banda not to reintroduce detention without trial, alter the law of treason retrospectively and provide for public executions. Only a person of outstanding strength of character, determination and commitment to the longer term good could survive these disappointments.

His steadfast protection and support of Banda, despite these many disappointments, and his preparedness to risk suffering private hurt and humiliation over many years – masked as they may have been by a generally excellent public reputation, public praise and official honours – was all the more remarkable because it was done with his eyes open and under few, if any, illusions. Although he may have been optimistically charmed by his first meeting with Banda – and he was not the only person to be so charmed[32] – by the time he released the final detainees six months later he was unsure whether Banda would fulfil his undertaking to control them ('One would have to accept that for what it was worth') and he was aware that if he did not fulfil the undertaking, he, Jones, would come in for strong criticism and would be discredited. Once he became Governor he was never under any doubt as to the doctor's ruthless and dictatorial tendencies. At a very early stage and on several occasions Banda emphasized that he was personally and exclusively responsible for party policy and the line to be adopted in cabinet by the elected ministers. He made it clear that he laid down the policy without consulting any of his colleagues: 'If they do not like it they can either lump it or sack me.' Jones saw that this attitude carried all the dangers found in a dictatorship. At the same time he was fully aware of the possible consequences of the doctor's behaviour, including his ultimate downfall. His policies would be obeyed while they remained popular but if he tried to impose unpopular policies 'his dictatorial methods could sink him' – as they very nearly did in 1964.

Few Governors in the final years of colonial rule really governed. Usually, by the time they were appointed the basic decisions on early independence had already been taken or were asssumed, and this was borne in mind when appointing them; official dominance of the legislative and executive councils had or very soon disappeared; effective control was in the hands of indigenous people; and there was a substantial feeling that the sooner they were released from Britain the better for both Britain and the country concerned, if not, as many doubted, for the country's people. This scenario was particularly valid for Nyasaland where in Jones's time the Governor's power to govern and his scope for influence were minimal, and certainly less than elsewhere, because of Banda's extraordinary gifts as a political leader, his singlemindedness, ruthlessness, dominant behaviour and personal supremacy in the country's affairs.

Jones's success, having quickly recognized that the leadership most likely to secure the people's well-being had changed from the traditional chiefs to the professional politicians, lay in speedily becoming, and then continuing to be, Banda's devoted supporter, advocate, defender, apologist and channel of communication with the British government. He was able to play this role so successfully, indeed brilliantly, because, in his unwavering devotion to the best interests of Nyasaland–Malawi and its people, he could look past the doubts and difficulties, and in many cases the evils, of the nearby trees, to see the broader wood and its greater long-term contribution to the social and economic prosperity of the country and its people. He would not allow any personal or short-term considerations to blur his vision of that greater good and to render its fulfilment less likely. His outstanding qualities were the ability and determination to gain and retain Banda's trust and to be restrained, patient and forebearing in the face of the doctor's outbursts and excesses and quietly courageous in the face of his own short-term failures.

The question remains why Jones stayed in Nyasaland–Malawi as long as he did. At fifty-three, he was no longer a young man when he was apppointed Governor. Indeed, only one of his predecessors was older when appointed,[33] and Jones was five years older than the average of his twelve predecessors when made Governor.[34] He was already fifty-six years of age when the country became independent, older than the vast majority of colonial service officers when they retired. Four and a half years earlier, he had been about to start, and enjoy, his last tour of duty, when he received the offer of appointment to Nyasaland. By 1964 he had thirty-three years service in Central Africa behind him, a great deal of it fulfilling but much of it in the Nyasaland years trying, exhausting and probably privately distressing. He had already had a cardiac scare. His family commitments were not financially onerous. Furthermore, many others, lacking his competitiveness, determination, commitment and ability to see beyond the short-term set-backs to the longer-term benefits, would have been tempted to resign at various earlier points. It is understandable that he did not do so, despite what must have been a growing realization of his inability to influence Banda, and despite having to agree to legislation of which he profoundly disapproved, and to stand impotent while politically motivated atrocities were being inflicted by members of the governing party, as the country sank into the evils of a one-party dictatorship. To have resigned would have been quite unlike him, out of character and an admission of failure; and would almost certainly, at least in the short term, have done no good and have made matters much worse. He declined to take advantage of the offer of the governorship of British Guiana which would have provided an honourable means of escape, which may have been the Colonial Office's intention. His acceptance would have been seen by Banda as a betrayal. The doctor reposed a personal trust in him which he would not have reposed in others following a resignation or transfer, and so long as that trust remained, Nyasaland stood a chance of reaching independence without a major bust up. Jones's task was to see Nyasaland through to statehood without Britain having to declare a state of emergency and impose its will by costly use of force. Banda, in the last months of colonial rule, spoke of being prepared unilaterally to declare the country's independence. Jones's resignation, which could only have been a hollow gesture, would have been an act likely to provoke Banda to cut its ties of dependence. In such an event, Britain would have had to intervene militarily in order to avoid internationally public humiliation. It would have rendered to no avail all the patient work, much of it deeply unpalatable to Jones, designed to avoid that intervention and would have removed all point from having tolerated the unredressed damage to lives, health, property, the rule of law and democratic principles during the preceding years of his governorship. The British government and he could not afford to let that happen.

The same considerations do not apply, however, to his staying in office after independence. It seemed at the time the natural point at which to retire. He had long been aware of Banda's dictatorial behaviour and where it could lead. He knew of the violent outrages against political opponents, including brutal murders, which had already made the country a *de facto* one-party state – the May elections had returned all candidates unopposed – and his intelligence reports told him, as they told Banda, of the part which various of the doctor's lieutenants were playing in the violence. He knew, too, from long experience, of Banda's reluctance and tardiness in appealing to his people to be peaceful. He need no longer put up with any of this. He knew that for the country to survive economically, severe and unpopular measures would have to be introduced. He had long believed that Banda's personal popularity would melt in the face of unpopular policies. His own reputation was closely tied to Banda's. Why not leave while the going was good? His task of seeing the country through to independence as quickly and as orderly as possible, was completed. Had he retired at the time of independence Malawi would certainly have become a republic straight away, as Banda intended at one stage and as the British government may partly have had in mind when they offered Jones the Governorship of British Guiana. Even when the doctor changed his mind on this point, he did not intend the country to remain a monarchy for more than a few months. The British government did not mind very much one way or the other whether Malawi was a monarchy or a republic. Safeguarding their financial interests in bridging the significant budgetary gap does not seem to have played a part in their reaction to the choice, though they thought a short period as a monarchy followed quickly by a republic, was 'undignified' and costly in terms of two expensive sets of public celebrations, which the country could ill afford and which they would resent, since it was Britain which was keeping Malawi financially afloat. Paying for two major firework displays would not have appealed to them.

So why did Jones stay in Malawi as Governor-General after independence? There is no evidence that the opportunity to retain a full-time and enhanced salary, secure an increased pension, be awarded a higher class of knighthood and continue to enjoy the considerable perks and status of office weighed at all in his mind. Indeed, it is extremely unlikely that these were given more than passing consideration, and much more likely that they were not considered at all. Additionally, although in private conversation he was known to challenge the view that most officers joined the colonial service for altruistic reasons, arguing on the contrary that it was power that they sought and valued,[35] it is unlikely that by this stage he, of all people, was influenced by the illusion of power.

It is improbable that, at the time, he really believed he could be of much, if any, further use to Banda, whom he still, and justifiably, believed was far and away the best person, indeed the only person, to be head of state in the full interests of Malawi and its people. It is true that he told Butler that a Governor-General in Malawi would possibly have the advantages of persuading expatriate civil servants to stay in the country – though his remaining in office did not prevent large numbers leaving prematurely, and his subsequent leaving was not accompanied by the departure of others.[36] He said, too, that his staying might have 'advantageous effects' on British businessmen and investors and provide 'someone to whom [Banda] could turn for advice and assistance'. On the other hand, he thought Banda might prefer not to forgo the status of being head of both government and state, and he knew the intention was that the republic should not be long delayed. He thought the balance was only slightly in favour of having a Governor-General. His experience over the past four years could have given him few illusions as to the influence he could bring to bear on Banda. Even his role as a channel of communication with the British government was no longer necessary, for Banda had got just about all he hoped to get from Britain, and the high commissioner now existed as the channel. Indeed, with his contacts in Britain, Jones could have been seen as being more useful to Banda there. The reasons for his staying in Malawi must be sought elsewhere.

Malawi itself exerted a considerable pull on Jones. We have seen how he enjoyed the squirearchical aspects of life in Central Africa with its opportunities for hunting, shooting, fishing, walking, visiting remote rural areas and – as Benson had done briefly on the Barotseland tour, reliving earlier and younger district officer days – being close to nature and the African people to whose interests he was so profoundly devoted. The prospect of being able to continue to enjoy, even for a short period, that kind of life and its pleasures, must have attracted him mightily. To enjoy it as a Governor-General without the heavy burdens of work and responsibility of a Governor, must have made the prospect even more glowing. But a fuller understanding of the pull which Malawi exerted on him lies still elsewhere.

Africa had become his life. There he had spent the whole of his career.

Proconsul of the Wind of Change · 309

There he had been married and there his children had been born and brought up. As to their profound and enduring love of Central Africa there can be no doubt. The summit of his professional career had been in Nyasaland, a country where, as elsewhere, in the course of time he became much admired and respected and where he came to enjoy an enviable and outstanding reputation. Perhaps the strongest of all the threads combining to tie him to the country and now pulling to keep him there for at least a while longer, was that which bound him to his son. On the slopes of Zomba mountain, on whose plateau top he had so often walked, in whose streams he had so often fished, and from which his eyes had so frequently explored the magificently beautiful and seemingly endless panoramic views, lay Government House with its colourful flower gardens and broad sweeping lawns. This had been their home for the past three years. This, too, was where Timothy spent his last days. But a short distance downhill is the Zomba cemetery. Here Timothy was buried and here, in the fullness of time, he wished his own and his wife's remains to be interred. Whatever the counter influences, he decided not to leave Malawi at independence but to stay a little longer – understandably so.

His final two years in Malawi were not professionally happy ones. All that for which he had striven, and suffered, came to the very brink of destruction and he was no more able to influence events than he had been over the preceeding four years. It is difficult to see how the cabinet crisis would have been much, if any, different had he not been there. He was unable to bring about a reconciliation and to hold the cabinet together. Indeed, far from there being a rapprochement, Banda and his former ministers became bitter enemies, and the cabinet disintegrated, to be replaced by all but two new members. Many of the most able and experienced Malawians went into exile. All the important steps which Banda took during the crisis were taken on his own initiative: sticking to his guns, sacking the ministers, proposing to resign momentarily and be reinstated instantaneously, calling an informal private meeting of parliamentarians, summoning a formal meeting the following day to debate a motion of confidence, passing restriction and detention legislation, and pursuing a repressive regime particularly in the Fort Johnston district. In matters of detail, it fell to the expatriate officers of the Malawi government to keep the machinery of government operating. It fell to Youens and Roberts to persuade the African civil servants of Zomba to return to work. It fell to Roberts both to point out to Banda that there was no need to resign even momentarily and also to draft the motion of confidence. And it fell to Lomax to work out and effect Chipembere's evacuation.

Nevertheless, once the peak of the crisis passed with Chipembere's departure, there were many periods of relaxation and contentment. Jones enjoyed fishing on Zomba plateau and in Lake Malawi, he enjoyed drives with his wife in their private Jaguar car, he took an increasing interest in the colourful and fascinating variety of birds in the Government House grounds, he continued to enjoy entertaining friends and other guests, he played a good deal of golf and he still climbed Mlanje mountain. Somehow, his departure when Malawi became a republic rather than two years earlier, seems in retrospect to have been the 'natural' time to leave. And yet, it was as if he could still not let go of Africa – the pull was too strong and enduring. Nearly all of the many tasks he undertook in retirement involved dealings with Africa, and were directed, as had been virtually the whole of his adult life, to the well-being of that continent's people. When his ashes were laid to rest beneath the tall, cool, dark green conifers in Zomba's peaceful, quiet, cemetery, Africa absorbed into her being one of her most devoted servants.

Notes

1. Early Life

1. *Chester Observer*, 11 January 1908; *Chester Chronicle*, 11 January 1908.
2. Mrs D. Read to author, October 1998; Hugh Hughes, Secretary of the St John's Street former Calvinistic Methodist Church, Chester, to author, 7 and 11 September 1998.
3. Notes provided by Elisabeth Perchard.
4. Hugh Hughes to author, 7 and 11 September 1998; G. Longrick, Senior Steward, St John's Street Wesley Methodist Church, Chester, to author, 5 September 1998.
5. *Chester Chronicle*, 11 January 1908, p. 1.
6. W. J. Bennett to author, correspondence February and March 1995.
7. R. E. Rooke to author, 5 December 1994; Jones Papers, (hereafter JP), Robbins to Jones, 13 January 1930; *Chester Directories*, various years – in none of these does his name appear in the lists of private residences in Chester.
8. Material in the following paragraphs dealing with Jones's time at the King's School, Chester, except where otherwise stated, is from *The King's School Yearbook 1914–15 to 1922–23* and its successor *The King's School Magazine 1924 to 1927*.
9. W. J. Bennett to author, correspondence February and March 1995; R. E. Rooke to author, 5 December 1994; R. Clegg to author, 12 December 1994; S. N. Downs to author, 21 October, 18 November, 24 December 1994, 24 January 1995; A. J. Pickett to author, 2 December 1994; A. S. Turner, interview with author, 6 January 1995; C. W. Wilson to author, 17 and 22 November 1994.
10. W. J. Bennett to author, 24 November 1994.
11. S. N. Downs to author, 18 November 1994.
12. Ted Shephard to Lady Jones, n.d. but 1995.
13. St Catherine's College archives, A. H. Bennett, 19 September 1927, open reference.
14. The King's School Chester Rowing Club Centenary, 1883–1983.
15. JP, Trinity College of Music, London, certificate.
16. E. Sheperd to E. Perchard, n.d. (probably 1994), privately held.
17. S. N. Downs to author, 21 October and 18 November 1994.
18. St Catherine's College archives, H. H. Willis, 23 September 1927, open reference.
19. S. N. Downs to author, 18 November 1994; A. Pickett to author, 2 December 1994; R. E. Rooke to author, 5 December 1994; C. W. Wilson to author, 14 October 1994.
20. S. N. Downs to author, 21 October and 18 November 1994.
21. JP, H. W. Ralph, no addressee, 8 February 1930.

22. W. J. Bennett to author, 26 March 1995.
23. W. J. Bennett to author, 26 January 1995.
24. St Catherine's College archives, Jones to Censor, 4 and 23 September 1927; 10 January, 27 April and 13 July 1929.
25. JP, St Catherine's musical society and debating society programmes, 1927–29; A. Fountain to Lady Jones, 26 November 1994, privately held.
26. King's School Chester Magazine, April 1930, p. 48.
27. L. Frewer to author, 15 October and 20 November 1994.
28. King's School Chester Magazine, April 1929. Except where otherwise stated, material on Jones's career at Oxford is from JP, unreferenced newspaper cuttings.
29. JP, St Catherine's AFC fixture lists 1928.
30. Standard, 10 December 1930.
31. JP, R. M. Montgomery – also a non-collegiate student – to Jones, 14 December 1928; Standard, 10 December 1930.
32. He was extremely proud of having played in this match, and he kept the green cap with its red dragon, red tassel and inscription on the peak – '1928–1929 F. A. W.' (Football Association of Wales) – for the remainder of his life.
33. JP, T. Robbins to Jones, 13 and 15 January 1930.
34. A. Fountain to Lady Jones, 26 November 1994, privately held.
35. St Catherine's College archives, Jones to Censor, 24 March and 22 September 1930, G. Fisher to J. B. Baker, 30 April 1930 and R. D. Furse to J. B. Baker, 6 May 1930; Sir Patrick Nairne to author, 22 January 1995.
36. JP, A. J. Carlyle, no addressee, 11 February 1930.
37. Material in this paragraph is from Ralph Furse, *Aucuparius: Recollections of a Recruiting Officer* (London: Oxford University Press, 1962), Ch. 10.
38. JP, C. W. Dixon to Jones, 4 October 1930.
39. St Catherine's College archives, non-collegiate students' records.
40. Barbara Castle, *Fighting All the Way* (London: Macmillan, 1993), pp. 51–2; Baroness Castle to author, 17 November 1994 and 17 October 1999.
41. Sir Douglas Hall, interview with author, 10 July 1998.
42. JP, Colonial Office to Jones, 23 June 1931. Although in later years Jones claimed that the letter of appointment was signed personally by Lord Passfield, the colonial secretary, it was in fact signed – as was invariably the case – by an official, on this occasion J. Green: JP, Green to Jones, 23 June 1931.
43. E. Ursell to author, 9 November 1998.
44. Sir Douglas Hall, interview with author, 10 July 1998; Furse, *Acuparius*, Appendix I.

2. Northern Rhodesia: the Districts

1. *The Dominions Office and Colonial Office List, 1933* (London: Waterlow and Sons, 1933), p. 422 et seq.
2. C. Duff to author, 6 September 1994.
3. JP, Typescript, 'Journey in Africa 1932'; T. D. Carter (ed.), *The Northern Rhodesia Record* (privately printed, 1992), p. 14 – Jones is unnamed but the dates precisely fit his tour of service in the Zambezi valley.
4. Lady Jones, interview with author, 7 January 1995.
5. Carter, *The Northern Rhodesia Record*, p. 27.

Notes to Chapter 2 · 313

6. Material in the following pages covering Jones's first tour, unless otherwise stated, is from JP, Jones's private diary (hereafter Diary), 1932 and 1933.
7. Carter, *The Northern Rhodesia Record*, p. 42.
8. Lady Jones, interview with author, 7 January 1995.
9. JP, Walters of Oxford to Jones, 25 June 1931.
10. Duff to author, October 1994.
11. Ibid.
12. *Dominions Office and Colonial Office List, 1933*, p. 422.
13. Duff to author, October 1994.
14. *The Chester Association of Old King's Scholars Year Book 1934*, p. 17.
15. R. G. Miller to author, 7 August 1994.
16. Carter, *The Northern Rhodesia Record*, p. 208.
17. *Report of a Commission Appointed to Enquire into the Disturbances in the Copperbelt of Northern Rhodesia, October 1935*, Cmnd 5009, para. 60.
18. G. Clay, interview with author, 26 October 1994; marriage certificate, Family Records Office, London; correspondence with secretary, Tottenham football club, 1997.
19. R. Hill to author, 27 June 1995.
20. Clay, interview with author, 26 October 1994.
21. Diary, 11 March 1939.
22. Father Brian Browne to author, 6 February 1995.
23. Clay, interview with author, 26 October 1994.
24. J. P. MacDonnell to Jones, 13 May 1939.
25. *Report of the Commissioner* (Lusaka: Government Printer, November 1939), p. 197.
26. Material for the following account of Jones's relations with Miss Featherstone is from Diary, January–May 1939.
27. Lady Jones, interview with author, 7 January 1995.
28. S. C. Mbilishi to author, 2 May 1995.
29. JP, Jones to Branigan, 2 August 1939.
30. JP, Lynn-Allen to Jones, 11 August 1939.
31. JP, provincial commissioner, Mongu, to chief secretary.
32. JP, Jones to chief secretary, 16 and 28 September 1939.
33. JP, Jones to provincial commissioner, Mongu, 8 June 1940.
34. JP, provincial commissioner, Mongu to Jones, 21 June 1940.
35. JP, provincial commissioner, Mongu to Jones, 28 June 1940.
36. The High Court of Justice, Case no. 1941/4592, Certificate of making Decree Nisi Absolute (Divorce), Principal Registry of the Family Division, 1942, Folio 112.
37. Material for the following account of the journey to and from Jones's wedding is from Diary, 31 October to 9 December 1942.
38. Lady Jones, interview with author, 7 January 1995.
39. Ibid.
40. Ibid.; E. B. Smith, Memorial address, 13 March 1993.
41. Lady Jones, interview with author, 7 January 1995; Diary, 9 December 1942.
42. John Took to Editor, *Independent*, 26 July 1989.
43. L. Nell to author, 14 October 1994.
44. Lady Jones, interview with author, 7 January 1995.
45. C. Johnson to author, 23 January 1994.

46. L. Bean to author, 15 March 1995.
47. JP, chief secretary to Jones, 25 September 1946 and Jones to chief secretary, 28 September 1946.
48. Material in this and the following paragraphs dealing with life at Mongu, except where otherwise stated, is from I. Mackinson to author, 20 January 1995; Mrs S. Glennie to author, 3 January and 23 February 1995. Correspondence on Mongu was also conducted with the author by Mrs P. Allanson, R. Brown, J. M. Burnie, G. Clay, R. I. Cunningham, A. d'Avray, T. E. Dorman, I. M. Eldridge, J. H. Ellison, B. Hastie, Mrs R. Heath, R. G. Heath, R. G. Hodkinson, G. Labuschagne, M. C. Mortimer, M. Priestley, C. Rawlins and I. H. Wethey.
49. *Horizon*, vol. 6, no. 7, July 1964, p. 38.
50. Wethey to author, 6 September 1994.
51. Ellison to author, 15 September 1994.
52. Hastie to author, 10 February 1995.
53. Labuschagne to author, 13 October 1994.
54. Hastie to author, 10 February 1995.
55. Eldridge to author, 14 November 1994.

3. Northern Rhodesia: the Provinces and Secreteriat

1. *The Northern Rhodesia Handbook* (Lusaka: Government Printer, 1950); *NR Handbook* hereafter.
2. Material on the work of the commissioner for native development, except where otherwise stated, is from *Northern Rhodesia, Commissioner for Native Development, Annual Report for the Year 1954* (Lusaka: Government Printer, 1955).
3. Material on Jones's time as commissioner for native development is from Eldridge to author, 14 and 17 October 1994; C. Rawlins to author, 9 December 1994; R. C. Andrew to author, 6 January 1995; K. Carter to author, 27 June 1994; Mrs B. Clothier to author, 10 October and 7 November 1994.
4. JP, clerk of executive council to Jones, 27 June 1955.
5. Northern Rhodesia *Staff List*, 1958.
6. F. Finch to author, 31 July 1994; Macgregor to author, 17 June 1995.
7. *NR Handbook*.
8. JP, handwritten undated and unsigned note by Jones.
9. E. Dunlop to author, 19 January 1995.
10. Northern Rhodesia *Staff List*, 1958.
11. T. Dorman to author, 5 December 1994.
12. Material in this and the following two paragraphs is from R. Cunningham to author, 18 October 1994.
13. Material on the gubernatorial tour is from M. Priestley to author, 5 February 1995 and I. Mackinson to author, 20 January 1995.
14. G. Clay to author, 27 February 1995.
15. Lord Hastings to author, 7 March 1995.
16. JP, menu, Adelphi Club, 6 March 1931.
17. Material in this and the following paragraph is from Priestley to author, 5 February 1995.
18. Diary, 21 August and 5 December 1957.
19. Hall to author, 5 June 1997.
20. The following account of the work of the SNA is based on Bean to author, 15 March 1995.

21. Eldridge to author, 14 November 1994.
22. Bean to author, 15 March 1995.
23. Material in this paragraph is from Davies to author, 20 October 1994 and Hastie to author, 10 February 1995.
24. Material for the remainder of the account of the Gwembe affair is from David Howarth, *The Shadow of the Dam* (London: Collins, 1961); J. Sugg to author, 13 March 1995; and Eldridge to author, 14 November 1994.
25. Colleagues, including his immediate predecessor who had introduced the change and given the titles to 'illustrate the two distinct functions of the head of the Administration', went out of their way to emphasize that there was absolutely 'no change whatsoever in the status or salary of the position'.
26. Hall, interview with author, 10 July 1998.
27. JP, Benson to Jones, 28 September 1955. 'Jonas', the widespread African pronunciation of 'Jones', was the familiar name used by Jones's colleagues, family and friends.
28. JP, Benson to Jones, n.d., but September 1958.
29. Unattributable interviews 28 April 1999 and letters to author, 15 September and 7 October 1994, and 7 May 1999. These sources, who nevertheless thought highly of Jones, admitted that they might be somewhat overstating the case by the use of words such as 'sychophantic', 'pontifical', 'bogus' and 'the Jonas Jones admiration society', but could not find better words to convey their feelings.

4. Nyasaland: Chief Secretary

1. JP, Brimblecoombe to Jones, 15 September 1959.
2. Armitage Papers, Poynton to Armitage, 21 September 1959.
3. Foster, interviews with author, 20 April 1994 and 14 August 1997. See also Baker, *Retreat From Empire*, pp. 255–64.
4. Baker, *State of Emergency*, Chs 4 and 5.
5. Robert Shepherd, *Iain Macleod, A Biography* (London: Hutchinson, 1994), p. 187.
6. Baker, *Retreat from Empire*, pp. 254–65.
7. Diary, 1–15 January 1960.
8. JP, Chambers to Jones, 6 January 1960.
9. JP, Poynton to Jones, 6 January 1960.
10. Lady Jones, interview with author, 20 July 1994.
11. Armitage Papers, Poynton to Armitage, 20 November 1959; and Armitage to Poynton, 9 December 1959
12. Diary, 15–31 January 1960.
13. Armitage Papers, private diary for 18 and 19 December 1959; CO 1015/1518, Macleod to Perth, 20 December 1959; Theunissen, interview with author, 26 June 1994.
14. CO 1015 1518, Macleod to Perth, 20 December 1959 and note by secretary of state (hereafter SS) on Nyasaland emergency, 24 December 1959; DO 35 7476, Minute, unsigned, dated 24 December 1959, and Minute by Shannon, 29 December 1959; Macmillan Diaries for 3 and 4 January 1960, Bodleian Library, Oxford, dep.d. 37.
15. DO 35 7564, Macmillan to Macleod, 28 January 1960.
16. Lady Jones, interview with author, 20 July 1994.

316 · Notes to Chapter 4

17. Material in this and the following three paragraphs is from Diary, 4 February to 9 March 1960.
18. JP, handwritten note by Jones, 'My Visit to Gwelo, 10 February 1960', dated 14 January 1969.
19. JP, Brian Lapping and Sarah Curtis interview with Jones, 31 May 1983.
20. JP, handwritten notes by Jones, one dated 14 January 1969 and headed 'My visit to Gwelo, 10 February 1960', the other undated but headed '3 March 1959 to 1 April 1960'.
21. Material in this and the following two paragraphs is from JP, handwritten notes by Jones, n.d. but probably 1985.
22. Diary, 12–14 March 1960 and Armitage Diary, 14 March 1960.
23. JP, handwritten notes by Jones, n.d. but probably 1985.
24. JP,. Banda to Jones, 16 March 1960.
25. Armitage Diary, 19, 21 and 24 March 1960.
26. Armitage Diary, 1 April 1960; Oxford University Colonial Records Project (OUCRP), Youens, interview with Bradley, 26 November 1970; Youens, interview with author, 4 January 1995. See also Colin Baker, 'Dr. Banda's Arrest and Release from Detention, 1959–60', *Society of Malawi Journal*, vol. 49, no. 3, 1996, pp. 1–14.
27. Diary, 1 April 1960.
28. Watson to author, 20 January 1994; Haskard to author, 27 February 1994; Codrington to author, 12 February 1994.
29. JP, meeting between the chief secretary and Dr Banda on 20 June 1960.
30. JP, Chipembere to secretary for African affairs, 13 May 1960.
31. Cmnd 1132, *Report of the Nyasaland Constitutional Conference Held in London in July and August 1960*.
32. JP, Monson to Jones, 19 August 1960 and Jones to Monson, 24 August 1960.
33. JP, Jones Record of Discussion with Mr A. C. W. Dixon on 23 August 1960.
34. JP, Jones to Monson, 17 and 24 August 1960; Jones to Armitage, 25 August 1960; Record of Discussion with Mr A. C. W. Dixon on 23 August 1960.
35. JP, Jones to Macleod, 17 August 1960.
36. JP, minute, Jones to Youens 13 August 1960.
37. JP, Note for the Record, 16 August 1960.
38. JP, colonial secretary to commonwealth relations secretary, copied to Jones, 12 August 1960.
39. JP, Record of a Discussion between Dr Banda and the acting chief secretary on Friday 12 August 1960; Jones to Macleod, 17 August 1960.
40. Armitage, Diary, 9 August 1960.
41. JP, Record of a Discussion between Dr H. K. Banda and the acting chief secretary on Monday, 5th September 1960.
42. Banda interview with Hans Germani, cited in Attati Mpakati, 'Malawi: the Birth of a Neo-Colonial State', *Africa Review*, 1973, Vol. 3, Pt. 1, p. 51.
43. JP, Note for the Record, 6 September 1960.
44. JP, Jones to Macleod, 6 September 1960.
45. Ibid.
46. JP, Record of a Discussion between Dr H. K. Banda and the acting chief secretary on Wednesday, 7th September 1960; JP, Jones to Macleod, 8 September 1960.
47. JP, Jones to Macleod, 8 September 1960.

48. JP, Jones to Monson, 9 September 1960.
49. JP, colonial secretary to commonwealth secretary, 12 September 1960.
50. JP, Macleod to Jones, 12 September 1960, No.536.
51. JP, Macleod to Jones, 12 September 1960, No. 537.
52. JP, Jones to Macleod, 14 September 1960.
53. Ibid.
54. JP, Note for the Record, 15 September 1960 and Jones to Macleod, 15 September 1960.
55. JP, Jones to Macleod, 20 September 1960.
56. JP, Jones to Dixon and Jones to Blackwood, 19 September 1960; Blackwood to Jones, 22 September 1960.
57. JP, Jones to Macleod, 23 September 1960; Draft n.d. but probably 22 September 1960.
58. JP, Finney to private secretary to the Governor, 28 September 1960; E. Bailey to author, 12 July 1994.
59. Short, op. cit., p. 139.
60. JP, Note of meeting with Dr Banda, 28 October 1960.
61. JP, Jones, no addressee but probably Macleod, 28 October 1960.
62. Armitage Memoirs 1960, vol. 2, pp. 42–53.
63. JP, Jones to the president of the Zomba gymkhana club, 14 October 1960; Jones to Robin Palmer, 25 January 1973; Elisabeth Perchard, interviews with author, 4 August 1998 and 15 September 1999.
64. JP, Record of a Discussion between Dr Banda and the acting chief secretary on 12 August.
65. JP, Note for the Record, 16 August 1960.
66. JP, chief secretary to provincial commissioners, 22 September 1960, ref. no. 35339/21.
67. The pun about the government being determined to achieve the end of responsible government in Nyasaland was, presumably, unintended.
68. JP, no author or addressee but Jones probably to Macleod, 28 September 1960.
69. JP, Poynton to Jones, 5 September 1960; Macleod to Jones, 7 October 1960.
70. Armitage Diary, 26 July 1960.
71. JP, Armitage to Jones, 18 September 1960.
72. Armitage Memoirs 1960 vol. 2, p. 50.
73. *New Daily*, 13 October 1960.
74. *Nyasaland Times*, 13 October 1960.
75. JP, note by Jones, headed 'Iain Macleod', n.d. but probably 1970.
76. *The Times*, 19 June 1992.
77. J. McCracken to author, 12 August 1992.
78. *Daily Express*, 19 February 1960; *News Chronicle*, 19 February 1960.
79. CO 1015 1543, Morgan to Gorell Barnes, 5 June 1959.
80. Rhodes House Library, Oxford, *End of Empire*, Mss. Brit. Emp. s.527.
81. See also A. H. M. Kirk-Greene, *On Crown Service: a History of H M Colonial and Overseas Civil Services, 1837–1997* (London: I.B.Tauris, 1999), p. 101.
82. Jones's seniors in Northern Rhodesia felt that it was the chief secretary and secretary for native affairs, and not the provincial commissioner, who were the real trouble-shooters: Hall to author, 17 September 1997.
83. Armitage Diary, 6 December 1960.

84. H. E. I. Phillips, interview with author, 28 August.1997; JP, Armitage to Jones, 11 December 1960; Short, op. cit., pp. 144–5; J. R. T. Wood, *The Welensky Papers: a History of the Fedration of Rhodesia and Nyasaland* (Durbam: Graham, 1983), pp. 848–56. For Macmillan's account of the conference see H. Macmillan, *At the End of the Day* (London: Macmillan, 1973), pp. 301ff.
85. Armitage Diary, 6 December 1960.
86. Diary, 30 July and 7 October 1960; JP, Jones to Armitage, 25 August 1960; Wyndham to Jones, 14 December 1960; Armitage to Jones, 1 and 15 January 1961.
87. Armitage to Jones, 21 February 1961; Diary, January–April 1961 passim.
88. Malawi Government Gazette, 2 December 1961, p. 362; Diary; and Armitage Memoirs 1961.

5. Nyasaland: Governor

1. JP, acting chief secretary to heads of department, 6 April 1961.
2. Royal Instructions under the Nyasaland (Constitution) Order in Council, 1961 (a).
3. Diary, 3 July 1961.
4. For details of the events of the previous year, see Baker, *Retreat from Empire* and Baker, *State of Emergency*.
5. DO 158 60, Minutes of Informal Conference Between the British High Commissioner, Salisbury, and the Two Northern Governors, Salisbury, 31 May 1961.
6. B. Jones-Walters to A. Mell, 17 June 1961, privately held.
7. JP, Jones to Macleod 27, 29 and 31 July 1961.
8. Short, *Banda*, p. 152.
9. Ibid., p. 153.
10. JP, Jones to Macleod, 16 August 1961; SS to Jones, 16 August 1961.
11. Diary, 16 August 1961.
12. JP, Jones to Macleod, 19 August 1961.
13. JP, draft note by Jones, probably to chief secretary, on his meeting with Banda on 22 August 1961.
14. Ibid.
15. JP, Jones to Macleod, 23 August 1961; draft note by Jones, probably to chief secretary, on his meeting with Banda on 22 August 1961.
16. JP, Jones to Macleod, 29 August 1961.
17. Ibid.
18. JP, Jones to Macleod, 19 August 1961.
19. JP, draft note by Jones, probably to chief secretary, of his meeting with Banda on 22 August 1961; Jones to Macleod, 23 August 1961.
20. JP, Jones to SS, 23 August 1961.
21. JP, Jones to SS, 29 August 1961.
22. CO 1015 2491, Jones to Macleod, 4 October 1961. See also JP, Jones to Macleod, 2 September 1960.
23. *Nyasaland Government Gazette*, 1961, p. 303.
24. JP, Jones to Macleod, 4 October 1961.
25. G. Landreth to author, 5 April 1995.
26. JP, SS to Governor, Zomba, Circular Letter no. 8, 9 October 1961; JP, Maudling to Jones, 16 October 1961.

27. JP, Note of a meeting between His Excellency the Governor and certain members of executive council and parliamentary secretaries, 11 September 1961.
28. JP, Note of a meeting held at Government House, Zomba, on 30 November 1961, with non-official ministers and parliamentary secretaries.
29. CO 1015 2552, Brief: Nyasaland Current Political Questions.
30. JP, Maudling to Jones, 8 February 1962.
31. JP, Note of a meeting held at Government House, Zomba, on 30 November 1961, with non-official ministers and parliamentary secretaries.
32. JP, Note of a meeting held at Government House, Zomba on 1 December 1961, with official ministers.
33. JP, Record of meeting with the SS at Government House on 1 December 1961.
34. Ibid.
35. JP, Secret Note, 'Mr Rolf Gardiner's letter to Lord Colyton dated 20 January – material for possible reply', attached to Jones to Colyton 6 February 1962.
36. JP, Jones to chief secretary, 6 December 1961.
37. R. Foster, interviews with author, 20 April 1995 and 14 August 1997.
38. JP, Jones to Maudling, 29 January 1962.
39. JP, Jones to Maudling, 30 December 1961; Jones to Maudling, 29 January 1962; Jones, note for the record, 18 December 1961; Cmnd 1132, p. 5, para. A(v).
40. JP, Minutes of a meeting between Alport, Hone and Jones on 10 January 1962.
41. JP, draft note of meeting between Jones and Banda on 22 August 1961, probably Jones to chief secretary.
42. Ibid.
43. JP, Jones to British High Commission, Salisbury, 28 May 1962.
44. JP, Jones to SS, 26 June 1961.
45. JP, Jones to Macleod, 4 October 1961.
46. JP, British High Commission, Salisbury, to Commonwealth Relations Office, 3 November 1961.
47. Chiume to author, 8 July 1999.
48. JP, Jones to chief secretary, 27 September 1961.
49. JP, British High Commission, Salisbury, to Commonwealth Relations Office, 18 October 1961.
50. JP, SS to Governor, Lusaka, and Secretary of State to Jones, both 17 October 1961; British High Commission, Salisbury, to Commonwealth Relations Office, 3 November 1961.
51. JP, Note of a meeting at the Commonwealth Relations Office, 15 November 1961.
52. JP, press conference held by Dr Banda, 26 November 1961.
53. JP, Jones to Butler, 26 June 1962.
54. SS to British High Commission, Salisbury, 5 July 1962. Jones's advice not to proceed was given in JP, Jones to Maudling, 1 February 1962.
55. Phillips, *From Obscurity to Bright Dawn*, pp. 167–8 and Ch. 13, passim.
56. JP, Jones to Maudling, 21 November 1961; Jones to Alport, 24 November 1961.
57. JP, Note on Two Meetings between His Excellency and Dr. The Honourable H. K. Banda on 22 and 26 November 1961; Jones to SS, 27 November 1961.
58. JP, Jones to British High Commission, Salisbury, 2 December 1961.

59. JP, Nicholson to Banda, 20 December 1961.
60. JP, Fisher to Banda, 28 December 1961.
61. JP, Banda to Jones, 2 January 1962.
62. JP, Jones to Maudling, 18 December 1961; Jones to chief secretary, 18 December 1961.
63. JP, Jones to chief secretary, 18 December 1961.
64. JP, Jones to SS, 21 December 1961.
65. JP, Minutes of Meeting on 10 January 1962.
66. Draft, The Provincial and District Administration, September 1962, privately held.
67. JP, Alport to Sandys, 15 January 1962.
68. JP, Jones to Alport, 24 January 1962.
69. JP, Jones to Maudling, 24 January 1962.
70. JP, Jones to Monson 17 February 1962.
71. JP, Note by Jones, sent by him to the chief secretary for information and return, 16 February 1962.
72. JP, Sandys to Commonwealth Relations Office for the cabinet, 12 February 1962; Jones to Monson, 17 February 1962.
73. JP, Top Secret note by Jones, n.d. but probably 13 February 1962; CO 1015 2554, Jones to Monson, 17 February 1962.
74. JP, Jones to Maudling, 15 January, 12 and 21 February 1962.
75. JP, Jones to Sandys, 14 and 15 February 1962.
76. JP, Jones to Monson, 17 February 1962.
77. JP, Jones to SS, 18 December 1961.
78. Foster, interviews with author, 20 April 1995 and 14 August 1997.
79. CO 1015 2554 Jones to Monson, 17 February 1962.
80. CO 1015 2554 Jones to Monson, 9 March 1962.
81. Butler Papers, G38, Macmillan to Butler, 9 March 1962; Watson to Howard-Drake, 23 February 1962; Minute to Tennant, 21 March 1962.
82. Foster, interviews with author, 20 April 1995 and 14 August 1997.
83. R. A. Butler, *The Art of the Possible: the Memoires of Lord Butler, KG, CH* (London: Hamish Hamilton, 1971), p. 211. Butler seems to have been confusing the occasion with an earlier visit by Jones to London.
84. JP, Jones to SS, 9 March 1962.
85. Butler, op. cit., p. 208; JP, SS to Governors of Nyasaland and Northern Rhodesia, 13 March 1962; Hone to SS, 14 March 1962; British High Commission, Salisbury, to Commonwealth Relations Office, 15 March 1962.
86. JP, Butler to Alport, 28 April 1962.
87. JP, Central African Federation, home secretary's discussions with the high commissioner and Governors, March 1962.
88. JP, Records of SS's discussions with high commissioner and Governors, 26–30 March 1962.
89. Diary, 25 March 1962 to 5 April 1962; JP, SS to British High Commission, Salisbury, 5 April 1962.
90. JP, Jones to Butler, 9 April 1962.
91. JP, Jones to SS, 9 April 1962.
92. 'Mission' was the term now used for what in London had been described as a 'commission' to examine the consequences of secession.
93. JP, Jones to Butler, 14 April 1962.
94. JP, Alport to Butler, 16 April 1962.

95. JP, SS to Jones, 14 April 1962.
96. JP, Jones to Butler, 14 April 1962.
97. JP, Jones to Butler, 14 and 15 April 1962; Butler to Jones, 16 April 1962.
98. JP, Jones to Butler, 27 April 1962.
99. JP, Jones to Butler, 2 May 1962.
100. Ibid.
101. JP, Butler to Jones, 5 May 1962.
102. JP, Record of Meetings between Mr. R. A. Butler and Dr Banda at Government House, with Sir Glyn Jones Present, 16 and 17 May 1962.
103. Butler, op. cit., p. 212.
104. JP, Cabinet Paper, Nyasaland: Discussions with Dr. Banda in London, 20 June 1962.
105. JP, Meetings between Mr. R. A. Butler and Dr. Banda at Government House 16–17 May 1962; Sir Glyn Jones was also present.
106. JP, Minutes of a meeting at Marimba House, Salisbury, 26 May 1962.
107. JP, Jones to Butler, 19 May 1962. See also Butler, op. cit., pp. 214–15.
108. JP, Cabinet paper C (62) 100 of 20 June 1962.
109. JP, Butler to Jones, 26 June 1962.
110. JP, Notes of meetings between the SS, the Governor of Nyasaland and Dr Banda, 2–4 July 1962.
111. JP, Jones to Butler, 12 July 1962.
112. Diary, July–August 1962.
113. JP, Stevens to Commonwealth Relations Office, 3 August 1962.
114. Material in this and the following seven paragraphs, unless otherwise stated, is from JP, Jones to Butler, 7 August 1962.
115. DO 183 168, Governor to SS, 7 August 1960.
116. Cameron, interview with author, 21 March 1998.
117. Ibid.
118. DO 183 168, Governor to SS, 7 August 1962.
119. Cameron, interview with author, 21 March 1998.
120. Chiume, interview with author, 13–14 December 1998.
121. Tape recording of Chipembere seminar at California Institute of Technology, 1 February 1971, privately held.
122. Sir Michael Caine, interview with author, 15 October 1997.
123. JP, and DO 183 168, Jones to SS, 7 August 1962.
124. JP, D. K. Chisiza to Jones, 4 August 1962.
125. JP, Governor to SS, 15 August 1962; and SS to Governor, 31 August 1962.
126. JP, Jones to SS, 24 August 1962.
127. JP, Jones to SS, 7 August 1962.
128. DO 183 168, CAO to Jones, 14 August 1962.
129. Excerpt from Banda's private papers, enclosed with T. Walker, to author 20 April 1998.
130. DO 183 126 Intelligence Reports, Nyasaland, Report (hereafter NICR) for September 1962. See also Power, 'Remembering Du'.
131. JP, Governor to SS, 31 July 1962.
132. *Nyasaland, Report for the Year 1962* (London: HMSO, 1963), pp. 2, 165.
133. JP, Jones to Banda, 25 August 1962.
134. NICR for October 1962.
135. Draft, the Provincial and District Administration September 1962, privately held.

136. JP, Note of a Meeting held at Government House, Zomba, on 30 November 1961 with non-official ministers and parliamentary secretaries.
137. Though it was not said, the 'new men' brought in clearly included, primarily, Jones, the Governor, and Foster, the chief secretary. Other former colleagues of the Governor from Northern Rhodesia recently transferred to Nyasaland included the chief justice, the solicitor-general and secretary for justice, the registrar-general, the under-secretary and two other members of the ministry of local government, the director of agriculture and the deputy director of veterinary services.
138. The Governor's private secretary noted on a different occasion how Jones carried out fewer district tours than had his predecessors.
139. *Report of the Nyasaland Constitutional Conference, held in London in July and August 1960* (London: HMSO, 1960, Cmnd 1132), p. 8; *Report of the Nyasaland Constitutional Conference held in London in November 1962* (London: HMSO, 1962, Cmnd 1887), p. 16; *Nyasaland Government Gazette*, 26 May 1962, pp. 196–8; conversations, N. Wenban-Smith with author, January 2000; W. Wenban-Smith to N. Wenban-Smith, 1 June 1992, privately held. See also H. Phillips, op. cit, pp. 174–6; and P. Mullins, *Retreat from Africa* (Edinburgh: 1992), pp. 89–90. The members of the Commission were: W. Wenban-Smith, chairman, D. G. Ansell, L. M. Bandawe and N. Chilemba.
140. JP, Roberts to Jones, 24 October 1962.
141. JP, Jones to SS, 10 October 1962.
142. JP, Jones to SS, 26 October 1962.
143. JP, Butler to Alport, Jones and Hone, 25 October 1962; SS to British High Commission, Salisbury, 10 November 1962; Jones to Foster, 10 November 1962.
144. JP, SS to British High Commission, Salisbury, 25 October 1962.
145. JP, Private Meeting with Dr. Banda: Brief for the First SS, n.d. but October 1962.
146. JP, Record of a discussion between Dr. Banda and the Governor of Nyasaland, Thursday, 8th November 1962.
147. Diary, 9 November 1962.
148. JP, pencilled note n.d., but 9 November 1962.
149. Diary, 10–11 November 1962.
150. Diary, 12 November 1962. For details see Cmnd 1887, *Report of the Nyasaland Constitutional Conference*.
151. DO 183 97, Nyasaland Constitutional Conference 1962, Record of Meetings, First meeting on 12 November 1962.
152. JP, Jones to Foster, 14 November 1962.
153. JP, Record of meeting between Dr Banda and the Governor of Nyasaland on the morning of Tuesday, 13 November 1962.
154. JP, Note of First SS's discussion with the Governor of Nyasaland and Dr. Banda on Wednesday 14th November 1962.
155. JP, Jones to SS, 2 December 1962.
156. JP, Jones to Butler, 29 December 1962.
157. JP, Note of a meeting between the First SS and Dr. Banda, the Governor of Nyasaland being present, at 12 noon 16th November 1962.
158. Diary, 17–24 November 1962.
159. Record of a meeting between the SS and Dr. Banda with the Governor of Nyasaland present on 22nd November.
160. This and other constitutional provisions mentioned in the following para-

graphs are contained in Cmnd 1887 *Report of the Nyasaland Constitutional Conference*.
161. DO 183 97, Nyasaland Constitutional Conference 1962, Record of Meetings, 13th and final meeting.
162. Diary, 24-25 November 1961; JP, Meeting between the First SS and Dr. Banda, the Governor of Nyasaland being present, on 28 November 1962.
163. Diary, 29 November–1 December 1962.
164. JP, Minutes of a meeting of the Executive Council held at 9.30 am. on Wednesday 23 January 1963.
165. JP, Note of a meeting with Dr. Banda, Mr. Butler and His Excellency the Governor on 28 February 1963.
166. JP, Butler to Jones, 2 September 1962.
167. JP, Jones to SS, 11 January 1963.
168. Ibid.
169. Ibid.
170. *Proceedings of Malawi Parliament* (hereafter Hansard), Third meeting, First Session, October 1964, p. 224.
171. JP, Jones to Alport, 15 January 1963; Diary, 15-16 January 1963.

6. Nyasaland: Self-government

1. Diary, 1 February 1963.
2. DO 183 136 and 137, NICR for February 1963.
3. NICR for June 1963.
4. NICR for July 1963.
5. JP, Jones to SS, 23 January 1963.
6. JP, Governor to SS, 25 February 1963.
7. JP, Notes of Meetings with Dr. Banda, Mr. Butler and the Governor on 28 and 29 January 1963.
8. JP, SS to BHC Salisbury, 23 February 1963.
9. JP, SS to Governor, 24 February 1963.
10. JP, Foster to SS, n.d. but late February 1963.
11. JP, SS to Foster 27 February 1963.
12. JP, Record of a meeting between the Governor, Sir Glyn Jones, and the Prime Minister, Dr. The Hon. H. K. Banda, on 19th May.
13. JP, Note for the record, by Jones, meeting with Banda on 20 May 1963.
14. The fiscal year was changed to coincide with the calendar year.
15. D. A. G. Reeve to author, 23 March 1995.
16. JP, Diary, 9 June to 4 July 1963; Gore to Butler, 31 July 1963; Youens to Butler, 11 and 15 June 1963; Jones to Butler, 26 June, 31 July and 26 August 1963.
17. JP, Welensky to Jones, 11 June 1963; Youens to Welensky, 19 June 1963; BHC Salisbury to SS, 20 June 1963; Jones to BHC Salisbury, 27 June 1963; Jones to SS, 9 July 1963.
18. JP, Jones to SS, 28 June 1963. Since Jones had not yet returned to work, it is likely that this letter was drafted by Youens.
19. JP, Watson to Jones, 17 July 1963.
20. Neale, interview with author, 15 March 1999.
21. JP, Jones to Watson, 8 August 1963.
22. K. Neale, interview with author, 15 March 1999.
23. JP, BHC Salisbury to SS, 1 July 1963.

24. JP, Jones to SS, 3 July 1963.
25. JP, Jones to SS, 9 July 1963.
26. JP, Jones to SS, 13 July 1963.
27. A. Kerr to author, 28 January 1995.
28. JP, Jones to Banda, 25 August 1962.
29. JP, Jones to SS, 13 July 1963.
30. JP, Jones to SS, 8 July 1963.
31. JP, Jones to SS, 9 July 1963..
32. B. S. Ward to author, 7 February 1995.
33. JP, Jones to Butler, 19 July and 7 August 1963. There were other cases of consuls being persuaded not to pursue complaints on behalf of their nationals: Reeve to author, 23 March 1995.
34. E. L. T. Richardson to author, 4 September 1995.
35. JP, SS to Jones, 9 and 10 July 1963.
36. J. Clement to author, 10 April 1995.
37. Hansard, 76th session, 9–16 July 1963.
38. JP, Jones to SS, 11 July 1963.
39. Armitage Papers, *The Erosion of the Rule of Law in Nyasaland; The Erosion of the Rule of Law in Nyasaland: The Local Courts; Rule of Law in Nyasaland, Reply to the Hon J. M. Greenfield; QC*; Alport to Butler, 31 July 1963 and Jones to Butler, 2 August 1963.
40. JP, SS to Jones, 16 August 1963.
41. Ibid.
42. JP, Jones to SS, 19 August 1963.
43. JP, Unsworth to Jones, 28 May 1963.
44. I. R. Strachan to author, 16 November 1995.
45. JP, Jones to SS, 19 June 1963.
46. Ibid.
47. JP, Butler to Unsworth, October 1963.
48. D. McLinden to author, 4 July 1995.
49. C. Bean to author, 3 July 1995.
50. The Police Ordinance, Chapter 64 Laws of Nyasaland, section 4.
51. Cmnd 1887, para. 74.
52. E. Bult to author, 14 March 1995.
53. Kerr to author, 28 January 1995.
54. Bult to author, 14 March 1995.
55. Bean to author, 3 July 1995.
56. JP, Jones to Banda, 9 August 1963.
57. JP, Jones to Banda, 20 August 1963.
58. Material in this and the following three paragraphs is from JP, Record of a meeting with Dr. Banda at Government Lodge, Blantyre, 31st July, 1963.
59. JP, Jones to SS, 9 and 13 August 1963, 29 November 1963; SS to Jones, 2 August 1963.
60. Examples are found in DO 183 468.
61. JP, Brief for First SS, Dr. Banda's visit, n.d. but mid-September 1963.
62. JP, Note of Meeting held on 23 September 1963.
63. JP, Meeting of 23 September 1963.
64. JP, Meeting of 23 September 1963; Record of meeting with Dr. Banda, 16 August 1963.
65. Elisabeth Perchard, interview with author, 4 August 1998; JP, Jones to

Poynton, 15 October 1963, Jones to Watson, 26 October 1963, Tennant to Jones, 22 November 1963.
66. JP, Jones to SS, 10 December 1963 and 9 January 1964.
67. JP, Jones to SS, 9 January and 8 February 1964.
68. JP, Jones to SS, 30 December 1963. See also NICR for December 1963.
69. JP, Record of a meeting with Dr. Banda at Government Lodge, Blantyre, in the afternoon of 31st December 1963. See also JP, Jones to Sandys, 21 April 1964.
70. JP, Jones to SS, 8 February 1964. Chiume later claimed that Banda would not allow members of the cabinet to see the post mortem report on Pondeponde (nor, earlier, that on Dunduzu Chisiza) when they asked for it: Chiume interview with author, 13–14 December 1998.
71. JP, Jones to SS, 9 January 1964.
72. NICR for January 1963.
73. JP, Jones to Sandys, 3 February and 21 April 1964.
74. JP, Jones to SS, 3 February 1964.
75. JP, Jones to Banda, 8 February 1964.
76. JP, Jones to SS, 3 and 24 February and 21 April 1964.
77. JP, Jones to SS, 9 March 1964.
78. NICR for February 1964.
79. DO 183 137, Neale to Snelling, 10 April 1964.
80. JP, Jones to SS, 3 February 1964.
81. JP, Jones to SS, 16 March and 24 May 1964; NICR for March 1964.
82. JP, Jones to Sandys, 21 April 1963.
83. JP, Jones to SS, 23 January 1964.
84. Ibid.
85. JP, Jones to SS, 10 March 1964.
86. In a subsistence economy such as Nyasaland, the destruction of a family's crops removed their source of food for a year.
87. JP, Jones to Chirwa, 28 February 1964.
88. JP, Jones to Chirwa 11 March 1964.
89. JP, Chirwa to Jones, 13 March 1964.
90. JP, Note for the Record by Jones, n.d. but 18 March 1964.
91. JP, Jones to Chirwa, 6 April 1964.
92. JP, Chirwa to Jones, 17 April 1964.
93. JP, Jones to SS, 21 April 1964.
94. JP, Jones to Chirwa, 18 April 1964.
95. DO 183 137, Central Africa Division, CRO, For Ministers' Own Information, May 1964.
96. JP, Jones to SS, 26 May 1964.
97. *Nyasaland Government Gazette* 1964, p. 232.
98. Reeve to author, 23 March 1995.
99. JP, Jones to SS, 13 April 1964.
100. JP, Jones to Banda, 27 April 1964.
101. JP, Jones to SS, 30 April 1964
102. JP, SS to Jones, 5 February and 26 March 1964; Jones to Whitley, 6 February 1964; Jones to SS, 8 April 1964.
103. JP, Sandys to H.M. The Queen, 26 June 1964.
104. JP, Banda and Blackwood to Butler, 2 July 1963; Jones to Commonwealth and Colonial Secretary, 29 November 1963.

326 · Notes to Chapters 6 and 7

105. JP, Butler to Jones, 2 August 1963.
106. JP, Butler to Jones, 31 July 1963.
107. JP, Jones to Butler, 7 August 1963.
108. DO 183 444, Tennant to Garner, 12 November 1963.
109. DO 183 444, Garner to Chadwick, 13 November 1963.
110. DO 183 444, Chadwick to Garner, 14 November 1963.
111. A. H. M. Kirk-Greene, *A Bibliographical Dictionary of the British Colonial Governor, Vol. I: Africa* (Stanford, CA: Hoover Institution Press, 1980), pp. 63, 118.
112. DO 183 444, Neale to Whitley and Tennant, n.d. but probably early January 1964.
113. JP, Banda to Sandys, 13 January 1964.

7. Malawi: Governor-General

1. DO 183 457, Cole to Sandys, Despatch no. 3, 14 October 1964.
2. DO 183 457, Cole to Bottomley, Despatch no. 4, 27 October 1964.
3. DO 183 168, Cole, no addressee but probably Sandys, 11 August 1964.
4. Short, *Banda*, pp. 194–6; Chipembere seminar, California Institute of Technology, 1 February 1971: tape recording provided to author by Dr D. Brody (hereafter Chipembere seminar).
5. M. W. K. Chiume, *Kwacha* (Nairobi: East African Publishing House, 1975), pp.195–200.
6. OUCRP, Youens, interview with Sir Kenneth Bradley, 26 November 1970.
7. Chiume, interview with author, 13–14 December 1998.
8. JP, Secret Record of Meeting with Dr. Banda, 28 July 1964.
9. DO 183 457, Cole to Sandys, Despatch no. 3, 14 October 1964.
10. OUCRP, Youens interview with Bradley, 26 November 1970.
11. DO 183 168, Cole, no addressee but probably to Sandys, 11 August 1964.
12. JP, Note of Meeting, 29 July 1964.
13. H. B. M. Chipembere, 'Malawi in Crisis: 1964', *Ufahamu*, Vol. 2, 1970, pp. 17–18.
14. Material in this and the following paragraph, except where otherwise stated, is from JP, Secret Record of Meeting with Dr. Banda, 31 July 1964.
15. Diary, 1 August 1964.
16. JP, Record of Meeting of 6 August 1964.
17. Diary, 12 August 1964.
18. Undated paper, probably early 1990s, by Moxon, *The Malawi Cabinet Crisis*, enclosed with Tovey to author, 1 July 1999.
19. Unattributable letter to author, 29 July 1998.
20. Material in this and the following three paragraphs is from Chipembere, 'Malawi in Crisis: 1964', pp. 11–12.
21. Chiume, interview with author, 13–14 December 1998.
22. JP, Note of meeting with Dr Banda, 11 August 1964.
23. Except where otherwise stated, material in the following paragraphs dealing with events between 24 August and 26 October 1964 is from JP, Notes made by Sir Glyn Jones, Governor-General.
24. Chipembere, 'Malawi in Crisis: 1964', p.18.
25. DO 183 168, Cole to Snelling, 24 August 1964.
26. Ibid.

27. Details of the cabinet meeting are from JP, Minutes of a Meeting of the Cabinet held on Wednesday 26 August 1964 at 9.30 a.m. in the No. 1 Committee Room of the National Assembly Building, Zomba; and from Youens, interviews with author, 4 January 1995 and 8 December 1997.
28. *Malawi Government Gazette*, 28 August, p. 49.
29. Statutory Instrument, 1964, no. 916, s.59.3 and s.61.1.
30. OUCRP, Youens interview with Bradley, 26 November 1970.
31. DO 183 457, Cole to Sandys, Despatch no. 3, 14 October 1964.
32. D. Trelford, 'An Editor in Malawi', *The Listener*, 6 January 1977, p. 16.
33. DO 183 457, Cole to Sandys, Despatch No. 3, 14 October 1964.
34. Youens, interviews with author, 4 January 1995 and 8 December 1997.
35. Oxford Development Records Project (ODRP), Youens, interview with Kettlewell, 19 February 1985.
36. Hansard, Second Meeting, First Session, 8 and 9 September 1964, p. 12.
37. Roberts, interviews with author, July–August 1982.
38. Chiume, *Kwacha*, p. 214.
39. JP, Matters on Which Ministers Want Immediate Action: Paper submitted to Dr. Banda by Ministers, August 1964.
40. Hansard, Second Meeting, First Session, 8 and 9 September 1964, p. 12.
41. Hansard, Second Meeting, First Session, September 1964, p. 141.
42. Chipembere seminar.
43. Hansard, Second Meeting, First Session, September 1964, pp. 12–13, 73–4.
44. Chipembere, 'Malawi in Crisis: 1964', p. 19.
45. DO 183 168, Cole to Snelling, 3 September 1964.
46. Hansard, Second meeting, First Session, September 1964, pp. 12–13.
47. Ibid., pp. 73–4. See also pp. 52, 101.
48. Chipembere, 'Malawi in Crisis: 1964', pp. 7–9.
49. JP,. Meeting held at Government House on Monday 31 August 1964.
50. Ibid.
51. OUCRP, Youens interview with Bradley, 16 November 1970; DO 183 457, Cole to Sandys, Despatch no. 3, 14 October 1964.
52. JP, Meeting at Government House at 6.30 p.m. on Wednesday 2 September 1964.
53 DO 183 168, Cole to Snelling, 6 September 1964.
54. Ibid.; Phillips, interview with author, 3 December 1997.
55. JP, Banda to Jones, 7 September 1964.
56. Chiume, *Kwacha*, pp. 203–4.
57. Chiume, interview with author, 13–14 December 1998.
58. Chiume, *Kwacha*, pp. 203–4.
59. JP, Chisiza, Chokani and Msonthi, separately, to Governor-General, 7 September 1964. See also *Malawi Government Gazette*, 11 September 1964, p. 71, where Chokani's and Chisiza's resignations are gazetted but not Msonthi's.
60. Chokani to author, 28 January 1999.
61. Youens, interview with author, 8 December 1997.
62. Hansard, Second Meeting, First Session, 8 and 9 September 1964.
63. DO 183 457, Cole to Sandys, Despatch no. 3, 14 October 1964.
64. Ibid.
65. See also Hansard, Second Session, First Meeting, September 1964, p. 90.
66. JP, Chipembere to Governor-General, 9 September 1964.
67. Youens, interview with author, 8 December 1997.

68. Ibid.
69. See also *Malawi Government Gazette*, 12 September 1964, p. 83.
70. Chipembere, 'Malawi in Crisis: 1964', p. 18.
71. JP, Secret Note for the Record, 26 September 1964.
72. DO 183 457, Cole to Sandys, Despatch no. 3, 14 October 1964.
73. Ibid.
74. P. Lewis, interviews with author, 31 January 1996 and 13 October 1998.
75. DO 183 457, Cole to Sandys, 14 October 1964.
76. JP, Youens, note of telephone conversation with Jones, n.d., probably 30 September 1964.
77. DO 183 457, Cole to Sandys, 14 October 1964.
78. Ibid.
79. Ibid.
80. *Malawi Government Gazette*, Supplement, 30 September 1964, pp. 331, 334.
81. Hansard, Third Meeting, First Session, October 1964, p. 224.
82. OUCRP and ODRP, Youens interviews with Bradley, 26 November 1970 and with Kettlewell, 19 February 1985.
83. JP, Jones to Banda, 10 November 1964.
84. JP, Secret Note for the Record, 17 October 1964.
85. JP, Note for the Record; Jones to Watson, 5 November 1964.
86. JP, Secret Note for the Record, 17 October 1964.
87. OUCRP, Youens, interview with Bradley, 26 November 1970.
88. Ibid. Jones's account in JP says that Youens, not he, rang Banda to tell him what had happened.
89. Ibid. The account of the attack on Chirwa, and of Miss Kadzamira's and Youen's part is corroborated by Wilfred Chipande to author, 18 January 1998.
90. Roberts, interviews with author, July–August 1982.
91. OUCRP, Youens interview with Bradley, 26 November 1970.
92. JP, Jones to Watson, 5 November 1964; Diary, c. 24 October 1964.
93. Youens, interview with author, 8 December 1997.
94. Statutory Instrument, 1964, no. 916, s.66.1.
95. JP, handwritten note by Jones, November 1964.
96. The Malawi Independence Order, 1964, Statutory Instrument, 1964, no. 916, s. 54.2.
97. W. Chokani to author, 28 January 1999.
98. L. Bean, telephone conversation with author, 4 November 1997.
99. JP, Secret Record, 29 October 1964.
100. Hansard, Third Meeting, First Session, October 1964, p. 225.
101. *Sunday Telegraph*, 1 November 1964; *Rhodesia Herald*, 5 November 1964; C. Cameron, interview with author, 21 March 1998; A. Macadam, interview with author, 3 October 1996. See also Jackson, *Send Us Friends*, p. 280.
102. JP, Chipembere to Jones, 7 March 1965.
103. Material in this and the following paragraph, except where otherwise stated, is from Hansard, Second Session, Fifth Meeting, April 1965, pp. 504ff., and Third Session, Fourth Meeting, January 1966, p. 449.
104. Lewis, interview with author, 13 October 1998.
105. JP, Banda to Jones, 28 January 1965; *Malawi Government Gazette*, 1965, p. 59.
106. JP, Chipembere to Jones, 7 March 1965. As a precaution against the possibility of the letter not arriving safely, Chipembere repeated its substance in

another letter, sent to Lady Jones on 16 March. It is likely that Chipembere felt that Lady Jones's contacts with Miss Kadzamira might ensure that its contents became known to Banda if other methods failed.

107. JP, Secret Note, n.d. but probably 10 March 1964.
108. JP, Jones to Chipembere, 17 March 1965.
109. *Malawi Government Gazette*, Supplement, 19 March 1965.
110. JP, draft letter, Jones to Banda, n.d. but between 17 and 22 March 1965.
111. Hansard, Second Session, Fifth Meeting, April 1965, pp. 639ff.
112. Diary, 27 March 1971.
113. Material in this and the following three paragraphs is from JP, Jones, secret record, 6 April 1965.
114. The details of the following account of Chipembere's evacuation are from Denton to author, 2 April 1996, 9 July 1996, 23 July 1996, 19 November 1996, 12 August 1997, 17 December 1997 and 1 December 1998; and Lewis, interview with author, 13 December 1998.
115. JP, Note of Meeting, 12 May 1965.
116. JP, Chipembere to Jones, 26 October 1965.
117. Hansard, Third Session, First Meeting, July 1965, pp. 12, 35–7.
118. Lewis, interview with author, 13 October 1998
119. Hansard, Third Session, Third Meeting, November 1965, pp. 249ff. and pp. 271–2; Banda to Nkrumah, 31 January 1966, privately held.
120. H. S. Peters, conversations with author, early 1966.
121. M. Tadman, conversation with author, 6 March 1999; Tadman to author, 30 March 1999; and JP, Jones, handwritten notes dated 11 June 1969.
122. JP, Jones, handwritten notes, dated 11 June 1969.
123. JP, Chipembere to Jones, 26 October 1965.
124. JP, Gondwe to Banda, n.d. but probably 9 November 1965.
125. JP, Jones, handwritten note of meeting with Banda, 24 November 1965.
126. JP, Jones, confidential record, n.d. but probably about 10 June 1966.
127. Hansard, Third Session, Third Meeting, November 1965, pp. 219ff. and Third Session, Sixth Meeting, May 1966; *Malawi Government Gazette*, Extraordinary, Bill no. 8B, 25 April 1966; The Republic of Malawi (Constitution) Act, no. 23 of 1966.
128. Diaries 1966, passim.
129. D. Arden to author, 19 February 1999.
130. JP, Farewell Message, n.d. but early July 1966.
131. Details of Jones's departure are from John Boyd-Carpenter, 'African Sunset', *Spectator*, 5 August 1966, p. 185.

8. Retirement

1. JP, Jones to McGee (CRO), and Jones to McMullen (CRO), 27 June 1966. Material in this and the following paragraph, unless otherwiswe stated, is from Diary, 4 July to 31 December 1966.
2. JP, Lomax to Jones, 12 August 1967.
3. JP, Jones to Banda, 27 June 1967.
4. Hansard, Fifth Session, Second Meeting, 12–14 December 1997, passim; Roberts, interviews with author, July–August 1982..
5. Material in this and the following four paragraphs is from JP, Secret Note by Jones, 22 March 1968.

6. Earl Phillips,'H. B. M. Chipembere, 1930–1975, Malawi Patriot', *Ufahamu*, vol. vii, no. 1, 1976, pp. 4–17.
7. JP, telegram from Foreign and Commonwealth Office to Jones, 31 January 1984.
8. JP, Jones to Banda, 16 August 1984.
9. Doig, *It's People That Count*, pp. 122–5.
10. Brind, *Lying Abroad*, pp. 229–31.
11. JP, Roberts to Jones, 21 September 1966.
12. Banda to Jones, 24 October 1966, cited in JP, Jones to Banda, 2 May 1974.
13. JP, Roberts to Jones, 25 November 1966.
14. JP, Banda to Jones, 22 April 1974.
15. Elisabeth Perchard, interview with author, 4 August 1998.
16. JP, Banda to Jones, 22 April 1974; Jones, Mr W. J. R. Pincott, Appraisal by Sir Glyn Jones, March 1974, privately held.
17. Jones to Banda, referred to in JP, Banda to Jones, 22 April 1974.
18. JP, Jones to Banda, 11 April 1974.
19. JP, Banda to Jones, 22 April 1974.
20. JP, Jones to Banda, 2 May 1974.
21. As a comparison, the prime minister of Great Britain's annual salary at the time did not exceed £20,000.
22. JP, Banda to Jones, 23 May 1974.
23. JP, Pincott to Jafu, 31 May 1974.
24. Material in this and the following paragraphs dealing with the Lesotho assignment, unless otherwise stated, is from JP, Report on Five Visits to Lesotho Made by Sir Glyn Jones, GCMG as Adviser on Governmental Matters to the Prime Minister of Lesotho, London, 18 March 1970.
25. Material in this and the following paragraphs dealing with Rhodesia, unless otherwise stated, is from Cmnd 4964, *Rhodesia*.
26. Massingham to author, 13 January 1995.
27. Smedley to author, 24 October 1994.
28. Massingham to author, 13 January 1995.
29. E. B. Smith, A Memorial Address, Oxford, 13 March 1993.
30. *Guardian*, 4 December 1972.
31. Ibid.
32. JP, Cousins to Richard Banda, 15 December 1972.
33. The following details concerning Jones's attempt to have the book withdrawn by Routledge are from JP, Minute of Meeting held at the Office of Coward Chance, lawyers, on 13 February 1973 Concerning the Biography of H.E. President Banda of Malawi Written by Mr. Philip Short.
34. JP, decree nisi dated 25 April 1955, Cause Undefended 6211.
35. JP, Richard Banda to Robert Allen of Longman Group, 14 December 1972.
36. JP, various undated handwritten notes by Jones; Jones to Banda, 17 April 1983; Jones to Verrier, 6 September 1983; Rex Collings to Jones, 10 September 1984; undated note, Jones to Miss Neville Rolfe.
37. JP, Banda to Jones, 2 May 1983.
38. Lapping to author, 8 September 1998.
39. Connors to author, 10 July 1997.
40. Elisabeth Perchard, interview with author, 4 August 1998.
41. Shepperd to author, July 1997.
42. Material in this and the following two paragraphs is from Connors to

author, 10 July 1997.
43. JP, Jones to Lapping, 19 June 1985
44. Lapping to author, 8 September 1998.
45. Ibid.
46. Lapping to author, 12 May 1997.
47. JP, Jones to Lapping, 19 June 1985.
48. Lapping to author, 8 September 1998.
49. B. Lapping, *End of Empire* (London: Paladin 1989), p. 21.
50. Lapping to author, 8 September 1998.
51. JP, Jones to A.R. Munday, headmaster, 1 October 1972.
52. JP, Nairne to Jones, 29 July 1987 and undated notes by Jones.
53. G. Brookes to author, 1 February 1995
54. Elisabeth Perchard, interview with author, 4 August 1998.
55. W. Knapp to author 14 September 1994.
56. Lady Jones and Elisabeth Perchard interview with author 20 July 1994.
57. St Catherine's College, Oxford, Order of Service and Memorial Address, Memorial Service for Sir Glyn Jones, GCMG, MBE, MA, 13 March 1993, p1. _ _ _y held.
58. Elisabeth Perchard, interviews with author, 20 July 1994, 4 August 1998 and 15 September 1999. Earlier in 1993, Helen Kittermaster laid to rest her mother's ashes, next to the grave of Sir Harold Kittermaster who died in office as Governor in 1939: Helen Kittermaster, telephone conversation with author, 7 March 1999.

9. Proconsul of the Wind of Change

1. S. N. Downs to author, 21 October 1994.
2. Unattributable.
3. Sir Patrick Nairne commented: 'He was not, in my experience, a man of many words': *St Catherine's Year*, (Oxford, 1992), p. 36. Jones's frequent long pauses before replying were commented on by members of the Granada television team, by some of his closest official colleagues and by businessman who wondered if he had heard what was being said. They also commented kindly on the way he would frequently, just before replying, loudly clear his throat and hitch up his trouser waistband.
4. For a pen picture of Benson, see Short, *African Sunset*, chs VIII and IX.
5. JP, Meeting at Goudhurst, 31 May 1983, with Brian Lapping and Sarah Curtis.
6. Ibid.; Lady Jones, interview with author, 20 July 1994.
7. Lady Jones, interview with author, 20 July 1994.
8. Other former Governors, when asked, said they had never known a secretary of state to address the chief secretary rather than the Goveror in this way and believed it to be both unprecedented and improper: Sir Douglas Hall to author, 5 September 1997; Sir Cosmo Haskard to author, 29 June 1997, and Sir Robert Foster, interview, 20 April 1995.
9. JP, Meeting at Goudhurst, 31 May 1983, with Brian Lapping and Sarah Curtis.
10. There has been a fairly widespread belief that it was Jones who brought Banda back to Zomba from Gwelo (see, for example, Jackson, *Send Us Friends*, p. 263) but it was in fact Youens who did so.

332 · Notes to Chapter 9

11. JP, Jones to Monson, 19 December 1961.
12. JP, Meeting at Goudhurst, 31 May 1983, with Brian Lapping and Sarah Curtis.
13. Foster, interview with author, 20 April 1995.
14. JP, manuscript note by Jones on fifth independence anniversary celebrations.
15. Brind, *Lying Abroad*, p. 225.
16. DO 208 2 Cole to Bottomley, Despatch No. 3, 7 April 1966.
17. Brind, *Lying Abroad*, p. 199.
18. DO 208 334, biographical notes, nd., probably 1966.
19. I. H. Wethey to author, 9 January 1996; Elisabeth Perchard, interview with author, 15 September 1999.
20. P. Swan to author, 26 January 1995.
21. P. Howard, interview with author, 30 July 1994.
22. Swan to author, 26 January 1995.
23. Brody, telephone conversation with author, 30 October 1999. In the early days, Chiume got away with addressing Banda as 'Doc'. In the front of a book which he sent to Banda, Chipembere and the Chisizas in Gwelo gaol in February 1960, Chiume inscribed the words, 'With love and good wishes to the Doc, Chip and the Chis's from Kanyama': ibid.
24. The Malawi Independence Order, 1964, Schedule 2, s.54.2.
25. JP, manuscript note by Jones in retirement.
26. Ibid.
27. DO 208 28, Memorandum to Steering Committee on the Importance of Malawi, 8 March 1966.
28. Reeve to author, 23 March 1995.
29. JP, P. F. C. Nicholson to Jones, from Beira, 12 February 1964.
30. Jones showed great kindness to Kettlewell and Ingham when they became constitutional casualties in 1962. When chiefs were to be removed from office, he persuaded Banda to allow them to retire on pension. One of the police officers who was involved in investigating the assaults on Europeans in 1963 was able to secure a transfer to another territory with Jones's help, unknown to the officer concerned.
31. JP, Jones to Banda, 12 March 1962.
32. Devlin, for example, found Banda charming.
33. Sir George Smith, Governor from 1913 to 1923.
34. A. H. M. Kirk-Greene, *A Biographical Dictionary of the British Colonial Governors Vol. 1: Africa* (Stanford, CA: Hoover Institution Press, 1980), p. 313.
35. Unattributable.
36. Of the 1136 expatriate civil servants on 1 October 1962, 681 (60 per cent) had left by 6 July 1965: Nyasaland Staff List 1962 and Malawi Staff List 1965.

Biographical Notes

ALPORT, Cuthbert James McCall, b. 1912; lawyer and politician; educated Haileybury and Cambridge; MP 1950–61; various ministerial posts in Commonwealth Relations Office; created Life Peer, 1961; British high commissioner, Federation of Rhodesia and Nyasaland, 1961–3; d. 1999.

ARMITAGE, Robert Perceval, b. 1906; educated Winchester and Oxford; Colonial administrative service, Kenya, 1929; administrative secretary, 1947; financial secretary, Gold Coast, 1948; minister of finance, 1951; Governor of Cyprus, 1954–55; Governor of Nyasaland, 1956–61; MBE, 1944; CMG, 1951; KCMG, 1954; d. 1990.

BANDA, Aleke, b. 1939; educated Southern Rhodesia; secretary of Que Que branch of Nyasaland African Congress; arrested 1959 and briefly detained; deported to Nyasaland; co-founder, with Orton Chirwa, of Malawi Congress Party, 1959; founder of *Malawi News*; secretary-general Malawi Congress Party, 1966; held various ministerial posts, 1966–72; dismissed 1973 and subsequently twice detained; re-entered political life with return of multi-party elections in 1994.

BANDA, Hastings Kamuzu, b. 1898; medical practitioner and politician; worked in Southern Rhodesia and South Africa as a young man; educated USA and Scotland; practised medicine Liverpool, Tyneside and London, 1939–52 and Ghana 1953–8; returned to Nyasaland 1958 and took over leadership of Nyasaland African Congress; detained March 1959 to April 1960; leader of majority party and minister of natural resources and local government 1961–63; prime minister of Nyasaland and then Malawi 1963–66; President of Republic of Malawi 1966–94; d. 1997.

BENSON, Arthur Edward Trevor, b. 1907; colonial administrative service, Northern Rhodesia, 1932; Colonial Office, 1939; Prime Minister's Office, 1940–42; Cabinet Office, 1942–43; Colonial Office, 1943–44; Northern Rhodesia, 1944–46; administrative secretary, Uganda, 1946–49; chief secretary, Central Africa Council, 1949–51; Chief Secretary, Nigeria, 1951–54; Governor, Northern Rhodesia, 1954–59; CMG, 1952; KCMG, 1954; GCMG, 1959; d. 1987.

BLACKWOOD, Michael Hill, b. 1917; lawyer and politician; member of legislature of Nyasaland and Malawi, 1954–74; member of executive council 1956–61; CBE, 1963.

BWANAUSI, Augustine, b. 1930; schoolmaster and politician; educated at Makerere College, Uganda; worked in Tanganyika and became a senior member of the Tanganyika African National Union; returned to Nyasaland, 1959; held various ministerial posts, 1961–64; dismissed 1964; exile in Zambia and Tanzania; died in car crash in Zambia, 1968.

CAMERON, Colin; lawyer; elected to legislature, 1961; minister of works and Transport, 1961; resigned ministerial post, July 1964; fled country and returned to Scotland, November 1964.

CHIBAMBO, Rose; organizer and leader of women's league, 1958–64; dismissed from parliamentary secretary post and suspended from Malawi Congress Party, September 1964; exile in Zambia, 1964; returned to Malawi with multi-party elections in 1994.

CHIPEMBERE, Henry Blasius Masauko, b. 1930; politician; graduated Fort Hare, South Africa; district assistant, Nyasaland Civil Service; member of legislature, 1956–64; treasurer of Nyasaland African Congress, 1958; detained March 1959 to September 1960; convicted of sedition, January 1961; released from prison, January 1963; minister of local government, 1963–64; minister of education, 1964; resigned from office, September 1964; led unsuccessful *coup d'état*, February 1965; evacuated to live in USA, 1965 to 1975, with temporary return to Tanzania, 1966–69; d. 1975.

CHIRWA, Orton Edgar Ching'oli, b. 1919; teacher, lawyer and politician; educated Zambia and Fort Hare, South Africa, 1947–51, graduating BA and BEd with diploma in education; returned to Nyasaland 1951 and taught at teacher training college; London, studying law, 1955–58; called to Bar, 1958; returned again to Nyasaland and became legal adviser to Nyasaland African Congress, 1958; briefly detained 1959; co-founder, with Aleke Banda, Malawi Congress Party and was its first president, 1959; various ministerial posts, 1961–64: parliamentary secretary to the ministry of justice, minister of justice, attorney-general; dismissed September 1964; lived in exile in Tanzania; abducted and returned to Malawi in 1981, convicted of treason in 1984; sentence of death commuted; died in prison 1992.

CHISIZA, Dunduzu, b. 1930; younger brother of Yatuta Chisiza; worked in Southern Rhodesia; secretary-general of Nyasaland African Congress, 1958–59; detained March 1959 to September 1960; reinstated as secretary-general; parliamentary secretary to ministry of finance, 1961–6; killed in car crash, September 1962.

Biographical Notes · 335

CHISIZA, Yatuta, b. 1926, elder brother of Dunduzu Chisiza; police officer, Tanganyika; returned to Nyasaland, 1958; detained March 1959 to September 1960; personal bodyguard to Dr Banda, 1958–64; parliamentary secretary, ministry of labour, 1963–6; minister of home affairs, 1964; dismissed September 1964; lived in exile in Tanzania and Zambia, 1964–67; killed in armed invasion of Malawi, 1967.

CHIUME, Murray William Kanyama, b. 1929; teacher and politician; educated Tanganyika and Uganda; taught in Tanganyika; returned to Nyasaland; member of legislature, 1956–64; publicity secretary of Nyasaland Congress Party and later Malawi Congress Party; overseas during state of emergency, 1959–60; minister of education, 1961–64; minister of external affairs, 1964; dismissed September 1964; lived in exile in East Africa, 1964–94; returned to Malawi, 1994.

CHOKANI, Willie, b. 1930; schoolmaster and politician; educated in Blantyre; graduated Delhi, India; detained, 1959; minister of labour, 1962; dismissed 1964; exile in Zambia, 1964; Malawi ambassador to the USA, 1994.

FOOTMAN, Charles Wothington Fowden, b. 1905; graduated, Oxford; colonial administrative service, Zanzibar, 1930; East African Governors' Conference, 1942; Colonial Office, 1943–46; financial secretary, Nyasaland, 1947; chief secretary, 1951; chairman public services commission, Tanganyika and Zanzibar, 1960; Commonwealth Relations Office, 1962; ministry of overseas development, 1964–70; d. 1997.

FOSTER, Robert, b. 1913; graduated Cambridge; colonial administrative service, Northern Rhodesia, 1936; provincial commissioner, 1957; secretary, ministry of native affairs, 1960; chief secretary, Nyasaland, 1961–63; Deputy Governor, 1963–64; high commissioner, Western Pacific, 1964–68; CMG, 1961; KCMG, 1964; KCVO, 1970; GCMG, 1970.

HONE, Evelyn Dennison, b. 1911; colonial administrative service, Tanganyika, 1935; secretary to the government of the Seychelles, 1944; assistant secretary, Palestine, 1946; colonial secretary, British Honduras, 1948; chief secretary, Aden, 1953; chief secretary, Northern Rhodesia, 1957; Governor, Northern Rhodesia, 1959–64; OBE, 1946; CMG, 1953; CVO, 1954; KCMG, 1959; GCMG, 1965; d. 1979.

KETTLEWELL, Richard Wildman, b. 1910; colonial agricultural service, Nyasaland, 1934; served in army in East Africa, Middle East and Ceylon, 1939–43; director of agriculture, 1951; secretary for natural resources, 1959; secretary for lands and mines, 1961; retired, 1962; CMG, 1955; d. 1994.

LOMAX, Douglas George, b. 1915; Hampshire constabulary, 1936–42; special police corps, Germany, 1946–50; Nyasaland police force 1950–71; senior assistant commissioner, 1966; head of Special Branch, 1964–71; CPM; QPM, 1966; OBE, 1969; d. 1998.

MKANDAWIRE, Mikeka; b. early 1920s; store-keeper, Soche, Blantyre; detained 1959; minister without portfolio, 1961–64; exile in Scotland, 1965; returned to Malawi; d. 1995.

MSONTHI, John, b. 1928; schoolmaster and politician; educated Zomba Secondary School and graduated Bombay, India; detained 1959; minister of transport, 1962; suspended from cabinet and then reinstated, 1964; temporarily resigned as minister, 1964; various ministerial posts from 1964.

PHILLIPS, Henry Ellis Isadore, b. 1914; Institute of Historical Research, University of London, 1936–39; served in war, 1939–45; prisoner of war, 1942; colonial administrative service, Nyasaland, 1946; development secretary, 1952; seconded to federal treasury of Rhodesia and Nyasaland, 1953–57; deputy secretary, Nyasaland, 1956; financial secretary, Nyasaland, 1957–64 and minister of finance, 1961–64; MBE, 1946; CMG, 1960; Kt 1964.

TEMBO, John, b. 1932; schoolmaster and politician; educated Malawi, Botswana and Zimbabwe; parliamentary secretary to ministry of finance, 1962; minister of finance, 1964; minister of trade and industry, 1969; governor of reserve bank, 1971.

WATSON, Noel Duncan, b. 1915; educated Bedford and Oxford; colonial administrative service, Cyprus, 1938–43; Colonial, Commonwealth Relations and Foreign and Commonwealth Offices, 1946–74: principal, 1946; assistant secretary, 1950; under-secretary, 1963; assistant under-secretary of state, 1964; deputy under-secretary of state, 1972; CMG, 1960; KCMG, 1967.

WELENSKY, Roy, b. 1907; started work at age of fourteen, became a railway engine driver and heavyweight boxer; became leader of railway workers' union, Northern Rhodesia; member of legislative council of Northern Rhodesia, 1938; director of manpower, 1941; member of war committee, 1941; leader of Northern Rhodesia non-official members, 1946; federation of Rhodesia and Nyasaland minister of transport, 1954; deputy prime minister, 1955; prime minister, minister of defence, minister of external affairs, 1956–63; KCMG, 1953; d. 1991.

YOUENS, Peter William, b. 1916; colonial administrative service, 1939; naval service, 1939–40; Sierra Leone, assistant district commissioner, 1942;

district commissioner, 1948; colony commissioner, 1950; assistant secretary, Nyasaland, 1951; deputy chief secretary, 1953–63; secretary to the prime minister and cabinet, Malawi, 1964–66; company director, London, 1966–94; OBE, 1960; CMG, 1962; Kt 1965.

Sources

Primary Sources

1. *The Jones Papers*
Some of these are deposited in Rhodes House Library, Oxford, and others – in the possession of his daughter, Elisabeth Perchard – will in due course also be deposited there. They are comprised of Jones's diaries from 1932 to 1969, with gaps; official papers which he retained from Nyasaland and Malawi; private papers relating to his career; and private notes that he made at various times during his Nyasaland–Malawi period.

2. *The R.A. Butler Papers*
These are deposited in the Library, Trinity College, Cambridge.

3. *The Harold Macmillan Papers*
These are deposited in the Bodleian Library, Oxford.

4. *The Roy Welensky Papers*
These are deposited in the Rhodes House Library, Oxford.

5. *The Robert Armitage Papers*
These are deposited in Rhodes House Library, Oxford.

6. *The* End of Empire *papers*
These are deposited by Brian Lapping of Granada Television in Rhodes House Library, Oxford, Mss. Brit. Emp. s.527.

7. *The Oxford University Colonial Records Project and Oxford Development Records Project papers*
These include transcripts of interviews with Sir Peter Youens, Sir Bryan Roberts, Sir Roy Welensky, and are deposited in Rhodes House Library, Oxford.

8. *Files in the Public Record Office, Kew*

CO 1015 2491, Governor's Reports on Current Situation, Nyasaland.
CO 1015 2552, 2553 and 2554, Visit of Secretary of State for the Colonies to Federation of Rhodesia and Nyasaland, November–December 1961.
CO 1015 2629, Matters Arising From Prime Minister's Tour of Nyasaland, January 1960.
DO 158 60 and 296, Informal Conference Between the British High Commissioner, Salisbury, and the Two Northern Governors.

Sources · 339

DO 183 61, Republican Status of Malawi.
DO 183 95, 96 and 97, Nyasaland Constitutional Conference 1962.
DO 183 136 and 137, Intelligence Reports, Nyasaland.
DO 183 140, Briefs prepared for the Visit of Lord Alport and the Governors of Northern Rhodesia and Nyasaland to the UK on the future of the Federation.
DO 183 142, Briefs prepared for Mr Butler's Visit to the Federation, May 1962.
DO 183 168, Executive Council (now Cabinet), Nyasaland (now Malawi).
DO 183 176, British Embassy Washington to Foreign Office.
DO 183 444, Appointment of Governor-General When Nyasaland Becomes Independent.
DO 183 445, Despatches from the Governor-General of Malawi.
DO 183 457, Despatches from the British High Commissioner in Malawi.
DO 183 467, Visit of Dr H. Banda to the UK, 1962.
DO 183 468, Visit of Dr Banda to Europe, USA and UK.

9. *Correspondence*

Correspondence with over 400 former colleagues of Jones, including those who were at school and university with him, those who worked with him in Northern Rhodesia and Nyasaland–Malawi, and those who knew him socially. Some of this correspondence has been used as background material and specific sources are shown in the Notes to the text.

10. *Interviews*

Donald Arden, Jeremy Armitage, Humphry Berkeley, John Blunden, Sir Michael Caine, Frank Chevallier, Dr W.M. Chirwa, Gervas Clay, Bob Dewar, Ian Dinwithey, John Durrant, Sir Robin Foster, Eileen Gilespie, Sir Douglas Hall, Sir David Hunt, Lady Jones, Richard Kettlewell, Paul Lewis, Charles Lucas, Nicholas Maxwell-Lawford, Lady Nicholson, Colin Perchard, Elisabeth Perchard, Syd Peters, Sir Henry Phillips, Coralie Pincott, Eric Pocklington, Sir Bryan Roberts, John Sheriff, Peter Smith, Sir Peter Tapsell, Sir Edgar Unsworth, Sir Edgar Williams, Sir Peter Youens.

11. *Miscellaneous*

Extracts from the private papers of Dr H.K. Banda, provided by Dr D. Brody and T. Walker.
Tape recording of H. B. M. Chipembere's political geography seminar at California Institute of Technology, 1 February 1971, copies provided by Dr D. Brody and David Stuart-Mogg.

Secondary Sources

1. *Government publications*

Cmnd 5009 (1935) *Report of a Commission Appointed to Enquire Into Disturbances on the Copperbelt of Northern Rhodesia.*

Cmnd 814 (1959) *Report of the Nyasaland Commission of Inquiry.*
Cmnd 1132 (1960) *Report of the Nyasaland Constitutional Conference, Held in London in July and August 1960.*
Cmnds 1148–1151 (1960) *Report of the Advisory Commission on the Review of the Constitution of the Federation of Rhodesia and Nyasaland.*
Cmnd 1887 (1962) *Report of the Nyasaland Constitutional Conference.*
Cmnd 4964 (1972) *Rhodesia. Report of the Commission on Rhodesian Opinion Under the Chairmanship of the Right Honourable the Lord Pearce.*
Statutory Instrument, 1964, No. 916, *The Malawi Independence Order in Council 1964.*
The Southworth Commission Report, 1960 (Zomba, May 1960).
The Erosion of the Rule of Law in Nyasaland (Salisbury, July 1963).
The Erosion of the Rule of Law in Nyasaland: The Local Courts (Salisbury, September 1963).
Rule of Law in Nyasaland: Reply to the Hon. J. M. Greenfield, QC (Zomba, 1963).
Proposals for the Republican Constitution of Malawi (Zomba, November 1965).
Republic of Malawi (Constitution) Act 1966 (Zomba, June 1966).
Report of the McDonnell Commission (Lusaka, November 1939).

2. Journals

Intimidation in Central Africa: Vote for me or else (London: East Africa and Rhodesia, 1962).
Chipembere, H. B. M., 'Malawi in Crisis: 1964', *Ufahamu*, Vol. 2, 1970, pp. 1–22.
Power, Joey, 'Remembering Du: An Episode in the Development of Malawi's Political Culture', *African Affairs*, (1998), 97, 369–96.

3. Books

Baker, Colin, *State of Emergency: Crisis in Central Africa, Nyasaland 1959-1960* (London: Tauris Academic Press, 1997).
— *Retreat from Empire: Sir Robert Armitage in Africa and Cyprus* (London: Tauris Academic Press, 1998).
Bell, Vivienne, *Blown by the Wind of Change* (Sussex: Book Guild, 1986).
Brind, Harry, *Lying Abroad: Diplomatic Memoirs* (London: Radcliffe Press, 1999).
Butler, R. A., *The Art of the Possible: the Memoires of Lord Butler, KG, CH* (London: Hamish Hamilton, 1971).
Doig, Andrew, *It's People That Count* (Edinburgh: Pentland Press, 1997).
Jackson, Bill, *Send Us Friends* (Malawi: CLAIM, n.d., probably 1997).
Lwanda, John, *Kamuzu Banda of Malawi: A Study in Promise, Power and Paralysis* (Glasgow: Dudu Nsomba, 1993).
Phillips, Henry, *From Obscurity to Bright Dawn: How Nyasaland became Malawi, an Insider's Account* (London: Radcliffe Press, 1998).
Short, Philip, *Banda* (London: Routledge and Kegan Paul, 1974).

Index

administrative officers, functions of, 20
African membership of social and sporting clubs, 204, 304
Africanization, 146, 201, 214, 225
Alport, Lord, 117, 118, 124, 125, 129, 131, 133, 161, 297
anonymous letters sent to Banda, 219, 227
Armitage, Sir Robert, 61, 62, 64, 65, 67, 68, 69, 70, 71, 72, 73, 75, 84, 91, 94, 95, 145, 231, 273, 275, 288, 289, 292, 293, 297; announces retirement, 88; Jones's letter to, 83; leaves Nyasaland, 94; prosecution of MCP activists, 96; retirement of, 92; threat to resign, 90
arson attacks, 97, 185, 295

'Babs', 31; Jones's relationship with, 29
Baker, Maxine, 273, 274
Balovale, Jones's posting to, 34, 37, 38
Banda, Aleke, 68, 89, 189, 217, 226, 239; increasing authority of, 206
Banda, Gideon, pseudonym for Chipembere, 250
Banda, Hastings Kamuzu, 62, 70, 73, 79, 87, 88, 109, 112, 195; attends football match in Blantyre, 170; attends OAU conference in Cairo, 201, 202; called on to renounce violence, 93; campaign against Central African Federation, 112, 113, 115, 118; Chileka speech, 202, 204; control of Malawi Congress Party, 110; coup attempt against, 246, 259; criticism of, 201, 206, 208, 209, 210, 211, 216, 217, 225, 228, 236, 238, 254; description of, 66, 75; domination of the executive council, 110, 111; excessive responsibilities of, 205, 209, 210, 214, 218, 235, 304; imprisonment of, 68 (release from prison, 64, 67, 68, 69, 91, 95, 114, 287, 288, 289); intervention in juridical cases, 180; invited to sherry party, 96; letters (from Sir Godfrey Nicholson, 115–16; to Butler, 197; to Jones, 67, 75 (regarding employment, 262–3, 265, 266–7)); motorcade issue, 178; plan for autobiography, 272; positions of (appointed minister, 103; as leader of party, 82; as prime minister, 160 (proposed, 151); proposed as chief minister, 104–5, 106, 107, 119–20, 130, 131; question of membership of executive council, 71, 72, 81); pressure for release of prisoners and amnesty, 71, 73, 74, 78; relationship with Chiume, 138, 139, 140; relationship with Jones see Jones, relationship with Banda; resignation threat, 150, 211, 212, 213, 214, 215, 216, 218, 219, 220, 221, 222, 223, 224, 233, 293; responsibility for MCP policy, 104; return to Nyasaland, 61; statements against violence, 190, 191, 247, 290, 295–6;

suggestion of schizophrenia, 272; threat to return to prison *see* Gwelo card; tour of Europe and USA, 69, 182, 184; view of Nkula Falls scheme, 114; views on secession, 125, 126, 164, 166; violent outbursts of, 294; visits to London, 134–5, 177, 184, 201 (planned, 124, 132, 168); visited by Chirwa, 241–2; visited by Jones in prison, 65–6; Zomba speech, 173, 175 *see also* Banda, meetings and correspondence of

Banda, meetings and correspondence of: with Butler, 131–3, 150, 157; with Jones, 66, 74–5, 76, 79, 81–2, 98, 100, 101–2, 108, 113, 116, 118, 120, 121, 128, 129, 130, 140, 141, 144, 145, 152, 153, 155, 156, 162, 163, 164, 165–6, 173, 177, 183, 188–9, 195–6, 203, 211, 213, 215, 217–19, 220, 222, 224, 226–7, 229, 230–1, 232, 235, 236, 237, 239, 240, 242, 243, 247, 248, 249, 250, 254, 261, 288; with Sandys, 116, 117; with Youens, 73–4, 76–7; with Welensky, proposed, 115, 116, 120, 121, 304

Banda, Richard, 270

Barotseland Province: description of, 51; Jones as resident commissioner of, 283; special status of, 56

Bean, Leonard, 246

Bell, Kenneth, 16

Benson, Anna, 59

Benson, Sir Arthur, 63, 284, 285, 303; tour in Northern Rhodesia, 52–4 (Jones's involvement in organizing, 283, 308); relationship with Jones, 56, 59–60

Benson, Daphne, 59

Betts, Barbara, 16

Betts, James, 16

Bill of Rights for Nyasaland, 133

Blackwood, Michael H., 79, 80, 89, 97, 100, 102, 153, 161, 163, 183, 195, 215, 273, 292; letter to Butler, 197; meeting with Jones, 99

Bonfield, A.W., 32

British South Africa Company, 34

Bullock, Lord, 278

Butler, R.A., 123, 124, 125, 127, 128, 129, 151, 152, 154, 156, 161, 162, 163, 166, 170, 172, 173, 175, 176–7, 179, 182, 183, 184, 188, 192, 200, 225, 265, 276; discussion with Macmillan, 150; handling of Banda, 135; letter to Jones, 131; letter to Unsworth, 181; meetings with Banda, 131–3, 150, 153, 162, 168 (in London, 134–5); meeting with Jones, 133, 157; returns to London, 134; view of Stevens report, 148; visit to Nyasaland, 124, 158, 162

Bwanausi, Augustine, 136, 137, 139, 160, 196, 207, 208, 210, 219, 227, 228, 232, 234, 237, 243, 304; appointed minister, 103; cocktail party in Blantyre, 236; in exile, 259; meeting with Jones, 234, 235; proposed as development and housing minister, 196

cabinet meeting, crisis, 207–15, 304, 309

Callaghan, James, 240

Cameron, Colin, 99, 100, 102, 111, 128, 136, 137, 152, 160, 204, 225, 226, 304; appointed minister, 103; proposed as public works minister, 196; resigns, 203, 207

cannibalism: reports of, 25; trial of women, 54–5

Carlyle, A.J., reference for G.S. Jones, 14–15

Catholic Church, attacks on, 87, 88

census activities carried out by Jones, 20–1, 37, 40

Central Africa Federation, 61, 62, 106, 112, 136; British government

Index · 343

view of, 111, 118–19 (agrees Nyasaland withdrawal, 151); dissolution of, 176 (costs of, 157); Jones's attitude to, 113 *see also* Banda, campaign against Federation
Central Africa Office, 167, 169, 197; closure of, 187
Chadwick, G.W., 198–9
Chakuamba, Gwanda, 110, 186, 221, 239; proposed as minister for community development, 231
Chibambo, McKinley, 207, 230; appointed regional minister, 231
Chibambo, Rose, 226, 227
Chidzanja, Richard, 207, 221; appointed regional minister, 231; proposed as minister of works and transport, 231
chiefs, traditional, role and significance of, in Jones's view, 269, 283, 284, 303, 305
Chikowi, Chief, 185
Chinyanja, Jones's learning of, 31
Chipembere, Henry B.M., 62, 66, 71, 73, 78, 79, 81, 82, 84, 160, 175, 194, 204, 205, 207, 212, 218, 221, 231, 232, 233, 234, 237, 241, 242, 243, 247, 292, 303, 304; addresses audiences in US, 254; arrest for sedition, 275 (Jones's part in, 277); attempted coup by, 247–8; call for amnesty, 248–9, 253, 254; cocktail party in Blantyre, 236; confinement order on, 239; contact with Jones, 230, 260; death of, 261; departure for USA, 250–2, 309; imprisonment of, 69, 96, 111, 137, 178; in exile, 259; letter to Jones, 248; meetings banned, 237, 238; possible visit to London, 254; proposed as education minister, 196; release of, 139, 158, 159; restriction order on, 247
Chirwa, Orton E.C., 68, 101, 110, 111, 137, 146, 160, 178, 179, 180, 181, 200, 207, 208, 210, 211, 212, 218, 219, 226, 228, 235, 237, 238, 241, 243, 244, 245, 246; abducted, 261–2; as minister of justice, relations with Jones, 191; as parliamentary secretary, 103, 110; attack on Jones, 193–4; death of, 262; in exile, 259; leaves Malawi, 243; meeting with Banda with demands, 217; meeting with Jones, 211, 220, 223 (secretly, 205–6); proposed as justice minister, 196; report to Jones, 210; visit to Banda's house, 241–2 (attacked, 242, 243)
Chirwa, Vera, 259; abducted, 261–2; released from gaol, 262
Chisiza, Dunduzu, 66, 71, 73, 78, 79, 81, 82, 84, 101, 102, 105, 110, 111, 113, 136, 137, 139, 164, 292, 304; as parliamentary secretary, 103, 110; killed in car crash, 140, 159; letter to Jones, 138; view of Nkula Falls scheme, 114
Chisiza, Yatuta, 66, 71, 73, 78, 79, 81, 82, 84, 137, 140, 175, 205, 207, 209, 210, 214, 218, 221, 226, 227, 231, 232, 234, 237, 241, 243, 244, 247, 292, 303; approach to Lomax of Special Branch, 201; cocktail party in Blantyre, 236; death of, 260; in exile, 259; meeting with Jones, 234, 235; proposed as commissioner of police, 139; proposed as home affairs minister, 196; resignation of, 228
Chiume, Mrs, 140
Chiume, Murray W.K., 71, 88, 101, 104, 105, 111, 113, 137, 142, 160, 175, 194, 205, 207, 208, 209, 210, 212, 214, 216, 218, 219, 221, 222, 223, 224, 225, 226, 227, 228, 232, 233, 237, 245, 247, 262, 292; appointed minister, 103; criticisms of, 136–40; in exile, 259; meeting with Banda, 165;

proposed as information minister, 196; relations with Banda, 215
Chokani, Willie, 110, 111, 136, 137, 139, 160, 207, 208, 210, 231, 232, 233, 234, 237, 243; as minister of labour, 208 (proposed, 196); in exile, 259; meetings with Jones, 234, 235, 245–6; phoned by Jones, 236; resignation of, 228, 229
Christian Democratic Party (CDP), 83, 93
circumcision ceremony, Jones's attendance at, 37
civil servants, 173, 203, 256; adjustment to new regime, 141, 144, 148; African, 207, 218, 240, 309 (salaries of, 265 (restricted, 205)); animosity towards, 142; Banda's criticism of, 303; expatriate, 205, 209, 210, 239, 309 (attitude to Jones, 144, 286; meeting of, 172; possible exodus of, 152, 166, 308; retirement fund for, 157); loyalties of, 154; question of governor's responsibility for, 154; strike of, 238; threat of violence to, 239
Clarke, Sir Charles Arden, 198
Cleak, D.S., 26
Cole, David, 201, 206, 213, 225, 230, 239, 245, 252, 262, 298
Colonial Office, 294, 296, 297, 300, 301, 306
Commonwealth Relations Office (CRO), 124, 243, 245, 298, 301, 302
Congo, 233
Congress Liberation Party, 89, 161
Connors, Peter, 273, 274
constitution of Nyasaland, 98, 103, 105, 130, 131, 132–3, 156; new, 156
copper, government revenues from, 50
Copperbelt, 49, 50; labour unrest in, 32

corporal violence: at school, Jones's attitude to, 10, 35, 282; Jones's attendance at a whipping, 34; Jones's reaction to, 19; Jones's whipping of drummers, 31, 35; on African women, Jones's views on, 282
corruption, 203, 218
Council of State for Nyasaland, 133
Coutts, Sir Walter, 199
Crown Agents, 262–3
Curtis, Sarah, 273

Davies, J.T. ('Jit'), 11
defederalization committee, setting-up of, 161
Denton, Keith, 250
detainees, release of, 141, 144, 292, 305
detention without trial, proposed, 203, 204, 225
development plans for Nyasaland–Malawi, 164, 165, 208
Devlin, Sir Patrick, 67, 286
Devlin commission of inquiry, 62
diary of Jones, 19, 20, 21, 22, 23, 24, 25, 29, 30, 31, 35, 36–7, 53, 55, 66, 71, 81, 89, 116, 117, 150, 186, 187, 215, 224, 230, 231, 232, 233, 234, 236, 237, 241, 267–8
diseases, Jones's knowledge of, 24
district officers, effects of animosity on, 143–6
Dixon, C.W., 15, 79, 80, 292
Doig, Andrew, 262
Dorman, Sir Maurice, 199, 268
Duff, Colin, 33
Duke of York camps *see* education of Jones
Duncan, 'Jerry', 5

education of Jones: academic record, 5–6; attendance at Duke of York's Camp, 10, 282; elementary, 3, 277, 280; examination record, 6; known as 'Ocky Jones', 3; made head boy,

9–10; made prefect, 9; membership of Cadet Corps, 4–5; secondary, at King's School, Chester, 3–12
elected ministers, meeting with Banda, 136–7
elections: in Nyasaland, 96–7; orderly nature of, 103; results of, 97
Elizabeth, Queen, 59, 197, 199, 240; Jones lunches with, 258
Ellams, David, 207, 211, 213
End of Empire series, 273–7
executions, in public, 252–3, 304
expatriates, 207; Banda's warning to, 170, 173; fear among, 160, 221; Malawi's need for, 204; possible exodus of, 168, 174, 197, 247; threats to, 197; violence against, 175 *see also* civil servants

Featherstone, Nancy, Jones's relationship with, 36–40, 39 *see also* Jones, Nancy
Feira, Jones's posting to, 40
financial problems of Nyasaland, 184
Fisher, Geoffrey, 14
Fisher, Nigel, 116, 121, 122, 128
fishing *see* sports interests of Jones
Fold, Superintendent, 32, 33
food, provision of, at Mongo, 43
Foot, Dingle, 66
Footman, Charles W.F., 62, 64, 65, 67, 288; house taken over by Jones, 287
foreign policy of Malawi, 202, 208, 210, 214, 217, 218
Foster, Sir Robert, 56, 61, 63, 90, 92, 103, 104, 121, 122, 123, 163, 185, 290; appointed deputy Governor, 155
French, Mrs, Banda's association with, 270, 272
French, William Henry, 272
Furse, Sir Ralph, 15

Garner, Sir Saville, 198
Ghana, 172, 220

Gilstrap, Sam, 249, 250, 252, 254
Gondwe, Vincent, 254
Greenfield, Sir Julian, 176
Gulliver, Colonel R.F.L., 171
Gwelo card, 84, 111, 113, 118, 255, 291, 293, 295
Gwembe valley, 29; battle fought in, 59; description of, 25; displacement of Tonga villagers, 57–60; Jones's posting to, 19

Hall, Sir Douglas, 56–7
Harlech, Lord, 268
Hastings, Lord, 54
Hazell, C.H., 27
Hollis, Roger, 128
Holt, Charlie, 5
Hone, Sir Evelyn, 63, 65, 119, 124, 125, 126, 133
hospital fees, issue of, 225
hunting *see* sports interests of Jones
hyenas, attacks by, 19

image of Malawi and Nyasaland, 168, poor, 176, 178–9, 192, 193, 200, 208, 209, 210, 233, 246, 300
independence of Nyasaland, 130, 133, 149, 154, 173, 195, 197, 198, 199; date for, 150, 151, 153, 165, 183–4; financial, 184; in view of Banda, 183; timetable for, 132
indirect rule, 55–6; Jones view of, 283
Ingham, John, 61, 62, 92, 93, 102, 103, 110, 303
Isaac, a servant, sacking of, 30
Israel, doctors recruited from, 168

Jafu, George, 264
Jardim, George, 218, 258
Jehovah's Witnesses, attacks on, 187, 188, 189, 190, 192, 304
Johannsen, Jerker, 189
Jonathan, Chief, 267
Jones, Agnes, 1–2, 282; death of, 284
Jones, Bertha, 2
Jones, Glyn Smallwood: academic

record of, 281; affinity for African people, 45, 48, 57; and issue of violence against expatriates, 174; applications to join armed forces turned down, 38; applies for teaching posts, 14; applies to join Northern Rhodesia Regiment, 38; attends Marlborough House conference, 150, 152; attends Zambian independence celebrations, 243, 246; birth of, 2; colleagues' view of, 298; concern to prevent violence, 188; confirmed in Anglican Church, 92; death of, 278 (buried in Zomba, 310; memorial service for, 278); debating skills of, 281; decides on allocation of ministers, 100–2; description of, 50 (attention to detail, 52; competitiveness of, 22, 281, 286, 301, 306; gift of leadership, 281; reputation as a trouble shooter, 92); employed at Malawi Buying and Trade Agency, 263–4, 270; Fellow of the Royal Empire Society, 29; financial arrangements of, 30; health of, 25–6 (cardiac indisposition, 166, 200, 306; liver failure, 278; malaria, 278); interviews Banda for television, 273, 274; leaves England for Africa, 17, 18; length of service in Nyasaland–Malawi, 306; letters and correspondence of (from Armitage, 83–4; to Banda, 239–40 see also Banda, meetings and correspondence; to Butler, 133; to Chirwa, 194–5; to Macleod, 83, 87; to Maudling, 124; to Monson, 122–3; to Watson, 168, 169, 243, 245); marriages of (first, to Margaret Florence McWilliam, 33, 298 (divorce, 39); second, to Nancy Featherstone, 39–40, 47, 55, 308 (honeymoon, 40) see also Jones, Nancy); meetings with Banda see Banda, meetings with Jones; meeting with Butler, 130; meeting with Macmillan, 128; meeting with London publishers, 271; organises tour for Governor Benson, 53–4, 55; political beliefs of, 268; postings (to Eastern Province, 40; to Luanshya district, 31–3; to Mongu, 35, 42, 51; to Mwinilunga, active in tax collecting, 20); pro-Banda stance of, 122, 126, 170, 186, 244, 246, 264, 268, 276, 294, 297, 301, 302, 305; public criticism of, 302; relationship with Banda, 67, 75, 82–3, 152, 159, 198, 256, 267, 287, 289–90, 291, 295, 296, 297, 299, 300, 305, 306, 308; relationship with Benson, 59–60; relationship with Maudling, 106; relationship with staff, 48, 49; reports by (to Butler, 167, 175, 178, 180, 190, 194; to Macleod, 76, 79, 80, 82, 93, 103, 143; to Maudling, 112–13; to Sandys, 190; to Welensky, 80); resignation threat, 243, 306; resigns fron Zomba gymkhana club, 84; returns cheque to Granada TV, 276; sees Armitage off as Governor, 92; social life, 282, 298; 'squirearchical feel' to his life, 283, 308; studies on Tropical African Services course, 16; tour of Fort Johnston district, 249; travels to London, 125, 134, 185; view on releasing Chipembere, 158; visit to Gwembe valley, 58; visit to Welensky, 72; visits to Banda in prison, 65–6; warning regarding Alport's visit, 117–18; work on Rhodesia commission, 268–9 see also education of Jones, musical interests of Jones and positions held by Jones

Jones, Gwilym Ioan, 1–2, 280; work as errand boy, 2

Jones, John, 2
Jones, Judge Elder, 272
Jones, Elizabeth Eleanor *née*
 Smallwood, 2, 41, 42, 75, 94, 185,
 256, 278, 279
Jones, Madeline (Linnie), 2
Jones, Margaret Florence *née*
 McWilliam, 33; refuses to go to
 Africa, 34
Jones, Nancy *née* Featherstone, 41,
 64, 75, 185, 231, 256, 262–3, 267,
 273–4, 287
Jones, Nesta, 2, 3, 33
Jones, 'Patagonia', 2
Jones, Timothy, 42, 55, 256, 279;
 breaks a leg, 93–4, 95, 309; death
 of, 284, 299
judicial system, traditional, 261
judiciary, 200; commission of
 inquiry into, 179, 181;
 establishment of, 180–1
Judith, Lady Listowel, meeting with
 Jones, 260

Kadzamira, Cecilia, 140, 184, 195,
 217, 223, 242, 262, 263, 267, 273,
 279, 297, 298
Kadzamira, Mary, 184
Kangoni, a headman, 31
Kanjedza, Banda's threatened march
 on, 80
Kapwepwe, Simon, 160
Kariba dam, 57
Katsonga, Chester, 93; house
 stormed, 93
Kaunda, Kenneth, 160; arrest of, 50
Kenema, Jones's servant, 19
Kettlewell, Richard W., 68, 101, 103,
 110, 303
King's African Rifles (KAR), 171,
 249, 287
King's School, Chester, 3–12, 280–1;
 academic record of, 5; colonial
 tradition of, 10; egalitarian
 elements of, 282; Jones's offer of
 grant to, 277
knighthood of Jones, 307

Kota Kota case, 146
Kuchawe manifesto, 216–17, 219,
 235
Kumbikano, federal MP, 185
Kumtumanji, Gomile, 207, 239;
 appointed regional minister, 231

labour unrest in Malawi, 209
Lancaster House agreement, 74, 75,
 77, 80, 81, 85, 86, 87, 88, 102, 107,
 108, 110, 114, 303
Lancaster House conference, 69, 70,
 72, 73, 88, 95, 99, 107, 112, 145,
 289, 292
Lapping, Brian: *End of Empire* series,
 273–7; with Sarah Curtis,
 interview with Jones, 91
law and order, 166–8, 172, 173, 175,
 176, 179, 181, 182, 297, 302;
 Banda's responsibility for, 191
League of Malawi Youth (LMY), 97,
 174, 176, 180, 189, 239; special
 action squads, 186
Lennox-Boyd, Alan, 55, 288
Lesotho, 267
Lewis, Paul, 244, 250
Litunga, 34, 54
locusts, 25
Loft, George, 67
Lomax, Douglas G., 244, 248, 250,
 259, 260, 309
Long, Peter, 244, 248, 250
Longman publisher, and Banda
 biography, 270
Lovale tribe, 34, 36
Luanshya, social life at, 32
Lukulu mission station, 42
Lunda dialect, Jones's mastery of,
 34, 36
Lunda tribe, 34
Lusaka, life in, 63

MacDonnell, Sir Philip, 34–6;
 appreciation of Jones's work, 36
MacDonnell Commission, Jones's
 work as secretary, 39
Mackinson, Ian, 53–4

Macleod, Iain, 64, 65, 68–9, 70, 77, 78, 79, 80, 81, 87, 88, 89, 91, 93, 99, 107, 108, 113, 128, 276, 286, 287, 288, 289; appointed colonial secretary, 62; Jones's letter to, 82, 87; message to Banda, 78; replaced by Maudling, 104; visit to Nyasaland, 68

Macmillan, Harold, 64, 89, 93, 94, 118, 125, 150, 199, 286, 287, 288, 289; 'wind of change' speeches, 62, 65, 285, 288

malaria, 14, 19, 25, 278

Malawi Buying and Trade Agency, Jones works with, 258, 263–4, 270, 301

Malawi Congress Party (MCP), 66, 68, 72, 81, 82, 83, 85, 88, 89, 93, 96, 98, 101, 103, 104, 107, 108, 109, 110, 117, 128, 137, 138, 141, 142, 145, 146, 147, 160, 167, 170, 174, 175, 177, 179, 180, 181, 182, 186, 187, 190, 193, 194, 195, 202, 221, 222, 229, 238, 260, 284, 285, 303; pay for Rolls-Royce, 196; relations with civil service, 140, 142, 148

Malawi Freedom Movement, 261

Malawi News, 189, 190; attacks on Catholic Church, 82; comments on Europeans, 160

'Malawi police', 170–5, 178, 181; excesses of, 302–3

Malawi Rifles, 239, 248, 250

Malawi Youth League, 83, 161, 237–8, 251

Malinki, Alex, 270

Marlborough House conference, 141, 150, 152, 157, 158, 162, 166, 182

Marlborough House constitution, 145

Matthews, Major, 248

Maudling, Reginald, 106–7, 114, 116, 117, 118, 119, 120, 122, 123, 124, 131, 140, 142; discussion with Banda, 108; replaces Macleod as secretary of state, 104; visit to Nyasaland, 105

Maxwell, Inspector, 32–3

Mazabuka, Jones's transit stay at, 26, 28, 30

Mbadwa party, 185, 186

McCracken, John, interview with Jones, 90

McWilliam, Margaret Florence *see* Jones, Margaret, 33

McWilliam, Peter, 33

mercy, prerogative of, 155

mining industry, in Copperbelt, 50

Mkandawire, Mikeka, 102, 111, 136, 137, 160; appointed minister, 103

Mombelo, witchcraft charge against, 24

Monckton, Lord, 95

Monckton report, 70, 72, 78

Mongu: description of, 45; Jones's posting as district commissioner, 35, 42, 51; ordering of provisions by Europeans, 43

Monson, Sir Leslie, 70, 72, 122

movement of people, legislation to restrict, 183

Moxon, Major Peter, 204

Mozambique, 208, 209

Msonthi, John, 110, 111, 136, 147, 160, 207, 216, 229, 230; as minister for transport and communications, 231 (proposed, 196, 213); dropped from cabinet, 201, 202, 205, 212; resignation of, 228, 229; sobriety criticized, 213; visit to Jones, 212

musical interests of Jones: enjoys singing of Africans, 26–7; organ-playing, 8, 44; piano-playing, 8–9, 26, 282; singing, 8–9, 26, 278, 282

Muwalo, 219, 221, 226, 239; proposed as minister of information, 231

Mwanambi, raid on, 21

Mwinilunga, 25, 28; description of, 19; Jones's posting to, 19, 24, 31

Nacala rail link, issue of, 218
Nairne, Sir Patrick, 278
nature, Jones's appreciation of, 24
Ndola, description of, 49–50
Neale, Kenneth, 297
Nicholson, Sir Godfrey, 115–16, 121, 122, 128, 271
Nkata Bay, violence in, 160, 161
Nkrumah, Kwame, 198, 298
Nkula Falls hydro-electricity scheme, 111, 112, 113, 304; Banda's views on, 114; Chisiza's views on, 114
nominated officials, replacing of, 109, 110
Norman-Walker, Hugh, 160, 185
Northern Rhodesia, 61, 124, 126, 133, 136, 160, 210, 276, 287, 303; description of, 18; development plan for, 47; Jones's enjoyment of, 30; Jones's service in, 282–3, 284
Northern Rhodesia Regiment, 58
Northern Rhodesia Rifles, 33
Nyampasa, sister of Mombelo, 24
Nyasaland: constitution of *see* constitution of Nyasaland; development plans for, 66; elections in, 96–7; relationship with Federation, 106, 111
Nyasaland African Congres, 61
Nyasaland Constitutional Party, 195
Nyasaland Independence Bill, royal assent, 199
Nyasulu, Alex, 226, 227; proposed as minister for natural resources, 231
Nyerere, Julius, 220, 222

one-party state, 307; Jones's view of, 268
Operation Stunt, 82
Organization of African Unity (OAU), 202

Parslow, John, 279
Pearce, Lord, 268, 269

Perchard, Colin, 278
Petauke: formation of producers' association, 41; relocation of *boma* to, 40–1
Phillips, Sir Henry, 93, 103, 107, 108, 114, 140, 154, 160; as minister of finance, 185, 195, 196
Pigg, James Bennett, 33
Pincott, W.J.R, appointed deputy chief agent of MBTA, 263; letter to George Jafu, 267
Pine, John, 103
Plymouth Brethren, 34, 39
police, 146, 170, 171, 172, 174, 175, 178, 181–2, 188, 190, 192, 193, 238, 239, 256, 302; allegedly partisan, 146; divided responsibility for, 156; fearing for families, 182; no action against MCP officials, 182; officers seen as reactionary, 181 *see also* Malawi police
political murders, 302
Portugal, 208, 210, 214, 218
positions held by Jones: Acting Governor, Nyasaland, 69, 70, 87; commissioner for native development, 47–8, 285; government advisor to Lesotho, 267; Governor of Nyasaland, 88–9, 91, 95–159, 306; Governor-General of Malawi, 185, 201–57 (appointed, 197; continuation after independence, 307; farewell ceremony, 256–7; resignation threat, 233; returns to Britain, 258); offered chief secretaryship of Nyasaland, 63; offered governorship of British Guiana, 185; provincial commissioner, Western Province, 49; refuses transfer to Palestine, 42; resident commissioner of Barotseland, 51; secretary for native affairs, 56, 57, 285; secretary of MacDonnell inquiry, 34; selected as administrative officer cadet, 15–16;

turns down governorship of British Guiana, 198, 306
Poynton, Hilton, 61, 88, 91, 185; letter to Jones, 63
preventive detention bill, proposed, 245, 247, 304
Priestley, Michael, 52, 56
public meetings banned by Banda, 237
public schools emigration league, 10
Public Services Commission, 145, 146

Ralph, H.W., 11
recreation pursuits of Jones, 26; at Zomba, 68; company of other people, 27, 28, 32, 44; dancing, 44; reading, 27 see also sports interests of Jones
registration of voters, 96
relationship with children, 55
release of prisoners, 74, 77, 78, 79, 80, 82, 83, 87, 89, 293; demanded, 72, 73
republican future for Malawi, 184, 206, 215, 220, 240, 255, 307, 308, 310
resettlement of populations, 41
restriction orders, signed by Jones, 285
Rhodesia, 268–9; independence of, 268
Richardson, Sir John, 94
Roan Antelope mine, 31; strike by workers, 32–3
Roberts, Sir Bryan, 146, 147, 154, 216, 221, 222, 224, 225, 229, 236, 243, 244, 248, 249, 250, 253, 260, 262, 263, 273, 297, 299, 309; appointed as secretary to cabinet, 300; excluded as director of public prosecutions, 171; interview with Banda, 147; proposed as attorney-general, 231; visit to Banda, 223
Roberts, Hilda, 16, 31
Roberts, Dr John, 3
Rolls-Royce car used by Banda, 196

Routledge and Kegan Paul publisher, 271

Sacranie, Sattar, 225, 226, 270
salary of Jones, 307
Sandys, Duncan, 116, 117, 118, 119, 120, 121, 124, 125, 131, 151, 164, 187, 189, 197, 199, 299, 304; view of secession, 121, 122, 123, 124; visit to Nyasaland, 118, 122, 131
secession, 124, 136, 148, 150, 156; Banda's view of, 115, 116, 117, 118, 119, 123, 125, 126, 135; British government policy on, 133, 149; date of, 153, 157, 162, 167; economic and political implications of, 120, 132, 149, 150, 163; Sandys' view of see Sandys, Duncan
self-government of Nyasaland, 111, 148, 156, 255, 301; limitations on, 154
Sesheke, Jones's visit to, 51–2
Shepperd, John, 274
Shepperson, Professor George, 273
shooting see sports interests of Jones
Short, Philip, biography of Banda, 270
Silombela, Medson, 252–3; execution of, 291
Skinner report, 205, 210, 211, 217, 218, 225, 240
Smallwood, Edward, 2
Smallwood, Edward William, 2
Smallwood, Mary Ann, 2
Smallwood, Mary née Bishall, 2
Smallwood, Mary née Davies (Mair y Cymau), 2
Smallwood, Sarah Jane, 2
Smallwood, William, 2
Snelling, Sir Peter, 245
social activities of Europeans, 43–4
South Africa: Banda abstains from boycott vote, 202; Malawians working in mining industry, 208
Southern Rhodesia, 61, 116, 118, 124, 210, 218

specialist staff: recruiting of, 192; shortages of, 141
sports interests of Jones, 49: at school (athletics, 6, 281; boxing, 6–7; rowing, 7–8, 281 (Sheriff of Chester's prize, 8); soccer, 7); cricket in Africa, 44; fishing, 44, 52, 53–4, 55, 56, 65, 68, 136, 283, 298, 308, 310; golf, 310; hunting, 56, 72, 308; rowing, at university, 14; shooting, 22–4, 44, 55, 56, 136, 155, 157, 258, 283, 308 (of crocodiles, 40; of hippopotamuses, 31); skiing, 258; soccer, 31, 32, 40, 281 (asked to play football for North Wales, 14; awarded blue, 13; captain of St Catherine's, 13; continues playing soccer at university, 16; playing with Africans, 37); swimming, 281; tennis, 52; walking, 21, 22, 26, 166, 283, 308
St Catherine's association of alumni, 277
St Catherine's Society, 277
state of emergency, 76, 156, 191, 206, 225, 292; avoidance of, 294, 295, 301, 307; declared in Nyasaland (1959), 62, 141, 142, 286, 287, 288, 289
Stevens report, 136, 148
strikes: by government employees in Zomba, 238–9; by mineworkers, 50
string, Jones's ordering of, 20
Suckling, George, 34
Surtee, I.K., 99
Symonds, Reverend H.H., 11

Tanzania, 248
tax, collecting of, 37, 40
taxation: system in Africa, 32; tribal refusal to pay, 34
Tembo, John, 140, 160, 184, 185, 195–6, 206, 207, 208, 210–11, 217, 230, 240, 304; appointed minister of finance, 202, 231 (proposed, 196)

termites, tunnelling of, in Jones's house, 41
Thomas, T.W., 5
treason law, proposed, 249, 304
Trelford, Donald, 273
tsetse fly, 19, 26
Turnbull, Sir Richard, 199

United Federal Party (UFP), 96–7, 98, 99, 100, 153, 303
United Kingdom (UK): budget adjustment for Nyasaland, 163–4; policy on Nyasaland, 111, 124, 289, 291, 292, 293, 294, 303; view of Federation, 118–19, 126, 127; view of secession, 122, 127
United Nations, 172, 202
university career of Jones, 11–15; at St Catherine's Society, 12; chosen as President of Alumni, 278; graduates, 15; made honorary fellow of St Catherine's, 278; reputation as a debater, 12
University of Malawi, proposed, 207
Unsworth, Sir Edgar, 179, 186, 195, 200; letter to Jones, 179, 180
urban politicians, importance of, in Jones's view, 285–6

Victoria, Queen, 54, 55
Vincent, member of MBTA staff, 264
violence, 70, 93, 95, 96, 97, 103, 160, 161, 167, 170, 179, 186, 188, 192, 193, 237, 238, 240, 246, 247, 249, 290, 295, 296, 302, 304; against expatriates, 174, 200; pre-election, 185, 186, 187, 195, 303; statistics of, 190 *see also* corporal violence

walk-out technique of Banda, 137, 150, 222
Watson, Sir Duncan, 170, 185, 192, 198, 200, 243, 245; letters to Jones, 167–8, 176
Welensky, Sir Roy, 66, 71, 72, 80,

100, 114, 115, 119, 124, 126, 127, 129, 149, 161, 162, 167, 173, 175, 292
Welsh church, attendance at, 1, 2, 3
Welsh language, speaking of, 1, 2
Western Province, description of, 49
Westminster, Duke of, 1, 4
Whitehead, Sir Edgar, 119, 124, 127, 149
Wilfred, chauffeur, 242
Williams, B.T., 5, 10
Willis, H.H., 5
Wilson, Harold, 262
witchcraft: accusations of, 24; beliefs in, 19; murders, 253
Witwatersrand Native Labour Association (WNLA), 208, 209, 210
women: hanging of, 291; Jones's descriptions of, 29; white, presence of, 28

Youens, Sir Peter, 68, 71, 72, 73, 74, 75, 76, 77, 78, 148, 155, 172, 199, 202, 207, 211, 213, 216, 220, 221–2, 223, 225, 231, 236, 238, 239, 240, 241, 242, 243, 244, 248, 250, 289, 296, 299, 309; appointed as secretary to cabinet, 300; as potential head of civil service, 155; meeting with Banda, 98, 147–8; meeting with Blackwood, 98; report to Jones, 148; visit to Banda, 84
Young Pioneers Movement, 183, 195

Zambezi valley, flooding of, 57–60
Zomba, 65; Jones's liking of, 309, 310; life in, 63